Multi-Agent Coordination

Multi-Agent Coordination

A Reinforcement Learning Approach

Arup Kumar Sadhu
Amit Konar

IEEE PRESS

WILEY

Registered Office
John Wiley & Sons, Inc., 111 River Street, Hoboken, NJ 07030, USA

Editorial Office
111 River Street, Hoboken, NJ 07030, USA

For details of our global editorial offices, customer services, and more information about Wiley products visit us at www.wiley.com.

Wiley also publishes its books in a variety of electronic formats and by print-on-demand. Some content that appears in standard print versions of this book may not be available in other formats.

Library of Congress Cataloging-in-Publication Data

Names: Sadhu, Arup Kumar, author. | Konar, Amit, author.
Title: Multi-agent coordination : a reinforcement learning approach / Arup Kumar Sadhu, Amit Konar.
Description: Hoboken, New Jersey : Wiley-IEEE, [2021] | Includes bibliographical references and index.
Identifiers: LCCN 2020024706 (print) | LCCN 2020024707 (ebook) | ISBN 9781119699033 (cloth) | ISBN 9781119698999 (adobe pdf) | ISBN 9781119699026 (epub)
Subjects: LCSH: Reinforcement learning. | Multiagent systems.
Classification: LCC Q325.6 .S23 2021 (print) | LCC Q325.6 (ebook) | DDC 006.3/1–dc23
LC record available at https://lccn.loc.gov/2020024706
LC ebook record available at https://lccn.loc.gov/2020024707

Cover design: Wiley
Cover image: © Color4260/Shutterstock

Contents

Preface

Coordination is a fundamental trait in lower level organisms as they used their collective effort to serve their goals. Hundreds of interesting examples of coordination are available in nature. For example, ants individually cannot carry a small food item, but they collectively carry quite a voluminous food to their nest. The tracing of the trajectory of motion of an ant following the pheromone deposited by its predecessor also is attractive. The queen bee in her nest directs the labor bees to specific directions by her dance patterns and gestures to collect food resources. These natural phenomena often remind us the scope of coordination among agents to utilize their collective intelligence and activities to serve complex goals.

Coordination and planning are closely related terminologies from the domain of multi-robot system. Planning refers to the collection of feasible steps required to reach a predefined goal from a given position. However, coordination indicates the skillful interaction among the agents to generate a feasible planning step. Therefore, coordination is an important issue in the field of multi-robot coordination to address complex real-world problems. Coordination usually is of three different types: cooperation, competition, and mixed. As evident from their names, cooperation refers to improving the performance of the agents to serve complex goals, which otherwise seems to be very hard for an individual agent because of the restricted availability of hardware/software resources of the agents or deadline/energy limits of the tasks. Unlike cooperation, competition refers to serving conflicting goals by two (team of) agents. For example, in robot soccer, the two teams compete to win the game. Here, each team plans both offensively and defensively to score goals and thus act competitively. Mixed coordination indicates a mixture of cooperation and competition. In the example of a soccer game, inter-team competition and intra-team cooperation is the mixed coordination. Most of the common usage of coordination in robotics lies in cooperation of agents to serve a common goal. The book deals with the cooperation of robots/robotic agents to efficiently complete a complex task.

In recent times, researchers are taking keen interest to employ machine learning in multi-agent cooperation. The primary advantage of machine learning is to generate the action plans in sequence from the available sensory readings of the robots. In case of a single robot, learning the action plans from the sensory readings is straightforward. However, in the context of multi-robot, the positional changes of the other robots act as additional inputs for the learner robot, and thus learning is relatively difficult. Several machine learning and evolutionary algorithms have been adopted over the last two decades to handle the situations. The simplest of all is the supervised learning technique that requires an exhaustive list of sensory instances and the action plan by the robots. Usually, a human experimenter provides these data from his/her long acquaintance with such problems or by direct measurement of the sensory instances and decisions. The training instances being too large, sometimes has a negative influence to the engineer, and he/she feels it uncomfortable not to miss a single instance that carries valuable mapping from sensory instance to action plan by the robots.

Because of the difficulty of generating training instances and excessive computational overhead to learn those instances, coupled with the need for handling dynamic situations, researchers felt the importance of reinforcement learning (RL). In RL, we need not provide any training instance, but employ a critic who provides a feedback to the learning algorithm about the possible reward/penalty of the actions by the agent. The agent/s on receiving the approximate measure of penalty/reward understands which particular sensory-motor instances they need to learn for future planning applications. The dynamic nature of environment thus can easily be learned by RL. In the multi-agent scenario, RL needs to take care of learning in joint state/action space of the agents. Here, each agent learns the sensory-motor instances in the joint state/action space with an ultimate motive to learn the best actions for itself to optimize its rewards.

The superiority of evolutionary algorithms (EAs) in optimizing diverse objective functions is subjected to the No Free Lunch Theorem (NFLT). According to NFLT, the expected effectiveness of any two traditional EAs across all possible optimization problems is identical. A self-evident implication of NFLT is that the elevated performance of one EA, say A, over the other, say B, for one class of optimization problems is counterbalanced by their respective performances over another class. It is therefore practically difficult to devise a universal EA that would solve all the problems. This apparently paves the way for hybridization of EAs with other optimization strategies, machine learning techniques, and heuristics.

In evolutionary computation paradigm, hybridization refers to the process of integrating the attractive features of two or more EAs synergistically to develop a new hybrid EA. The hybrid EA is expected to outperform its ancestors with respect to both accuracy and complexity over application-specific or general benchmark problems. The fusion of EAs through hybridization hence can be regarded as the key to overcome their individual limitations.

Hence, apart from the RL, hybridization of the EAs is also an effective approach to serve the purpose of multi-robot coordination in a complex environment. The primary objective of an EA in the context of multi-robot coordination is concerned with the minimization of the time consumed by the robots (i.e. the length of the path to be traversed by the robots) for complete traversal of the planned trajectory. In other words, robots plan their local trajectory, so that robots shifted from given positions to the next positions (subgoals) in a time-optimal sense avoiding collision with the obstacles or the boundary of the world map. The optimization algorithm is executed in each local planning step to move a small distance. Hence, cumulatively robots move to the desired goal position using the sequence of local planning. There are traces of literature on hybridization of the EAs.

Several algorithms for multi-agent learning are available in the literature, each with one specific flavor to optimize certain learning intents of the agents. Of these algorithms, quite a few interesting works on the MAQL have been reported in the literature. Among the state-of-the-art MAQL algorithms, the following need special mentions. Claus and Boutilier, aimed at solving the coordination problem using two types of reinforcement learners. The first one, called independent learner (IL), takes care of the learning behavior of individual agents by ignoring the presence of other agents. The second one, called joint action learner (JAL), considers all agents including the self to learn at joint action-space. Unlike JAL, in Team Q-learning proposed by Littman, an agent updates its Q-value at a joint state–action pair without utilizing associated agents' reward; rather the value function of the agent at the next joint state is evaluated by obtaining the maximum Q-value among the joint actions at the next joint state. Ville proposed Asymmetric-Q learning (AQL) algorithm, where the leader agents are capable of maintaining all the agents' Q-tables. However, the follower agents are not allowed to maintain all the agents' Q-tables and hence, they just maximize their own rewards. In AQL, agents always achieve the pure strategy Nash equilibrium (NE), although there does exist mixed strategy NE. Hu and Wellman extended the Littman's Minimax Q-learning to the general-sum stochastic game (where the summation of all agents' payoff is neither zero nor constant) by taking into account of other agents' dynamics using NE. They also offered a proof of convergence of their algorithm. In case of multiple NE occurrences, one is selected optimally. Littman proposed Friend-or-Foe Q-learning (FQL) algorithm for general-sum games. In this algorithm, the learner is instructed to treat each other agent either as a friend in Friend Q-learning or as a foe in Foe Q-learning. FQL provides a stronger convergence guarantee in comparison to that of the existing NE-based learning rule. Greenwald and Hall proposed correlated Q-learning (CQL) employing correlated equilibrium (CE) to generalize both Nash Q-learning (NQL) and FQL. The bottlenecks of the above MAQL algorithms are update policy selection for adaptation of the Q-tables in joint state–action space and the curse of dimensionality with an increase in the number of learning agents. Several attempts have been made to handle the curse of dimensionality in MAQL. Jelle and Nikos proposed Sparse Cooperative Q-learning, where a sparse representation of the joint state–action space of the agents is done by identifying the need for coordination among the agents at a joint state. Here, agents undertake coordination by their actions only in a few joint states. Hence, each agent maintains two Q-tables: one is the individual-action Q-table for uncoordinated joint states and another one is the joint action Q-table to represent the coordinated joint states. In case of uncoordinated states, a global Q-value is evaluated by adding the individual Q-values. Zinkevich offers a neural network-based approach for generalized representation of the state-space for multi-agent coordination. By such generalization, agents (here robots) can avoid collision with an obstacle or other robots by collecting minimum information from the sensors. Reinaldo et al. proposed a novel algorithm to heuristically accelerate the TMAQL algorithms.

In the literature of MAQL, agents either converge to NE or CE. The equilibrium-based MAQL algorithms are most popular for their inherent ability to determine optimal strategy (equilibrium) at a given joint state. Hu et al. identified the phenomenon of similar equilibria in different joint states and introduced the concept of equilibrium transfer to accelerate the state-of-the-art equilibrium-based MAQL (NQL and CQL). In equilibrium transfer, agents recycle the previously computed equilibria having very small transfer loss. Recently, Zhang et al. attempted to reduce the dimension of the Q-tables in NQL. The reduction is done by allowing the agents to store the Q-values in joint state–individual action space, instead of joint state–action space.

In the state-of-the-art MAQL (NQL and CQL), balancing exploration/exploitation during the learning phase is an important issue. Traditional approaches used to balance exploration/exploitation in MAQL are summarized here. The greedy exploration, although has wide publicity, needs to tune the value of which is time-costly. In the Boltzmann strategy, the action selection probability is controlled by tuning a control parameter (temperature) and by utilizing the Q-values due to all actions at a given state. Here, the setting of temperature to infinity (zero) implies pure exploration (exploitation). Unfortunately, the Boltzmann strategy antagonistically affects the speed of learning. Evolution of the Boltzmann strategy toward better performance is observed in a series of literature. However, the above selection mechanisms are not suitable for selecting a joint action preferred for the team (all the agents) because of the dissimilar joint Q-values offered by the agents at a common joint state–action pair. There are traces of literature concerning joint action selection at a joint state during learning. However, with the best of our knowledge, there is no work in the literature, which considers the work, presented in this book.

The book includes six chapters. Chapter 1 provides an introduction to the multi-robot coordination algorithms for complex real-world problems, including trans-portation of a box/stick, formation control for defense applications and soccer playing by multiple robots utilizing the principles of RL, the theory of games, dynamic programming, and/or EA. Naturally, this chapter provides a thorough survey of the existing literature of RL with a brief overview of the evolutionary optimization to examine the role of the algorithms in the context of multi-agent coordination. Chapter 1 includes multi-robot coordination employing evolution-ary optimization, and especially RL for cooperative, competitive, and their compo-sition for application to static and dynamic games. The latter part of the chapter deals with an overview of the metrics used to compare the performance of the algo-rithms while coordinating. Fundamental metrics for performance analysis are defined to study the learning and planning algorithms.

Chapter 2 offers learning-based planning algorithms, by extending the tradi-tional multi-agent Q-learning algorithms (NQL and CQL) for multi-robot coordi-nation and planning. This extension is achieved by employing two interesting properties. The first property deals with the exploration of the team-goal (simul-taneous success of all the robots) and the other property is related to the selection of joint action at a given joint state. The exploration of team-goal is realized by allowing the agents, capable of reaching their goals, to wait at their individual goal states, until the remaining agents explore their individual goals synchronously or asynchronously. Selection of joint action, which is a crucial problem in traditional multi-agent Q-learning, is performed here by taking the intersection of individual preferred joint actions of all the agents. In case the resulting intersection is a null set, the individual actions are selected randomly or otherwise following classical techniques. The superiority of the proposed learning and learning-based planning algorithms are validated over contestant algorithms in terms of the speed of con-vergence and run-time complexity, respectively.

In Chapter 3, it is shown that robots may select the suboptimal equilibrium in the presence of multiple types of equilibria (here NE or CE). In the above perspec-tive, robots need to adapt to such a strategy, which can select the optimal equilib-rium in each step of the learning and the planning. To address the bottleneck of the optimal equilibrium selection among multiple types, Chapter 3 presents a novel consensus Q-learning (CoQL) for multi-robot coordination, by extending the equi-librium-based multi-agent Q-learning algorithms. It is also shown that a consensus (joint action) jointly satisfies the conditions of the coordination-type pure strategy NE and the pure strategy CE. The superiority of the proposed CoQL algorithm over traditional reference algorithms in terms of the average reward collection are shown in the experimental section. In addition, the proposed consensus-based planning algorithm is also verified considering the multi-robot stick-carrying problem as the testbed.

Unlike CQL, Chapter 4 proposes an attractive approach to adapt composite rewards of all the agents in one Q-table in joint state–action space during learning, and subsequently, these rewards are employed to compute CE in the planning phase. Two separate models of multi-agent Q-learning have been proposed. If the success of only one agent is enough to make the team successful, then model-I is employed. However, if an agent's success is contingent upon other agents and simultaneous success of the agents is required, then model-II is employed. It is also shown that the CE obtained by the proposed algorithms and by the traditional CQL are identical. In order to restrict the exploration within the feasible joint states, constraint versions of the said algorithms are also proposed. Complexity analysis and experiments have been undertaken to validate the performance of the proposed algorithms in multi-robot planning on both simulated and real platforms.

Chapter 5 hybridizes the Firefly Algorithm (FA) and the Imperialist Competitive Algorithm (ICA). The above-explained hybridization results in the Imperialist Competitive Firefly Algorithm (ICFA), which is employed to determine the time-optimal trajectory of a stick, being carried by two robots, from a given starting position to a predefined goal position amidst static obstacles in a robot world map. The motion dynamics of fireflies of the FA is embedded into the sociopolitical evolution-based meta-heuristic ICA. Also, the trade-off between the exploration and exploitation is balanced by modifying the random walk strategy based on the position of the candidate solutions in the search space. The superiority of the proposed ICFA is studied considering run-time and accuracy as the performance metrics. Finally, the proposed algorithm has been verified in a real-time multi-robot stick-carrying problem.

Chapter 6 concludes the book based on the analysis made, experimental and simulation results obtained from the earlier chapters. The chapter also examines the prospects of the book in view of the future research trends.

In summary, the book aimed at developing multi-robot coordination algorithms with a minimum computational burden and less storage requirement as compared to the traditional algorithms. The novelty, originality, and applicability of the book are illustrated below.

Chapter 1 introduces fundamentals of the multi-robot coordination. Chapter 2 offers two useful properties, which have been developed to speedup the convergence of TMAQL algorithms in view of the team-goal exploration, where team-goal exploration refers to the simultaneous exploration of individual goals. The first property accelerates exploration of the team-goal. Here, each agent accumulates high (immediate) reward for team-goal state-transition, thereby improving the entries in the Q-table for state-transitions leading to the team-goal. The Q-table thus obtained offers the team the additional benefit to identify the joint action leading to a transition to the team-goal during the planning, where TMAQL-based planning stops inadvertently. The second property directs an alternative approach to speedup the convergence of TMAQL by identifying the preferred joint action for the team. Finding preferred joint action for the team is crucial when robots are acting synchronously in a tight cooperative system. The superiority of the proposed algorithms in Chapter 2 is verified both theoretically as well as experimentally in terms of the convergence speed and the run-time complexity.

Chapter 3 proposes the novel CoQL, which addresses the equilibrium selection problem. In case multiple equilibria exist at a joint state, by adapting the Q-functions at a consensus. Analytically it is shown that a consensus at a joint state is a coordination-type pure strategy NE as well as a pure strategy CE. Experimentally, it is shown that the average rewards earned by the robots are more when adapting at consensus, than by either NE or CE.

Chapter 4 introduces a new dimension in the literature of the traditional CQL. In traditional CQL, CE is evaluated both in learning and planning phases. In Chapter 4, CE is computed partly in the learning and the rest in the planning phases, thereby requiring CE computation once only. It is shown in an analysis that the CE obtained by the proposed techniques is same as that obtained by the traditional CQL algorithms. In addition, the computational cost to evaluate CE by the proposed techniques is much smaller than that obtained by traditional CQL algorithms for the following reasons. Computation of CE in the traditional CQL requires consulting m Q-tables in joint state–action space for m robots, whereas in the present context, we use a single Q-table in the joint state–action space for evaluation of CE. Complexity analysis (both time- and space-complexity) undertaken here confirms the last point. Two schemes are proposed: one for a loosely- and the other one for a tightly coupled multi-robot system. Also, the problem-specific constraints are taken care of in Chapter 4 to avoid unwanted exploration of the infeasible state-space during the learning phase, thereby saving additional run-time complexity during the planning phase. Experiments are undertaken to validate the proposed concepts in simulated and practical multi-agent robotic platform (here Khepera-environment).

Chapter 5 offers the evolutionary optimization approach to address the multi-robot stick-carrying problem using the proposed ICFA. ICFA is the synergistic fusion of the motion dynamics of a firefly in the FA and the local exploration capabilities of the ICA. In ICA, an evolving colony is not guided by the experience of more powerful colonies within the same empire. However, in ICFA, each colony attempts to contribute to the improvement of its governing empire by improving its sociopolitical attributes following the motion dynamics of a firefly in the FA. To improve the performance of the above-mentioned hybrid algorithm further, the step-size for random movement of each firefly is modulated according to its relative position in the search space. An inferior solution is driven by the explorative force while a qualitative solution should be confined to its local neighborhood in the search space. The chapter also recommends a novel approach of evaluating the threshold value for uniting empires without imposing any serious computational overhead on the traditional ICA. Simulation and experimental results confirm the superiority of the proposed ICFA over the state-of-the-art techniques. Chapter 6 concludes the book with interesting future research directions.

Arup Kumar Sadhu
Amit Konar
Artificial Intelligence Laboratory and Control Engineering Laboratory
Department of Electronics and Telecommunication Engineering
Jadavpur University, Kolkata, India

Acknowledgments

The authors sincerely like to thank Prof. *Surnajan Das*, the vice-chancellor of Jadavpur University (JU), and Prof. *Chiranjib Bhattacharjee* and Dr. *Pradip Kumar Ghosh*, the pro-vice-chancellors of JU, Kolkata, for creating a beautiful and lively academic environment to carry out the necessary scientific work and experiments for the present book. They also would like to acknowledge the technical and moral support they received from Prof. *Sheli Sinha Chaudhuri*, the HoD of the Department of Electronics and Tele-Communication Engineering (ETCE), Jadavpur University, where the background research work for the present book is carried out. Special thanks go to the reviewers of the previous publications by the authors on the selected subject. Their suggestions helped a lot to develop the present book in its current shape.

The authors like to thank their family members for their support in many ways for the successful completion of the book. The first author wishes to mention the everlasting support and words of optimism he received from his parents, Mrs. *Purnima Sadhu* and Mr. *Prabhat Kumar Sadhu*, without whose active support, love, and affection, it would not have been possible to complete the book in the current form. He likes to acknowledge the strong gratitude he has for his elder sisters, Dr. *Sucheta Sadhu* and Mrs. *Mithu Sadhu*, who have nurtured him since his childhood and always remained as a source of inspiration in his life. The second author acknowledges the support he received from his family members for sparing him from many family responsibilities while writing this book.

The authors like to thank their students, colleagues, and coresearchers of the AI Lab, Jadavpur University, for their support in many ways during the phase of writing the book. Finally, the authors thank all their well-wishers, who have contributed directly and indirectly toward the completion of the book.

Arup Kumar Sadhu
Amit Konar
Artificial Intelligence Laboratory
Department of Electronics and Telecommunication Engineering
Jadavpur University, Kolkata, India
12 April 2020

About the Authors

Dr. Arup Kumar Sadhu received his PhD (Engineering) degree in Multi-robot Coordination by Reinforcement Learning from Jadavpur University, India, in 2017. Currently he is working with Research & Innovation Labs, Tata Consultancy Services, India, as a scientist. His research interests include Reinforcement Learning, Artificial Intelligence, Robotics, Path planning for unmanned aerial vehicle, Evolutionary Computation, Fuzzy Logic, and Human–Computer Interaction. He has many international conference, journal papers, and patents. He served as a reviewer of IEEE Transactions on Fuzzy Systems and IEEE Transactions on Emerging Topics in Computational Intelligence, Neurocomputing, and Applied soft computing, IJSI and FUZZ-IEEE.

Prof. Amit Konar received his PhD (Engineering) degree from Jadavpur University, India, in 1994. Currently he is a Professor with the Department of Electronics and Tele-Communication Engineering (ETCE), Jadavpur University, where he is the Founding Coordinator of the M. Tech. program on intelligent automation and robotics. He has supervised 28 PhD theses. He has over 350 publications in international journal and conference proceedings. He is the author of 15 books. He served as the Associate Editor of IEEE Transactions on Systems, Man and Cybernetics, Part-A, and is currently serving IEEE Transactions on

Fuzzy Systems and IEEE Transactions on Emerging Topics in Computational Intelligence. He was the recipient of All India Council for Technical Education (AICTE)-accredited 1997–2000 Career Award for Young Teachers and Fellowship of National Academy of Engineers (FNAE) in 2015 for his significant contributions in Artificial Intelligence and Robotics.

1

Introduction

Multi-agent Coordination by Reinforcement Learning
and Evolutionary Algorithms

This chapter provides an introduction to the multi-agent coordination by reinforcement learning (RL) and evolutionary algorithms (EAs). A robot (agent) is an intelligent programmable device capable of performing complex tasks and decision-making like the human beings. Mobility is part and parcel of modern robots. Mobile robots employ sensing-action cycles to sense the world around them with an aim to plan their journey to the desired destination. Coordination is an important issue in modern robotics. In recent times, researchers are taking keen interest to synthesize multi-agent-coordination in complex real-world problems, including transportation of a box/stick, formation control for defense applications, and soccer playing by multiple robots by utilizing the principles of RL, theory of games (GT), dynamic programming (DP), and/or evolutionary optimization (EO) algorithms. This chapter provides a thorough survey of the existing literature of RL with a brief overview of EO to examine the role of the algorithms in the context of multi-agent coordination. The study includes the classification of multi-agent coordination based on different criterion, such as the level of cooperation, knowledge sharing, communication, and the like. The chapter also includes multi-robot coordination employing EO, and specially RL for cooperative, competitive, and their composition for application to static and dynamic games. The later part of the chapter deals with an overview of the metrics used to compare the performance of the algorithms in coordination. Two fundamental metrics of performance analysis are defined, where the first one is required to study the learning performance, while the other to measure the performance of the planning algorithm. Conclusions are listed at the end of the chapter with possible explorations for the future real-time applications.

Multi-agent Coordination: A Reinforcement Learning Approach, First Edition.
Arup Kumar Sadhu and Amit Konar.
© 2021 The Institute of Electrical and Electronics Engineers, Inc.
Published 2021 by John Wiley & Sons, Inc.

1.1 Introduction

A robot is an intelligent and programmable manipulator, targeted at developing the functionality similar to those of a living creature [1]. It can serve complex and/or repetitive tasks efficiently. Based on the ability of locomotion, robots are categorized into two basic types: fixed base robots and mobile robots. Depending upon the type of locomotion, mobile robots are categorized into three types: wheeled/legged robots, winged/flying robots, and underwater robots, where for the last one, locomotion is controlled by water thrust. In this chapter, we would deal with wheeled robots only.

Agency is a commonly used jargon in modern robotics [1]. An agent is a piece of program/hardware that helps a robot to serve a directed goal. Like humans, when complexity of the problem grows, collective intelligence of the agents is required to achieve the target. The book is on collective/group behavior of agents, who can sense and act rationally. On occasions, agents can share the sensory information or its decision with its teammates directly through a communication network or by displaying its gestural/postural patterns, carrying a specific signature, to communicate a message to its team members.

Communication is a vital issue to generate plans by the agents. However, communication is time-costly and thus is often disregarded for real-world robotic applications. In the present book, we attempted to learn the agent behavioral patterns by a process of learning, and thus avoid communication overhead in real-time planning [1].

There exists quite a vast literature on planning algorithms [2–29]. One of the early robot planning algorithms is due to Nilsson in connection with his research on reasoning-based planning undertaken in Stanford AI research laboratory, which later was adopted in STRIPs [30–32]. In late 1980s to early 1990s, several planning algorithms, including A^* [31, 32], Voronoi diagrams [33], Quad tree, and potential field [34] were evolved. These algorithms presume static world. At the beginning of the 1990s, Michalewicz in one of his renowned papers introduced genetic operators to undertake dynamic planning with local adaptation in trial solutions by specialized mutation operators. The period 1990–2000 has seen significant changes in the planning algorithm with the introduction of supervised/unsupervised neural learning in planning algorithms [32]. The neural algorithms worked in both static and dynamic environments. Typically, in dynamic environments, they predict the direction and speed of motion to determine possible avoidance of collisions. However, they had limited learned experience, and thus were unable to handle planning in the presence of random motions of dynamic obstacles/persons in the environment. Almost at the beginning of the first quarter of the

1990s, Sutton proposed RL algorithm [35], which can help the robot learn its environment through semi-supervised learning. We would deal with multi-agent RL (MARL) in this chapter.

Planning and coordination are two closely used terms in multi-agent robotics [30]. While planning is concerned with determining the sequence of steps to achieve a goal, coordination refers to skillful interaction among the agents to serve their individual short-run/long-run purposes. Apparently, coordination among the agents is required to implement the steps of planning. In centralized planning, the agents need not require coordination, as the central manager takes care of all the agents' states as if its own state and generate a planning cycle by taking care of all the agents' states and goals jointly. Unfortunately, centralized planning is very slow and single-point failure may occur. Thus, centralized planning is not amenable for real-time applications, when the number of agents is excessive. In distributed planning, each agent generates one step of planning by coordinating with other active agents.

Coordination is broadly divided into two types: cooperation [36] and competition [37]. As the names indicate, cooperation requires agents to work hand-in-hand to purposefully serve the common objective of the team. Competition, on the other hand, leads to the success of one team against the failure of its opponent. For instance, in robot soccer, teammates work harmoniously in a cooperative manner, while each team of agents competes for winning at the cost of defeat of the other team.

Researchers are taking keen interest to model agent cooperation/competition by various models/tools. A few of these that need special mention include RL, GT [38–45], DP [46, 47], EO [48–56], and many others [6, 15–28, 57–59]. In RL, agents learn the most profitable joint action at each joint state through a feedback from the environment, and use them for subsequent planning applications [35]. GT requires for strategic analysis in multi-agent domain. In GT, agents evaluate the equilibrium, representative of the most-profitable joint action for the team in a joint state, and execute the joint action for joint state-transition in a loop until the joint goal is explored [38, 41–43, 60]. In DP [46], a complex problem is divided into finite overlapping subproblems. Each subproblem is solved by a DP algorithm and the solution is stored in a database. In the subsequent iterations, if a subproblem already addressed reappears, then that subproblem is not readdressed, but its solution is exploited from the database. In EO algorithm [48, 61–70], the constraint to satisfy the cooperation is checked on the members of the trial solutions before the solutions are entertained for the next generation. Recently, researchers aimed at developing MARL fusing RL, DP, and GT [71, 72]. In this book, we would explore new algorithms of MARL and novel EO.

1.2 Single Agent Planning

In single agent planning [5], an agent searches for the sequence of actions, for which it reaches its predefined goal state from a given state optimally in terms of predefined performance metric. The section describes the single agent planning terminologies and algorithms. Here, single agent planning algorithm includes search-based and learning-based planning algorithms.

1.2.1 Terminologies Used in Single Agent Planning

Definition 1.1 An *agent* [1] is a mathematical entity that acts on its environment and senses the changes in the environment due to its action. The agent is realized by hardware/software means. A hardwired agent has an actuator (motors/levers) and a sensor to serve the purpose of actuation and sensing, respectively.

A learning agent learns its right action at a given location/grid, called state, from its sensory-action doublets. A planning agent identifies its best action at its current state to obtain maximum reward for its action in the given environment.

In a single agent system, the environment includes a single agent. Naturally, the learning/planning steps/moves of the agent is undisturbed by the environment. Figure 1.1 offers architecture of a single agent system.

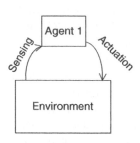

Figure 1.1 Single agent system.

Definition 1.2 The *state* of an agent represents a situation of the agent, concerning the position and/or orientation of the agent in the environment at an instant.

A state-space is a collective set of states of an agent. The definition of the state-space is required *a priori*, to address a planning problem. Such description of the state-space is problem specific. The state-space may be discrete or continuous. We in this book, however, deal with discrete state-space. Figure 1.2 illustrates three discrete states ($s1$, $s2$, and $s3$) of an environment.

| s_1 | s_2 | s_3 |

Figure 1.2 Three discrete states in an environment.

Definition 1.3 The *action selection* by an agent is done randomly or using specific strategies, such as ε-greedy strategy [35] or the Boltzmann strategy [73]. Random action selection sometimes is inefficient, when the same action is selected repeatedly during the learning phase.

Figure 1.3 Robot executing action Right (R) at state *s*1 and moves to the next state *s*2.

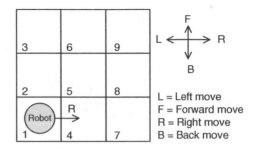

L = Left move
F = Forward move
R = Right move
B = Back move

The ε-greedy strategy [35] allows an agent to select random actions from a pool with a probability $=\varepsilon$. For example, if $\varepsilon = 0.2$, then the agent would select 20 actions randomly and 80 greedy actions out of 100 trials from a pool of actions.

Unlike the above, the Boltzmann strategy [73] employs a probability distribution based on the reward function value obtained for individual actions. Usually, an exponential distribution is used to determine the probability of an action in a pool of actions. The larger is the individual reward, the higher is the action selection probability. One control parameter temperature is used to tune the action selection probabilities.

In Figure 1.3, we consider one agent capable of state-transitions using only four actions: Left-move (L), Forward-move (F), Right-move (R), and Back-move (B).

Definition 1.4 A *state-transition* [35] function at state $s \in \{s\}$ due to action $a \in \{a\}$ is a mapping from (s, a) to $s' \in \{s\}$, where s' be a next state, i.e.

$$s' \leftarrow \delta(s, a). \tag{1.1}$$

In deterministic system, for each pair of (s, a), we have a fixed s'. In non-deterministic (or stochastic) situation, for each pair of (s, a), we may have different s'. Traditionally, non-determinism is handled in an easier way by assigning a probability mass for each state-transition $\delta(s, a)$, such that the sum of the state-transition probabilities is equal to one.

Non-determinism creeps into the system by various ways. For instance, in robot planning application, the condition of floor, such as its "slippery condition" is a guiding factor to determine the transition probabilities.

Suppose, in Figure 1.4, a robot executes an action a at state s and moves to the next state s', receiving an immediate reward $r(s, a)$ as a feedback from the environment. Suppose the floor on which the robot moves on is slippery. In that case, from a state s because of an action a the robot can have more than one

Figure 1.4 Deterministic state-transition.

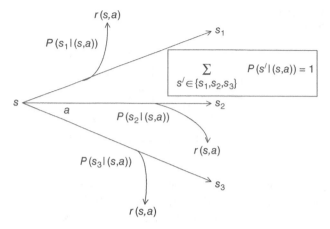

Figure 1.5   Stochastic state-transition.

state-transition, each with a state-transition probability of $P(s' \mid (s, a))$, $s' \in [s_1, s_2, s_3]$, where,

$$\sum_{\forall s'} P\left(s' \mid (s, a)\right) = 1 \tag{1.2}$$

as shown in Figure 1.5. For each state-transition, the agent receives an individual immediate reward $r(s, a)$ with its corresponding state-transition probability.

Definition 1.5   A *policy* [35] π is a decision-making mapping function, representing the probability assignment to a set of actions $\{a\}$ at a given state $s \in \{s\}$ such that, $\sum_{\forall a} \pi(s, a) = 1$, i.e.

$$\pi : s \times \{a\} \rightarrow [0, 1], \tag{1.3}$$

subject to

$$\sum_{\forall a} \pi(s, a) = 1 \tag{1.4}$$

holds for each state s.

In Figure 1.3, at state s_1 there is a set of finite possible actions: L, F, R, and B. Now, random selection of an action from this finite set infinite times results in a policy, $\pi(s_1, a) = 0.25$, $a \in \{L, F, R, B\}$.

In a planning problem, an agent starts by executing its individual action from a predefined state (starting state) with an aim to reach its individual predefined absorbing state (goal state), optimally in terms of time, path length, energy, and the like. Feasibility and optimality are two desired criterions need to be satisfied while addressing the planning problem [30].

Definition 1.6 *Feasibility* refers to the locomotion of an agent to a feasible next state because of an action form the current state.

Definition 1.7 *Optimality* indicates the performance optimization of the planning algorithm in each step, by minimizing the system resource utilization.

Definition 1.8 The sequence of actions lead to the predefined goal state from a given starting state maintaining the feasibility and optimality jointly in each step is well known as *plan*.

To understand the concept of planning, Example 1.1 is given to realize the movement of a single agent (here robot) in a two-dimensional discrete environment.

Example 1.1 Suppose a robot moves in a two-dimensional 5×5 grid environment as shown in Figure 1.6. There are 25 states and each state is represented by an integer or the Cartesian coordinate (x, y), where $x \in [1, 5]$ and $y \subset [1, 5]$. An agent can execute one among the four possible actions $a \in \{L, F, R, B\}$ at a state $s \in [1, 25]$. After executing an action a at a state s, a state-transition takes place and the robot moves from s to the next state $s' \in [1, 25]$ by (1.1). The collection

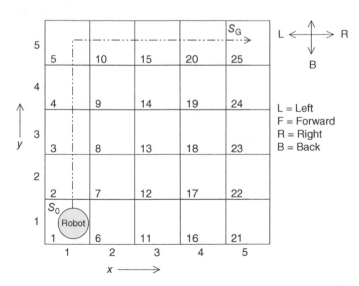

Figure 1.6 Two-dimensional 5×5 grid environment.

of state-transitions for which the robot moves from its current state "1" to the goal state "25" is called a feasible path. Among the feasible paths, the optimal one is chosen. One optimal path (here in terms of number of state-transitions) is shown in Figure 1.6 by dotted lines. The example can be made more interesting by adding obstacles in the optimal path.

After finalizing a plan (sequence of actions) by an agent, the agent follows the plan either by execution, refinement, or hierarchical approach.

Execution: In the execution phase, planner's plan is executed in a simulator or by a robot connected to the real environment. There are two types of robots for execution. In the first type, the robot is programmable and acts as an autonomous agent. This approach has the provision of updating the plans after finite time interval. However, most planning algorithms are designed to tackle new situations during the planning phase and hence, the above type of execution is not preferred. The second one is the special-purpose robot designed to solve a specific task given to it.

Refinement: Refinement is the evolution of the planning algorithms toward the better performance as shown in Figure 1.7. In Figure 1.7, agents first compute a collision-free path in the presence of obstacles after that agents optimize (smoothen) the path. Finally, a trajectory is planned following the path and a feedback controller is added for that.

Hierarchical: In hierarchical model, each plan is considered as an action under a larger plan. The same plan may also be defined as a subroutine under the larger plan. In Figure 1.8, the master plan is known as the *root node*. Remaining subsequent plans act as an action for the master plan or plan. There may be infinite number of plans under a master plan or plan. In Figure 1.8, n, m, and p are the real positive integer number. In Figure 1.9 (hierarchical model), agent 1 interacts with environment 1 and agent 2 with environment 2. Again in Figure 1.9,

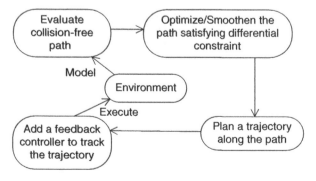

Figure 1.7   Refinement approach in robotics.

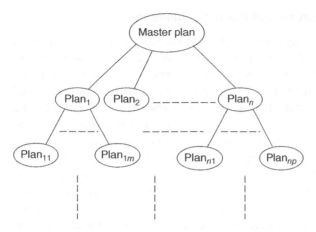

Figure 1.8   Hierarchical tree.

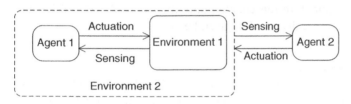

Figure 1.9   Hierarchical model.

environment 2 includes agent 1 and environment 1. So, Agent 2 interacts with the environment 2 as well as 1.

The search-based planning algorithms are employed to evaluate low-cost planning paths in terms of path length, time, energy, and the like, for single-robot planning. The search-based planning algorithms are popular mainly because of their simplicity. The search-based algorithm compromises of the following two parts:

1) In the first part, the realization of the goal following a number of feasible plans is done by employing a search algorithm.
2) The second part is related to the optimal planning, which employs principle of optimality to reduce the computational effort in the planning algorithms.

The search-based planning algorithms avoid the geometric models or differential equations. The search-based algorithms also avoid uncertainty and hence they avoid complications due to probability calculation.

1.2.2 Single Agent Search-Based Planning Algorithms

By search-based planning algorithms, a plan (or sequence of feasible actions) is searched by one of the following methods: forward search, backward search, and bidirectional search [30]. Forward search algorithm deals with the three variant of states. First one is the state which has not been visited yet or the unexplored one is known as *unvisited* state. If all possible state-transitions are explored in a given state, then the state is referred to as a *dead* state. The state which has been visited but still there exist a few unexplored next state is defined as *alive* state. Breadth first [30], Depth first [30], Dijkstra's [74], Best first search [30], Iterative deepening [30], A-star (A*) [32], and D-star (D*) [6] are the examples of forward search algorithms. The above forward search algorithms are extendable to the backward search algorithm, by solving the same planning problem by traversing from the goal state to the starting state. The bidirectional search is the combination of forward and backward search. In every search-based planning algorithm, a tree is maintained. For the forward (backward) search, initial (goal) state is the root node of the tree. The advantage of bidirectional search is the radical reduction in the exploration required. In this chapter, only the Dijkstra's, A* and D*, and STRIPS like algorithms are discussed as given below.

1.2.2.1 Dijkstra's Algorithm

Dijkstra's algorithm was proposed by computer scientist Edsger W. Dijkstra's [74]. Dijkstra's algorithm is employed to find out the shortest path between two nodes in a graph. In case of robotics, each state is represented by a node of the graph. The starting state is denoted by the source node and instead of finding the shortest path from the source node to all other nodes, the shortest path is obtained from the source node to a specific goal node (goal state of the robot).

The Dijkstra's algorithm is explained for the 3×3 grid shown in Figure 1.10. In Figure 1.10, there are nine states (nodes). State 1 is the source node and state 9 is

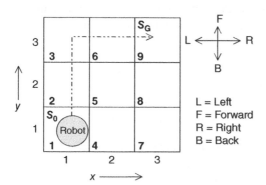

Figure 1.10 Two-dimensional 3×3 grid environment.

L = Left
F = Forward
R = Right
B = Back

Figure 1.11 Corresponding graph of Figure 1.10.

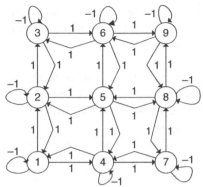

the goal node. From each node there are maximum four possible paths as shown in the graph (Figure 1.11). Weights of all the edges are 1, ∞, and −1. 1 is assigned for a feasible edge. The self-loop and/or collision between robot and the boundary in Figure 1.11 signify the penalty with reward of −1. ∞ is assigned for an invalid edge. The steps of Dijkstra's algorithm are given in Algorithm 1.1.

The trace of the Dijkstra's algorithm for robot path planning is given in Table 1.1. The bold numbers are the selected node corresponding to the column's node from the current node. The run-time complexity of the Dijkstra's algorithm is $O(|V| \log |V| + |E|)$, where $|V|$ and $|E|$ are the number of edges and nodes, respectively.

1.2.2.2 A* (A-star) Algorithm

A^* is a heuristic search-based algorithm [32]. In A^* algorithm, the quality of a node is measured by introducing two cost functions: one is heuristic cost and another is the generation cost. The heuristic cost, denoted by $h(x)$, is a measure of distance (here city block distance) between the current node x to the goal node. The generation cost of a node x, denoted by $g(x)$, measures the distance of node x from the source node. Total cost function at node x is the summation of $f(x)$ and $g(x)$. The following definitions are required before explaining the A^* algorithm [32].

Definition 1.9 A node x is called *open* if the node x has been generated and the heuristic cost $h(x)$ has been computed over it but it has not been expanded yet.

Definition 1.10 A node x is called *closed* if it has been expanded for generating offspring.

The steps of A^* algorithm is given Algorithm 1.2. Example 1.2 is given for better understanding of A^* algorithm in the perspective of robot path planning problem.

Algorithm 1.1 Dijkstra's Algorithm

Input: Mark all the unvisited nodes and the current node is set as the source node; Generate a search graph G, including the starting node x. Mark node x as an open;
Output: The optimal path;
Begin
Initialize: Set a distance value to all the nodes in the graph. Set zero for the source node (here state 1) and ∞ for the remaining nodes;
Repeat
1) From the current node, explore all the unvisited neighbors and evaluate their distances from the initial node. (For example, let the current node, x has a distance of 3 unit from the source node, and an edge connecting x with another node y has distance of 2. Now, the distance to y through x from the source node becomes 3 + 2 = 5. Compare the currently evaluated distance with the previously recorded distance (∞ at the beginning). If the currently evaluated distance is less than previously recorded distance, then update the database by the currently evaluated distance, otherwise do nothing.
2) Once all the neighbors of the current node have been explored, the current node is marked asvisited (not checked further), and the evaluated distances are recoded as the final and minimal distances.
3) Select one unvisited node with smallest distance as the next current node;
Until goal state reached;
End.

Table 1.1 Trace of Dijkstra's algorithm for Figure 1.11.

		Nodes →								
		1	2	3	4	5	6	7	8	9
Visited ← nodes	{1}	−1	1	∞	1	∞	∞	∞	∞	∞
	{1,2}	1	−1	2	2	2	∞	∞	∞	∞
	{1,2,3}	2	1	−1	3	2	3	∞	∞	∞
	{1,2,3,6}	3	2	1	4	3	−1	5	6	4

Algorithm 1.2   A* Algorithm

Input: Generate a search graph G, including the starting node x. Mark node x as an open;

Output: The optimal path;

Begin

Initialize: Create a list of *closed* node keeping them initially empty;

Repeat

  1) If list of *open* node is empty, then exit with failure;

  2) Let node n is selected from the list of open nodes and removes it from the set. Put the node n on the closed nodes list;

  3) If n is the goal node, then exit and return the solution obtained to trace a path from the node n to node x in the search graph G;

  4) Expand node n and generate the set M, which contains its successors that are not already the ancestors of n in G. Add the elements of M as successors of n in G;

  5) Point n from each members of M, which does not belong to G and add them in the open list. If for all the members of M already belong to open or closed list of nodes, then redirect the pointer to n, subject to the shortest path is found through n. If all the members of M are belong to closed list of nodes, then redirect the pointers of its entire offspring in G, so that they point toward the back along the best paths found till now to these offspring;

  6) Sort the elements of open list in order of increasing cost function (sum of heuristic cost and generation cost);

  Until goal state reached;

End.

Example 1.2   In this example, the A* algorithm is employed to find the shortest path between source node 1 to the goal node 9 as shown in Figure 1.10. The heuristic cost $h(x)$ of node x (x_x, x_y) is given by the city-block distance and it is defined in (1.5).

$$h(x) = |x_g - x_x| + |y_g - y_x|,\tag{1.5}$$

where (x_g, y_g) is the goal coordinate.

The trace of the A* algorithm is given in Table 1.2. In step 0, robot starts from node 1 and its heuristic cost is 4 and generation cost is 0. Hence, total cost is 4.

Table 1.2 Trace of A* algorithm from Figure 1.10.

Step	State-space		Heuristic cost	Generation cost	Total cost
0	①		4	0	4
1		For node 2 **(selected)**	**3**	**1**	**4**
		For node 4	3	1	4
2		For node 3 **(selected)**	**2**	**2**	**4**
		For node 5	2	2	4
3			1	3	4
4			0	4	4

The bold values signifies the selected node and its corresponding cost.

In step 1, node 1 is expanded by the action forward (F) to node 2 and by the action right (R) to node 4. The total cost of both the nodes 2 and 4 is $3 + 1 = 4$. Node 2 is selected and it is expended further by the actions forward (F), right (R), and back (B) to the nodes 3, 5, and 1, respectively. The total cost of the nodes 3 and 5 is $2 + 2 = 4$. Node 1 is not selected following Definition 1.10. Node 3 is selected and it is extended further to node 2 and 6 by the action back (B) and right (R), respectively. Here, node 2 is a closed node by Definition 1.10 and hence it is eradicated. So, node 6 is expanded to node 6 and 9 by the action back (B) and forward (F). Again node 6 is eradicated by Definition 1.10 and node 9 is the goal state. The total cost function of node 9 is 4 with 0 heuristic cost. Hence, optimal path is generated by sequentially following the nodes 1, 2, 3, 6, and 9.

1.2.2.3 D* (D-star) Algorithm

Unlike A^* [68], D^* [6] algorithm may be employed to efficiently plan in dynamic unknown or partially known environments, by adjusting the weights of the edges (arcs). In the present path-planning application, each state is assumed as a node and weight of each edge (arc) connecting two nodes represents the cost of moving from one node to another. Initially, a path is planned from current node to the goal employing the A^* algorithm using the known information. In the journey of the robot toward the goal state, it discovers the presence of obstacles in its path and the graph is modified by adapting the arc weight. The robot again computes the shortest path from its node position to the goal. The process continues until it reaches its goal position or it concludes that the goal is inaccessible. The trace of the D^* algorithm is shown below in Table 1.3 by adding an obstacle in state 3 of Figure 1.10 as shown in Figure 1.12. Steps 0 and 1 are same as A^* algorithm. In step 2, node 3 is expanded to node 1 and 5 by action right (R) and back (B), respectively.

Node 3 is not accessible as there is an obstacle at node 3. So, node 5 is expanded by left (L), forward (F), right (R), and back (B) actions to nodes 2, 6, 8, and 4, respectively. Nodes 2 and 4 are closed nodes following Definition 1.10. Selecting node 6 and expanding it to nodes 5 and 9 by actions back (B) and right (R), respectively, the goal node 9 is reached. So, optimal path is generated by sequentially following the nodes 1, 2, 5, 6, and 9.

1.2.2.4 Planning by STRIPS-Like Language

Representation is the main bottleneck of the earlier explained search-based planning techniques due to enormous state-space. To address such representation problem, STRIPS-like language [30] is proposed by the Stanford Research Institute Problem Solver group, which is expressive enough to characterize a planning problem logically. STRIPS stands for Stanford Research Institute Problem Solver.

Table 1.3 Trace of D∗ algorithm from Figure 1.12.

Step	State-space		Heuristic cost	Generation cost	Total cost
0	①		4	0	4
1	(tree with node 1 branching F→②, R→④)	For node 2 **(selected)**	**3**	**1**	**4**
		For node 4	3	1	4
2	(tree: 1→F→2→R→⑤, B→1; R→4)	For node 5	2	2	4
3	(tree: ...→5→L→②, F→⑥, R→⑧, B→④)	For node 6 **(selected)**	**1**	**3**	**4**
		For node 8	1	3	4
4	(tree: ...→6→B→⑤, R→⑨ Goal)		0	4	4

The bold values signifies the selected node and its corresponding cost.

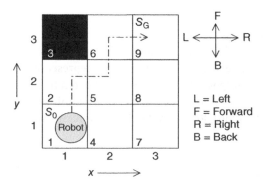

Figure 1.12 Two-dimensional 3 × 3 grid environment with an obstacle.

L = Left
F = Forward
R = Right
B = Back

STRIPS is the first well-known logic-based representation of the discrete planning algorithm, which is the extension of first-order logic (propositional logic). The following representations are employed in STRIPS.

State: In STRIPS, an agent decomposes the environment into logical conditions (TRUE or FALSE), and then the state is represented by conjunctions of function-free ground literals. Ground literal refers to the predicates, which cannot break any more. Suppose, a home service robot is instructed to bring a cup of tea with a biscuit and a magazine. So, in STRIPS, the initial state is formed using the following predicates "at(home)," "¬ have(tea)," "¬ have(biscuit)," and "¬ have (magazine)." Here, home represents the initial position. Now, initial state is the conjunctions of the function-free predicates (ground literals), i.e. "at(home) ^¬ have(tea)^¬ have(biscuit)^¬ have(magazine)." However, the goal state is the "at(home)^have(tea)^have(biscuit)^have(magazine)". Now, the task is to find out the sequence of actions to reach from the initial state to the goal state.

Action: An action follows the following two conditions: preconditions and effect. In precondition, an agent needs to satisfy certain feasibility condition before executing an action. For example, for "have(tea)" the agent must go to a nearby tea stall because tea is not available at(home). Also the preconditions are always positive ground literals. On the other hand, effects are the conjunction of positive and negative ground literals. For example, if there is an action "go(tea stall)" from "at(home)", then the precondition is "at(home)^path(here, there)" and the effect is "at(tea stall)^¬ at(home)". Hence, to reach the goal state "at(home)^have(tea)^have (biscuit)^have(magazine)," an agent must satisfy all the preconditions and effects.

1.2.3 Single Agent RL

In the above perspective, learning can assist an agent to select actions. In single agent RL [35, 75–77] (Figure 1.13), an agent receives a reward/penalty as a feedback due to an action at its present (current) state or situation from the surrounding (environment). Such scalar feedback measures the quality of the action in that state. In the literature of RL, this quality value is well known as state–action value. The robot remembers or stores the <state, action, reward> profile as an experience for future reference. Once the robot learns all possible <state, action, reward> profiles, it plans optimally in terms of time and/or energy, from any state within the environment it learns. The single agent RL can be explained by the well-known multiarmed bandit problem [78, 79].

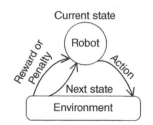

Figure 1.13 Structure of reinforcement learning.

1.2.3.1 Multiarmed Bandit Problem

In the literature of English, a bandit refers to a robber or gambler, who belongs to a gang typically isolated from the human society. If a bandit has only one arm, then the bandit is called one-armed bandit. The one-armed bandit is also well known as a slot machine, because a slot machine is operated by a button located on the front panel of the machine. A *slot machine* is a casino gambling machine, which rolls three or more times once the button is pushed. As the slot machine stops rolling, it pays off the bandit based on the pattern formed by the symbols visible on the front side of the machine. A multiarmed bandit consists of a series of slot machines arranged in a row. In multiarmed bandit problem [78, 79], the bandit has to decide which slot machine to play and for how many times to maximize the sum of the rewards earned.

The gambler starts playing the multiarmed bandit problem without any knowledge about the slot machines. In each trial, the gambler faces a trade-off between the "exploration" of a new slot machine to obtain better reward than the present rewards, and "exploitation" of a slot machine that has already obtained highest expected rewards. Similar trade-off is experienced by a reinforcement learner in RL. Hence, the multiarmed bandit is employed to manage several projects in a large organization, where initially the properties of the projects are partially known or unknown, but as time passes, the properties becomes fully known to the bandit.

Suppose, a multiarmed bandit [78, 79] has N-slot machines (or N-arms), which are being played by the bandit, and the bandit receives different rewards for each arm, with an aim to determine the arm having the maximum reward. To choose the best arm, i.e. an arm corresponding to the maximum reward (or greedy reward); the agent (or bandit) may compute the running average of rewards of all the arms given in (1.6).

$$Q_t(a) = \frac{r_1 + r_2 + \cdots + r_k}{k}, \tag{1.6}$$

where $Q_t(a)$ refers to the estimated value of the action a in t trials (play). We assume that action a was played k times in t trials and r_k was the reward of choosing the action (arm) a at kth time step. As choosing an arm is analogous to choosing an action, the value of each arm may also be defined as the expected reward of the arm. Let the expected optimal reward of the action a is $Q^*(a)$. Based on the greedy action selection policy, the optimal action a^* is chosen by (1.7).

$$a^* = \underset{a}{\mathrm{argmax}}\, Q^*(a). \tag{1.7}$$

The said greedy action selection may trap the agent (bandit) in local minima. To overcome the problem of trapping in local minima, an agent has to explore a new arm to receive new reward (well known as exploration), which might be better than the present reward. Randomization of the probability of choosing an arm, which is not the greedy one, is referred to as the exploration. In RL, always there is a trade-off between the exploration and exploitation. For example, let $N = 10$ in the said multiarmed bandit problem. Each arm (analogous to an action) $a \in [1, 10]$ has a random reward given in (1.8) drawn from a normal random distribution with mean zero and variance one, $N(0, 1)$. Equation (1.8) represents the true value or expected reward of the 10 arms.

$$Q^*(a) = [0.0325, 0.8530, 0.1341, 0.0620, -0.2040, 0.6525, 0.8927, -0.9418,$$
$$-1.4122, 0.8089].$$

(1.8)

By (1.7) and (1.8),

$$a^* = \underset{a}{\operatorname{argmax}} Q^*(a)$$

$$= \operatorname{argmax}[0.0325, 0.8530, 0.1341, 0.0620, -0.2040, 0.6525, 0.8927,$$

$$-0.9418, -1.4122, 0.8089]$$

$$= 7.$$

(1.9)

By (1.9), seventh action is the optimal action denoted by a^*. The learning process is started by estimating the true values from the earlier distribution of $N(0, 1)$ setting the exploration parameter ε to 0.2 and the first estimate is given in (1.10).

$$Q^0_{est}(a) = [0.6761, -1.4321, -0.1824, 3.1140, -1.5285, -2.4264, -1.6687,$$

$$-0.5252, -0.1021, -0.7124].$$

(1.10)

By (1.7), (1.10), and assuming $Q^*(a) = Q^0_{est}(a)$,

$$a^* = \underset{a}{\operatorname{argmax}} Q^*(a)$$

$$= \operatorname{argmax}[0.6761, -1.4321, -0.1824, 3.1140, -1.5285, -2.4264,$$

$$-1.6687, -0.5252, -0.1021, -0.7124]$$

$$= 4.$$

(1.11)

By (1.11), the bandit should choose the fourth action but by (1.9), the optimal action is the seventh one. So, the greedy choice is misleading the action selection. Several estimations are done to update the $Q_{est}(a)$ vector using (1.6). The learning process continues until the agent recognizes the seventh action as its best choice among the 10 actions. The variation of average reward with the number of trial for different ε is given in Figure 1.14.

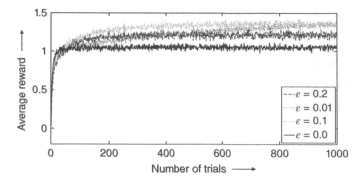

Figure 1.14 Variation of average reward with the number of trial for different ε in 10-armed bandit problem.

1.2.3.2 DP and Bellman Equation

DP [46] is an optimization technique, which transforms a large complex problem into a sequence of simple problems, by dividing it into finite overlapping subproblems, where overlapping indicates that the subproblems can recursively form the actual large complex problem. Breaking a large complex problem into finite overlapping subproblems is the condition of applying DP upon the large complex problem. In DP, there is a relation between the solution offered by the large problem and solutions offered by the subproblems. In the literature of optimization, this relationship is well known as the Bellman equation (BE) or DP equation.

Each subproblem is solved by a DP algorithm and the solution is stored in a database. In the subsequent iterations, if a subproblem already addressed reappears, then that subproblem is not readdressed, but its solution is exploited from the database. Finally, one optimal solution is chosen from the evaluated value functions. The basic four steps for a DP algorithm are given below [46].

1) Divide the large complex problem into finite overlapping subproblems.
2) A value function is defined recursively based on the overlapping subproblems.
3) Compute and memorize the value functions of the overlapping subproblems to avoid repetition.
4) Obtain an optimal solution from the evaluated value functions.

Value function is the heart of DP, as it expresses the quality of a state because of an optimal action in terms of numerical value. If one needs to maximize the value function $v(s)$ at a state $s \in \{s\}$, then using the principle of DP, the problem can be expressed in the BE as given in (1.12).

$$v(s) = \max_a \left[r(s,a) + \gamma v\left(s'\right) \right], \quad \gamma \in (0,1), \tag{1.12}$$

where $r(s, a)$ refers to the reward received at state s because of an action a and $v(s')$ denotes the value function at next state s'.

1.2.3.3 Correlation Between RL and DP

It is apparent from the earlier sections that the RL works on the principle of reward/penalty received by the agents as a feedback from the environment, DP is nothing but an optimization technique, which optimizes the BE [71, 72]. Figure 1.15 indicates that the single agent Q-learning (QL) is the combination of the RL and the DP. The details of single agent Q-learning are given in the next section.

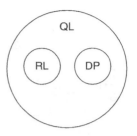

Figure 1.15 Correlation between the RL and DP.

1.2.3.4 Single Agent Q-Learning

Q-learning is one well-known paradigm among the RL techniques coined by Watkins and Dayan [80] in 1989. In Q-learning, an agent (robot) adapts in an unknown environment, and receives two types of rewards due to an action at a given state within the environment. One reward is immediate reward received as a feedback from the environment as explained earlier in Section 1.2.3. Another reward is evaluated at the next state. The evaluated reward at the next state is of two types based on the nature of the environment. If the environment is deterministic, then best (or optimal) future reward is evaluated at the next state, shown in Figure 1.16. Since, in deterministic environment, an agent can move from a given state to the next state with probability one due to an action. On the other hand, in stochastic environment, a robot moves from a given state to the next one by assigning a probability in [0, 1] due to an action. Hence, in stochastic environment, the robot evaluates the expected best (or optimal) future reward at the next state. The expected best future reward in the next state is the expectation of selecting the best action in the next state in terms of numerical value. The mechanism of evaluating the expected best future reward in Q-learning is shown in Figure 1.17.

In Figure 1.16, initially all the Q-values at Q-table are set to zero. At the current state 1, the robot executes an action right (R) and receives an immediate reward r $(1, R) = 0$ from the environment. In the next state 3, maximum future reward is evaluated from the Q-table. Until $(3, F)$ is not explored, in the next state, $Q(3, L) = 81$ is the best future reward and updated Q-value at $(1, R)$ is $Q(1, R)=72.9$. On the other hand, once $(3, F)$ is explored in the next state, $Q(3, F) = 100$ is the best future reward and updated Q-value at $(1, R)$ is $Q(1, R) = 90$.

In Figure 1.17, "R" inside the circle symbolizes a robot. Here, each state 1 to 3 has distinct frictional properties. In such stochastic environment, any one next state among the three possible next states may be reached due to left action executed

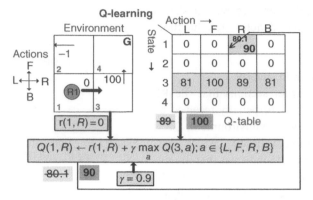

Figure 1.16 Single agent Q-learning.

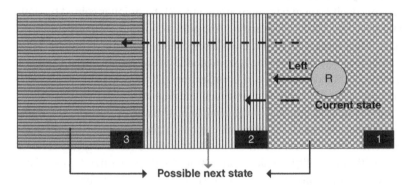

Figure 1.17 Possible next state in stochastic situation.

by *R* at 1. So, there is a probability of moving to the next state from the current state due to an action. In the literature, such probability is well known as the state-transition probability and the expected future reward is evaluated thereof.

In Q-learning, the future reward prediction depends on the current state–action pair. It is apparent that the future reward prediction in Q-learning of an agent depends exclusively upon the current state but not on the past state–action pairs, which is the Markov property. The Markov property is also well known as the memoryless property. This idea is framed inside the Markov Decision Process (MDP). In Q-learning, the MDP plays a significant role in finding the optimal value function corresponding to the optimal policy π^*. The definition of the MDP is given in Definition 1.11 [81].

Definition 1.11 *A MDP* is a 4-tuple $\langle S, A, r, p \rangle$ [82], [83], where *S* refers to a finite set of states, *A* denotes a finite set of actions, $r: S \times A \to \mathbb{R}$ refers to the reward function of the agent, and $p: S \times A \to [0, 1]$ indicates the state-transition probability.

$$v(s, \pi^*) = \max_a \left[r(s, a) + \gamma \sum_{s'} p\big[s' \mid (s, a)\big] v\big(s', \pi^*\big) \right], \tag{1.13}$$

where $v(s, \pi^*)$ and $v(s', \pi^*)$ represent the value at current state *s* and next state s' due to optimal policy π^*, γ denotes the discounting factor, $p[s' \mid (s, a)]$ is the state-transition probability to reach next state s' from current state *s* due to action $a \in A$, and $r(s, a)$ is the immediate reward at state *s* due to action *a*.

If an agent directly learns its optimal strategy without knowing either reward function or the state-transition probability, then the learning policy is called model-free RL [84]. Q-learning is one such model-free learning, involving the basic equation given in (1.14).

$$Q^*(s, a) = \left[r(s, a) + \gamma \sum_{s'} p\big[s' \mid (s, a)\big] v\big(s', \pi^*\big) \right]. \tag{1.14}$$

Here, $Q^*(s, a)$ is the optimal Q-value. After infinite revisit of state *S* due to action *a*, $Q(s, a)$ turns to $Q^*(s, a)$. If next state is deterministically known for each action, then the Q-learning is called deterministic. In deterministic situation, $p[s' \mid (s, a)] = 1, \forall s'$.

Combining (1.13) and (1.14), we can write,

$$v(s, \pi^*) = \max_a [Q^*(s, a)]. \tag{1.15}$$

Hence, the problem transforms to determining $Q^*(s, a)$ for all (s, a). If $Q^*(s, a)$ is found, one can identify the action which maximizes the $v(s, \pi^*)$. So, the Q-learning update rule becomes,

$$Q(s, a) = r(s, a) + \gamma \max_{a'} Q\big[\delta(s, a), a'\big], \tag{1.16}$$

where

$$s' \leftarrow \delta(s, a) \tag{1.17}$$

be the state-transition function. Hence, $Q(s', a') = Q(\delta(s, a), a')$. By combining (1.16) and (1.17), we obtain (1.18).

$$Q(s, a) = r(s, a) + \gamma \max_{a'} Q\big(s', a'\big), \tag{1.18}$$

Algorithm 1.3   Single Agent Q-Learning

`Input:` Current state `s` and action set `A`;
`Output:` Optimal Q-value $Q^*(s, a)$, $\forall s$, $\forall a$;
`Begin`
`Initialize:` $Q(s, a) \leftarrow 0$, $\forall s$, $\forall a$ and $\gamma \in [0, 1)$;
`Repeat`
`Select` an action $a \in A$ randomly and execute it;
`Receive` an immediate reward $r(s, a)$;
`Evaluate` next state $s' \leftarrow \delta(s, a)$;
`Update:` $Q(s, a)$ by (1.19) for deterministic situation,
by (1.20) for stochastic situation and $s \leftarrow s'$;
`Until` $Q(s, a)$ converges;
`Obtain:` $Q^*(s, a) \leftarrow Q(s, a)$, $\forall s$, $\forall a$;
`End.`

---

where $\max_{a'} Q(s', a')$ indicates the action $a' \in A$ for which maximum Q-value, $Q(s', a')$ is received at next state s'. Now, the Q-learning update rule with learning rate $\alpha \in (0, 1]$ is given by (1.19).

$$Q(s, a) \leftarrow (1 - \alpha)Q(s, a) + \alpha \left[r(s, a) + \gamma Q\left(s', a^*\right) \right]. \tag{1.19}$$

However, in the stochastic situation, the state-transition probability to reach the next state $s' \in \{s\}$ from the state s because of action a, is $P[s' \mid (s, a)] \neq 1$. So, Q-value adaption rule in the stochastic situation is given by (1.20) [84]:

$$Q(s, a) = (1 - \alpha)Q(s, a) + \alpha \left[r(s, a) + \gamma \sum_{s'} P\left[s' \mid (s, a)\right] \max_{a'} Q\left(s', a'\right) \right]. \tag{1.20}$$

After infinite revisit of (s, a), Q-value, $Q(s, a)$ turns to the optimal Q-value $Q^*(s, a)$. The convergence proof of (1.20) is given in [2]. Single agent Q-learning steps are given in Algorithm 1.3.

1.2.3.5   Single Agent Planning Using Q-Learning

Figure 1.18 explains the single robot planning mechanism. At first, the robot (R1) observes its current state 3 and its corresponding Q-values from the Q-table. Then at 3, the robot evaluates the action corresponding to the maximum Q-value using

Figure 1.18 Single agent planning.

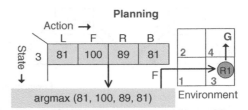

the learned Q-table. In Q-table, at the row of 3, the action R corresponds to the maximum Q-value. Robot executes the action R and moves to the next state 4. The above steps are repeated until the robot reaches it goal state.

1.3 Multi-agent Planning and Coordination

Multi-agent planning and coordination are two almost similar terminologies both belonging to the multi-agent systems. Multi-agent planning refers to determining the sequence of feasible actions of the agents to achieve individual goals maintaining optimality. However, coordination refers to skillful and effective interaction among the agents to serve the purpose of all the agents. The section describes the multi-agent planning and coordination terminologies with corresponding algorithms.

1.3.1 Terminologies Related to Multi-agent Coordination

A multi-agent system (MAS) includes several agents. Naturally, the action of an agent influences the rewards received by the other agents. This calls for special arrangement for learning and planning in a MAS. Figure 1.19 outlines the architecture of a MAS.

In the MAS, a state-space is a collective set of states of an agent. The definition of the state-space is required a priori, to address a planning problem. Such description of the state-space is problem specific. In a multi-robot coordination problem, instead of states, the joint state is defined.

Definition 1.12 A *joint state* is the collection or union of individual states in a fixed order following the ascending order of the agents.

Suppose s_i is the individual state of agent $i \in [1, m]$, then the joint state for m agents system is given by $S = \ <s_i>\ _{i=1}^{m}$.

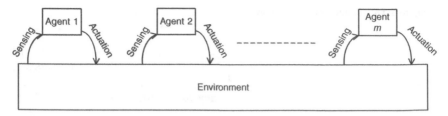

Figure 1.19 Multi-agent system with *m* agents.

Definition 1.13 The phrase: *joint-action* is a widely used term in the MAS and is defined by the collection or union of individual actions in a fixed order following the ascending order of the agents.

Suppose a_i is the individual action of agent $i \in [1, m]$, then the joint action for the m agent system is given by $A = < a_i >_{i=1}^{m}$. In Figure 1.20, due to joint action <R, L> at <1, 8> robots move to the joint next state <4, 5> as shown in Figure 1.20.

1.3.2 Classification of MAS

There exist several state-of-the-art attributes, based on which the MAS is classified [1, 37]. Attributes relevant to the present book are employed here to classify the MAS. Basically MAS is of two types: cooperative and competitive. Like any social living beings, an agent belonging to cooperative MAS cooperate with remaining agents. However, in the competitive MAS, agents do compete among themselves to acquire limited resources required for livelihood. In this chapter, we consider only the cooperative MAS.

Classification based on cooperation: Classification of MAS based on the cooperative aspect of the agents is done by measuring the ability of an agent to cooperate with remaining agents while performing a task. Agents cooperate with the

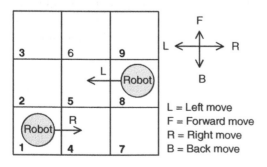

Figure 1.20 Robots executing joint action <R, L> at joint state <1, 8> and move to the next state <4, 5>.

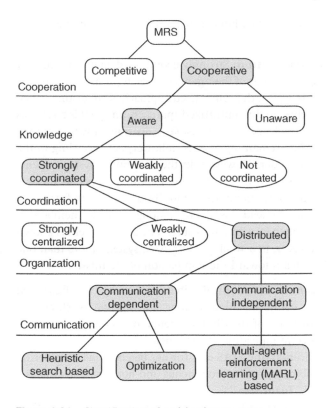

Figure 1.21 Classification of multi-robot systems.

remaining agents are well known as cooperative agent and those do not cooperate rather they compete with others are distinguished as noncooperative agent. The goal of cooperative agents is to achieve a common objective. On the other hand, the noncooperative agents have always conflicting objectives. Figure 1.21 provides a detailed classification of cooperative agents only based on the knowledge level.

Classification based on knowledge level: Further classification of cooperative MAS can be done based on the knowledge level of an agent about the remaining agents in the same team. In Figure 1.21, one is aware agent, which has knowledge about its teammates and the unaware agent does not have such knowledge about the remaining agents in the environment.

Classification based on coordination: Next, the aware agents are classified based on the coordination procedure employed by the agents. There are three types of coordination. In strong (weak) coordination, agents strictly (do not strictly) follow the coordination protocols. In the third type, i.e. not coordinated, agents do not coordinate with other agents. Classification based upon the coordination is shown in Figure 1.21.

Classification based on organization: Strongly coordinated agents are further classified based on the responsibilities of the agents in a team (or organization) as shown in Figure 1.21. By this aspect, the centralized approaches are distinguished from the distributed approaches. In the centralized approach, an agent is elected as a leader for the entire team. The leader is responsible to distribute the task among all the agents in the team. The remaining agents (follower) act according to the instructions provided by the leader. However, in the distributed system, agents are completely autonomous in view of the decision-making process, as there is no leader in the team. On the other hand, the centralized system can further be classified based upon the way the leader is elected among the team members. If only one robot leads the complete mission, then such centralized system is known as strongly centralized. However, in a weakly centralized system, more than one agent is allowed to lead the team toward the completion of the mission.

Classification based on communication: Distributed robots are classified based upon the dependency on communication among the agents as shown in Figure 1.21. There are two types of distributed agents, one is communication dependent, and another is communication independent.

Besides the above classification, the MAS can further be classified considering "Team Composition" (combination of heterogeneous and homogeneous robots), "System Architecture," and "Team Size."

Several approaches are available in the literature of multi-robot coordination. Among them, coordination by MAQL and EO algorithms are described in this chapter. To improve readability, GT and DP are briefly described below.

1.3.3 Game Theory for Multi-agent Coordination

GT formally analyzes the strategic situation of the MAS, where each agent potentially affects the interests of other agents in the environment [38, 41, 42]. Two types of game are considered in the present book: static and dynamic. The definitions of static and dynamic games are given below.

Definition 1.14 A *static game* with m player is defined by a tuple $\langle m, A_1, A_2, ..., A_m, r_1, r_2, ..., r_m \rangle$ [42], where $A_i, i \in [1, m]$ is the set of finite actions of player i and $r_i : \times_{i=1}^{m} A_i \to \mathbb{R}, i \in [1, m]$ refers to the reward function of player i, where, $\times$ denotes the Cartesian product.

Definition 1.15 If a static game is played repeatedly, then the game is well known as *repeated game*.

In static game, multiple agents execute their actions at a joint state and agents do not have any state-transition. Hence, a static game is also known as state-less game. Now, to handle the games with state-transitions, another version of game called dynamic game is defined below.

Definition 1.16   A *dynamic game* with m number of agents is defined as a 5-tuple $\langle m, \{S\}, \{A\}, r_i, p_i \rangle$ where $\{S\} = \times_{i=1}^{m} S_i$ is the joint state-space, $\{A\} = \times_{i=1}^{m} A_i$ is the joint action-space, $r_i = \{S\} \times \{A\} \to \mathbb{R}$ is the reward function at joint state–action of agent i, and $P_i = \{S\} \times \{A\} \to [0, 1]$ is state-transition function of agent i.

Suppose an agent $i \in [1, m]$ selects an action a_i from the pool of its action set A_i and plays the repeated game. The conjunction of the individually chosen actions for all the agents form a joint action $A \in \times_{i=1}^{m} A_i$. Let $\pi_i(a_i)$ refers to the probability of selecting an action $a_i \in A_i$ by agent i, where

$$\pi_i : A_i \to [0, 1]. \tag{1.21}$$

If $\pi_i(a_i) = 1$, then the strategy of agent i, π_i is deterministic for $a_i \in A_i$. The strategy profile for m agents is given by

$$\Pi = \{\pi_i : i \in [1, m]\}. \tag{1.22}$$

The strategy profile

$$\Pi_{-i} = \{\pi_1, ..., \pi_{i-1}, \pi_{i+1}, ..., \pi_m\} \tag{1.23}$$

denotes the strategy of all the agents except the strategy of agent i, π_i, where

$$\Pi = \Pi_{-i} \cup \{\pi_i\}. \tag{1.24}$$

It is apparent from Definitions 1.14 and 1.16 that a dynamic game is also a static game with state-transitions. In a static game, agents look for a balanced condition or equilibrium among them, such that no one would receive any incentive by unilateral deviation. In the literature, two well-known equilibria exist: Nash equilibrium (NE) and correlated equilibrium (CE).

Before understanding equilibrium, let at a given state s an agent (here robot) have an action set A. An action $a^* \in A$ corresponding to the maximum reward at state s refers to the optimal or greedy action. Collection of such optimal actions executed at each state is termed as optimal policy or strategy. In a particular state, if a robot executes an action, then the action is well known as a *pure strategy*. However, the *mixed strategy* is the randomization over the pure strategies. To understand mixed strategy, rock-paper-scissor game is given in Example 1.3.

Example 1.3   Rock-paper-scissor [41, 42] is a two player hand game, played for fun by kids and sometimes for decision-making by adults. Each player has three options: rock, paper, or scissor and a player can choose one in a trial. The player

(a)   (b)   (c)

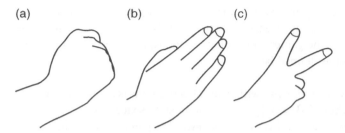

Figure 1.22 Hands gestures in rock-paper-scissor game: (a) rock, (b) paper, and (c) scissor.

expresses his/her choice to another player by using a hand to form one of the shapers as shown in Figure 1.22. With these options, this game can have three possible outcomes excluding a tie. The three possible outcomes are given one by one.

1) One rock crushes scissor. Here, player playing rock beats the player playing scissor.
2) But if paper covers rock, then the player chooses to play paper beats the player playing rock.
3) On the other hand, if scissors cut paper, then the play of paper is defeated by the play of scissor.

However, if the choices of both the players are same, then a tie occurs and the game is replayed until the tie is broken.

After finite trials of the game, the rewards of both the players are given in the reward matrix as shown in Figure 1.23. In Figure 1.23, one cell contains two rewards. The first reward is for Player 1 and second one is for Player 2. In case of a tie, both the players receive 0 reward. If a player wins the game, then the player is rewarded by 1. On the other hand, if the player loses, then the player is penalized by −1.

It is apparent that in the rock-paper-scissor game (Figures 1.22 and 1.23), optimal mixed strategy of Players 1 and 2 is to execute each action with a probability 1/3. Now, suppose Player 1 knows in advance that the Player 2 is playing the pure strategy "paper," then optimal pure strategy for Player 1 is "scissor" as it provides maximum reward to Player 1.

Figure 1.23 Rock-paper-scissor game.

		Player 2		
		Rock	Paper	Scissor
Player 1	Rock	(0,0)	(−1,1)	(1,−1)
	Paper	(1,−1)	(0,0)	(−1,1)
	Scissor	(−1,1)	**(1,−1)**	(0,0)

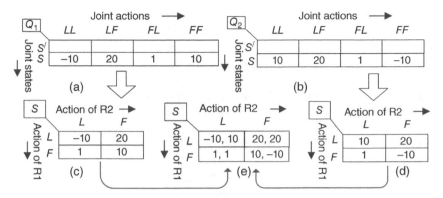

Figure 1.24 Reward mapping from joint Q-table to reward matrix.

1.3.3.1 Nash Equilibrium

NE is a solution concept of the multi-agent interactive system from where no player deviates to maintain its current reward, which is the maximum one. The Definition of NE is given in Definition 1.17. NE is of two types: pure strategy NE (PSNE) and mixed strategy NE (MSNE). To evaluate PSNE at a joint state, an agent selects an action from its own action set, which corresponds to its maximum reward due to joint action, where remaining agents' actions are kept fixed. The joint action at a joint state for which all the agents receive maximum reward and no one has any selfish intension to deviate from its chosen action is well known as PSNE at that joint state. An example is considered in Figures 1.24 and 1.25 to evaluate PSNE in a static game or state-less or one-stage or normal-form game [85].

Definition 1.17 *NE* is a stable joint action (or strategy) at a given joint state (S) of a system that involves m interacting agents, such that no unilateral deviation (deviation of an agent independently) can occur as long as all the agents follow the same optimal joint action $A_N = \; <a_i^*>_{i=1}^{m}$ at a joint state $S \in \{S\}$ for *PSNE*. Further, for a *MSNE*, agents perform the joint action $A = \; <a_i>_{i=1}^{m}$ with a probability $p^*(A) = \prod_{i=1}^{m} p_i^*(a_i)$, where $p_i^* : \{a_i\} \to [0, 1], p^* : \{A\} \to [0, 1]$.

Let $a_i^* \in \{a_i\}$ be the optimal action of agent i at s_i and $A_{-i}^* \subseteq A$ be the optimal joint action profile of all agents except agent i at joint state $S = \; <s_j>_{j=1, j\neq i}^{m}$ and $Q_i(S, A)$ be the joint Q-value of agent i at S because of joint action $A \in \{A\}$. Then the condition of PSNE at S is

$$Q_i(S, a_i^*, A_{-i}^*) \geq Q_i(S, a_i, A_{-i}^*), \quad \forall i$$
$$\Rightarrow Q_i(S, A_N) \geq Q_i(S, A'), \quad \forall i \; \left[\text{where } A_N = \; <a_i^*, A_{-i}^*> \quad \text{and} \quad A' = \; <a_i, A_{-i}^*>\right]$$

$$(1.25)$$

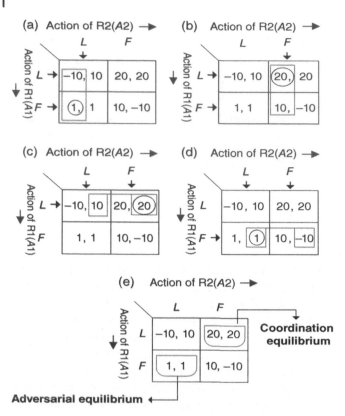

Figure 1.25 Pure strategy Nash equilibrium evaluation. (a) Fix $A1 = L$ and $A2 = L/F$ (b) Fix $A2 = F$ and $A1 = L/F$ (c) Fix $A1 = L$ and $A2 = L/F$. (d) Fix $A1 = F$ and $A2 = L/F$. (e) Nash equilibrium and FL and LF.

and condition of MSNE at S is

$$Q_i(S, p_i^*, p_{-i}^*) \geq Q_i(S, p_i, p_{-i}^*), \quad \forall i, \tag{1.26}$$

where $Q_i(S, p) = \sum_{\forall A} p(A) Q_i(S, A)$ and $p_{-i}^*(A_{-i}) = \prod_{j=1, j\neq i}^{m} p_j^*(a_j)$ be the joint probability of selecting joint action profile of all agents except agent i denoted by $A_{-i} \subseteq A$.

Agents follow Figure 1.25 to evaluate PSNE $A_N = <a_i^*, A_{-i}^*>$ and Figure 1.26 for MSNE $<p_i^*(a_i), p_{-i}^*(A_{-i})>$, respectively, at joint state S.

Pure Strategy NE

Assuming in the one-stage game there are two robots R1, R2 and each has two actions. Robot 1 (R1) selects one action from the set $\{L, F\}$ and robot 2 (R2) selects one from $\{L, F\}$. As a result there is a joint action set. The joint action set $\{LL, LF,$

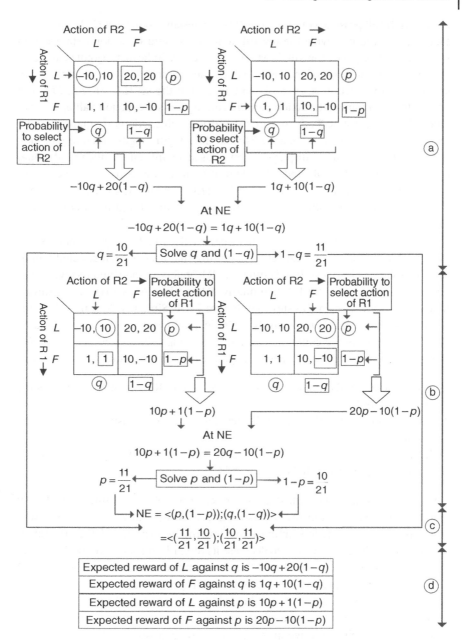

Figure 1.26 Evaluation of mixed strategy Nash equilibrium.

FL, FF} is the all possible combinations (the Cartesian product) of {*L, F*} and {*L, F*}. Figure 1.24a and b provide the reward tables of R1 and R2 at joint state–action space, respectively. The rows of the state–action tables indicate the joint state. Joint state is the conjunction of individual states, here *S* and *S'*. Each column corresponds to a joint action *A*. *A* can be any one from the set {*LL, LF, FL, FF*}. The entries for each joint state–action pair are called joint state–action value. To evaluate PSNE at joint state *S'*, the rewards at *S'* due to joint actions are mapped in the reward matrix, as shown in Figure 1.24c and d. In Figure Figure 1.24c and d, each cell of the reward matrices displays the rewards at a joint state *S'* due to individual actions, respectively, for R1 and R2. In Figure 1.24c–e, rows indicate the actions of R1 and columns indicate the actions of R2. However, in Figure 1.24e, each cell shows the rewards of both the agent. First entry is for R1 and the second one is for R2.

Figure 1.25a–d show the reward matrices of R1 and R2 at joint state *S'*. In Figure 1.25a, R1 selects its best action assuming that R2 has been selected *L* indicated by solid black arrows. In this situation, R1 prefers action *F* and receives 1 as a reward indicated in Figure 1.25a. Similarly, R1 receives 20 as a reward assuming that R2 has been selected *F* as shown in Figure 1.25b. Similarly, R2 earns 20 and 1, when R1 selects *L* and *F*, respectively, as indicated in Figure 1.25c and d. Finally, Figure 1.25e shows the common solution producing cells, which are the PSNE. Computation of PSNE for two agents is performed by the following three steps:

1) Fix the action of R1, then select the best reward of R2, considering all possible actions of itself.
2) Fix the action of R2, then select the best reward of R1, considering all possible actions of itself.
3) If the results of selection fall in the same cell, then PSNE = joint actions corresponding to the selected common grid.

Here, two PSNE are obtained: <*F, L*> and <*L, F*>. Let us examine them one by one. For the <*F, L*>, both the robots receive 1. Now, if any one robot selfishly attempts to change its action aiming at maximizing its own reward, then the robot, which changes its action, causes to decrease its reward from 1 to −10. Besides, if R1 changes its action from *F* to *L*, then R2's reward improves from 1 to 10. Again, if R2 changes its action from *F* to *L*, then R1's reward improves from 1 to 10. So, the joint action <*F, L*> is an adversarial equilibrium. Adversarial equilibrium is a PSNE in competitive situation. Now, the joint action <*L, F*> is coordination equilibrium, where both the robots receive maximum reward selflessly, i.e. 20. Coordination equilibrium is a PSNE in cooperative situation. The present book considers coordination equilibrium only.

Table 1.4 Expected reward of R1 and R2 at MSNE.

Expected reward of R1 by employing p against q	$p[-10q + 20(1-q)] + (1-p)[1q + 10(1-q)]$
Expected reward of R2 by employing q against p	$q[10p + 1(1-p)] + (1-q)[20p - 10(1-p)]$

Mixed Strategy NE

MSNE is stochastic. In MSNE, each robot randomizes its own pure strategies by assigning a probability in between zero and one for each pure strategy. Let R1 select its actions L and F with a probability p and $(1-p)$, respectively. Also, let R2 select its actions L and F with a probability q and $(1-q)$, respectively. The summary of rewards at MSNE is given in Figure 1.26. At MSNE, the expected rewards of L and F against q are equal. Equating these two expected rewards yield p and $(1-p)$ as shown in Figure 1.26a. Similarly, one can find q and $(1-q)$ as shown in Figure 1.26b. The expected reward of a mixed strategy is the weighted sum of the expected rewards of all the pure strategies in the mix. Finally, the expected reward of R1 by employing p against q and the expected reward of R2 by employing q against p are given in Table 1.4. Also it is listed in Figure 1.26d. Finally, the MSNE is $<(p, (1-p)); (q, (1-q))>$ given in Figure 1.26c. Table 1.4 provides the expected reward at MSNE for two players. Example 1.4 provides an example of MSNE for a two-player tennis game. Example 1.4 is given below to illuminate MSNE.

Example 1.4 Figure 1.27 shows the reward matrix for a two-player tennis game between Venus and Serena. Let in Figure 1.27, Venus is the row player and Serena is the column player. If Venus chooses Left (L), then she attempts to pass Serena to Serena's left (l). If Venus decides Right (R), then she is attempting to pass Serena to Serena's right (r). Serena chooses l, means that she bends slightly toward her l. Similarly, Serena chooses r means she slightly bends toward her r. There is no PSNE in Figure 1.27. Let's find MSNE for the tennis game. In MSNE, each agent's mix should be the best for the remaining agents' mix. To find Serena's NE mix $(q, 1-q)$, look at Venus's rewards. Now, Venus's rewards against q while choosing

Figure 1.27 Reward matrix for tennis game.

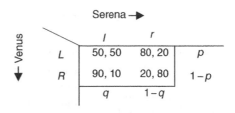

L and R is given by $50q + 80(1 - q)$ and $90q + 20(1 - q)$, respectively. In MSNE, L and R both themselves must be the best response against q. So,

$$50q + 80(1 - q) = 90q + 20(1 - q). \tag{1.27}$$

Therefore, solving (1.27), we obtain $q = 0.6$ and $1 - q = 0.4$. Now, to find Venus's NE mix $(p, 1 - p)$, look at Serena's rewards. Serena's reward against p while choosing l and r is given by $50p + 10(1 - p)$ and $10p + 80(1 - p)$, respectively. In MSNE, l and r both themselves must be the best response against p. So,

$$50p + 10(1 - p) = 10p + 80(1 - p) \tag{1.28}$$

Therefore, solving (1.28), we obtain $p = 0.7$ and $1 - p = 0.3$. Hence, the MSNE is given by $[(p, 1 - p); (q, 1 - q)] = [(0.7, 0.3); (0.6, 0.4)]$.

For multi-agent coordination without any communication among the agents, agents face coordination problem in the presence of multiple coordination equilibria [72]. Here, coordination problem refers to the problem of selecting unique equilibrium by all the robots. Such problem can be resolved by selecting a joint action based on a signal (e.g. traffic signal), which is commonly accessible by all the robots. Before discussing about the remedies of equilibrium selection, Example 1.5 is provided to realize the problem.

Example 1.5 The reward matrix for a common reward two-agent static game is given in Figure 1.28, where both a and b are the rewards. There are two action sets $\{x0, x1\}$ and $\{y0, y1\}$ for agent X and Y, respectively. Now, if $a > b > 0$, then there are two equilibria $<x0, y0>$ and $<x1, y1>$. But, only $<x0, y0>$ is the optimal and hence, one would expect that the agents play $<x0, y0>$. If $a = b > 0$, then none of the agents have any reason to prefer any one action.

In such situation, there exist multiple equilibria. Choosing one equilibrium among multiple equilibria by random selection or by focusing personal basing may lead to suboptimal (or uncoordinated) equilibrium.

A robot can resolve the problem of equilibrium selection [38] in a coordinated game by repeatedly playing a game by the same robot. In the literature, CE addresses the problem of equilibrium selection.

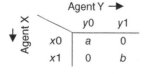

Figure 1.28 Reward matrix of in a common reward two-agent static game.

1.3.3.2 Correlated Equilibrium

CE is more general than the NE [72]. There are four variants of CE: Utilitarian, Egalitarian, Republican, and Libertarian equilibria [72]. In each variant, a numerical value is maximized and its corresponding index (joint action) is well known as CE. The former numerical value may be evaluated by one of the following techniques:

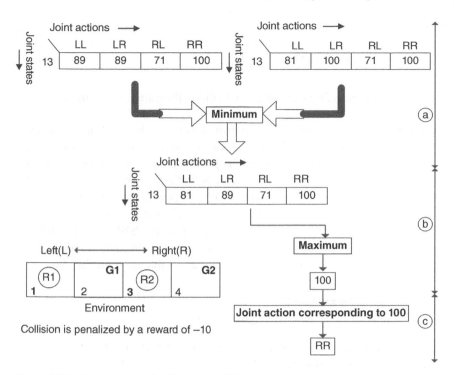

Figure 1.29 Pure strategy Egalitarian equilibrium, which is one variant of CE.

1) In Utilitarian equilibrium, the numerical value to be maximized is evaluated by adding all robots' rewards.
2) The least efficient robot's reward is maximized in the Egalitarian equilibrium.
3) Most efficient robot's reward is maximized in Republican equilibrium.
4) In Libertarian equilibrium, the numerical value to be maximized is evaluated by multiplying all the robots' rewards.

Like NE in CE, there are pure strategy and mixed strategy CE. The definition of CE is given in Definition 1.18. The pure strategy Egalitarian equilibrium evaluation is shown in Figure 1.29.

Definition 1.18 *CE* at a joint state, $S = \, <s_i>_{i=1}^{m}$ with m interacting agents is the pure strategy CE, A_C and mixed strategy CE, $p^*(A_C)$ if agents follow (1.29) and (1.30), respectively.

$$A_C = \underset{A}{\mathrm{argmax}}[\Phi(Q_i(S,A))], \tag{1.29}$$

$$p^*(A_C) = \underset{p(A)}{\mathrm{argmax}}\left[\Phi\left[\sum_A p(A)(Q_i(S,A))\right]\right], \tag{1.30}$$

where

$$\Phi \in \left\{ \sum_{i=1}^{m}, \mathrm{Min}_{i=1}^{m}, \mathrm{Max}_{i=1}^{m}, \prod_{i=1}^{m} \right\}. \tag{1.31}$$

Game of chicken reflects the idea of CE and is illustrated in Example 1.6.

Example 1.6 In the game of chicken, two players play by heading toward each other as shown in Figure 1.30. If both the players move (*M*) on the same way, then they collide, which results in penalty for both the agents. If one player moves and another player waits (cooperate (*C*)), then both the players are rewarded. The player which successfully moves receives more reward, than the player which cooperates. Both the players receive zero reward if none of them move. In Figure 1.31, both the joint action (*M*, *C*) and (*C*, *M*) is the PSNE. To achieve PSNE without establishing any communication among the players, they should follow a signal (like traffic signal), which is commonly accessible for both the players.

1.3.3.3 Static Game Examples
A few examples of static games are given below.

Constant-sum-game: In constant-sum game [41], summation of the two players' rewards is constant as shown in Figure 1.32, where *<a, b>* and *<x, y>* are the action sets of player 1 and 2, respectively. In Figure 1.32, the value of the constant is 1.

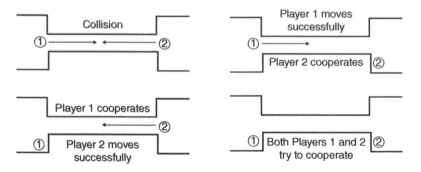

Figure 1.30 Game of chicken.

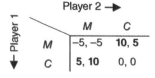

Figure 1.31 Reward matrix in the game of chicken.

Player 1 ↓ / Player 2 →	M	C
M	−5, −5	10, 5
C	5, 10	0, 0

Zero-sum game: Zero-sum game is a special case of constant-sum game [41]. It is a two-player game, where the summation of the two players' reward is always zero. This indicates that one player's gain is equivalent to another player's loss. Hence, net change in reward is zero. Chess and tennis are the examples of zero-sum game, where there is a winner and a loser. Financial market is also an example of zero-sum game. In the literature of GT, matching pennies and rock-paper-scissor (given in Example 1.3) are the well-known examples of zero-sum game. Example 1.7 illustrates the game of matching pennies.

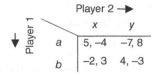

Figure 1.32 Constant-sum game.

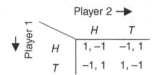

Figure 1.33 Matching pennies.

Example 1.7 In matching pennies, two pennies are thrown by two players simultaneously. The rewards of the players depend on whether the pennies match or not. If both pennies result in head (H) or tail (T), then player 1 wins and rewarded by player 2's penny. If there is a mismatch, then player 2 wins and rewarded by player 1's penny. As one player's gain is other player's loss, hence, matching pennies is a zero-sum game as shown in Figure 1.33. In matching pennies, there is no PSNE instead there exists MSNE.

In some situation, a game does not have a PSNE but every game have a MSNE [42]. For example in the rock-paper-scissor game, there is no PSNE but there exists MSNE.

General-sum-stochastic game: In general-sum-stochastic game, the summation of all the players' rewards is neither zero nor constant. Prisoner's Dilemma is an example of general-sum-stochastic game and is illustrated in Example 1.8.

Example 1.8 In Prisoner's Dilemma, two criminals are suspected of committing a crime and are being interrogated in two separate cells. From human physiology, both the criminals want to minimize their jail sentence. Both of them face the same scenarios as follows (Figure 1.34):

- If Players 1 and 2 each Deny (D) each other, then each of them are sentenced by nine year jails.
- If Player 1 Deny (D) but Player 2 remains Confess (C), then Player 1 will be set free and Player 2 will serve 10 year jails (and vice versa).

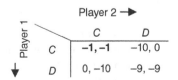

Figure 1.34 Reward matrix in Prisoner's Dilemma game.

- If both Players 1 and 2 remain Confess (C), then both of them will only serve one year jail.

Hence, in Prisoner's Dilemma game, (C, C) is the PSNE.

1.3.4 Correlation Among RL, DP, and GT

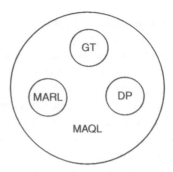

Figure 1.35 Correlation among the MARL, DP, and GT.

It is apparent from the earlier sections that the RL works on the principle of reward/penalty received by the agents as a feedback from the environment. DP is nothing but an optimization technique, which optimizes the BE. On the other hand, GT helps in analyzing the strategic situation of the agents in the MAS, where an agent significantly affects the interests of other agents in the environment. Figure 1.35 indicates that the multi-agent Q-learning (MAQL) comprising of the MARL, GT, and DP. However, in the literature, MARL is well known as MAQL for simplicity.

1.3.5 Classification of MARL

Based on the task type, MARL is classified as cooperative, competitive, and mixed as shown in Figure 1.36 [85]. Now, the cooperative and mixed algorithms may be designed for static (stateless) games or for stagewise (dynamic) games. However, there are only two competitive algorithms for two agents, namely Minimax-Q and heuristically accelerated multi-agent RL (HAMRL).

Joint Action Learners (JAL) and Frequency Maximum Q-value (FMQ) heuristic are classified as cooperative static algorithm. Team-Q, Distributed-Q, Optimal Adaptive Learning (OAL), Sparse Cooperative Q-learning (SCQL), Sequential Q-learning (SQL), and Frequency of the maximum reward Q-learning (FMRQ) fall within the scope of cooperative dynamic algorithms.

The mixed static algorithms are classified based on the belief on the other agents' policy of an agent and the steps required in searching the optimal policy (direct policy search). Belief-based learning include Fictitious play (FP), Meta Strategy, *AWESOME*, and Hyper-Q. The direct policy search-based algorithms are classified based on variation of the learning rate: fixed learning rate and variable learning rate. Fixed learning rate includes Infinitesimal Gradient Ascent (IGA) and Generalized IGA (GIGA). Win or Learn Fast-IGA (WoLF-IGA) and GIGA-Win or Learn Fast (GIGA-WoLF) are under the variable learning rate. The dynamic mixed

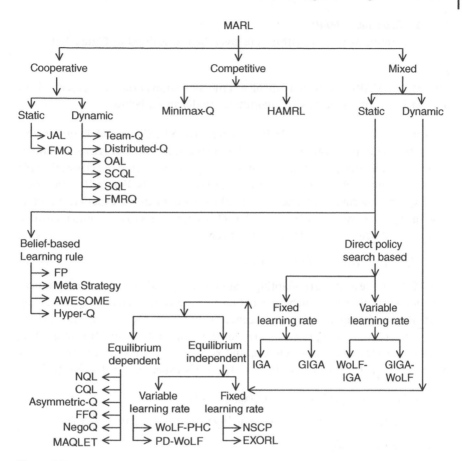

Figure 1.36 Classification of multi-agent reinforcement learning.

strategy algorithms are classified as equilibrium dependent and equilibrium independent. Equilibrium-dependent algorithms are Nash Q-Learning (NQL), Correlated Q-Learning (CQL), Asymmetric-Q learning, Friend-or-Foe Q-Learning (FFQ) (for more than two agents), Negotiation-based Q-learning (NegoQ), and MAQL with equilibrium transfer (MAQLET). Again equilibrium-independent learning algorithms are classified as fixed learning rate and variable learning rate. Fixed learning rate includes Nonstationary Converging Policies (NSCP) and Extended Optimal Response Learning (EXORL) heuristic. WoLF Policy Hill-Climbing (WoLF-PHC) and PD-WoLF are under the variable learning rate. The details of all the algorithms are given in the subsequent sections.

1.3.5.1 Cooperative MARL
The cooperative MARL algorithms are given below as listed in Figure 1.36.

Static
The static MARL does not involve any state-transitions as described in Section 1.3.3. The static MARL algorithms are discussed below.

Independent Learner and Joint Action Learner   In [81], Claus and Boutilier proposed two variants of learners. One is the Independent Learner (IL) and another is the JAL. IL learns Q-value at its own action–space employing the classical single agent Q-learning rule ignoring the presence of other agents. For an IL i, the single agent Q-learning rule (1.19) becomes (1.32) with $<a, r>$ as the experience profile. Also the Q-value earned by IL denoted by $Q_i(a_i)$ converges to the optimal Q-value $Q_i^*(a_i)$ for all action $a_i \in A_i$ in the single agent system.

$$Q_i(a_i) \leftarrow Q_i(a_i) + \alpha[r_i(a_i) - Q_i(a_i)]. \tag{1.32}$$

In MAS, all the agents are adapting simultaneously and hence, the environment is no longer stationary, which does not ensure the convergence of Q-values any more. Reconsidering the 1.5, in IL, Agent X learns for the actions x_0 and x_1. However, if Agent X is a JAL, then it learns for the four joint actions. It is interesting that the expected value of selecting x_0 and x_1 exclusively depends on the strategy played by Y. In 1.5, if $a = b = 10$, then Agent X's expected Q-value for x_0 is

$$
\begin{aligned}
\widehat{Q}_x(x_0) &= \widehat{Q}_x(x_0, y_0) \times P(y_0 \mid x_0) + \widehat{Q}_x(x_0, y_1) \times P(y_1 \mid x_0) \\
&= 10 \times P(y_0 \mid x_0) + 0 \times P(y_1 \mid x_0) \quad \left[\text{by } 1.5\,\widehat{Q}_x(x_0, y_0) = 10 \text{ and } \widehat{Q}_x(x_0, y_1) = 0\right] \\
&= 10 \times 0.5 + 0 \times 0.5 \\
&= 5,
\end{aligned}
$$
$$\tag{1.33}$$

where $P(y_0 \mid x_0)$ and $P(y_1 \mid x_0)$ refer to the probability of y_0 and y_1 being executed, respectively, by agent Y subject to x_0 is being selected by agent X. To handle the above explained dynamics in multi-agent systems, the JAL maintains a belief about the other agents' strategies and the expected value of action a_i by agent i is given below.

$$\widehat{Q}_i(a_i) = \sum_{a_{-i} \in A_{-i}} Q_i(a_{-i}, a_i) \prod_{j \neq i} P^i_{a_{-i[j]}}, \tag{1.34}$$

where

$$Q_i(a_{-i}, a_i) \leftarrow Q_i(a_{-i}, a_i) + \alpha[r_i(a_{-i}, a_i) - Q_i(a_{-i}, a_i)]. \tag{1.35}$$

The experience tuple of JAL is denoted by $<a_i, a_{-i}, r_i>$.

So, JAL learns the Q-value at joint action–space considering the presence of other agents by synergistically combining the RL and equilibrium (or coordination) learning methods [45, 86–88]. Learning equilibrium depends on the rewards corresponding to the joint actions at a given joint state and these rewards are obtained by the well-known RL more especially by Q-learning. The convergence of Q-learning does depend on the already explained trade-off between the exploration and exploitation. If an agent i chooses an action a_i with probability $P_i(a_i)$, then probability of choosing remaining actions is $1 - P_i(a_i)$. The said trade-off can be balanced by tuning the temperature parameter T of the Boltzmann strategy given by (1.36). The variation of T is done in such a way so that the convergence is guaranteed [89].

$$P_i(a_i) = \frac{e^{Q_i(a_i)/T}}{\sum\limits_{\forall \widetilde{a_i}} e^{Q_i(\widetilde{a_i})/T}}. \tag{1.36}$$

The following conditions are required to satisfy for convergence of both the IL and JAL [81]:

1) The learning rate α decreases with respect to time, i.e. $\sum_{\alpha=0}^{t} \alpha = \infty$ and $\sum_{\alpha=0}^{1} \alpha^2 < \infty$.
2) Each agent selects each of its actions infinitely.
3) The probability of choosing action a by agent i, $P_t^i(a) \neq 0$.
4) All the agent's exploration strategy is exploitive. That is, $\lim_{t \to \infty} P_t^i(X_t) = 0$, where X_t is a random variable denoting the event that some nonoptimal action was taken based on i's estimated value at time t.

Finally, myopic heuristic-based optimistic exploration strategies are proposed in [81] for optimal action selection.

1) **Optimistic Boltzmann (OB):** Choose the action a_{-i} using the Boltzmann strategy, assuming $MaxQ_i(a_i) = Max\ Q_i(a_i, a_{-i})$.
2) **Weight OB (WOB):** Explore using the Boltzmann strategy using the factor P_i(optimal match a_{-i} for a_i), i.e. $MaxQ_i(a_i) \cdot P_i$(optimal match a_{-i} for a_i).
3) **Combined:** Employ the Boltzmann strategy, assuming $V(a_i) = \rho\ Max\ Q_i(a_i) + (1 - \rho)EV(a_i)$ as the value of action a_i, where $\rho \in [0, 1]$.

Considering the biasing $\rho = 0.5$ in [81], it is shown that combined exploration strategy outperforms the OB, WOB, and the Boltzmann strategy in terms of the average accumulated reward. The algorithm for IL and JAL are given in Algorithms 1.4 and 1.5, respectively.

Algorithm 1.4   Independent Learners

Input: Action set of agent i, A_i, $\alpha \in [0, 1)$;
Output: Optimal Q-value of agent i, $Q_i^*(a_i)$, $a_i \in A_i$;
  Initialize: $Q_i(a_i) \leftarrow 0$;
Begin
  Repeat
    Execute an action a_i by agent i employing the
    Boltzmann strategy;
    Receive immediate reward $r_i(a_i)$;
    Update: $Q_i(a_i) \leftarrow Q_i(a_i) + \alpha [r_i(a_i) - Q_i(a_i)]$;
    $Q_i^*(a_i) \leftarrow Q_i(a_i)$;
  Until $Q_i(a_i)$ converges;
End.

Algorithm 1.5   Joint Action Learners

Input: Action set A_i, $\forall i$, $\alpha \in [0, 1)$;
Output: Optimal joint Q-value $Q_i^*(a_i, a_{-i})$, $\forall i$;
Initialize: $Q_i(a_i, a_{-i}) \leftarrow 0$;
Begin
  Repeat
    Execute an action a_i by agent i employing the
    Boltzmann strategy;
    Receive immediate reward $r_i(a_i, a_{-i})$ by
    observing other agents' rewards;
    Update: $\begin{aligned} & Q_i(a_i, a_{-i}) \leftarrow Q_i(a_i, a_{-i}) + \\ & \alpha[r_i(a_i, a_{-i}) - Q_i(a_i, a_{-i})] \end{aligned}$ and
    $P_{a_j}^i$, $\hat{Q}_i(a_i)$ by (1.50), (1.51) respectively;
    $Q_i^*(a_i, a_{-i}) \leftarrow Q_i(a_i, a_{-i})$;
  Until $Q_i(a_i, a_{-i})$ converges;
End.

Unfortunately, the above conditions do not guarantee convergence to equilibrium in the practical and complicated games such as in the climbing game [3, 81] and the penalty game [3, 81].

Frequency Maximum Q-Value heuristic The independent agent in [90] and [2] including the JAL in [81] does not guarantee convergence to the optimal joint action in the absence of coordination with high penalties. In the FMQ heuristic [3], a novel action selection strategy is proposed assuming agents can observe other agents' actions and are tested in two coordination problems mentioned in [81]: the climbing game and the penalty game. The said games are repeated cooperative single-stage games and they provide suitable platforms for studying the multi-agent coordination problem.

Agent 2 →

Agent 1		x	y	z
	x	11	−30	0
	y	−30	7	0
	z	0	6	5

Figure 1.37 The climbing game reward matrix.

Climbing game: It is apparent from Figure 1.37 that in the climbing game [3, 81], (x, x) is the optimal joint action and both the agents should go for it. Now, if Agent 1 plays x and Agent 2 plays y, then both the agents receive negative reward (−30). After learning this situation, both the agents avoid joint action (x, y). Later, if Agent 1 plays action z, then Agent 2 plays either y or z as due to both the joint action (z, y) and (z, z) agents receive positive rewards of 6 and 5, respectively. Suppose, Agent 2 is playing x but Agent 1 does not play x as it receives negative reward in the past due to x, and also Agent 1 does not play y as it provides negative reward. Hence, Agent 1 plays z and both the agents receive reward of 0. Similarly, if Agent 2 plays z, then agents receive at least 0 independent of Agent 1's choice. From the above analysis it is apparent that in the climbing game, agents always move away from the optimal joint action.

Penalty game: Similar to the climbing game, the presence of multiple equilibria in the penalty game [3, 81] is also challenging to check the performance of the coordination in the MAS. In the penalty game (Figure 1.38), both the agents should avoid the joint actions (x, z) and (z, x) to avoid the negative reward of −10. Now, in the penalty game, there are two optimal joint actions (x, x) and (z, z). Agents can play for any one of them. Suppose, Agent 1 plays x with an expectation that Agent 2 also plays x to receive maximum reward of 10. In this situation, if Agent 2 plays z, expecting Agent 1 plays z to receive maximum reward of 10. In the above circumstances, y is the safe choice for both the agents regardless of what other agent's play and is guaranteed to receive a reward of 0 or 2. Hence, it is challenging to identify the optimal joint action in penalty game for multi-agent coordination.

From the climbing game and the penalty game it is apparent that an agent should select its action wisely for convergence. Maintaining a balance between the exploration and exploitation is an intelligent approach for action selection. Balancing the exploration/exploitation is a trade-off and is addressed by the well-known

Agent 2 →

Agent 1		x	y	z
	x	10	0	−10
	y	0	2	0
	z	−10	0	10

Figure 1.38 The penalty game reward matrix.

Boltzmann strategy given in (1.36). In (1.36), the probability of selecting an action a_i for agent i is evaluated by utilizing the Q-value and the tuning parameter temperature (T). If $T \to \infty$, then each action has an equal probability to execute and hence, pure exploration occurs. If $T \to 0$, then the action has a probability of one to execute and hence, exploitation occurs. In [3], T is given by

$$T(t) = e^{-st} \times T_{\max} + 1, \tag{1.37}$$

where t is the learning epoch, s is a parameter to control the exploration rate, and $T_{\max}$ is initial value of temperature.

In [91], an optimistic assumption-based algorithm is proposed. By optimistic assumption, an agent updates its Q-value only if the new value is greater than the current one. Unfortunately, the optimistic assumption fails to converge to the optimal joint action due to misleading maximum reward. FMQ heuristic is based on the experience of the agent. Agent counts the frequency of the action which yields the best reward. Instead of optimistic assumption, an agent i uses the Boltzmann strategy with the modified Q-value $\tilde{Q}_i(A)$ given in (1.38).

$$\tilde{Q}_i(A) = Q_i(A) + f \times \frac{c_{\max}(A)}{c(A)} \times r_{\max}(A), \tag{1.38}$$

where $c_{\max}(A)$ is the number of times agent i receives maximum reward $r_{\max}(A)$ after executing the action A $c(A)$ times. f refers to the control parameter to control the importance of the FMQ heuristic. The value of f increases proportionally with the increase in problem difficulty.

Algorithm 1.6   FMQ heuristic

Input: Action set A_i, $\forall i$, $\gamma \in [0, 1)$, $\alpha \in [0, 1)$, f;
Output: Optimal joint Q-value $Q_i^*(A)$, $\forall i$, $i \in [1, m]$;
Initialize: $Q_i(A) \leftarrow 0$, $\forall i$;
Begin
  Repeat
    Execute action $a_i \in A_i$, $\forall i$ employing FMQ heuristic;
    Receive immediate reward $r_i(A)$, $\forall i$;
    Update: $Q_i(A) \leftarrow Q_i(A) + \alpha [r_i(A) - Q_i(A)]$ and modify
Q-value $\tilde{Q}_i(a_i)$, $\forall i$ by (1.54) for
    modified Boltzmann strategy (FMQ heuristic);
    $Q_i^*(A) \leftarrow Q_i(A)$;
  Until $Q_i(A)$, $\forall i$ converge;
End.

It is observed from the experiments that the FMQ heuristic outperforms the baseline experiments in terms of the convergence to the optimal joint action both in the climbing game and the penalty game [3]. To compare the FMQ heuristic with optimistic assumption, a partially stochastic version of the climbing

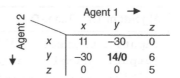

Figure 1.39 The penalty game reward matrix.

game is given in Figure 1.39. In the partially stochastic climbing game, at least one of the rewards is stochastic as shown in Figure 1.39. In Figure 1.39, the joint action (y, y) yields a reward of 14 or 0 with probability 0.5. So, in the long run both the agents receive a reward of 7 due to joint action (y, y). Hence, the reward matrix given in Figures 1.37 and 1.39 are equivalent in the long run. The FMQ heuristic also outperforms the baseline experiment and the optimistic assumption in the partially stochastic climbing game, in terms of the convergence to optimal joint action. Unfortunately, the FMQ heuristic fails to convergence to optimal joint action in the fully stochastic penalty game and climbing game. The algorithm for FMQ heuristic is given in Algorithm 1.6.

Dynamic
Dynamic RL is stochastic Markov game with more than one joint state.

Team-Q   Team-Q is a cooperative dynamic Q-learning algorithm. Dynamic indicates the existence of state-transitions. In [92], Littman proposed Team-Q learning designed for team games in the framework of team Markov games (Coordination game). In Team-Q learning, the value function $VQ_i(S')$ of agent $i \in [1, m]$ at joint next state S' for the m agents' team is given in (1.39).

$$VQ_i\left(S'\right) = \underset{a_1, a_2, \ldots, a_m}{\text{Max}} Q_i(S; a_1, a_2, \ldots, a_m). \tag{1.39}$$

The update rule in Team-Q learning for agent i is given in (1.40), without using reaming agents' model like in [81].

$$Q_i(S, A) \leftarrow (1 - \alpha)Q_i(S, A) + \alpha\left[r_i(S, A) + \gamma VQ_i\left(S'\right)\right], \tag{1.40}$$

where $A = \, <a_1, a_2, \ldots, a_m>$ be the joint action at joint state $S = \, <s_1, s_2, \ldots, s_m>$. The Team-Q learning is convergent following the generalized Q-learning algorithm [93, 94]. Team-Q learning is similar to NQL [95] for the coordination games. Still there exists a challenge regarding the equilibrium selection among multiple equilibria in noisy environment. The algorithm for Team-Q learning is given in Algorithm 1.7.

Algorithm 1.7   Team-Q

Input: Action set A_i, $\forall i$, $\gamma \in [0, 1)$, $\alpha \in [0, 1)$;
Output: Optimal joint Q-value $Q_i^*(S, A)$, $\forall i$, $i \in [1, m]$;
Initialize: $Q_i(S, A) \leftarrow 0, \forall i$;
Begin
  Repeat
    Execute action $a_i \in A_i$, $\forall i$;
    Receive immediate reward $r_i(S, A)$, $\forall i$;

    Update: $Q_i(S, A) \leftarrow (1-\alpha)Q_i(S, A) + \alpha\left[r_i(S, A) + \gamma \max_A Q_i(S; A)\right]$

    and $S \leftarrow S'$;
    $Q_i^*(S, A) \leftarrow Q_i(S, A)$;
Until $Q_i(S, A)$, $\forall i$ converge;
End.

Distributed-Q In [91], model-free Distributed Q-learning is proposed for cooperative MAS in deterministic situation with a motivation to compute an optimal policy in a cooperative multi-agent environment. The Distributed Q-learner solves two problems. The first problem is concerned with determination of the optimal policy. The second problem deals with selection of one optimal policy among alternatives, which is optimal for the entire team.

To handle multi-agent dynamics, MDP is extended to Multi-agent MDP (MMDP), where each agent maximizes its own reward having different goals (i.e. reward-function). However, in the cooperative MMDP, all the agents have identical reward function. Such identical reward-functions are advantageous in finding an equilibrium point, which is an optimal joint action and it maximizes the reward of all the agents. In cooperative MMDP, the learning algorithm is responsible in making cooperation among the agents. Here, also two types of agents are considered: one is JAL and another is IL as mentioned in [81]. IL cannot distinguish the difference between the individual (elementary) action [91] and joint action. Hence, IL maintains a Q-table of smaller size, i.e. $S \times A$, instead of maintaining the Q-table at joint state–action space, $S \times A^m$. In [91], the smaller Q-tables are assumed as the projection from the larger central Q-table with a conjecture about the strategies of teammates. So, in [91], a projection approach is proposed by evaluating the individual Q-table in a distributed way without adapting Q-table in joint state–action space by weighting the Q-values from larger Q-table given in (1.41).

$$q_i(S, a_i) \leftarrow \sum_{\forall A = <a_i>_{i=1}^m} \left[P(S, A \mid a_i) \cdot \left[r_i(S, a_i) + \gamma \max_{a_i'} q_i\left(S', a_i'\right) \right] \right],$$

(1.41)

where $P(S, A \mid a_i)$ refers to the probability of joint action A to be executed at joint state S including the action of agent i, a_i.

Another way of projection is the "pessimistic assumption." By pessimistic assumption, the individual smaller Q-value is the least efficient agent's Q-value obtained from larger central Q-value. Such approach creates robust policies but is not extended in [91], because of its cautious nature. Instead of pessimistic assumption, its dual form is utilized to obtain the smaller Q-value from the central Q-table as given in (1.42).

$$q_i(S, a_i) \leftarrow \max_A Q(S, A).$$

(1.42)

It can also be written in terms of small Q-table given in (1.43).

$$q_i(S, a_i) = \max_{a_i \in A} q_i(S, a_i).$$

(1.43)

Algorithm 1.8   Distributed Q-learning

Input: Action set A_i, $\forall i$, $\gamma \in [0, 1)$;
Output: Optimal Q-value $q_i^*(S, a_i)$, $\forall i$, $i \in [1, m]$, $a_i \in A$;
Initialize: $q_i(S, a_i) \leftarrow 0$, $\forall i$;
Begin
  Repeat
    Execute action $a_i \in A_i$, $\forall i$;
    Receive immediate reward $r_i(S, a_i)$, $\forall i$;

    Update: $q_i(S, a_i) \leftarrow \max\left\{ q_i(S, a_i), r_i(S, a_i) + \gamma \max_{a_i'} q_i\left(S', a_i'\right) \right\}$

    and $S \leftarrow S'$;
    $q_i^*(S, a_i) \leftarrow q_i(S, a_i)$;
  Until $q_i(S, a_i)$, $\forall i$ converge;
End.

The projection technique introduced in (1.43) is also known as optimistic assumption. It is assumed that all agents are acting optimally and the conjunction of the individual optimal actions is also an optimal joint action. However, such assumption is necessarily not true. This inspires the researchers in [91] to propose a Proposition, which states that in cooperative deterministic MMDP

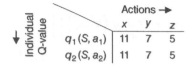

Figure 1.40 Individual Q-values obtained in the climbing game reward matrix by Distributed Q-learning.

	Agent 2 →		
	x	y	z
x	10	0	9
y	0	2	0
z	9	0	10

↓ Agent 1

Figure 1.41 The penalty game reward matrix.

		Actions →		
		x	y	z
$q_1(S, a_1)$		10	2	10
$q_2(S, a_2)$		10	2	10

Individual Q-value

Figure 1.42 Individual Q-values obtained in the penalty game reward matrix by Distributed Q-learning.

$$q_i^t(S, a_i) = \max_{A = <a_i>_{i=1}^m} Q^t(S, A) \quad (1.44)$$

holds and also its proof is given in [91], where t is the learning epoch. The steps of the Distributed Q-learning are given in Algorithm 1.8. The climbing game and the penalty game are extended for the Distributed Q-learning, respectively, in Examples 1.9 and 1.10.

Example 1.9 To extend the climbing game for Distributed Q-learning as shown in Figure 1.40, let both the agents are at joint state S and for brevity discount factor γ is set to 0. The reward function $q_i(S, a_i)$ is evaluated employing Algorithm 1.8. Such greedy approach of Algorithm 1.8 yields highest Q-value for both the agents as shown in Figure 1.40. In Figure 1.40, the optimal joint action is (x, x). However, in the IL, JAL, and the FMQ-heuristic algorithm, agents are supposed to find the suboptimal joint action (y, y) as explained in Figure 1.37.

Example 1.10 Like Example 1.9 to extend the penalty game for Distributed Q-learning as shown in Figure 1.42, the discount factor γ is set to 0 and Algorithm 1.8 is employed to evaluate distributed rewards. In the FMQ-heuristic algorithm (Figure 1.41), there are four optimal joint actions:(x, x), (x, z), (z, x), and (z, z) but only (x, x) and (z, z) are optimal joint actions with reward 10 as shown in Figure 1.42 offered by Algorithm 1.8. Unfortunately, application of the Distributed Q-learning is limited to the deterministic system only.

Optimal Adaptive Learning There are many straightforward solutions to choose optimal equilibrium among multiple equilibrium solutions, like enforce convention [96] and FP [39, 81]. In [81], the JAL guarantees the convergence to NE in a team game. However, it is not guaranteed that the selected NE is the optimal one. Similar problem arises in game theory like Adaptive play (AP) [86] and evolutionary model proposed in [40].

In model-free RL, agents do not have any idea about the environment; in addition, they may receive noisy rewards. Hence, it is impossible to converge

Joint actions of Agents 2 and 3 →

↓ Agent 1	b_1c_1	b_1c_2	b_1c_3	b_2c_1	b_2c_2	b_2c_3	b_3c_1	b_3c_2	b_3c_3
a_1	10	−20	−20	−20	−20	5	−20	5	−20
a_2	−20	−20	5	−20	10	−20	5	−20	−20
a_3	−20	5	−20	5	−20	−20	−20	−20	10

Figure 1.43 Reward matrix of a three-player coordination game.

properly. In [91] and [96], the MDP is extended to Team Markov Game (cooperative MMDP) with an aim to find a deterministic joint strategy to maximize the expected sum of discounted rewards. In [96], the OAL algorithm is proposed with convergence proof where agents learn to choose the optimal NE among multiple NE with probability one. Let in a three-player coordination game, $<a_1, a_2>$, $<b_1, b_2>$, and $<c_1, c_2>$ be the individual action sets of agent 1, 2, and 3, respectively. The reward matrix of this coordination game is shown in Figure 1.43. It is apparent from Figure 1.43 that there are three PSNEs $<a_1b_1c_1, a_2b_2c_2, a_3b_3c_3>$ and six suboptimal NEs. The rewards corresponding to the suboptimal NE are italicized.

Before discussing about the OAL algorithm, the AP algorithm [86] is discussed. In AP game, it is assumed that agents know the game before playing it and one virtual game (VG) is designed. In Team Markov Game, to eliminate the suboptimal NE, the following arrangement is made. Suppose, in cooperative situation $VG(S, A)$ be the payoff of the agents at joint state S because of joint action A. In VG, it is assumed that at optimal NE, the reward denoted by $VG^*(S, A)$ is equal to one and else it is set to zero; e.g. in Figure 1.43, $VG^*(S, A)$ is equal to one if A is an optimal NE, i.e. $A \in \{a_1b_1c_1, a_2b_2c_2, a_3b_3c_3\}$ and else it is zero. Considering weakly acyclic game (WAG) [86] as a VG, where each joint action $A \in \{A\}$ is considered as a vertex. The vertices are connected with the directed edge avoiding self-loop, where for an agent i the action $a_i \in A_i$ is the best response to A_{-i}, here $-i$ stands for all except agent i. By the principle of WAG represented as a best-response graph, from any starting vertex A there exists a directed path to some vertex $A^* \in \{A\}$ and from A^* there is no outgoing path [86].

To eliminate the suboptimal NE or tackle the equilibrium selection problem in WAG, Young proposed AP in [86]. In AP, suppose in a $m-$ player matrix game the joint action at time t is denoted by $A^t \in \{A\}$. Also assume two integers k and n such that $1 \leq k \leq n$ and $t \leq n$. After acting randomly, agents look at its experience and restart the learning at $t = n + 1$. At $t = n + 1$, each agent looks reverse at their most recent n experiences and randomly choose k samples from that. Now, the expected reward of agent i's action a_i is given in (1.45). After evolution of $ER(a_i)$ randomly, an action is chosen from a set of best response given in (1.46).

$$ER(a_i) = \sum_{A_{-i} \in \{A_{-i}\}} u_i(\{a_i\} \cup A_{-i}) \frac{K_{t+1}(A_{-i})}{k}, \tag{1.45}$$

where $K_{t+1}(A_{-i})$ refers to the count the joint action A_{-i} in the k samples and $u_i(\{a_i\} \cup A_{-i}) = u_i(A)$ is the reward of agent i because of joint action A.

$$BR_i^t = \left\{ a_i \mid a_i = \arg\max_{a_i' \in A_i} ER\left(a_i'\right) \right\}. \tag{1.46}$$

It is shown in [86] that by AP, WAG converges to a strict NE. Unfortunately, all the VGs are not WAG and hence, the AP may not converge to a strict NE for all VGs. To address the said problem, the WAG and AP algorithms are modified as follows.

The WAG and AP are modified as WAG with respect to a biased set (WAGB). In WAGB, there is a set D containing a few Nash equilibria of the WAGB. A game is a WAGB if from any vertex A one path exists leading to the NE belongs to set D or a strict NE [96]. In AP, agents randomly select the NE among multiple best responses of the agents. On the other hand, in biased AP (BAP) [96], agents deterministically select the best-response action as a NE belongs to D. Suppose, W_t denotes the set of k samples drawn from the most recent n joint actions. The following two conditions are satisfied. First condition is that the joint action $A' \in D$ such that $\forall A, A \in W_t, A_{-i} \subset A$, and $A_{-i} \in A'$. Second condition is that there must exist at least a joint action $A \in D$ so that $A \in W_t$ and $A \in D$. If the above two conditions are satisfied, then agent i chooses its best-response action a_i such that $a_i \in a^{t'}$, where

$$t' = \max \left\{ T \mid a^T \in W_t \wedge a^T \in D \right\}. \tag{1.47}$$

The philosophy of (1.47) is that the action a_i is the component of the most recent NE belonging to D. If the above two conditions are not satisfied, then AP is implemented. Hence, it can be concluded that the BAP on WAGB converges to either a NE belongs to D or a strict NE. The above techniques are applicable only when the game structure is known. To learn in an unknown game structure multi-agent $\in$−optimality is employed. By definition, a joint action is ε−optimality at joint state S and time t if $Q_t(S, A) + \in \geq \max_{A'} Q_t(S, A'), \forall A' \in \{A\}$. Let the set of ε−optimal joint action, which converges Q_t to Q^* with slower rate, then VG_t converges to VG^*. Here, ε varies proportionately to the function $B(N_t) \in [0, 1]$, where $B(N_t)$ decreases slowly and monotonically to zero with N_t. N_t refers to the minimum time required to sample a state–action pair. The algorithm for OAL is given in Algorithm 1.9 [96]. The convergence proof of the OAL algorithm is given in [96].

Algorithm 1.9 Optimal Adaptive Learning

Input: Action set A_i, $\forall i$ at joint state S, $\gamma \in [0, 1)$;

Output: Optimal Q-value $Q^*(S, A)$;

Initialize:

$t = 0$, $n_t(S, A) = 1$, $T_t(S' \mid (S, A)) = \dfrac{1}{|S|}$, $R_t(S, A) = 0$, $\epsilon_t = C$, $A^{\epsilon_t}(S) = A$, $D = A$;

Repeat $//n_t(S, A)$ is the number of times the joint action A has been executed in joint state S up to time t

If $t \leq m$,

 Then randomly select an action a_i, $\forall i$;

Else do

 Begin

 Update the virtual game VG_t at joint state S;

 Randomly select records from n recent observations of other agents' joint actions played at joint state S;

 Evaluate expected payoff of individual action a_i of the VG at joint state S by (1.45) and construct the best response set by (1.46);

 If condition 1 and 2 in BAP are TRUE

  Then choose best response action with respect to the biased set D;

 Else randomly select a best response action from $BR_i^t(S)$;

 End If.

 End.

End If.

 Receive immediate reward $r_i^t(S, A)$;

 Update: $n_t(S, A) \leftarrow n_t(S, A) + 1$, $R_t(S, A) \leftarrow R_t(S, A) + \frac{1}{n_t(S, A)}\left(r_i^t(S, A) - R_t(S, A)\right)$,

 $T_t(S' \mid (S, A)) \leftarrow T_t(S' \mid (S, A)) + \frac{1}{n_t(S, A)}\left(1 - T_t(S' \mid (S, A))\right)$,

 $Q_{t+1}(S, A) \leftarrow R_t(S, A) + \gamma \sum\limits_{\forall S' \in \{S\}} T_t(S' \mid (S, A)) \times \max\limits_{\forall A' \in \{A\}} Q_t(S', A')$, $t \leftarrow t + 1$, $N_t \leftarrow$

$\min\limits_{S, A} n_t(S, A)$;

 If $\epsilon_t > CB(N_t)$

  Then do

   Begin

   $\epsilon_t > CB(N_t)$, $Q^*(S, A) \leftarrow Q(S, A)$, $\forall i$ and $A^{\epsilon_t}(S)$

   $\leftarrow \left\{ A \mid Q_t(S, A) + \epsilon_t \geq \max\limits_{A' \in \{A\}} Q_t(S, A') \right\}$;

  End;

 End If.

Until $Q(S, A)$, $\forall i$ converge;

Sparse Cooperative Q-learning One of the principal bottlenecks of the MAS is the exponential increase in the space and time complexity, with the increase in number of agents. Kok et al. [97] observed that in most of the MAS, agents are required to coordinate their actions only in a few states and in the remaining, they act independently. In the coordinated joint state S, the Q-value of an agent i is denoted by $Q_i(S, A)$. However, if S be the uncoordinated joint state, then the Q-value of agent i is denoted by $Q_i(S, a_i)$. In case of uncoordinated joint state, the global Q-value $Q(S, A)$ for m number of agents is defined as the summation of individual Q-values given by (1.48).

$$Q(S,A) = \sum_{i=1}^{m} Q_i(S, a_i). \tag{1.48}$$

Based on the above observations, in [97], Kok and Vlassis proposed SCQL, where the Q-tables of the agents are sparsely maintained as discussed above.

Sequential Q-learning In [98], Wang and Silva proposed SQL to handle conflicting behavior of the agents that arises in tightly coupled multi-robot object transportation. In SQL, robots do not select their actions simultaneously; rather they do it sequentially based on their predefined priorities. In SQL, the problem of behavior conflict is addressed by avoiding the selection of same actions those already selected by the preceding robots. Assuming ith robot is denoted by R_i, $i \in [1, m]$ and all the robots are arranged in a special sequence. The subscript i in R_i indicates its position in the sequence. All the robots repeat steps given in Algorithm 1.10 to

---

Algorithm 1.10   Joint Action Formation in SQL

Initialize $\Psi = \phi$; // ϕ be the empty set.
Observe current joint state S;
For $i = 1$ to m
    Evaluate the currently available action set Δ_i, where A_i the action set of robot be i.
    $\Delta_i = (A_i - (A_i \cap \Psi))$;
    R_i selects the action $a_i^j = \Delta_i$ by probability $P\left(a_i^j\right) = \dfrac{e^{Q_i\left(S, a_i^j\right)}}{\displaystyle\sum_{r=1}^{|\{\Delta i\}|} e^{Q_i\left(S, a_i^r\right)}}$.

    Include the action a_i^j to the set Ψ;
End For
Execute the corresponding selected action a_i^j, $\forall i$;

form a joint action avoiding the conventional steps in the classical step MAQL. The joint action offered by Algorithm 1.10 avoids the bottleneck of behavior conflict in tightly coupled multi-robot object transportation.

Frequency of the Maximum Reward Q-learning   In [99], Zhang et al. proposed a MARL algorithm for fully cooperative tasks, namely FMRQ, which aims at achieving the optimal NE to maximize the system performance with respect to the metric of interest. In FMRQ, a modified immediate reward signal is used, which is obtained by identifying the highest global immediate reward. In FMRQ, an agent needs to share only its state and reward at each learning epoch with remaining agents.

In FMRQ, the authors considered two issues: first, they investigated whether the NE is good enough for the fully cooperative MAS; second, the curse of dimensionality of the MARL is considered by storing the Q-value at joint state–individual action space.

To describe the dynamics of the FMRQ, differential equations are formulated for the four cases including two-agent two-action repeated game, and a three-agent two-action repeated game. In each case, the critical points of the differential equations are analyzed and it is observed that FMRQ converges to equilibrium with maximum global rewards in all the five cases [99]. In case 1, there exists only one global immediate reward. Cases 2 and 3 have two maximum immediate rewards in diagonal positions and in the same row, respectively. In case 4, three maximum immediate rewards exist and in case 5, only one global immediate reward exists [99].

In FMRQ, the size of a Q-table for an agent i is $|\{S\}| \times |\{A_i\}|$. In the FMRQ algorithm (Algorithm 1.11), the immediate reward of an agent i, denoted by $r_i(a_i)$, is replaced by the frequency of getting the maximum global immediate reward by the same action a_i, denoted by $fre(a_i)$.

$$fre(a_i) = \frac{n_{\max a_i}}{n_{a_i}}, \tag{1.49}$$

where n_{a_i} refers to the number of times action a_i is selected by agent i and $n_{\max\_a_i}$ is the number of times agent i achieves the maximum global immediate reward. Moreover, the superiority of the FMRQ algorithm is verified by two case studies: one is the 12-vertex box-pushing by 4-agents and the other one is the distributed sensor network optimization problem. The FMRQ algorithm is provided in Algorithm 1.11 for an agent i in repeated games.

Algorithm 1.11 FMRQ for an Agent *i* in Repeated Games

Input: Action set $a_i \in A_i$, $\forall i$ and learning rate $\alpha \in [0, 1)$;
Output: Optimal Q-value $Q^*(a_i)$;
Initialize: $Q(a_i) \leftarrow 0$, count of selecting action a_i, $n_{a_i} = 0$, number of times maximum global immediate reward received by action a_i, $n_{max\_a_i} = 0$ and frequency of getting maximum immediate reward after selecting action a_i, $fre(a_i) = 0$;
Repeat
  Select an action a_i by the Boltzmann exploration scheme;
  $n_{a_i} = n_{a_i} + 1$;
  Execute the action a_i and update $n_{max\_a_i}$ and $rh(a_i)$;
  For each action $a_i \in A_i$ **do** //$rh(a_i)$ refers to history of global immediate reward obtained by action a_i
  Begin
    Evaluate $fre(a_i)$ by (1.49);
    $Q(a_i) = Q(a_i) + \alpha(fre(a_i) - Q(a_i))$;
    Set $n_{a_i} = 0$, $n_{max\_a_i} = 0$ and $fre(a_i) = 0$;
  End
  End For
Until $Q^*(a_i)$; converges;

1.3.5.2 Competitive MARL

The competitive MARL algorithms are discussed below. Here, two competitive MARL algorithms are discussed. One is Minimax Q-learning for two agents and its extension for general-sum game for more than two agents called HAMRL.

Minimax-Q Learning

In [100], Littman proposed a competitive algorithm, namely minimax-Q learning for two agents. In minimax-Q learning, both the agents have conflicting goals with an objective of maximizing the sum of its own discounted expected reward. In other words, an agent tries to maximize a reward function and simultaneously the opponent agent tries to minimize it. In [2] and [90], the authors realized that an agent must interact with other agents and the environment during the learning phase without proposing any supporting mathematical model. In addition, the theory of MDP [46, 84], which is an extension of game theory, also cannot handle the multi-agent dynamics. Even sometimes it is assumed that the environment is stationary. Littman [100] considered only two-player zero-sum Markov game. In zero-sum game, the summation of the rewards of two agents is zero [41]. In every

MDP, there is at least one strategy that is stationary, deterministic, and optimal [100]. But in most of the cases, the optimal strategies are probabilistic. For example, in Figure 1.23 (rock, paper, and scissor, Example 1.3), selection of a deterministic policy by any one player leads to punishment and hence, the player is defeated. The probabilistic strategy is required to represent the uncertainty about the agents' action choice. Suppose, the opponent agent has an action $O \in \{O\}$ and Q-value is denoted by $Q(S, A, O)$ as introduced in (1.50).

$$Q(S, A, O) \leftarrow r(S, A, O) + \gamma \sum_{S'} P\left(S' \mid (S, A)\right) \times V\left(S'\right), \tag{1.50}$$

where

$$V\left(S'\right) = \max_{\pi \in P(\{A\})} \min_{O \in \{O\}} \pi_A \cdot Q(S, A, O). \tag{1.51}$$

(1.51) indicates the expected reward to the agent for playing strategy π against the opponent's choice $O \in \{O\}$. $P(\{A\})$ refers to the probability distribution over the action set $\{A\}$. The algorithm for Minimax Q-learning is given in Algorithm 1.12 [100]. Algorithm 1.12 is tested in a two-player Markov game and it is compared with Q-learning. The convergence of Minimax-Q learning is guaranteed and the strategy offered by it is a safe choice against the opponent even in the worst situation.

Algorithm 1.12   Minimax Q-learning

Input: Action $A \in \{A\}$, opponent's action $O \in \{O\}$ at joint state S, $\alpha \in [0, 1)$ and $\gamma \in [0, 1)$;
Output: Optimal Q-value $Q^*(S, A, O)$;
Initialize: $Q(S, A, O) \leftarrow 0$, $\pi(S, A) = \frac{1}{|A|}$;
Begin
   Repeat
      Choose an action to execute by $\pi(S, A)$;
      Receive immediate reward $r(S, A, O)$;
      Update: $Q(S, A, O) \leftarrow (1 - \alpha) Q(S, A, O) + \alpha [r(S, A, O) + \gamma V(S')]$,
      $S \leftarrow S'$,
      $\pi(S, A) = \arg\max_{\pi(S, A)} \left[\underset{O}{Min} \sum_{\forall A} \pi(S, A) \times Q(S, A, O) \right]$ and $V(S') = \max_{\pi \in P(\{A\})} \min_{O \in \{O\}} \pi_A \cdot Q(S, A, O)$;
      $Q^*(S, A, O) \leftarrow Q(S, A, O)$;
   Until $Q(S, A, O)$ converges;
End.

Heuristically Accelerated Multi-agent Reinforcement Learning

In [101], Bianchi et al. proposed HAMRL, which attempts to speed up in convergence of MARL, by balancing exploration/exploitation employing a heuristic function for action selection. There exist a series of literature [101–104], where heuristic functions are used to increase the convergence speed of the MARL. The work of [101] is the extension of [104], whereas in [104], Littman's Minimax-Q is heuristically accelerated. Bianchi et al. defined a heuristic function $H : \{S\} \times \{A\} \times \{O\} \to \mathbb{R}$, which influences the action selection of the agents during the learning phase, when an agent executes an action $A \in \{A\}$ at state $S \in \{S\}$ against the opponent's action $O \in \{O\}$. In [101], the authors employ the modified ε-greedy learning rule including the heuristic function $H(S, A, O)$ given by (1.52).

$$\pi^c(S) = \arg\max_A \min_O \left[Q(S, A, O) + \xi H(S, A, O)^\beta \right] \tag{1.52}$$

and $\xi \in \mathbb{R}, \beta \in \mathbb{R}$ are the weightage on the confidence of the heuristic function. In (1.52), if $\xi = 0$, then (1.52) becomes (1.53), which is the standard ε-greedy.

$$\pi(S) = \begin{cases} \pi^c(S), & \text{if } p \geq \varepsilon, \varepsilon \in [0, 1] \\ \text{Select an action randomly,} & \text{otherwise} \end{cases}, \tag{1.53}$$

where $p \in [0, 1]$ is a random number. Considering $\xi = \beta = 1$, the heuristic function is given by

$$H(S, A, O) = \begin{cases} \max_i Q(S, i, O) - Q(S, A, O) + \eta, & \text{if } A = \pi^H(S) \\ 0, & \text{otherwise} \end{cases}, \tag{1.54}$$

where $\eta \in \mathbb{R}, \pi^H(S)$ is the heuristic policy. The superiority of the HAMRL (Algorithm 1.13) is validated by conducting the experiments in two robots soccer game.

Algorithm 1.13   HAMRL for Zero-sum Game

Input: Action $A \in \{A\}$, opponent's action $O \in \{O\}$ at joint state S, $\alpha \in$ [0, 1), $\gamma \in$ [0, 1) and $\varepsilon \in$ [0, 1);
Output: Optimal Q-value $Q^*(S, A, O)$;
Initialize: $Q(S, A, O) \leftarrow 0$, $H(S, A, O)$, π^H, η;
Begin
  Repeat
    Choose an action $A \in \{A\}$ using the modified ε-greedy rule;
    Execute $A \in \{A\}$, observe the opponent's action $O \in \{O\}$;
    Receive immediate reward $r(S, A, O)$;
    Update: $Q(S, A, O) \leftarrow (1 - \alpha)Q(S, A, O) + \alpha[r(S, A, O) + \gamma V(S')]$,
    $S \leftarrow S'$ and $H(S, A, O)$,
    where $V(S') = \max_{A \in \{A\}} \min_{O \in \{O\}} Q(S, A, O)$;
    $Q^*(S, A, O) \leftarrow Q(S, A, O)$;
  Until $Q(S, A, O)$ converges;
End.

1.3.5.3 Mixed MARL

Mixed MARL includes the following algorithms. The mixed MARL may be cooperative or competitive. It can be categorized based on the number of joint states involved: static and dynamic.

Static

The static MARL algorithms are further extended in Figure 1.36.

Belief-Based Learning Rule In belief-based learning algorithm, an agent maintains a belief about the remaining agents' strategy. This section illustrates the belief-based learning rule.

Fictitious Play FP [105] is a belief-based learning rule. Here, belief indicates that a player adapts with the strategy about opponent players' and behaves as per the strategy learned. In FP, a robot can resolve the problem of equilibrium selection [38] in a coordinated game by repeatedly playing the game by the same robot. FP is an effective and efficient approach to reach equilibrium in a coordinated game. As per FP, agent i learns the models of all the other agents $j \neq i$ by the model given in (1.55).

$$P^i_{a_j} = \frac{C^j_{a_j}}{\sum_{\forall \tilde{a}_j} C^j_{\tilde{a}_j}},$$

(1.55)

where $P^i_{a_j}$ refers to the model of agent j's strategy evaluated by agent i or agent i's assumption of playing $a_j \in A_j$ by agent j or Π_{-i} and $C^j_{a_j}$ be the number of times agent i observed agent j executing action a_j. In cooperative games, the strategy offered by (1.55) leads to an equilibrium, where in case of multiple equilibrium, agents randomly choose any one. Also, in FP, a player does not need to learn about opponent players' reward, rather it maintains a belief about the opponents' feature strategy. If a FP converges to Π^*, then Π^* is a NE.

Meta Strategy In [106], Powers and Shoham proposed a straightforward MARL algorithm for repeated games, which have the following two requirements. The first requirement is to specify a class of opponents and against them the algorithm yields a reward that approaches the reward corresponding to the best response. Second requirement is that the reward offered by the algorithm fulfills a threshold of security-level reward. Constraining the above requirements, the algorithm achieves a close to optimal payoff in self-play. Based on the above conditions an algorithm is proposed in [106], for stationary opponents only. However, to learn in a repeated game a learning algorithm is required. In the learning algorithm, an agent plays its best response with a prior probability of its opponent's strategy. GAMUT [60] is employed to test the superiority of the proposed algorithm in [106].

In [107], two properties are presented related to the rationality and convergence. By rationality in a stage game, if the other players' strategies converge to stationary strategy, then the learning algorithm will converge to a stationary strategy and it is the best response to the other players' strategies. Another property is related to the convergence. By this property, the learner will necessarily converge to a stationary strategy.

In [107], Bowling and Veloso proposed an algorithm for known repeated game having two players and two actions. Conitzer and Sandholm in [108] extend the work in [107] for all repeated games. It is investigated in [106] that the algorithms considering self-play proposed in [107] and [108] are not convergent against all possible opponents. In Figures 1.30, 1.31, and 1.34, by Tit-for-Tat algorithm for the Prisoner's Dilemma and game of chicken offers higher average reward in self-play than the rewards at NE. To avoid encounter the opponent outside the target set, security value V_s is defined in (1.56).

$$V_s = \max_{\pi_1 \in \{\pi_1\}} \max_{\pi_2 \in \{\pi_2\}} V_e(\pi_1, \pi_2). \tag{1.56}$$

In summary, Powers and Shoham synergistically fuse the FP [39], Bully [109], and Minimax [100] strategy with an aim to create most powerful hybrid algorithm [106].

By FP, an agent plays best response against its stationary opponent utilizing the likelihood of other agents to select an action from history. In [106], the best response

$$B_r(\pi) \leftarrow \underset{x \in X}{\operatorname{argmax}}(OV_e(x, \pi)), \tag{1.57}$$

where

$$X = \left\{ y \in \Pi_1 : EV(y, \pi) \geq \max_{z \in \pi_1} (EV(z, \pi)) - \varepsilon \right\}. \tag{1.58}$$

In [106], Bully algorithm (Algorithm 1.14) is extended to handle multiple strategies with equal reward by maximizing opponent's values. In Bully algorithm, a full set of mixed strategies are

$$BullyMixed \leftarrow \underset{x \in X}{\operatorname{argmax}}(OV_e(x, B_r(x))), \tag{1.59}$$

$$X = \left\{ y \in \Pi_1 : V_e(y, B_{r0}(y)) = \max_{z \in \Pi_1} (V_e(z, B_{r0}(z))) \right\}. \tag{1.60}$$

Bully algorithm is the one which is employed to elect a coordinator dynamically among m number of agents with unique identify (ID) in the field of distributed

---

Algorithm 1.14   Bully Algorithm

```
Begin
  An agent i initiates an election;
  Agent i sends election message to all agents with higher IDs and
  waits for feedback;
  If feedback is not OK
    Then agent i becomes coordinator and sends coordination
    message to all agents with lower IDs;
  Else
    The agent i drops out and waits for a coordination message;
  End;
  If an agent receives an election message
    Then immediately sends coordination message subject to that
    the agent has highest ID;
  Else
    Return OK and starts an election;
  If an agent receives a coordination message
    Then the agent i treats the sender as the coordination;
End.
```

---

computing. In distributed artificial intelligence, an algorithm needs to act as a leader (or coordinator). In distributed algorithm, it is assumed that each agent has a unique ID and goal of the algorithm is to find out the agent with highest ID. The Bully algorithm is given in Algorithm 1.14. Finally, the Minimax strategy is defined as

$$\text{maximin} \leftarrow \underset{\pi_1 \in \Pi_1}{\text{argmax}} \; \underset{\pi_2}{\text{min}} \; V_e(\pi_1, \pi_2). \tag{1.61}$$

Initial portion of Algorithm 1.15 is related to coordination/exploration to identify the class of opponent and choose one strategy among three. If neither stationary strategy nor Bully strategy holds, then best-response strategy is applied. The algorithm plays with one of the three strategies maintaining the average reward within the security level and improving the maximum strategy when it is too low, where $d_{t_1}^{t_2}$ refers to the distribution of opponent actions for the period from t_1 to t_2. Avg_n represents the average value achieved by the agent during the last n epoch. V_{Bully} represents $V_e(BullyMixed, B_{r0}(BullyMixed))$.

Algorithm 1.15   Meta Strategy Algorithm

```
Begin
Set strategy = BullyMixed
```
  Play strategy at time step t_1;
  Play strategy at time step t_2;
  If strategy=BullyMixed AND $AVGValue_H < V_{Bully} - \varepsilon_1$ with probability P
    Then set strategy $= B_{r\varepsilon_2}(d_0^t)$ and play;
  End If
  If $\left\| d_o^{t_1} - d_{t-t_1}^t \right\| < \varepsilon_3$
    Set best Strategy $= B_{r\varepsilon_2}(d_0^t)$;
  Else if strategy=BullyMixed AND $AVGValue_H > V_{Bully} - \varepsilon_1$
    Then set Best strategy=BullyMixed;
  Else
    Set best Strategy=Best Response;
  End If
  Until end of the game;
  If $AVGValue_{t-t0} < V_{security} - \varepsilon_0$
    Play Maximin strategy for t_3 time steps
  Else
    Play best Strategy for t_3 time steps;
  End If
End

Adapt When Everybody Is Stationary, Otherwise Move to Equilibrium   As per [108], the minimum requirements of MAS are that agents learn optimally against stationary opponents and converge to a NE when all the agents are playing the same algorithm. WoLF-IGA [107] has satisfied the above criteria in a two-agent two-action repeated game assuming that the opponents' strategies are observable. In [108], Conitzer and Sandholm proposed *Adapt When Everybody is Stationary, Otherwise Move to Equilibrium* (AWESOME), which is guaranteed to have the above properties for more than two agents and actions assuming that the opponents' actions (not strategies) are observable. In AWESOME, either agents' aim at adapting with the present strategies of the opponent agents or they converge to an already learned NE. Once both of the above hypotheses are discarded, agents restart the learning by the AWESOME algorithm.

The basic idea of the AWESOME is straightforward. If other agents are following stationary strategies, then AWESOME offers its best strategy to the other agents.

On the other hand, if other agents adapt their strategies, then AWESOME follows an already learned equilibrium. In spite of the above basic idea, the following additional specifications are made before proposing the AWESOME algorithm.

- From the beginning it is specified which equilibrium to repeat and restart learning by the AWESOME to avoid confusion.
- After restarting, the learning agents forget whatever it learned for simplicity.
- Following one equilibrium strategy among the already computed other equilibrium strategies may lead to divergence from equilibrium. Although, a null hypothesis exists, AWESOME does not reject the hypothesis without sufficient confirmations.
- If an agent selects its own action by its own mixed strategy, then AWESOME rejects the equilibrium strategy to avoid the nonequilibrium strategy.
- After rejecting the equilibrium strategy by AWESOME, randomly an action is chosen from a pool and changes its strategy.
- In AWESOME, except actions the strategies of the remaining agents are not observable. Hence, one needs to specify how to reject an equilibrium strategy which is common to all the agents.

The AWESOME algorithm is given in Algorithm 1.16 [108], and is developed based on the above specifications. It is shown in [108] that AWESOME learns best responses against the stationary opponents, and AWESOME converges to NE in self-play.

Hyper-Q Q-learning is a well-known technique to learn optimal strategies by an agent utilizing the cumulative rewards earned by it in an infinite trial-and-error. Unfortunately, this is not applicable for nonstationary environment with multiple adaptive agents. Most of the multi-agent Q-learner [72, 95, 100] requires knowledge about other agents' rewards and Q-function at each learning epoch. These MAQL algorithms are convergent subject to the following conditions which are not realizable in practice. First, an agent can observe all agents' rewards. Second, all the learning agents follow the same learning algorithms. In [110], Gerald proposed Hyper-Q learning. Hyper-Q learner learns only the mixed strategies and the strategies of the remaining agents are estimated employing the Bayesian inference. Hyper-Q learner aims at overcoming the above limitations of MAS by modeling the environment as repeated stochastic game, where only the remaining agents' actions are observable but the rewards received due to the actions are not observable.

Assuming the Hyper-Q learner is playing in a stochastic Markov game and hence, the reward functions of the agents become the function the available joint actions. Now, instead of choosing the best joint action with probability one (pure

Algorithm 1.16 AWESOME Algorithm

For $i = 1$ to m

    $\pi_i^* \leftarrow ComEquStrategy(i)$; // compute equilibrium strategy
    for agent i

End For;

Repeat

  For $i = 1$ to m

     $Ini2Empty(h_i^{prev})$; $Ini2Empty(h_i^{curr})$;

  End For;

$APPE \leftarrow true$; // All players playing Equilibrium

$APS \leftarrow true$; // All players stationary

$\beta \leftarrow false$; // β is true if the equilibrium hypothesis is just rejected

$t \leftarrow 0$; // denotes the tth epoch and is initializes to zero in every restart.

$\phi \leftarrow \pi_{Me}^*$; // refers to the AWESOME player's current strategy

While APPE

  For $j = 1$ to N^t

    $Play(\phi)$; // Play the strategy ϕ

    For $i = 1$ to m

      $Update(h_i^{curr})$;

    End For;

  End For;

  If APPE=false

    If β =false

      For $i = 1$ to m

       If $\left(\|h_i^{cur} - h_i^{prev}\| > \varepsilon_s^t\right)$

         Then $APS \leftarrow false$;

       End If;

      End For;

    End If;

    Then $\beta \leftarrow false$; $a \leftarrow \underset{a}{\arg\max} V\left(a, h_{-Me}^{curr}\right)$;

    If $V\left(a, h_{-Me}^{curr}\right) > V\left(\phi, h_{-Me}^{cur}\right) + n \mid A \mid \varepsilon_s^{t+1}\mu$;

     Then $\phi \leftarrow a$;

    End If;

  End If;

  If APPE=true

    For $i = 1$ to m

     If $\left(\|h_i^{cur} - \pi_i^p\| > \varepsilon_e^t\right)$

       Then $APS \leftarrow false$; $\phi \leftarrow RandAct()$; $\beta \leftarrow true$;

     End If;

    End For; **End If**;

  For $i = 1$ to m

    $h_i^{cur} \leftarrow h_i^{prev}$; $Ini2Empty(h_i^{curr})$;

  End For; $t \leftarrow t + 1$;

End While;

strategy), in stochastic Markov game, an agent chooses actions with the best probability (mixed strategy). The Hyper-Q learning update rule is given in (1.62).

$$\Delta Q(S, p_i, p_{-i}) \leftarrow \alpha \left[r(S, p_i, p_{-i}) + \gamma \max_{a_i'} Q\left(S, p_i', p_{-i}'\right) - Q(S, p_i, p_{-i}) \right],$$

(1.62)

where p_i and p_i' denote the mixed strategy to select action a_i and a_i' at joint state S and joint next state S', respectively. p_{-i} and p_{-i}' refer to the joint mixed strategy of all the agents except i to select joint action A_{-i} and A_{-i}' at joint state S and joint next state S', respectively. It is indicated in [110] that establishing the convergence for the function, approximation-based Q-learning is more difficult than the same for the Q-learning. If all the agents do explore in a similar exploration strategy, then like Q-learning in Hyper-Q learning, agents may fail to spot the optimal mixed strategy in the strategy space after infinite visit of the joint states. In case of stationary opponent strategy, the stochastic game becomes a MDP with stationary state-transitions and stationary rewards. Under the above circumstance, Hyper-Q learning converges. Remaining convergence conditions are given in [110]. To estimate opponent strategy, Bayesian strategy estimation is done in [110]. By Bayesian estimation, one can write

$$P(S \mid H) = \frac{P(H \mid S)P(S)}{\sum_{S'} P(H \mid S')P(S')},$$

(1.63)

where H refers to the history of observed actions, S and S' are the discrete state and next state, respectively. The outstanding performance of Hyper-Q learning in terms of convergence rate and opponent agent's strategy modeling is tested in the framework of two-player, three-action matrix game rock-paper-scissors game (Example 1.3).

Direct Policy Search Based Algorithm   Direct policy search-based algorithms are further classified as fixed learning rate and variable learning rate as shown in Figure 1.36.

Fixed Learning Rate   The algorithms with fixed learning rates are given below.

Infinitesimal Gradient Ascent   In [111], Singh and Kearns proposed IGA based on the positive changes in expected reward of the agents. The IGA is tested in a two-player, two-action iterated general-sum games. It is shown in [111] that agents converge to NE, but once they fail to converge to NE, they can never reach the

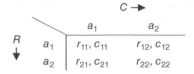

$c \rightarrow$

		a_1	a_2
R	a_1	r_{11}, c_{11}	r_{12}, c_{12}
$\downarrow$	a_2	r_{21}, c_{21}	r_{22}, c_{22}

Figure 1.44 Reward matrix in a two-player two-agent game.

NE. Literature shows that agents converge to NE, but with restriction and limiting the applicability of the NE [88]. Following the gradient ascent (positive change) is the most common trend in machine learning algorithm. It is not guaranteed that the strategies computed by gradient ascent in two-player, two-action iterated games will converge to NE. However, the average reward is guaranteed to converge NE. For example, let there is a two-player, two-action general-sum game. The reward matrix of the row (R) and column (C) player is given in Figure 1.44.

Let row player choose action a_1 stochastically with probability $0 \le r \le 1$ and column player choose action a_1 stochastically with probability $0 \le c \le 1$. The expected payoff of the row and column player is given by (1.64) and (1.65), respectively.

$$V_R(r,c) = r_{11}(rc) + r_{22}((1-r)(1-c)) + r_{12}(r(1-c)) + r_{21}((1-r)c), \tag{1.64}$$

$$V_C(r,c) = c_{11}(rc) + c_{22}((1-r)(1-c)) + c_{12}(r(1-c)) + c_{21}((1-r)c). \tag{1.65}$$

Here, the strategy pair (r, c) is called NE if and only if, the following two conditions hold.

- if for any mixed strategy r' (1.66) holds: i.e.

$$V_R\left(r',c\right) \le V_R(r,c) \tag{1.66}$$

- for any mixed strategy c' (1.67) holds: i.e.

$$V_C\left(r,c'\right) \le V_R(r,c). \tag{1.67}$$

Gradient for the row player and column player is given by (1.66) and (1.69), respectively, considering $u = (r_{11} + r_{22}) - (r_{21} + r_{12})$ and $u' = (c_{11} + c_{22}) - (c_{21} + c_{12})$.

$$\frac{\delta V_R(r,c)}{\delta r} = cu - (r_{22} - r_{12}), \tag{1.68}$$

$$\frac{\delta V_C(r,c)}{\delta c} = ru' - (c_{22} - c_{12}). \tag{1.69}$$

The mixed strategy update rules are given by (1.70) and (1.71), where η refers to the step size.

$$r \leftarrow r + \eta \frac{\delta V_R(r,c)}{\delta r}, \tag{1.70}$$

$$c \leftarrow c + \eta \frac{\delta V_C(r,c)}{\delta c}. \tag{1.71}$$

Assuming that the gradient ascent algorithm is a full information game and hence, both the players know the game matrices and the mixed strategies played by the opponent players in the previous step.

By game theory [43], the sequences of strategies over time may never converge to NE. However, in [111], it is shown that the average rewards of both the players always converge. The basic logic behind the analysis of two players acting according to IGA is a two-dimensional dynamic system. Considering the infinitesimal step size of $\eta(\eta \to 0)$, IGA is proposed in [111]. By (1.66)–(1.71) and setting $\eta \to 0$, the unconstraint dynamics of the strategy pair can be expressed as a function of time in (1.72).

$$\begin{bmatrix} \dfrac{\delta r}{\delta t} \\[2mm] \dfrac{\delta c}{\delta t} \end{bmatrix} = \begin{bmatrix} 0 & u \\ u' & 0 \end{bmatrix} \begin{bmatrix} r \\ c \end{bmatrix} + \begin{bmatrix} -(r_{22} - r_{12}) \\ -(c_{22} - c_{21}) \end{bmatrix}. \tag{1.72}$$

If the matrix U given in (1.73) is invertible, then trajectories of the unconstraint strategies of the two-player two-action stochastic game are of having either limit cycle behavior or have divergent nature. The direction and structure of these trajectories depend on the exact values of u and u'.

$$U = \begin{bmatrix} 0 & u \\ u' & 0 \end{bmatrix}. \tag{1.73}$$

By solving (1.72), (r^*, c^*) is given in (1.74).

$$(r^*, c^*) = \begin{bmatrix} \dfrac{c_{22} - c_{21}}{u'}, & \dfrac{r_{22} - r_{12}}{u} \end{bmatrix}. \tag{1.74}$$

The average expected reward of the IGA player converges to a NE following one of the following conditions. First condition is that the trajectories of the strategy pair will automatically converge to a NE. The other condition is that the trajectories due to the strategy pair will not converge but the average reward of the two players reward will converge to the NE. To prove these conditions, the following exclusive and exhaustive cases are considered [112].

1) U is non-invertible, if $u \neq 0/u' \neq 0$ or $u \neq 0$, $u' \neq 0$. Such cases can appear in team, zero-sum, and general-sum games.
2) U is invertible, if the Eigen values of (1.75) are imaginary with zero real part, i.e. when $uu' < 0$.

$$\begin{bmatrix} 0 & u \\ u' & 0 \end{bmatrix} \begin{bmatrix} x \\ y \end{bmatrix} = \lambda \begin{bmatrix} x \\ y \end{bmatrix}. \tag{1.75}$$

3) U is invertible, if its Eigen values are real with zero imaginary part. This condition may appear in team and general-sum games but not is zero-sum games, i.e. when $uu' > 0$.

If U has imaginary Eigen values with zero real part, then based on the location of the center (i.e. (r^*, c^*)) in the two-dimensional plane, there are three possibilities.

1) The center (r^*, c^*) is in the interior of the unit square,
2) Center (r^*, c^*) is on the boundary of the unit square, and
3) Center (r^*, c^*) is outside of the unit square.

Generalized Infinitesimal Gradient Ascent   Convex programming is the generalization of the linear programming having several applications in machine learning domain [113–115]. The convex programming aims at searching a point F which maximizes the cost function.

$$c : F \rightarrow R. \tag{1.76}$$

A convex programming comprises a feasible set $F \subseteq R^n$ and a convex cost function given in (1.76). In applications like industrial optimization, nonlinear facility location problems [113], network routing problems [116], and consumer optimization problems [117], the value of the end product is unknown until the end product is created. In [118], an online convex optimization programming is undertaken with identical feasible set but having dissimilar cost functions. An algorithm is proposed in [118], namely GIGA, which is generally reliable to solve former problems. GIGA is the extension of IGA [111] applicable for more than two agents. Following the definitions of convex, convex programming problem, online convex programming problem, and the assumptions made in [107], make clear idea about the online convex optimization. Interestingly, it is shown in [107] that the repeated games are online linear programming. Finally, GIGA tries to minimize regret [118].

Variable Learning Rate   The algorithms with variable learning rates are given below.

Win or Learn Fast-IGA   Referring from Section "Infinitesimal Gradient Ascent," if the center (r^*, c^*) is inside the unit square with imaginary Eigen values, then the performance of IGA and WoLF-IGA differs in terms of convergence. It is shown in [107] that IGA does not converge if (r^*, c^*) lies inside the unit square. But WoLF-IGA converges in such situation. The strategy-space where the player wins and loses is also indicated in the proof. In addition, it is shown in [107] that the trajectories due to Eigen values are pricewise elliptical in nature and take a spiral shapes toward the center. In [107], lemmas are proposed assuming that there are only imaginary Eigen values.

By lemma 6 in [107], if the learning rate for the row player (α_r) and the learning rate for the column player (α_c) remain constant, then the trajectory due to strategy pair forms an ellipse considering (r^*, c^*) as the center and $\begin{bmatrix} 0 \\ \sqrt{\dfrac{\alpha_c \mid u \mid}{\alpha_r \mid u/ \mid}} \end{bmatrix}$, $\begin{bmatrix} 1 \\ 0 \end{bmatrix}$ are as the axes of the ellipse. In [107], lemma 7 concludes that a player is winning if the strategy of the player is moving away from the center. It is also mentioned in [107] that in a two-person, two-action iterated general-sum game, both the players follow the WoLF-IGA algorithm with learning rates $\alpha_{\max}$ and $\alpha_{\min}$, then their strategies will converge to a NE subject to

$$\frac{\alpha^r_{\min}\alpha^c_{\min}}{\alpha^r_{\max}\alpha^c_{\max}} < 1. \tag{1.77}$$

GIGA-Win or Learn Fast   The most common problems in MARL, regret and convergence, are addressed in gradient-based GIGA-WoLF [119]. GIGA-WoLF is the synergism of GIGA's no-regret property and WoLF-IGA's convergence property [119]. A bound is assigned to test the GIGA-WoLF's regret against the unknown strategy of an opponent agent. For a two-agent, two-action normal-form game, if one agent follows the GIGA-WoLF algorithm and another agent follows the GIGA algorithm, then their strategies does converge to NE. Both the properties are validated theoretically and experimentally in [119]. In GIGA-WoLF, agents must know about the game and should have the model of opponent agent. In almost all the games (except "problematic" Shapley's game), unlike GIGA's strategies, GIGA-WoLF's strategies does converge in self-play to equilibrium.

Dynamic
The dynamic algorithms are categorized as equilibrium dependent and independent. The algorithms based on the equilibrium solution concept are listed below.

Equilibrium Dependent   The equilibrium-dependent MARL algorithms are given below.

Nash-Q Learning   NQL is the extension of Littman's Minimax-Q learning [100]. In other words, it's the extension of zero-sum-stochastic game to the general-sum-stochastic game. NQL is a MAQL algorithm, which converges under specific conditions. It looks for optimal joint action (NE) in a game. For multiple NEs in the game, the NQL algorithm is fused with other learning techniques to obtain optimal strategies for the entire team. The adopted framework in [95] is stochastic/Markov games. Markov game is the generalization of the MDP with more than two agents. Unlike, zero-sum game, here in general-sum-stochastic game, an agent's gain is no longer its opponent agent's loss. In general-sum game, an agent's reward depends on other agent's choices and hence, the NE is employed. In NE, an agent cannot deviate unilaterally and it is assumed that there is no communication among the agents. Only agents can observe other agents' strategies and rewards. In addition, the state-transition probabilities and reward functions are unknown. The NQL algorithm is designed in such a way that all the agents converge to the NE with restrictions. NQL is guaranteed that all the agents converge to the NE. But for multiple NE solutions, it is not guaranteed that all the agents converge the same NE. In [80], Filar and Vrieze proposed that every general-sum discounted stochastic game possess at least one equilibrium point in stationary strategy. Unlike single agent Q-learning [84] and Minimax Q-learning [100], in NQL the Q-learning update rule for agent i is given in (1.78).

$$Q_i(S,A) \leftarrow (1-\alpha)Q_i(S,A) + \alpha\left[r_i(S,A) + \gamma\, NashQ_i\left(S'\right)\right], \quad \forall i, \qquad (1.78)$$

where

$$NashQ_i\left(S'\right) = \pi_1\left(S'\right)\cdots\pi_m\left(S'\right)\cdot Q_i\left(S'\right). \qquad (1.79)$$

An online version of NQL and simulation results on Grid game 1 and 2 are given in [71]. The NQL for general-sum-stochastic game is given in Algorithm 1.17. The convergence proof of Algorithm 1.17 is given [71].

Algorithm 1.17   NQL in General-sum Game

Input: Action $a_i \in A_i$ at $s_i \in S_i$, $\forall i$, learning rate $\alpha \in [0, 1)$ and discount factor $\gamma \in [0, 1)$;
Output: Optimal Q-value $Q_i^*(S, A)$, $\forall i$; $// S = \{s_i\}_{i=1}^m$, $A = \{a_i\}_{i=1}^m$;
Initialize: $Q_i(A, A) \leftarrow 0$, $\forall i$;
Begin
   Repeat
      Choose an action $a_i \in A_i$, $\forall i$;
      Receive immediate reward $r_i(S, A)$, $\forall i$;
      Update: $Q_i(S, A) \leftarrow (1-\alpha)Q_i(S, A) + \alpha[r_i(S, A) + \gamma\, NashQ_i(S')]$,
      $\forall i$ and $S \leftarrow S'$;
      $Q_i^*(S, A) \leftarrow Q_i(S, A)$, $\forall i$; $// NashQ_i(S') = \pi_1(S') . \dots \pi_m(S') . Q_i(S')$
   Until $Q_i(S, A)$, $\forall i$ converge;
End.

Algorithm 1.18   Correlated-Q Learning

Input: Action $a_i \in A_i$ at state $s_i \in S_i$ for all the agents learning rate $\alpha \in [0, 1)$ and discount factor $\gamma \in [0, 1)$;
Output: Optimal Q-value $Q_i^*(S, A), \forall i$;
Initialize: $Q_i(S, A) \leftarrow 0, \forall i$;
Begin
    Repeat
        Choose an action $a_i \in A, \forall i$;
        Receive immediate reward $r_i(S, A), \forall i$;
        Update: $Q_i(S, A) \leftarrow (1 - \alpha) Q_i(S, A) + \alpha [r_i(S, A) + \gamma V_i(S')], \forall i$
        and $S \leftarrow S'$;
            $V_i(S') = CE(Q_1(S'), Q_2(S'), ..., Q_m(S')), \forall i$;
        $Q_i^*(S, A) \leftarrow Q_i(S, A), \forall i$;
        Until $Q_i(S, A), \forall i$; converge;
End.

Correlated-Q Learning   In [72], Greenwald and Hall introduced a MAQL algorithm, namely Correlated-Q Learning (CQL). In CQL, Q-value of an agent updates at CE. CQL generalizes both NQL and FFQ in general-sum-stochastic games. If NE and CE do not intersect, then the agent receives less reward at NE compared to the same at CE. Four variants of CE are defined in [72] and the definition of CE is given in Definition 1.18. The algorithm for CQL is given in Algorithm 1.18. Convergence analysis of the above equilibria in the framework of Markov games are done in [72].

Asymmetric-Q Learning   In [120], Ville proposed Asymmetric-Q Learning (AQL) algorithm, where an agent leads the follower agents by providing the information about the follower agents' strategy to the follower agents. AQL offers the following benefits:

- In each state the leader has unique equilibrium point.
- Asymmetric Q-learner always achieves the PSNE very fast. Though MSNE exists.
- The AQL algorithm enjoys the lower space and computational requirements than conventional algorithms.

In [120], the existing MAQL algorithms are divided into three clusters. One is the methods utilizing the direct gradients of agents' value function. Second one is the methods that estimate the value functions and then use this estimate to compute equilibrium of the process. Last one is the use of direct policy gradients. The AQL algorithm is developed by Stackelberg equilibrium (SE) [44]. The algorithm for the leader and the follower are given in Algorithms 1.19 and 1.20. The leader agents are capable to maintain all the agents' Q-tables. However, the follower agents are

---

Algorithm 1.19 Asymmetric-Q Learning for the Leader

Input: Action $a_i \in A_i$ at state $s_i \in S_i$ for all the agents learning rate $\alpha \in [0, 1)$ and discount factor $\gamma \in [0, 1)$;
Output: Optimal Q-value $Q_i^*(S, A)$, $\forall i$;
Initialize: $Q_i(S, A) \leftarrow 0$, $\forall i$;
Begin
  Repeat
    Choose an action $a_i \in A$, $\forall i$;
    Receive immediate reward $r_i(S, A)$, $\forall i$;
    Update: $Q_i(S, A) \leftarrow (1 - \alpha) Q_i(S, A) + \alpha [r_i(S, A) + \gamma V_i(S')]$, $\forall i$
    and $S \leftarrow S'$;
        $V_i(S') = SE(Q_1(S'), Q_2(S'), ..., Q_m(S'))$, $\forall i$;
    $Q_i^*(S, A) \leftarrow Q_i(S, A)$, $\forall i$;
  Until $Q_i(S, A)$, $\forall i$; converge;
End.

Algorithm 1.20 Asymmetric-Q Learning for the Follower

Input: Action $a_i \in A_i$ at state $s_i \in S_i$ for all the agents learning rate $\alpha \in [0, 1)$ and discount factor $\gamma \in [0, 1)$;
Output: Optimal Q-value $Q_i^*(S, A)$, $\forall i$;
Initialize: $Q_i(S, A) \leftarrow 0$, $\forall i$;
Begin
  Repeat
    Choose an action $a_i \in A$, $\forall i$;
    Receive immediate reward $r_i(S, A)$, $\forall i$;
    Update: $Q_i(S, A) \leftarrow (1 - \alpha) Q_i(S, A) + \alpha \left[r_i(S, A) + \gamma \max_{A'} Q_i(S', A') \right]$ and
    $S \leftarrow S'$;
    $Q_i^*(S, A) \leftarrow Q_i(S, A)$, $\forall i$;
  Until $Q_i(S, A)$, $\forall i$; converge;
End.

not able to maintain all the agents' Q-values and hence, they just maximize their reward. Experiments are performed in the grid world environment to demonstrate the superiority of the AQL algorithm.

Friend-or-Foe Q-learning   In [121], Littman proposed one variant of MAQL algorithm, namely FFQ algorithm with a strong convergence guarantee compared with NE in the framework of general-sum-stochastic game, where agents are instructed to consider other agents' either as a friend or foe. Though, FFQ learning is an improvement over the Nash-Q. In FFQ, two variants' of NE are employed. One is adversarial equilibrium and another is coordination equilibrium. In Minimax-Q (zero-sum game) [100], all the equilibria are adversarial equilibrium. However, in general-sum game, all the equilibria are not coordination equilibrium. Coordination equilibrium provides the highest possible reward of agent i, $i \in [1, m]$ given in (1.80) [121].

$$R_i(\pi_1, ..., \pi_m) = \max_{a_1 \in A_1, ..., a_m \in A_m} R_i(a_1, ..., a_m). \tag{1.80}$$

Except fully cooperative game, coordination equilibrium need not always exist. The adversarial and coordination equilibria are explained in Figure 1.25. The difference between the Nash operation and the maximization or minimax operations is that the latter two have unique solutions. However, the Nash operation offers two variant of solutions: adversarial and coordination equilibrium depending on the problem type.

Two Propositions are proposed and proved in [121]. As per the Propositions, if a one-stage game has a coordination/adversarial equilibrium, then all of the coordination/adversarial equilibrium have same value. There exist two conditions for convergence [121]. In summary, the conditions statement is that for a game there exists either adversarial/coordination equilibrium. Later, two stronger conditions of convergence are proposed in [95, 121]. These conditions can be summarized as follows. There exists an adversarial/coordination equilibrium in a game and every game is defined by the Q-functions adapted during the learning phase. The later conditions are also not sufficient to guarantee convergence. Hu and Wellman [95] state two theorems that by the latter two conditions Nash-Q converges to Nash-Q equilibrium until all the equilibria are adapted during the learning phase are unique. Also by the latter two conditions, Nash-Q converges to NE, until the required equilibria are employed in (1.82).

Now, in FFQ algorithm, *Nash* $Q_i(S')$ are given in (1.81) and (1.82) for Friend-Q (coordination equilibrium) and Foe-Q (adversarial equilibrium), respectively.

$$Nash \, Q_i\left(S'\right) = \max_{A'} \sum_{A'} P\left(A'\right) \cdot Q_i\left(S', A'\right), \tag{1.81}$$

Algorithm 1.21   Friend-or Foe-Q Learning

Input: Action $a_i \in A_i$ at state $s_i \in S_i$ for all the agents learning rate $\alpha \in [0, 1)$ and discount factor $\gamma \in [0, 1)$;
Output: Optimal Q-value $Q_i^*(S, A)$, $\forall i$;
Initialize: $Q_i(S, A) \leftarrow 0$, $\forall i$;
Begin
   Repeat
      Choose an action $a_i \in A$, $\forall i$;
      Receive immediate reward $r_i(S, A)$, $\forall i$;
      Evaluate *Nash* $Q_i(S')$, $\forall i$ by (1.81) and (1.82) respectively
      for Friend-Q and Foe-Q
      Update: $Q_i(S, A) \leftarrow (1 - \alpha) Q_i(S, A) + \alpha [r_i(S, A) + \gamma Nash\, Q_i(S')]$,
      $\forall i$ and $S \leftarrow S'$;
      $Q_i^*(S, A) \leftarrow Q_i(S, A)$, $\forall i$;
   Until $Q_i(S, A)$, $\forall i$; converge;
End.

$$Nash\, Q_i\left(S'\right) = \max_{a_1, \ldots, a_x} \min_{a_1, \ldots, a_y} \sum_{\forall A''} P\left(A''\right) Q_i\left(S', A''\right), \tag{1.82}$$

where $A' = <a_1, \ldots, a_m>$, $A'' = <a_1, \ldots, a_x, a_1, \ldots, a_y>$, and y refers to the number of foes (opponent agents). The convergence of FFQ learning is subject to that the Nash operator is max or minimax operator [121]. Like NQL, for simulation purpose two grid games are employed [95, 121] in FFQ. Six different variants' of opponents are described in [121]. Though, Nash-Q and FFQ cannot fix the problem of finding equilibria, if neither coordination nor adversarial equilibrium exists. The algorithm for FFQ learning is given in Algorithm 1.21.

Negotiation-Based Q-learning   In [122], Hu et al. proposed a MARL without mutually sharing their value functions. Authors in [122] mentioned that mutual exchange of value function is impractical because of the local restriction of the system and privacy of the agents in case of distributed agents. Doing so appears impossible to evaluate equilibrium in a one short game. In the above circumstances, authors propose a multi-step negotiation process to evaluate three types of pure strategies: PSNE, equilibrium-dominating strategy profile (EDNP), and nonstrict EDNP, instead of computing the computationally expensive MSNE. It is also shown that abovementioned three strategies are symmetric Meta strategies. Fusing the above techniques, Hu et al. proposed NegoQ in [122].

NegoQ deals with pure strategy equilibrium. However, in some games (e.g. rock-paper-scissor game, Example 1.3), PSNE does not exist. Another hindrance is that a strategy may be Pareto dominated and so not a PSNE. In Prisoners' Dilemma, only one PSNE (C, C) exist as shown in Figure 1.34. Though (D, D) is the better choice, but (D, D) is the Pareto optimal and not a PSNE. In this regard, a strategy profile Pareto dominates NE, i.e. EDNP is defined in Definition 1.19.

Definition 1.19 In an $m-$agent ($m \geq 2$) normal-form game, a joint action $A \in \{A\}$ is an EDNP if there is a PSNE $A_N \in \{A\}$ such that

$$Q_i(A) \geq Q_i(A_N), \quad i = [1, m]. \tag{1.83}$$

By Definition 1.19 one can conclude that each agent following EDNP receives more reward than the same by following PNSE.

Before defining the nonstrict EDSP, a normal-form game with the same is given in Figure 1.45. In Figure 1.45, there are two PSNEs: (a_1, b_1) and (a_2, b_2). It is apparent that the strategy profile (a_1, b_3) and (a_3, b_3) provide a greater reward to A than (a_1, b_1) and a greater reward to B than (a_2, b_2), respectively. So, the priority of (a_1, b_3) and (a_3, b_3) are more than (a_1, b_1) for A and (a_2, b_2) for B, respectively. Hence, for A and B the nonequilibrium strategy profile (a_1, b_3) and (a_3, b_3) partially dominate the existing PSNE. In [122], Hu et al. defined them as nonstrict EDSP as given in Definition 1.20.

Definition 1.20 In an $m-$agent ($m \geq 2$) normal-form game, a joint action $A \in \{A\}$ is an EDNP if there is a PSNE $A_N^i \in \{A\}$ such that

$$Q_i(A) \geq Q_i(A_N^i), \quad i = [1, m]. \tag{1.84}$$

In the multistep negotiation process of computing the abovementioned three pure strategy profiles, agents exchange their preferences of joint actions among themselves in terms of binary answers. An illustration of the multistep negotiation process is given in Figure 1.46. In Figure 1.46, "Y" and "N" represent as yes and no, respectively. A joint action is pure strategy profile if and only if both the agents' responses are yes. The negotiation process comprises of three types: (i) negotiation for finding the set of PSNE, (ii) negotiation for finding the set of

Figure 1.45 Nonstrict EDNP in normal-form game.

	B		
	b_1	b_2	b_3
a_1	**(20,40)**	(4,22)	(29,30)
a_2	(18,9)	**(36,19)**	(7,4)
a_3	(17,26)	(15,38)	(27,38)

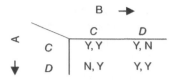

	B →	
	C	D
A C	Y, Y	Y, N
↓ D	N, Y	Y, Y

Figure 1.46 Multistep negotiation process between agent A and B.

nonstrict EDSP, and (iii) negotiation for choosing equilibrium (joint action) from the sets obtained by the above two steps. Evaluation of EDSP follows from the evaluation of the nonstrict EDSP, as EDSP is a special case of nonstrict EDSP. The negotiation to evaluate the PSNE for agent i is given in Algorithm 1.22. The negotiation to evaluate the nonstrict EDSP for agent i is given in Algorithm 1.23. Based on the Negotiation algorithms (Algorithms 1.22 and 1.23) to evaluate the pure strategy profiles the NegoQ algorithm for a Markov game is given in Algorithm 1.24. The superiority of

---

Algorithm 1.22 Negotiation to Evaluate the PSNE for Agent i in a Normal-form Game

Input: Action $a_i \in A_i$ only for the agent $i \in [1, m]$ and $Q_i(A)$;
$//A \in \{A\} = \times_{i=1}^{m} A_i$
Output: PSNE set $\{A_N\}$;
Initialize: $\{A_N\} \leftarrow \varphi$;
Evaluate maximal reward set for agent iMS_i;
For all $A_{-i} \in \{A_{-i}\}$
$\qquad a_i = \arg\max_{a'_i} Q\left(a'_i, A_{-i}\right)$;
$\qquad \{A_N\} \leftarrow \{A_N\} \cup \{a_i, A_{-i}\}$;
End For
For all joint action $A \in \{A_N\}$
$\qquad$ Ask remaining agents that is $\{A_N\}$ includes A; a
$\qquad$ **If** $\{A_N\}$ does not include A **then**
$\qquad\qquad \{A_N\} \leftarrow \{A_N\} \setminus \{A\}$;
$\qquad$ Inform other agents to exclude A from their $\{A_N\}$ sets
$\qquad$ **End If**
End For
For all joint action A' received from remaining agents
$\qquad$ **If** A' belongs to MS_i **then**
$\qquad\qquad$ Response as yes to the remaining agents;
$\qquad$ **else**
$\qquad\qquad$ Response as no to the remaining agents;
$\qquad$ **End If**
End For

Algorithm 1.23 Negotiation to Evaluate the Nonstrict EDSP for Agent i in a Normal-form Game

Input: Action $a_i \in A_i$ only for the agent $i \in [1, m]$, $\{A_N\}$ from Algorithm 1.13 and $Q_i(A)$; // $A \in \{A\} = \times_{i=1}^{m} A_i$
Output: nonstrict EDSP set $\{A_{nP}\}$;
Initialize: $\{A_{nP}\} \leftarrow \varphi$;
$\{X\} \leftarrow A \backslash \{A_N\}$;
For each PSNE $A_N \in \{A_N\}$
        For each joint action $A \in \{X\}$;
                If $Q_i(A) \geq Q_i(A_N)$ **then**
                      $\{X\} \leftarrow \{X\} \backslash \{A\}$;
                      $\{A_{nP}\} \leftarrow \{A_{nP}\} \cup \{A\}$;
                End If
        End For
End For
For all joint action $A \in \{A_{nP}\}$
        Ask remaining agents that is A_{nP} includes A;
        If answer is no **then**
                $\{A_{nP}\} \leftarrow \{A_{nP}\} \backslash \{A\}$;
        End If
End For
For all joint action A' received from remaining agents
        If A' belongs to A_{nP} **then**
                Response as yes to the remaining agents;
        else
                Response as no to the remaining agents;
        End If
End For

Algorithm 1.24 Negotiation-Q Learning for Agent i in a Markov Game

Input: Joint **action** space $\{A\}$, number of agents' m, state space $\{S\}$, learning rate α, discounting factor γ and exploration rate ε;
Output: Optimal joint Q-value $Q_i^*(S, A)$;
  Initialize: $Q_i(S, A) \leftarrow 0$;
Begin
   Repeat
     Negotiate with remaining agents employing Algorithms 1.13 and 1.14;
     Select the pure strategy equilibrium A' using ε-greedy;
     Receive experience tuple $<S, A, r_i(S, A), S'>$; // $r_i(S, A)$ and S' are the immediate reward and next joint state
     Update: $Q_i(S, A) \leftarrow (1-\alpha)Q_i(S, A) + \alpha[r_i(S, A) + \gamma Q_i(S', A')]$, and $S \leftarrow S'$;
     $Q_i^*(S, A) \leftarrow Q_i(S, A)$;
   Until $Q_i(S, A)$; converges;
End.

Algorithm 1.24 is tested in grid-world maps over the state-of-the-art reference algorithms.

MAQL with Equilibrium Transfer   Hu et al. [123] identified that agents evaluate the same equilibrium (NE or CE) at a joint state for different one-shot games. Here, two equilibria are declared as same if and only if the Euclidian distance between the probability distribution of the strategies is less than a predefined threshold. Reuse of the previously computed equilibrium (or equilibrium transfer) decreases as the convergence time of the equilibrium-based MAQL decreases with negligible transfer loss. Suppose G and G' are two one-short games that visit the same joint state S. Now, the Euclidian distance between the equilibrium strategy p of G and p' of G' are given in (1.85) and (1.86), respectively, for NE and CE.

$$d^{NE}\left(p, p'\right) = \sqrt{\sum_{i=1}^{n} \sum_{a_i \in A_i} \left(p_i(a_i) - p'_i(a_i)\right)^2}, \tag{1.85}$$

$$d^{CE}\left(p, p'\right) = \sqrt{\sum_{A \in \{A\}} \left(q(A) - q'(A)\right)^2}. \tag{1.86}$$

If the $d^{NE}(p, p')$ or $d^{CE}(p, p')$ is smaller than a threshold, then p and p' are considered as identical in G and G'. Hence, by equilibrium transfer one can directly use p in G'. As computation of equilibrium is more expensive than checking, hence, there is a significant saving in computational cost. Hu et al. [123] measures the equilibrium transfer loss and based on that loss the equilibrium transfer condition is defined. Let p^* and q^* denote the NE and CE of G and G', respectively. Now, loss because of transferring the equilibrium p^* and q^* from G to G' is given by (1.87) and (1.88), respectively.

Algorithm 1.25   Equilibrium Transfer-Based MAQL

Input: Action $a_i \in A_i$ at state $s_i \in S_i$ for all the agents learning rate $\alpha \in [0, 1)$, discount factor $\gamma \in [0, 1)$, exploration factor ε, threshold of transfer loss τ, G_c be the one-short game at joint state S and p^* previously computed equilibrium at S;
Output: Optimal joint Q-value $Q_i(S, A)$, $\forall i$; //$S \in \{S\} = \times_{i=1}^{m} S_i$ and $A \in \{A\} = \times_{i=1}^{m} A_i$
  Initialize: $Q_i(S, A) \leftarrow 0$, $\forall i$;
Repeat
  If joint state S has been visited
    then evaluate maximum utility loss ε^Ω, $\Omega \in \{NE, CE\}$ for transferring to G_c;
  Else

$\varepsilon^{\Omega} \leftarrow + \infty$;
End if
If $\varepsilon^{\Omega} > \tau$
  Then evaluate p^* for G_c;
Else
 Reuse p^* in G_c;
End if
Select joint action, A sampled from p^*;
Receive experience (S, A, r_i, S'), $\forall i$;
Evaluate equilibrium p' for the next joint state S';
Evaluate $V_i(S') \leftarrow$ expected value of p' in S', $Q_i(S, A) \leftarrow (1-\alpha)Q_i$
$(S, A) + \alpha(r_i + \gamma V_i(S'))$ and $S \leftarrow S'$;
Until $Q_i(S, A)$, $\forall i$ converge;

$$\varepsilon^{NE} = \max_{i \in N} \max_{a_i \in A_i} \left(Q_i^{G'}\left(a_i, p_{-i}^*\right) - Q_i^{G'}(p^*) \right), \tag{1.87}$$

$$\varepsilon^{CE} = \max_{i \in N} \max_{a_i \in A_i} \max_{a_i' \in A_i} \sum_{A_{-i}} q^*(a_i, A_{-i}) \times \left[Q_i^{G'}\left(a_i', A_{-i}\right) - Q_i^{G'}\left(a_i', A_{-i}\right) \right]. \tag{1.87}$$

Here, $Q_i^{G'}$ refers to the Q-value of agent i in G'.

Now the transfer loss condition for NE, p^* for an agent i is given by

$$Q_i^{G'}(p^*) + \varepsilon^{NE} \geq Q_i^{G'}(p^*) + \max_{a_i \in A_i}\left(Q_i^{G'}\left(a_i, p_{-i}^*\right) - Q_i^{G'}(p^*) \right)$$

$$= Q_i^{G'}(p^*) + \max_{a_i \in A_i} Q_i^{G'}\left(a_i, p_{-i}^*\right) - Q_i^{G'}(p^*) \tag{1.89}$$

$$= \max_{a_i \in A_i} Q_i^{G'}\left(a_i, p_{-i}^*\right).$$

Similarly, for CE, the following condition can be derived:

$$\sum_{A_{-i}} q^*(a_i, A_{-i}) \times Q_i^{G'}(a_i, A_{-i}) + \varepsilon^{CE} \geq \sum_{A_{-i}} q^*(a_i, A_{-i}) \times Q_i^{G'}\left(a_i', A_{-i}\right). \tag{1.90}$$

The algorithm for equilibrium transfer-based MAQL is given in Algorithm 1.25. Superiority of Algorithm 1.25 is tested in Grid World game, Wall game, and Soccer game.

Equilibrium Independent Equilibrium-independent MARL algorithms are again categorized based on the learning rate selection given below.

Variable Learning Rate RL algorithms with variable learning rate are given below.

Win or Learn Fast Policy Hill-Climbing In [124], Bowling and Veloso proposed WoLF policy hill-climbing algorithm for stochastic game in the presence of other adaptive agents, satisfying rationality and convergence. *Rationality* indicates that all agents' policies converge to stationary policies and then the learning algorithm will converge to a stationary policy, which is best response to their policies [124]. The convergence property states that agents necessarily converge to a stationary policy. Also, if all agents are rational and convergent, then it is guaranteed to converge NE. The learning algorithms in [31] and [125] either converge to a suboptimal policy or does not converge. Proposed WoLF is based on the principle of *learn quickly while losing and learn slowly while wining.*

Policy hill-climbing (PHC) is a straightforward extension of Q-learning to handle mixed strategies. The PHC algorithm is given in Algorithm 1.26. PHC learns the most recent mixed strategy. The updating of the mixed strategy in PHC is done by selecting the highest valued action as per the learning rate $\delta \in (0, 1]$. For $\delta = 1$, the algorithm behaves as single agent Q-learning. Both Q-values and the strategy are convergent following single agent Q-learning.

The main contribution of the proposed algorithm in [124] is the extension of PHC algorithm by employing a variable learning rate and the WoLF principle.

Algorithm 1.26   Policy Hill-Climbing (PHC)

Input: Action $a_i \in A_i$ at state $s_i \in S_i$ for all the agents learning rate $\alpha \in [0, 1)$ and discount factor $\gamma \in [0, 1)$;
Output: Optimal policy $\pi_i^*(S, A)$;
Initialize: $Q_i(S, A) \leftarrow 0$ and $\pi_i(S, A) \leftarrow \frac{1}{|A_i|}$;
Begin
    Repeat
        Choose an action $a_i \in A$ with probability $\pi_i(S, A)$;
        Receive immediate reward $r_i(S, A)$;

        Update: $Q_i(S, A) \leftarrow (1 - \alpha)Q_i(S, A) + \alpha\left[r_i(S, A) + \gamma\max_{A'} Q_i(S', A')\right]$,

        $S \leftarrow S'$ and

$$\pi_i(S, A) \leftarrow \pi_i(S, A) + \begin{cases} \delta, & \text{If } A = \arg\max_A Q(S, A') \\ \dfrac{-\delta}{|A_i| - 1}, & \text{otherwise} \end{cases}$$

        $\pi_i^*(S, A) \leftarrow \pi_i(S, A)$;
    Until $\pi_i^*(S, A)$ converges;
End.

In variable learning rate, the learning rate is used by the learning algorithm and is tuned in such a way so that the rationality is maintained. The WoLF principle motivates to learn quickly while losing and slowly while winning [124]. The WoLF-PHC algorithm employs two learning rate: losing learning rate δ_l and wining learning rate δ_w, where $\delta_l > \delta_w$. The winning/losing situation of the agent is determined by contrasting the current reward and the average reward taken over the time. If the agent is losing, then larger learning rate δ_l is employed. The WoLF-PHC [124] algorithm is given in Algorithm 1.27. The convergence and rationality of the WoLF-PHC algorithm is tested in Matrix games, Grid world game, and Soccer game. In all frameworks, WoLF-PHC outperforms reference algorithms.

Policy Dynamic-Based Win or Learn Fast (PD-WoLF) IGA [111] learner converges to NE rationally but they are not convergent to NE for all the general-sum games. Later, IGA was extended to WoLF-IGA in [107] and its convergence proof is shown in [107] for a 2×2 game assuming agents know the equilibrium policies of other agents. In [126], Banerjee and Peng did experimental-based comparisons of the

---

Algorithm 1.27   Win or Learn Fast-PHC (WoLF-PHC)

Input: Action $a_i \in A_i$ at state $s_i \in S_i$ for all the agents learning rate α, $\delta_l > \delta_w$ and discount factor $\gamma \in [0, 1)$;
Output: Optimal policy $\pi_i^*(S, A)$;
Initialize: $C(S) \leftarrow 0$, $Q_i(S, A) \leftarrow 0$ and $\pi_i(S, A) \leftarrow \frac{1}{|A_i|}$;
Begin
  Repeat
    Choose an action $a_i \in A$ with probability $\pi_i(S, A)$;
    Receive immediate reward $r_i(S, A)$;
    Update: average policy $\bar{\pi}$, $C(S) \leftarrow C(S) + 1$, $S \leftarrow S'$,
    $\bar{\pi}(S, A') \leftarrow \bar{\pi}(S, A') + \frac{1}{C(S)}[\pi_i(S, A') - \bar{\pi}(S, A')]$

    and $\pi_i(S, A) \leftarrow \pi_i(S, A) + \begin{cases} \delta, & \text{If } A = \operatorname*{argmax}_A Q(S, A'); \\ \dfrac{-\delta}{|A_i| - 1}, & \text{otherwise}; \end{cases}$

    $\delta = \begin{cases} \delta_w, & \text{If } \sum\limits_A \pi_i(S, A) Q_i(S, A) > \sum\limits_A \bar{\pi}(S, A) Q_i(S, A) \\ \delta_l, & \text{otherwise} \end{cases};$

    $\pi_i^*(S, A) \leftarrow \pi_i(S, A)$;
  Until $\pi_i^*(S, A)$ converges;
End.

WoLF and PD-WoLF to establish the superiority of the PD-WoLF both in the bimatrix and the general-sum games.

From Section "Infinitesimal Gradient Ascent," considering the sub case of purely imaginary Eigen values, U and the center (r^*, c^*) are within the unit square. The solution $r(t)$ of (1.72) for unconstraint dynamics [127] is given in (1.91), where the value of B and ϕ depends on the initial values of α, β.

$$r(t) = B\sqrt{u} \cos\left(\sqrt{uu't} + \phi\right) + r^*. \tag{1.91}$$

PD-WoLF criteria for a row player (agent) are given by (1.92).

$$\alpha_r(t) = \begin{cases} \alpha_{\min}, & \text{if } \Delta_t \Delta_t^2 < 0 \\ \alpha_{\max}, & \text{otherwise} \end{cases}, \tag{1.92}$$

where $\Delta_t = r_t - r_{t-1}$ and $\Delta_t^2 = \Delta_t - \Delta_{t-1}$. It is apparent that (1.92) is independent of other agents' policies.

Fixed Learning Rate   MARL Algorithms with fixed learning rate are given below.

Non-Stationary Converging Policies   One major shortcoming of MAQL is the assumption that the environment is stationary. In [128], Michael and Jeffrey proposed the NSCP, where agents are not interested in converging to an equilibrium rather they search for the best-response policy for the non-stationary opponents. NSCP predicts the opponents' non-stationary strategy with precision and act by its best-response strategy with respect to the opponents in the well-known test bench of general-sum-stochastic games (game with multiple joint states) or matrix games (game with one joint state). The MAQL algorithms [71, 72, 81, 95, 100] and [121] either converge to NE or CE. By [129], the equilibrium-based MAQL algorithms are problematic, as the learning stops at the equilibrium point and the equilibrium point is necessarily not a goal point. Also an additional problem arises in the presence of multiple equilibria. The NSCP algorithm aims at adapting an optimal reward considering the presence of other agents. In [130], an agent converges to best-response strategy subject to stationary opponents in two-player general-sum-stochastic games. The NSCP algorithm is given in Algorithm 1.28. Simulation results validate the superior performance of the NSCP with respect to reference algorithms.

Extended Optimal Response Learning   The zero-sum-stochastic game proposed by Littman [100] was extended to general-sum-stochastic game by Hu and Wellman [95] and agents converge to NE in stochastic games by these algorithms. On the contrary, in [95] and [100], agents always try to converge to NE ignoring strategies of other agents. Further, all the agents must agree upon to select a NE in the

---

Algorithm 1.28   Non-Stationary Converging Policies

Input: Action $a_i \in A_i$ at state $s_i \in S_i$, $\forall i$, $i \in [1, m]$, learning rate $\alpha \in [0, 1)$ and discount factor $\gamma \in [0, 1)$;

Output: Optimal Q-value $Q_i^*(S, A)$, $\forall i$;

Initialize: $Q_i(S, A) \leftarrow 0$, $\forall i$ and $\pi^i(S, A) = \frac{1}{|A|}$;

Begin

   Repeat

   Observe the actions taken by all the agents $A \in \{A\}$;

   Receive immediate reward $r_i(S, A)$, $\forall i$;

   Update: other agents' strategy $\pi_{-i}(S, A) = \frac{1}{|A|}$, $\forall i$;

   Select best-response strategy $\pi_i^{br}(S, A)$

   that maximizes $BR(S') = \sum_{a_1}\sum_{a_2}\cdots\sum_{a_m}\pi_i^{br}(S', a_i) \cdot \prod_{\forall -i}\hat{\pi}_i(S', a_i) \cdot Q_i(S', A)$;

   Update: Q-values using the following rules

   $Q_i(S, A) \leftarrow (1-\alpha)Q_i(S, A) + \alpha[r_i(S, A) + \gamma BR(S')]$ and $S \leftarrow S'$;

   Until $Q_i(S, A)$, $\forall i$; converges;

   Obtain $Q_i^*(S, A) \leftarrow Q_i(S, A)$, $\forall i$;

End.

---

presence of multiple NEs. Thus, the algorithms proposed in [95] and [100] are not adaptable in the above sense. In [131], Nobuo and Akira extended optimal response to EXORL, where agents converge to NE subject to adaptability of other agents. Similar to NQL [95], in EXORL, an agent maintains all agents' Q-tables assuming that it can observe other agents' state–action and reward. EXORL aims at realizing a policy which is optimal response to other agents' policies, where remaining agents are adaptable and attain NE. The EXORL algorithm is given in Algorithm 1.29. JAL [81] learns Q-value due to its own action and estimates teammates' strategy. Let π_i be the strategy of agent i at state S which maximizes (1.93).

$$Q_i(S, \pi_i) = (\pi_i)^T Q_i(S)\overline{\pi}_{-i}(S), \tag{1.93}$$

where $\overline{\pi}_{-i}(S)$ refers to estimate of all agents' joint policy except agent i. Now, if a policy diverges from NE, then the policy may not be suitable to estimate the remaining agents' strategy. This problem is addressed in [131] and the update rule is given by (1.94) and (1.95) tuning the value of ρ.

$$Q_i(S, \pi_i) = (\pi_i)^T Q_i(S)\overline{\pi}_{-i}(S) - \rho\sigma(S, \pi_i), \tag{1.94}$$

Algorithm 1.29   EXORL for Agent *i*

Input: Action $a_i \in A_i$ at $s_i \in S_i, \forall i$, learning rate $\alpha \in [0, 1)$ and discount factor $\gamma \in [0, 1)$;

Output: Optimal Q-value $Q_i^*(S, A), \forall i$; $//S = \{s_i\}_{i=1}^m, A = \{a_i\}_{i=1}^m$;

Initialize: $Q_i(A, A) \leftarrow 0, \pi_i(S, a_i) \leftarrow \frac{1}{|A_i|} \forall i, \overline{\pi}_{-i}(S, A_{-i}) \leftarrow \frac{1}{|\times_{j=1, j\neq i}^m A_j|}$;

Begin

    Repeat

        Choose an action $a_i \in A_i, \forall i$;

        Receive immediate reward $r_i(S, A), \forall i$;

        Update: $Q_i(S, A) \leftarrow (1 - \alpha) Q_i(S, A) + \alpha [r_i(S, A) + \gamma Q_i(S', A)]$,
        $\forall i, S \leftarrow S'$

    and $\overline{\pi}_{-i}(S) \leftarrow (1 - \beta)\overline{\pi}_{-i}(S) + \beta.\overline{\pi}_{-i}(S')$; $//\overline{\pi}_{-i}(S') = \begin{cases} 1 & \text{if } A_{-i} = A'_{-i} \\ 0 & \text{otherwise} \end{cases}$

    Until $Q_i(S, A), \forall i$ converge;

        Obtain $Q_i^*(S, A) \leftarrow Q_i(S, A), \forall i$;

End.

---

where

$$\sigma(S, \pi_i) = \max_{\pi_{-i}} \left[(\pi_i)^T Q_{-i}(S)\pi_{-i} \right] - (\pi_i)^T Q_{-i}(S)\overline{\pi}_{-i}(S), \tag{1.95}$$

here $\sigma(S, \pi_i)$ refers to the possible increase in expected discounted reward of agent *i*. Hence, to maximize the left part of (1.95), agent *i* has to maximize the first component of right part and also minimizes the second component of the right part. Also, (1.95) is a piece-wise linear concave function and it has a sole maximal point. It is shown in [131] that by EXORL an agent plays well subject to that the opponent agents play fixed policy considering small value of ρ. The EXORL is verified in Matching Pennies, Presidency Game [80], and Battle of sexes game in [131].

1.3.6 Coordination and Planning by MAQL

In the present book, for multi-robot coordination and planning without any communication among the agents, we focus on the equilibrium-based MAQL as explained in Section "Equilibrium Dependent". Because of the absence of communication among the agents, each agent needs to maintain all the agents' Q-tables at joint state–action space. Figure 1.47 explains the multi-robot coordination and planning mechanism for the well-known stick-carrying problem. Stick-carrying

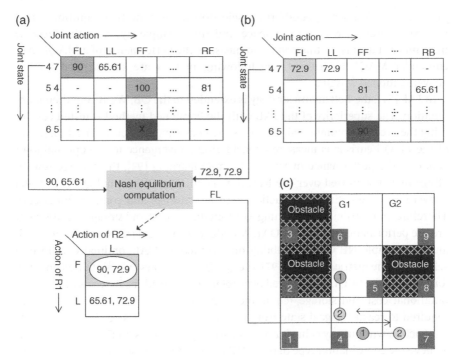

Figure 1.47 Multi-robot coordination for the well-known stick-carrying problem. (a) Joint Q-table of agent 1 by NQL. (b) Joint Q-table of agent 2 by NQL. (c) Stick-carrying by employing (a) and (b).

problem refers to the transportation of a stick from current positions to the desired destination. Presently, twin robots are at a joint state <4, 7> with a stick as shown in Figure 1.47c. As each robot have both robots' Q-tables at joint state–action space, a robot looks for the optimal joint action, i.e. PSNE at <4, 7> by evaluating equilibrium. To evaluate equilibrium, a robot extracts the information from the joint state <4, 7> (Figure 1.47a, b) and PSNE, "FL" is evaluated following the definition of NE as shown in Figure 1.47. Here, both the robots evaluate identical PSNE. Hence, without any communication between the robots, coordination occurred and the stick is shifted to the next joint state <5, 4> because of the joint action "FL" by the robots.

1.3.7 Performance Analysis of MAQL and MAQL-Based Coordination

The MAQL algorithms illustrated above have addressed several challenges of the MAQL. The main challenges of MAQL are suitable action selection for balancing exploration/exploitation, update policy selection for adaptation of the Q-table in joint state–action space, equilibrium selection among multiple equilibria, and the exponential increase in the space and time complexity, with the increase in number of agents. In this regard, to measure the performance of a MAQL over contender MAQL algorithms, the following metrics are summarized for the abovementioned MAQL.

In JAL [81], the Boltzmann strategy is extended to the OB, WOB, and their combination. The superiority of the JAL with the combined method is tested considering the average accumulated reward as the performance metric. The superiority of the FMQ heuristic is measured considering convergence to the optimal joint action as the performance metric. In Team-Q learning [92], the average reward of agents is maximized over the learning epoch. The Distributed Q-learner [91] converges to the optimal joint action with less storage and computational cost. Therefore, in Distributed Q-learning, computational cost and storage requirement are the performance metrics. In OAL [96] algorithm, agents select the optimal NE among multiple NE with probability one. Hence, in OAL, optimal equilibrium selection is the metric. In SCQL [97], the Q-tables are sparsely maintained and performance of the SCQL is measured over reference algorithms in terms of the computational cost and storage requirement. In SQL [98], the metric is the steps required to reach the goal state from the starting state, i.e. selection of the right joint action without any behavior conflict among the agents. In FMRQ [99], agents achieve the coordination-type optimal NE to maximize the system performance in terms of average steps per episode for box-pushing problem and average rewards per episode for distributed sensor network problem. In Minimax-Q learning algorithm [100], both the agents learn optimal policies and efficiency of the algorithm is tested in the framework of a two-player grid game by measuring the winning percentage of the game by the agent in an episode. Performance of the HAMRL algorithm [101] is measured in terms of the convergence speed. FP [105] addressed the equilibrium selection problem in coordination game. The performance of the Meta strategy [106] is measured in terms of the average reward achieved by the agents. AWESOME [108] learns the best response (NE) considering a stationary opponent and its performance is measured against FP in terms of the distance to equilibrium and distance to the best response. In Hyper-Q learning [110], online Bellman error and average reward variation with respect to the learning epoch are considered as the performance metrics. In [111], IGA proposed a scheme by which agents conditionally converge to the NE. Performance of the GIGA [118], WoLF-IGA [107], and GIGA-WoLF [119] algorithms are measured in terms of the convergence rate. In NQL [95], percentage of NE achieved in a game is considered as the performance metric. In CQL [72], mean Q-value difference is the performance metric. In AQL [120], change in Q-values of the agents with the learning epoch is considered as the performance metric. The FFQ [121] always converges to a NE and converging to a NE is a metric. Average reward with the episode and number of learning epoch required per episode are the metrics in NegoQ. In the equilib-rium transfer-based MAQL [123], three metrics are considered. First one is the learning speed, second one is the improved average reward, and finally the last one is the reduction in the space complexity. In WoLF-PHC [124], the policy either converges to NE or to a suboptimal NE and percentage of winning a game by an agent is considered as the performance metric. In PD-WoLF [111], average reward is the performance metric during the learning phase. Average time required to complete a task is considered the performance metric during learning in case of NSCP [128]. In EXORL [100], policy and Q-value learned with the learning epoch are considered as the performance metric.

In MAQL-based coordination, agents re-evaluate the NE/CE as explained in Section 1.3.6. As the computational cost of evaluating the NE/CE is very high, run-time complexity is one performance metric in the MAQL-based coordination. On the other hand, space-complexity, successful completion of the task, system resource utilization, and the like are considered as the performance metrics during the MAQL-based coordination [98].

1.4 Coordination by Optimization Algorithm

One common bottleneck of the search-based coordination and MARL-based algo-rithms is the memory requirement and suboptimal solution. Such bottlenecks are addressed by the Swarm Intelligence (SI) [61, 62] and EA [62]. The advantages of the SI algorithms are Scalability, Adaptability, Collective Robustness, and Individ-ual Simplicity. The scalability of the SI algorithms are remarkable, as the control mechanism adopted by the SI algorithms does not depend upon the swarm size, until the swarm size is not too small [45]. The SI algorithm has very fast response to the rapidly changing environment by employing the auto-configuration and self-organization capabilities, which allow the swarms to adapt online with the dynamic environment [66]. Collective robustness indicates that the SI algorithms are distributed and hence, there is no possibility of single point failure [67]. In spite of very simple behavior of every swarm in any SI algorithm, the group of a swarm can achieve sophisticated group behavior [67]. Particle Swarm Optimization (PSO) algorithm and Firefly algorithm (FA) are two examples of SI algorithms. In PSO, the fitness function is not differentiable and is employed to obtain quality solution for high-dimensional problems faster than other alternatives. However, there is a high probability to be trapped in local optima in high-dimensional problems. On the other hand, the FA has a very high probability of exploring the global optima. The advantages of EAs are that they can cope with discontinuities, nonlinear con-straints, multi-modalities, and multi-objective optimization problems.

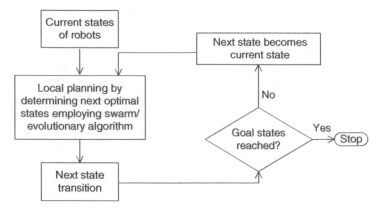

Figure 1.48 Multi-robot local planning by swarm/evolutionary algorithm.

However, the EAs do not provide any guarantee to provide optimal solutions within finite amount of time. Differential evolution is an example of EA. Stability is a very good attribute of DE over the GA. Another is Imperialist Competitive Algorithm (ICA) [67], which is a sociopolitical-based algorithm. ICA has neighborhood movements both in continuous and discrete search-space. However, the solutions provided by the ICA does not guarantee for optimal solution. In addition, the ICA requires tuning more number of parameters as compared with the PSO, FA, and DE. In the above circumstance, hybridization is a good approach. By hybridization, the efficient attributes of two or more algorithms are fused to produce a powerful algorithm. One approach for multi-robot stick-carrying problem is shown in [91], where the hybridization of the motion dynamics of fireflies of the FA [48] into a sociopolitical evolution-based meta-heuristic search algorithm is done and is named as Imperialist Competitive Firefly Algorithm (ICFA). The abovementioned algorithms are implemented for multi-robot coordination following scheme as shown in Figure 1.48. Brief description of the abovementioned algorithms are given below.

1.4.1 PSO Algorithm

In [61], Kennedy and Eberhart proposed a nonlinear function optimization technique following the behavior of flocking birds, namely PSO. Let an n-dimensional nonlinear function given by (1.96) to be optimized. The PSO aims at finding such a $\vec{X}$ so that (1.96) is either maximized or minimized depending upon the problem requirement. So, one can say that the solution of (1.96) is an n-dimensional hyperspace.

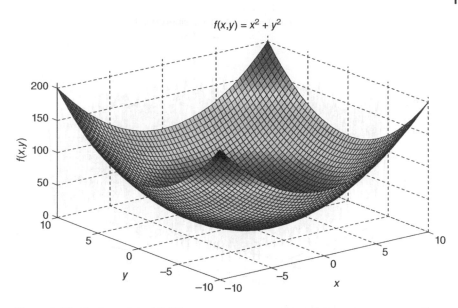

Figure 1.49 Surface plot of (1.97).

$$f\left(\vec{X}\right) = f(x_1, ..., x_n). \tag{1.96}$$

Let us consider a two-dimensional problem as given in (1.97) [48]. In (1.97), $x \in$ [−10, 10] and $y \in$ [−10, 10] and the plot of (1.97) is given in Figure 1.49. It is apparent from Figure 1.49 that (0, 0) is the only solution in the xy plane for which the $f(x, y)$ attains a minimum value of zero. It is quiet easy to identify the minima for the function (1.96) compared to the same for (1.98) [48]. The plot of (1.98) is shown in Figure 1.50. Unlike Figure 1.49, in Figure 1.50, there are multiple optimal points. It is difficult to identify the global optima among them. PSO employs the multi-agent parallel search technique and each agent starts from different initial positions and explores the landscape until a global optima is reached. It is assumed that in PSO, agents can communicate among themselves and share the values of fitness function explored by them.

$$f(x, y) = x^2 + y^2, \tag{1.97}$$

$$f(x, y) = x \sin(4\pi y) + y \sin(4\pi x + \pi) + 1. \tag{1.98}$$

In PSO, each agent flies through the multidimensional landscape with a unique position and velocity at each landscape. The population is initialized with random positions denoted by $\vec{X} = \{x_i\}_{i=1}^{S}$ each having a random velocity $\vec{V} = \{v_i\}_{i=1}^{S}$.

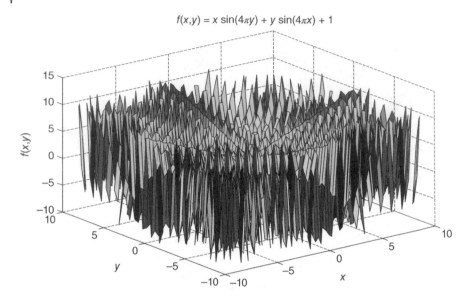

Figure 1.50 Surface plot of (1.98).

The position and velocity of the d-th dimension's i-th particle is given by (1.99) and (1.100), respectively.

$$x_{id}(t+1) = x_{id}(t) + v_{id}(t+1), \tag{1.99}$$

$$v_{id}(t+1) = \omega \cdot v_{id}(t) + C_1 \cdot \varphi_1 \cdot (P_{id}(t) - x_{id}(t)) + C_2 \cdot \varphi_2 \cdot (g_{id}(t) - x_{id}(t)). \tag{1.100}$$

In (1.100), the first component is the initial velocity of the i-th particle. ω refers to the inertial weight factor. C_1 and C_2 are the constant multiplier termed as self-confidence and swarm confidence, respectively. Two random numbers $\varphi_1 \in [0, 1]$ and $\varphi_2 \in [0, 1]$ are introduced in (1.100), which determine the influence of $\vec{p}(t)$ and $\vec{g}(t)$ on (1.100). $\vec{p}(t), \vec{g}(t)$, and $\vec{x}(t)$ are initialized to zero at $t = 0$, i.e. and $\vec{p}(0) = \vec{g}(0) = \vec{x}(0)$. After that the velocity and position of each particle update following (1.99) and (1.100). The algorithm for PSO is given in Algorithm 1.30 [48].

In [69], Pugh et al. proposed the noise-resistance PSO for obstacle avoidance in multi-robot systems. In [70], Pugh modified the noise-resistance PSO [69] by setting

$$x_i^{*'} = x_i^{*''}, \text{if } fitness\left(x_i^{*''}\right) > fitness\left(x_i^{*'}\right), \tag{1.101}$$

Algorithm 1.30 Particle Swarm Optimization (PSO)

Input: Enter the Swarm size (S), values of C_1, C_2, $\varphi_1 \in [0, 1]$, $\varphi_2 \in [0, 1]$, ω and $V_{\max}$;

Output: Approximate global optimal position $\vec{X}^*$;

Initialize: Initialized the position and velocity vectors: $\vec{X}_i(0)$ and $\vec{V}_i(0)$;

Begin

While termination condition is not reached **do**

  For $i = 1$ to S

  Evaluate the fitness $f\left(\vec{X}_i\right)$;

  Update $\vec{p}_i$ and $\vec{g}_i$;

  Adapt position and velocity of the partial by (1.99) and (1.100) respectively.

  End For;

End While.

End.

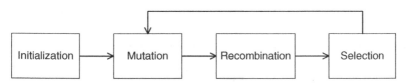

Figure 1.51 Steps of Differential evolution (DE) algorithm [132].

where $x_i^{*'}$ refers to the neighborhood best for particle (here robot) i and $x_i^{*''}$ denotes the new neighborhood best particle.

1.4.2 Firefly Algorithm

In FA [93], a potential solution to an optimization problem is encoded by the position of a firefly in the search space and the light intensity at the position of the firefly corresponds to the fitness of the associated solution. Each firefly changes its position iteratively by flying toward brighter fireflies at more attractive location in the fitness landscape to obtain optimal solutions.

1.4.2.1 Initialization

FA commences with a population P_t of NP, D-dimensional firefly positions, $\vec{X}_i(t) = \{x_{i,1}(t), x_{i,2}(t), x_{i,3}(t), ..., x_{i,D}(t)\}$ for $i = [1, NP]$ by randomly initializing in the search range $\left[\vec{X}^{min}, \vec{X}^{max}\right]$ where $\vec{X}^{min} = \{x_1^{min}, x_2^{min}, ..., x_D^{min}\}$ and $\vec{X}^{max} = \{x_1^{max}, x_2^{max}, ..., x_D^{max}\}$ at the current generation $t = 0$. Thus, the d-th component of the i-th firefly at $t = 0$ is given by (1.102).

$$x_{i,d}(0) = x_d^{min} + rand(0, 1) \times \left(x_d^{max} - x_d^{min}\right), \tag{1.102}$$

where $rand(0, 1)$ is a uniformly distributed random number lying between 0 and 1 and $d = [1, D]$. The objective function value $f\left(\vec{X}_i(0)\right)$ (which is inversely proportional to the light intensity for minimization problem) of the i-th firefly is evaluated for $i = [1, NP]$.

1.4.2.2 Attraction to Brighter Fireflies

Now the firefly $\vec{X}_i(t)$ is attracted toward the positions of the brighter fireflies $\vec{X}_j(t)$ for $i, j = [1, NP]$ but $i \neq j$ such that $f\left(\vec{X}_j(t)\right) < f\left(\vec{X}_i(t)\right)$ for minimization problem. Now the attractiveness $\beta_{i,j}$ of $\vec{X}_i(t)$ toward $\vec{X}_j(t)$ is proportional to the light intensity seen by adjacent fireflies. However attractiveness $\beta_{i,j}$ decreases exponentially with the distance between the fireflies, denoted by $r_{i,j}$ as given in (1.103).

$$\beta_{i,j} = \beta_0 \exp\left(-\gamma \times r_{i,j}^m\right), \quad m \geq 1, \tag{1.103}$$

where β_0 denotes the maximum attractiveness experienced by the i-th firefly at its own position (i.e. at $r_{i,j} = r_{i,i} = 0$) and γ is the light absorption coefficient, which controls the variation of $\beta_{i,j}$ with $r_{i,j}$. This parameter is responsible for the convergence speed of FA. A setting of $\gamma = 0$ leads to constant attractiveness while γ approaching infinity is equivalent to the complete random search [48]. In (1.103), m is a positive constant representing a nonlinear modulation index. The distance between $\vec{X}_i(t)$ and $\vec{X}_j(t)$ is computed using the Euclidean norm as follows:

$$r_{i,j} = \left\|\vec{X}_i(t) - \vec{X}_j(t)\right\|. \tag{1.104}$$

This step is repeated for $i, j = [1, N]$.

1.4.2.3 Movement of Fireflies

The firefly at position $\vec{X}_i(t)$ moves toward a more attractive position $\vec{X}_j(t)$ occupied by a brighter firefly (i.e. $f\left(\vec{X}_j(t)\right) < f\left(\vec{X}_i(t)\right)$) for $j = [1, N]$ but $i \neq j$ following the dynamic given in (1.105).

$$\vec{X}_i(t + 1) = \vec{X}_i(t) + \beta_{i,j} \times \left(\vec{X}_j(t) - \vec{X}_i(t)\right) + \alpha \times (rand(0, 1) - 0.5).$$

$$(1.105)$$

The first term in the position updating formula (1.105) represents the i-th firefly's current position. The second term in (1.105) denotes the change in the position of the firefly at $\vec{X}_i(t)$ due to the attraction toward the brighter firefly at $\vec{X}_j(t)$. Hence it is apparent that the brightest firefly with no more attractive firefly in the current sorted population P_t will have no motion due to the second term and may get stuck at the local optima. To circumvent the problem, the last term is introduced in (1.105) for the random movement of the fireflies with a step-size of $\alpha \in (0, 1)$. Here, $rand(0,1)$ is a random number generator uniformly distributed in the range $(0, 1)$. This step is repeated for $i = [1, NP]$. After completion of its journey mediated by the brighter ones, the updated position of the i-th firefly is represented by $\vec{X}_i(t + 1)$ for $i = [1, NP]$.

After each evolution, Sections 1.4.2.2 and 1.4.2.3 are repeated until one of the following conditions for convergence is satisfied. These conditions include restraining the number of iterations, maintaining error limits, or the both, whichever occurs earlier. In Algorithm 1.31, the number of iterations is considered as the condition of convergence.

1.4.3 Imperialist Competitive Algorithm

ICA is a population-based stochastic algorithm, which is inspired by the sociopolitical evolution and the imperialistic competitive policy of a government to extend its power beyond its boundaries. It has earned wide popularity because of its noticeable performance in computational optimization with respect to the quality of solutions [89]. Like any other EAs, ICA starts with an initial population of solutions, called countries. The countries are classified into two groups – imperialists and colonies, based on their ruling power (which is inversely proportional to their objective function values). The colonies (weaker countries) with their relevant imperialist (stronger country) form some empires. In each empire, the imperialist pursues an assimilation policy to improve the economy, culture, and political situation of its colonies, thus winning their loyalty. Moreover, the empires take part in the imperialistic competition in an attempt to gain more colonies. In ICA, the assimilation of colonies toward their respective imperialists along with the

---

Algorithm 1.31   Traditional Firefly Algorithm (FA)

Input: $\vec{X} = (x_1, x_2, ..., x_D)$, fitness function $f(X)$; **//** *D* dimension of the firefly

Output: $\vec{X}_i$, $i \in [1, n]$;

Initialize: Generate population $\vec{X}_i$, $i \in [1, n]$, $\alpha \in (0, 1)$, $\beta_0 = 1$ and $\gamma \in [0.1, 10]$;

While (*t* <MaxGeneration)

  For *k*=1 to *D*

    For *i*=1 to *n*

      For *j*=1 to *n*

        If $f\left(\vec{X}_i(t)\right) < f\left(\vec{X}_j(t)\right)$

        then Move $\vec{X}_i(t)$ towards $\vec{X}_j(t)$ in all *D* dimensions;
        End If;
        Update $x_{ik}(t+1) = x_{ik}(t) + \beta r_{ij} \times [x_{jk}(t) - x_{ik}(t)] + \alpha (rand - 0.5)$;
      End For;
    End For;
  End For;
  Rank the fireflies based on current fitness and find the current best one;
End While.

---

competition among empires eventually results in just one empire in the world with all the other countries as colonies of that unique empire. An overview of the main steps of the ICA is presented next.

1.4.3.1   Initialization

ICA starts with a population P_t of *NP*, *D*-dimensional countries, $\vec{X}_i(t) = \{x_{i,1}(t), x_{i,2}(t), x_{i,3}(t), ..., x_{i,D}(t)\}$ for $i = [1, NP]$ representing the candidate solutions, at the current generation $t = 0$ by randomly initializing in the range $\left[\vec{X}^{\min}, \vec{X}^{\max}\right]$ where $\vec{X}^{\min} = \{x_1^{\min}, x_2^{\min}, ..., x_D^{\min}\}$ and $\vec{X}^{\max} = \{x_1^{\max}, x_2^{\max}, ..., x_D^{\max}\}$. Thus the *d*-th component (sociopolitical feature) of the *i*-th country at $t = 0$ is given by

$$x_{i,d}(0) = x_d^{\min} + rand(0, 1) \times (x_d^{\max} - x_d^{\min}), \tag{1.106}$$

where *rand*(0, 1) is a uniformly distributed random number lying between 0 and 1 and $d = [1, D]$. The objective function value $f\left(\vec{X}_i(0)\right)$ of the country $\vec{X}_i(0)$ is evaluated for $i = [1, NP]$.

1.4.3.2 Selection of Imperialists and Colonies

The population P_0 is sorted in ascending order of $f\left(\vec{X}_i(0)\right)$ for minimization problem with $i = [1, NP]$. The first N countries with less cost function values are selected as imperialists while the remaining $M = NP - N$ countries are declared as colonies. Hence the population individuals are categorized into two groups of countries – imperialists and colonies.

1.4.3.3 Formation of Empires

The empire under the *j*-th imperialist is constructed based on its ruling power. To accomplish this, first the normalized power of the *j*-th imperialist country, p_j, is evaluated by (1.107) with $f\left(\vec{X}_{NP}(0)\right)$ representing the objective function value of the weakest country in the current sorted population P_0.

$$p_j = \frac{f\left(\vec{X}_{NP}(0)\right) - f\left(\vec{X}_j(0)\right)}{\sum\limits_{l=1}^{N} f\left(\vec{X}_{NP}(0)\right) - f\left(\vec{X}_l(0)\right)}. \tag{1.107}$$

It is evident from (1.107) that better the *j*-th imperialist (i.e. less objective function value $f\left(\vec{X}_j(0)\right)$ for minimization problem), higher is the difference $f\left(\vec{X}_{NP}(0)\right) - f\left(\vec{X}_j(0)\right)$ leading to the enhancement of its corresponding ruling power, p_j. Now the initial number of colonies under in the *j*-th empire, denoted by n_j, is computed by (1.108).

$$n_j = \left\lfloor M \times p_j \right\rfloor, \tag{1.108}$$

such that

$$\sum_{j=1}^{N} n_j = M. \tag{1.109}$$

Here, $\lfloor \rfloor$ represents the floor function. According to (1.108), the stronger imperialists with higher ruling power now possess larger empires. Hence p_j symbolizes the fraction of the colonies occupied by the *j*-th imperialist. Subsequently, the *j*-th empire is formed by randomly selecting n_j countries from M colonies provided that there will be no common colony between two different empires. Hence the number of countries within the j-th empire including its imperialist is $n_j + 1$. Let the k-th country belonging to the j-th empire be denoted by $\vec{X}_k^j(t)$ (at generation $t = 0$) for $k = [1, n_j+1]$. The countries within the j-th empire are now sorted in ascending order of their objective function values such that the imperialist $\vec{X}_1^j(t)$ in the j-th empire attains the first rank. This step is repeated for $j = [1, N]$.

1.4.3.4 Assimilation of Colonies

Each imperialist country now attempts to improve its empire by enhancing the sociopolitical influences of its colonies. To accomplish this, each country $\vec{X}_k^j(t)$ in the j-th empire now moves toward its corresponding imperialist $\vec{X}_1^j(t)$ by changing its characteristic features following (1.110) for $k = [2, n_j+1]$.

$$\vec{X}_k^j(t + 1) = \vec{X}_k^j(t) + \beta \times rand(0, 1) \times \left(\vec{X}_1^j(t) - \vec{X}_k^j(t) \right). \tag{1.110}$$

Here, $rand(0, 1)$ is a uniformly distributed random number lying between 0 and 1 and β is the assimilation coefficient. The objective function value of the modified colony $f\left(\vec{X}_k^j(t + 1) \right)$ is evaluated for $k = [2, n_j+1]$. After assimilation, all the countries in the j-th empire are sorted in ascending order of the objective function values and the first ranked country is declared as the imperialist $\vec{X}_1^j(t + 1)$ of the same empire for the next generation (i.e. $t = t + 1$). The step is repeated for $j = [1, N]$.

1.4.3.5 Revolution

Revolution creates sudden fluctuation in the economic, cultural, and political aspects of countries in an empire. The colonies in an empire are now equipped with the power of randomly changing their sociopolitical attributes instead of being assimilated by their corresponding imperialist. It resembles the mutation of trial solutions in the traditional EA. The revolution rate η in the algorithm indicates the percentage of colonies in each empire which will undergo the revolution process. A high value of revolution rate therefore fortifies the explorative power at a cost of poor exploitation capability. Hence a moderate value of revolution rate is favored. Revolution is implemented by randomly selecting $\eta \times n_j$ countries (including the imperialist) in the j-th empire (for $j = [1, N]$) and then they are replaced by randomly initialized countries characterized by new sociopolitical nature. After revolution, as in case of assimilation, all the countries in each empire are sorted in ascending order of the objective function values so that its imperialist is at the first position. The step is repeated for all empires.

1.4.3.6 Imperialistic Competition

All the N empires now participate in an imperialistic competition to take possession of colonies of other weaker empires based on their ruling power. The colonies
of the weaker empires will be gradually eluded from the ruling power of their corresponding imperialists and will be thereafter controlled by some other stronger
empires. Consequently, the weaker empires will be losing their power and ultimately may be eradicated from the competition. The imperialistic competition
along with the collapse mechanism will progressively result in an increment in
the power of more dominant empires and diminish the power of weaker ones.
The imperialistic competition encompasses the following steps.

Total Empire Power Evaluation
Once an empire is constructed under the dominance of the j-th imperialist
$\vec{X}_1^j(t+1)$, the power of the respective empire is compositely influenced by the
objective function value of $\vec{X}_1^j(t+1)$ as well as the constituent colonies
$\vec{X}_k^j(t+1)$ (after assimilation) under the respective j-th empire for $k = [2,\ n_j+1]$.
The total objective function value of the j-th empire is evaluated as follows:

$$tc_j = f\left(\vec{X}_1^j(t+1)\right) + \xi \cdot \frac{1}{n_j} \sum_{k=2}^{n_j+1} \vec{X}_k^j(t+1). \tag{1.111}$$

Here, $\xi < 1$ is a positive number which regulates the influence of the constituent
colonies to control the ruling power of the empire. A tiny value of ξ causes the total
power of the j-th empire to be determined by its imperialist $\vec{X}_1^j(t+1)$ only, while
increasing the value of ξ accentuates the importance of the colonies in deciding the
total power of the respective empire. The N empires now are sorted in ascending
order of tc_j for $j = [1, N]$. Then the normalized possession power of the j-th empire,
pp_j, is evaluated by (1.112) with tc_N representing the total objective function value
of the weakest empire in the current population P_t.

$$pp_j = \frac{tc_N - tc_j}{\sum\limits_{l=1}^{N} tc_N - tc_l}. \tag{1.112}$$

It is evident from (1.112) that stronger the j-th empire (i.e. less the total objective
function value tc_j for minimization problem), higher is the possession power, pp_j,
which consecutively increases its probability of seizing colonies from weaker
empires. This step is repeated for $j = [1, N]$.

Reassignment of Colonies and Removal of Empire

The empire with least possession power is interpreted as being defeated in the competition. Let the weakest colony of this weakest empire be denoted as $\vec{X}_{worst}$, which is now removed from the dominance of its currently ruling imperialist and reassigned as a new colony to one of the stronger empires based on their possession probabilities. It is noteworthy that $\vec{X}_{worst}$ will not be possessed by the most powerful empires, but stronger the empire, more likely to possess $\vec{X}_{worst}$. To accomplish this, the possession probability of the j-th empire is computed as follows for $j = [1, N]$:

$$prob_j = pp_j - rand(0, 1).$$ (1.113)

Now $\vec{X}_{worst}$ is assigned as a new colony to the j-th empire for which the possession probability $prob_j$ is maximum. However, if the worst colony consists of only its imperial before exclusion operation (i.e. $\vec{X}_{worst}$ is the imperialist of the weakest empire), the removal of $\vec{X}_{worst}$ will result in the collapse of the weakest empire.

Union of Empires

The disagreement between two empires may be assessed by the difference in their respective sociopolitical features. This dissimilarity between any two empires, j and l, is evaluated by taking the Euclidean distance between the respective imperialists $\vec{X}_1^j(t + 1)$ and $\vec{X}_1^l(t + 1)$ as in (1.114) for $j, l = [1, N]$.

$$Dist_{j,l} = \left\| \vec{X}_1^j(t + 1) - \vec{X}_1^l(t + 1) \right\|.$$ (1.114)

If $Dist_{j,l}$ is less than a predefined threshold, Th, the two empires are merged into one empire. The stronger country among $\vec{X}_1^j(t + 1)$ and $\vec{X}_1^l(t + 1)$ is declared as the imperialist of the newly formed empire.

After each evolution, we repeat from Section 1.4.3.4 until one of the following conditions for convergence is satisfied. Stop criteria include a bound by the number of iterations, achieving a sufficiently low error or aggregations thereof.

1.4.4 Differential Evolution Algorithm

Differential evolution (DE) algorithm is a stochastic, population-based global optimization algorithm, introduced by [133], to optimize real parameter, real-valued functions [48].

1.4.4.1 Initialization

Range of each parameter, i.e. the upper and lower boundaries for each parameter, is defined, and then randomly these parameters are initialized.

1.4.4.2 Mutation

The step mutation expands the search-space. Mutation is done by (1.115), where $F \in [0, 2]$ is the mutation factor. $x_{r_{1,G}}, x_{r_{2,G}}$ and $x_{r_{3,G}}$ are the randomly selected variables with i, r_1, r_2, r_3 and G are index. $v_{i,G+1}$ refers to the donor vector.

$$v_{i,G+1} = x_{r_{1,G}} + F\left(x_{r_{2,G}} - x_{r_{3,G}}\right). \tag{1.115}$$

1.4.4.3 Recombination

Employing the target vector $x_{i,G}$ and the elements of the donor vector $v_{i,G+1}$, the trial solution vector $u_{i,G+1}$ is evaluated by following (1.116).

$$u_{i,j,G+1} = \begin{cases} v_{i,j,G+1} & \text{if rand}() \leq CR \text{ or } j = I_{rand} \\ x_{i,j,G} & \text{if rand}() > CR \text{ or } j \neq I_{rand} \end{cases}, \tag{1.116}$$

where $i = [1, N], j = [1, D]$ and $v_{i,G+1} \neq x_{i,G}$ is checked by I_{rand}.

1.4.4.4 Selection

The target solution $x_{i,G}$ is compared with the trial solution vector $u_{i,G+1}$ and the next generation is selected by (1.117).

$$x_{i,G+1} = \begin{cases} u_{i,G+1} & \text{if } f(u_{i,G+1}) \leq f(x_{i,G}) \\ x_{i,G} & \text{otherwise} \end{cases}, \tag{1.117}$$

where $i = [1, N]$.

Sections 1.4.4.2 to 1.4.4.4 continue until the termination criterion as explained earlier is reached.

1.4.5 Off-line Optimization

By SI and EO algorithms only the off-line optimization is possible due to their huge run-time complexity. In case of multi-robot coordination, robots evaluate the optimal trajectory (collection of coordinates) off-line in the sense of system recourse (time and/or energy) utilization. After off-line optimization of the trajectory, it is executed in the real-robot.

1.4.6 Performance Analysis of Optimization Algorithms

The performance of SI, EA, and their hybridization can be analyzed by the following performance metrics. *Quality* of *solution* within a fixed epoch and the *convergence time* are two performance matrices of the SI and EA. In addition, mean best objective function versus function evaluation, accuracy versus function evaluation, and function evaluation versus search space dimensionality can be considered as the performance metrics. In spite of the abovementioned performance metrics, statistical test is conducted over the algorithms for performance measurement.

1.4.6.1 Friedman Test

Friedman test [64], which is a nonparametrical statistical test, may be carried out on the average objective function values of each of the algorithms for fixed independent runs, assuming a fixed dimension. To carry out the Friedman test, first the average ranking (R_i) for each of the considered algorithms is calculated as the mean of the individual ranks obtained by them over all the considered N number of benchmark functions, as shown in (1.118),

$$R_i = \frac{1}{N} \sum_{j=1}^{N} r_i^j. \tag{1.118}$$

Here, r_i^j refers to the individual rank attained by the i-th algorithm for the j-th benchmark function and the results have been computed considering N benchmark functions. In the next step, a term formally defining the Friedman statistic, which follows a χ_F^2 distribution with $(k-1)$ degrees of freedom, has been evaluated using (1.119),

$$\chi_F^2 = \frac{12N}{k(k+1)} \left[\sum_{i=1}^{k} R_i^2 - \frac{k(k+1)^2}{4} \right]. \tag{1.119}$$

1.4.6.2 Iman–Davenport Test

Moreover, Iman–Davenport test [65] can also been conducted in order to substantiate the findings of the former statistical analysis. It is basically a deviation from the Friedman test producing more precise results and the Iman–Davenport statistics is calculated as follows:

$$F_F = \frac{(N-1) \times \chi_F^2}{N \times (k-1) - \chi_F^2}. \tag{1.120}$$

Tabular analysis can be shown in case of Friedman test, which demonstrates that the null hypothesis has been rejected if the computed value of χ_F^2 is greater than the critical value of the χ_F^2 distribution with degrees of freedom $(k-1)$ at probability of α $(\chi_{3,\alpha}^2)$. For, Iman–Davenport test, the statistic is distributed with $(k-1)$ and $(k-1) \times (N-1)$ degrees of freedom. Likewise, the null hypothesis has been rejected as the calculated value of F_F is greater than the critical value of the F_F distribution with degrees of freedom $(k-1)$ and $(k-1) \times (N-1)$ at probability of α $(F_{(k-1),(N-1),\alpha})$. It is obvious that the proposed algorithm is the most efficient one, hence, in the post-hoc analysis, the proposed algorithm is assumed to be the control method.

For multi-robot trajectory (path) planning, Average total path deviation, Average Uncovered Target Distance, Average total path traversed, and numbers of steps required are considered as the performance metrics.

1.5 Summary

This chapter introduces multi-robot coordination algorithms for complex real-world problems employing the principles of RL, GT, DP, and/or EA. As expected, this chapter includes a thorough survey of the exiting literature of RL with a brief overview of the EO to examine the role of the algorithms in view of the multi-agent coordination. Here, multi-robot coordination is achieved by employing the EO, and specially RL for cooperative, competitive, and their composition for application to static and dynamic games. The remainder of the chapter provides an overview of the metrics used to compare the performance of the algorithms while coordinating.

References

1 Arkin, R.C. (1998). *Behavior-Based Robotics*. MIT Press.
2 Sen, S., Sekaran, M., and Hale, J. (1994). Learning to coordinate without sharing information. *Proceedings of the American Association for Artificial Intelligence* **94**: 426–431.
3 Kapetanakis, S. and Kudenko, D. (2002). Reinforcement learning of coordination in cooperative multi-agent systems. *Proceedings of the American Association for Artificial Intelligence* **18**: 326–331.
4 Konar, A., Chakraborty, I.G., Singh, S.J. et al. (2013). A deterministic improved Q-learning for path planning of a mobile robot. *IEEE Transactions on Systems, Man, and Cybernetics: Systems* **43** (5): 1141–1153.
5 Sadhu, A.K., Rakshit, P., and Konar, A. (2016). A modified Imperialist Competitive Algorithm for multi-robot stick-carrying application. *Robotics and Autonomous Systems* **76**: 15–35.
6 Stentz, A. (1997). Optimal and efficient path planning for partially known environments. In: *Intelligent Unmanned Ground Vehicles*, vol. **388** (eds. M. Hebert and C. Thorpe), 203–220. Boston, MA: Springer.

7 Xu, X., Zuo, L., and Huang, Z. (2014). Reinforcement learning algorithms with function approximation: recent advances and applications. *Information Sciences* **261**: 1–31.

8 Buşoniu, L., Lazaric, A., Ghavamzadeh, M. et al. (2012). Least-squares methods for policy iteration. In: *Reinforcement Learning* (eds. M. Wiering and M. van Otterlo), 75–109. Berlin Heidelberg: Springer.

9 Xu, X., Hu, D., and Lu, X. (2007). Kernel-based least squares policy iteration for reinforcement learning. *IEEE Transactions on Neural Networks* **18** (4): 973–992.

10 Golub, G. and Kahan, W. (1965). Calculating the singular values and pseudo-inverse of a matrix. *Journal of the Society for Industrial and Applied Mathematics, Series B: Numerical Analysis* **2** (2): 205–224.

11 Lagoudakis, M.G. and Parr, R. (2003). Least-squares policy iteration. *The Journal of Machine Learning Research* **4**: 1107–1149.

12 Martins, M.F. and Demiris, Y. (2010). Learning multirobot joint action plans from simultaneous task execution demonstrations. *Proceedings of the 9th International Conference on Autonomous Agents and Multiagent Systems* **1**: 931–938.

13 Cao, Y.U., Fukunaga, A.S., and Kahng, A.B. (1997). Cooperative mobile robotics: antecedents and directions. *Autonomous Robots* **4** (1): 7–27.

14 Farinelli, A., Iocchi, L., and Nardi, D. (2004). Multi-robot systems: a classification focused on coordination. *IEEE Transactions on Systems, Man, and Cybernetics, Part B: Cybernetics* **34** (5): 2015–2028.

15 Szer, D., Charpillet, F., and Zilberstein, S. (2005). MAA*: a heuristic search algorithm for solving decentralized POMDPs. *Proceedings of the 21st Conference on Uncertainty in Artificial Intelligence-UAI*, Edinburgh, Scotland (26–29 July 2005).

16 Dias, M.B., Zlot, R., Kalra, N., and Stentz, A. (2006). Market-based multirobot coordination: a survey and analysis. *Proceedings of the IEEE* **94** (7): 1257–1270.

17 Stentz, A. and Dias, M.B. (1999). A Free Market Architecture for Coordinating Multiple Robots. Technical Report, CMU-RI-TR-99-42, Robotics Institute, Carnegie Mellon University.

18 Dias, M.B. and Stentz, A. (2002). Opportunistic optimization for market-based multirobot control. *IEEE/RSJ International Conference on Intelligent Robots and Systems* **3**: 2714–2720.

19 Dias, M.B. (2004). Traderbots: a new paradigm for robust and efficient multirobot coordination in dynamic environments. Doctoral dissertation, Carnegie Mellon University Pittsburgh.

20 Sandholm, T. (2002). Algorithm for optimal winner determination in combinatorial auctions. *Artificial Intelligence* **135** (1): 1–54.

21 Berhault, M., Huang, H., Keskinocak, P. et al. (2003). Robot exploration with combinatorial auctions. *Proceedings IEEE/RSJ International Conference on Intelligent Robots and Systems, (IROS 2003)* **2**: 1957–1962.

22 Dias, M.B., Zlot, R., Zinck, M. et al. (2004). A versatile implementation of the TraderBots approach for multirobot coordination. *Proceedings of the 8th Conference on Intelligent Autonomous Systems (IAS-8)*, Amsterdam, Netherlands (10–12 March 2004).

23 Badreldin, M., Hussein, A., and Khamis, A. (2013). A comparative study between optimization and market-based approaches to multi-robot task allocation. *Advances in Artificial Intelligence* **2013**: 1–11.

24 Konar, A., Chakraborty, I.G., Singh, S.J. et al. (2013). A deterministic improved Q-learning for path planning of a mobile robot. *IEEE Transactions on Systems, Man, and Cybernetics: Systems* **43** (5): 1–13.

25 Marden, J.R., Arslan, G., and Shamma, J.S. (2009). Cooperative control and potential games. *IEEE Transactions on Systems, Man, and Cybernetics, Part B: Cybernetics* **39** (6): 1393–1407.

26 Fax, A. and Murray, R.M. (2004). Information flow and cooperative control of vehicle formations. *IEEE Transactions on Automation Control* **49**: 1465–1476.

27 Kashyap, A., Başar, T., and Srikant, R. (2006). Consensus with quantized information updates. *Proceedings of the 45th IEEE Conference on Decision and Control*, San Diego, CA (13–15 December 2006).

28 Olfati-Saber, R., Fax, A., and Murray, R.M. (2007). Consensus and cooperation in networked multi-agent systems. *Proceedings of the IEEE* **95** (1): 215–233.

29 Mohanty, M., Mishra, A., and Routray, A. (2009). A non-rigid motion estimation algorithm for yawn detection in human drivers. *International Journal of Computational Vision and Robotics* **1** (1): 89–109.

30 LaValle, S.M. (2006). *Planning Algorithms*. Cambridge university press.

31 Nilsson, N.J. (2014). *Principles of Artificial Intelligence*. Morgan Kaufmann.

32 Konar, A. (1999). *Artificial Intelligence and Soft Computing: Behavioral and Cognitive Modeling of the Human Brain*. CRC Press.

33 Bhattacharya, P. and Gavrilova, M.L. (2008). Roadmap-based path planning: using the Voronoi diagram for a clearance-based shortest path. *IEEE Robotics and Automation Magazine* **15** (2): 58–66.

34 Gayle, R., Moss, W., Lin, M.C., and Manocha, D. (2009). Multi-robot coordination using generalized social potential fields, *Proceedings of the IEEE International Conference on Robotics and Automation*. Kobe, Japan (12–17 May 2009), pp. 106–113.

35 Sutton, R.S. and Barto, A.G. (1998). *Reinforcement Learning: An Introduction*. Cambridge, MA: The MIT Press.

36 Krishna, K.M. and Hexmoor, H. (2004). Reactive collision avoidance of multiple moving agents by cooperation and conflict propagation. *IEEE International Conference on Robotics and Automation (ICRA)* **3**: 2141–2146.

37 Farinelli, A., Iocchi, L., and Nardi, D. (2004). Multirobot systems: a classification focused on coordination. *IEEE Transactions on Systems, Man, and Cybernetics, Part B (Cybernetics)* **34** (5): 2015–2028.

38 Myerson, R.B. (1991). *Game Theory: Analysis of Conflict.* Cambridge: Harvard University Press.

39 Brown, G.W. (1951). Iterative solution of games by fictitious play. *Activity Analysis of Production and Allocation* **13** (1): 374–376.

40 Kandori, M., Mailath, G.J., and Rob, R. (1993). Learning, mutation, and long run equilibria in games. *Econometrica: Journal of the Econometric Society* **61**: 29–56.

41 Neumann, L.J. and Morgenstern, O. (1947). *Theory of games and economic behavior*, vol. **60**. Princeton: Princeton University Press.

42 Nash, J. (1951). Non-cooperative games. *Annals of Mathematics* **54**: 286–295.

43 Owen, G. (1995). *Game Theory.* Academic Press.

44 Basar, T. and Olsder, G.J. (1999). *Dynamic Noncooperative Game Theory*, vol. **23**. SIAM.

45 Fudenberg, D. and Kreps, D.M. (1992). *Lectures on Learning and Equilibrium in Strategic Form Games.* Louvain-La-Neuve: Core Foundation.

46 Howard, R.A. (1960). *Dynamic Programming and Markov Processes.* The MIT Press.

47 Bellman, R.E. (1957). Dynamic programming. *Proceedings of the National Academy of Science of the United States of America* **42** (10): 34–37.

48 Yang, X.S. (2009). Firefly algorithms for multimodal optimization, stochastic algorithms: foundations and applications. *SAGA, Lecture Notes in Computer Sciences* **5792**: 169–178.

49 Narimani, R. and Narimani, A. (2013). A new hybrid optimization model based on imperialistic competition and differential evolution meta-heuristic and clustering algorithms. *Applied Mathematics in Engineering, Management and Technology* **1** (2): 1–9.

50 Subudhi, B. and Jena, D. (2011). A differential evolution based neural network approach to nonlinear system identification. *Applied Soft Computing* **11** (1): 861–871.

51 Ramezani, F., Lotfi, S., and Soltani-Sarvestani, M.A. (2012). A hybrid evolutionary imperialist competitive algorithm (HEICA). In: *Intelligent Information and Database Systems*, Part I, LNAI, vol. **7196** (eds. J.-S. Pan, S.-M. Chen and N.T. Nguyen), 359–368. Berlin Heidelberg: Springer.

52 Khorani, V., Razavi, F., and Ghoncheh, A. (2010). *A New Hybrid Evolutionary Algorithm Based on ICA and GA: Recursive-ICA-GA*, 131–140. IC-AI.

53 Nozarian, S. and Jahan, M.V. (2012). A Novel Memetic Algorithm with Imperialist Competition as Local Search. *International Proceedings of Computer Science and Information Technology* **30**: 54–59.

54 Lin, J.L., Tsai, Y.H., Yu, C.Y., and Li, M.S. (2012). Interaction enhanced imperialist competitive algorithms. *Algorithms* **5** (4): 433–448.

55 Coelho, L.D.S., Afonso, L.D., and Alotto, P. (2012). A modified imperialist competitive algorithm for optimization in electromagnetic. *IEEE Transactions on Magnetics* **48** (2): 579–582.

56 Bidar, M. and Rashidy, H.K. (2013). Modified firefly algorithm using fuzzy tuned parameters. *Proceedings of the 13th Iranian Conference on Fuzzy Systems (IFSC), IEEE*, Iran Qazvin (27–29 August 2013), pp. 1–4.

57 Seuken, S. and Zilberstein, S. (2007). Memory-Bounded Dynamic Programming for DEC-POMDPs. *IJCAI*, pp. 2009–2015.

58 Seuken, S. and Zilberstein, S. (2012). Improved memory-bounded dynamic programming for decentralized POMDPs. *arXiv preprint arXiv*. pp. 1206.5295.

59 K. Alton and I. M. Mitchell, Efficient dynamic programming for optimal multi-location robot rendezvous. *Proceedings of the 47th IEEE Conference on Decision and Control*, MEX Cancun (9–11 December 2008), pp. 2794–2799.

60 Nudelman, E., Wortman, J., Shoham, Y., and Leyton-Brown, K. (2004). Run the GAMUT: a comprehensive approach to evaluating game-theoretic algorithms. *Proceedings of the Third International Joint Conference on Autonomous Agents and Multiagent Systems* 2: 880–887.

61 Kennedy, J., Eberhart, R., and Shi, Y. (2001). *Swarm Intelligence*. Los Altos, CA: Morgan Kaufmann.

62 Das, S., Abraham, A., and Konar, A. (2008). Particle swarm optimization and differential evolution algorithms: technical analysis, applications and hybridization perspectives. In: *Advances of Computational Intelligence in Industrial Systems*, 1–38. Berlin Heidelberg: Springer.

63 Gargari, E.A. and Lucas, C. (2007). Imperialist competitive algorithm: an algorithm for optimization inspired by imperialistic competition. *Proceedings of the IEEE Congress in Evolutionary Computation, CEC*, Singapore (25–28 September 2007), pp. 4661–4667.

64 Horng, M.H. and Jiang, T.W. (2010). The codebook design of image vector quantization based on the firefly algorithm. In: *International Conference on Computational Collective Intelligence*, Part III, LNAI, vol. **6423** (eds. J.-S. Pan, S.-M. Chen and N.T. Nguyen), 438–447. Berlin, Heidelberg: Springer.

65 Abidin, Z.Z., Arshad, M.R., and Ngah, U.K. (2011). A simulation based fly optimization algorithm for swarms of mini-autonomous surface vehicles application. *Indian Journal of Marine Sciences* **40** (2): 250–266.

66 Belal, M., Gaber, J., El-Sayed, H., and Almojel, A. (2006). Swarm intelligence. In: *Handbook of Bioinspired Algorithms and Applications*, CRC Computer and Information Science, vol. **7** (eds. S. Olariu and A.Y. Zomaya). Chapman and Hall.

67 M. Dorigo, *In The Editorial of the First Issue of: Swarm Intelligence Journal*, Springer Science + Business Media, LLC, Vol.1, No. 1, pp. 1–2, 2007.

68 Hosseini, S. and Al Khaled, A. (2014). A survey on the Imperialist Competitive Algorithm metaheuristic: implementation in engineering domain and directions for future research. *Applied Soft Computing* **24**: 1078–1094.

69 Pugh, J., Zhang, Y., and Martinoli, A. (2005). Particle swarm optimization for unsupervised robotic learning. *Proceedings of the Swarm Intelligence Symposium*, Pasadena, CA (June 2005), pp. 92–99.

70 Pugh, J. and Martinoli, A. (2006). Multi-robot learning with particle swarm optimization. *International Proceedings of the Autonomous Agents and Multi-agent Systems*, Japan (8–12 May 2006), pp. 441–448.

71 Hu, J. and Wellman, M.P. (2003). Nash Q-learning for general-sum stochastic games. *The Journal of Machine Learning Research* **4**: 1039–1069.

72 Greenwald, A., Hall, K., and Serrano, R. (2003). Correlated Q-learning. *Proceedings of the International Conference on Machine Learning* **3**: 242–249.

73 Kaelbling, L.P., Littman, M.L., and Moore, A.W. (1996). Reinforcement learning: a survey. *Journal of Artificial Intelligence Research* **4**: 237–285.

74 Dijkstra, E.W. (1959). A note on two problems in connexion with graphs. *Numerische Mathematik* **1**: 269–271.

75 Najnin, S. and Banerjee, B. (2018). Pragmatically framed cross-situational noun learning using computational reinforcement models. In: *Frontiers in Psychology (Cognitive Science Section)*, vol. **9**, Article 5 (ed. J.L. McClelland).

76 Fraternali, F., Balaji, B., and Gupta, R. (2018). Scaling configuration of energy harvesting sensors with reinforcement learning. *Proceedings of the 6th International Workshop on Energy Harvesting and Energy-Neutral Sensing Systems*, Shenzhen, China (4 November 2018), pp. 7–13. ACM.

77 Lawhead, R.J. and Gosavi, A. (2019). A bounded actor–critic reinforcement learning algorithm applied to airline revenue management. *Engineering Applications of Artificial Intelligence* **82**: 252–262.

78 Schawartz, H.M. (2014). *Multi-Agent Machine Learning a Reinforcement Approach*. Wiley.

79 Berry, D. and Fristedt, B. (1985). *Bandit Problems*. Chapman and Hall.

80 Filar, J. and Vrieze, K. (2012). *Competitive Markov Decision Processes*. Springer Science & Business Media.

81 Claus, C. and Boutilier, C. (1998). The dynamics of reinforcement learning in cooperative multiagent systems. *Proceedings of the National Conference on Artificial Intelligence* **15**: 746–752.

82 Jain, R. and Varaiya, P. (2010). Simulation-based optimization of Markov decision processes: an empirical process theory approach. *Automatica* **46** (8): 1297–1304.

83 Kemeny, J.G. and Laurie Snell, J. (1960). *Finite Markov Chains*. New York, Berlin, Tokyo: Springer-Verlag.

84 Barto, A.G., Sutton, R.S., and Watkins, C.J. (1989). *Learning and Sequential Decision Making*. Amhers: University of Massachusetts.

85 Busoniu, L., Babuska, R., and De Schutter, B. (2008). A comprehensive survey of multiagent reinforcement learning. *IEEE Transactions on Systems, Man, and Cybernetics, Part C: Applications and Reviews* **38** (2): 156–172.

86 Young, H.P. (1993). The evolution of conventions. *Econometrica: Journal of the Econometric Society* **61** (1): 57–84.

87 Fudenberg, D. and Levine, D.K. (1993). Steady state learning and Nash equilibrium. *Econometrica: Journal of the Econometric Society* **61**: 547–573.

88 Kalai, E. and Lehrer, E. (1993). Rational learning leads to Nash equilibrium. *Econometrica: Journal of the Econometric Society* **61**: 1019–1045.

89 Singh, S., Jaakkola, T., Littman, M.L., and Szepesvari, C. (1998). Convergence results for single-step on-policy reinforcement learning algorithms. *Machine Learning* **38** (3): 287–308.

90 Tan, M. (1993). Multi-agent reinforcement learning: independent vs. cooperative agents. *Proceedings of the Tenth International Conference on Machine Learning*, Amherst (27–29 June 1993), pp. 330–337.

91 Lauer, M. and Riedmiller, M. (2000). An algorithm for distributed reinforcement learning in cooperative multi-agent systems. *Proceedings of the Seventeenth International Conference on Machine Learning*, Stanford, CA (29 June to 2 July 2000).

92 Littman, M.L. (2001). Value-function reinforcement learning in Markov games. *Cognitive Systems Research* **2** (1): 55–66.

93 Littman, M.L. and Szepesvári, C. (1996). A generalized reinforcement-learning model: convergence and applications. *Proceedings of the International Conference on Machine Learning* **13**: 310–318.

94 Szepesvári, C. and Littman, M.L. (1999). A unified analysis of value-function-based reinforcement-learning algorithms. *Neural Computation* **11** (8): 2017–2060.

95 Hu, J. and Wellman, M.P. (1998). Multiagent reinforcement learning: theoretical framework and an algorithm. *Proceedings of the International Conference on Machine Learning* **98**: 242–250.

96 Wang, X. and Sandholm, T. (2002). Reinforcement learning to play an optimal Nash equilibrium in team Markov games. *Advances in Neural Information Processing Systems* **2**: 1571–1578.

97 Kok, J.R. and Vlassis, N. (2004). Sparse cooperative Q-learning. *Proceedings of the International Conference on Machine Learning*, Banff, Alberta (4–8 July 2004).

98 Wang, Y. and de Silva, C.W. (2008). A machine learning approach to multi-robot coordination. *Engineering Application of Artificial Intelligence* **21**: 470–484.

99 Zhang, Z., Zhao, D., Gao, J. et al. (2016). FMRQ: a multiagent reinforcement learning algorithm for fully cooperative tasks. *IEEE Transactions on Cybernetics* **47**: 2168–2267.

100 Littman, M.L. (1994). Markov games as a framework for multi-agent reinforcement learning. *Proceedings of the Eleventh International Conference on Machine Learning* **157**: 157–163.

101 Bianch, R.A.C., Martins, M.F., Ribeiro, C.H.C., and Costa, A.H.R. (2014). Heuristically: accelerated multiagent reinforcement learning. *IEEE Transactions on Cybernetics* **44** (2): 252–265.

102 Bianchi, R.A.C., Ribeiro, C.H.C., and Costa, A.H.R. (2008). Accelerating autonomous learning by using heuristic selection of actions. *Journal Heuristics* **14** (2): 135–168.

103 Bianchi, R.A.C. (2012). Heuristically accelerated reinforcement learning: theoretical and experimental results. *Frontiers in Artificial Intelligence and Applications* **242**: 169–174.

104 Bianchi, R.A.C. (2007). Heuristic selection of actions in multiagent reinforcement learning. *Proceedings of the 20th International Joint Conference on Artificial Intelligence*, Hyderabad, India (6–12 January 2007), pp. 690–695.

105 Conitzer, V. (2009). Approximation guarantees for fictitious play. *Proceedings of the 47th Annual Allerton Conference on Communication, Control, and Computing, IEEE*, Allerton House, IL (30 September to 2 October 2009), pp. 636–643.

106 Powers, R. and Shoham, Y. (2004). New criteria and a new algorithm for learning in multi-agent systems, *Advances in Neural Information Processing Systems*, Vancouver, British Columbia (13–18 December 2004), pp. 1089–1096.

107 Bowling, M. and Veloso, M. (2002). Multiagent learning using a variable learning rate. *Artificial Intelligence* **136** (2): 215–250.

108 Conitzer, V. and Sandholm, T. (2007). AWESOME: a general multiagent learning algorithm that converges in self-play and learns a best response against stationary opponents. *Machine Learning* **67** (1–2): 23–43.

109 Stone, P. and Veloso, M. (2000). Multiagent systems: a survey from a machine learning perspective. *Autonomous Robots* **8** (3): 345–383.

110 Tesauro, G. (2003). Extending Q-learning to general adaptive multi-agent systems. *Advances in Neural Information Processing Systems*, Vancouver and Whistler, British Columbia (8–13 December 2003), pp. 871–878.

111 Singh, S., Kearns, M., and Mansour, Y. (2000). Nash convergence of gradient dynamics in general-sum games. *Proceedings of the Sixteenth Conference on Uncertainty in Artificial Intelligence*, San Francisco, CA (30 June to 3 July 2000), pp. 541–548. Morgan Kaufmann Publishers Inc.

112 Reinhard, H. (1986). *Differential Equations: Foundations and Applications*. North Oxford: Academic.

113 Boyd, S. and Vandenberghe, L. (2004). *Convex Optimization*. Cambridge University Press.

114 Friedman, J., Hastie, T., and Tibshirani, R. (2001). *The Elements of Statistical Learning*, Springer series in statistics, vol. **1**. Berlin: Springer.

115 Boser, B.E., Guyon, I.M., and Vapnik, V.N. (1992). A training algorithm for optimal margin classifiers. *Proceedings of the Fifth Annual Workshop on Computational Learning Theory*, Pittsburgh, PA (27–29 July 1992), pp. 144–152. ACM.

116 Bansal, N., Blum, A., Chawla, S., and Meyerson, A. (2003). Online oblivious routing. *Proceedings of the Fifteenth Annual ACM Symposium on Parallel Algorithms and Architectures*, San Diego, CA, (7–9 June 2003), pp. 44–49. ACM.

117 Boot, J.C. (1964). *Quadratic Programming: Algorithms, Anomalies, Applications.* Rand McNally.

118 Zinkevich, M. (2003). Online convex programming and generalized infinitesimal gradient ascent. *Proceedings of the International Conference on Machine Learning,* Washington, DC (21–24 August 2003).

119 Bowling, M. (2005). Convergence and no-regret in multiagent learning. *Advances in Neural Information Processing Systems* **17**: 209–216.

120 Könönen, V. (2004). Asymmetric multiagent reinforcement learning. *Web Intelligence and Agent Systems: An International Journal* **2** (2): 105–121.

121 Littman, M.L. (2001). Friend-or-foe Q-learning in general-sum games. *Proceedings of the International Conference on Machine Learning* **1**: 322–328.

122 Hu, Y., Gao, Y., and An, B. (2015). Multiagent reinforcement learning with unshared value functions. *IEEE Transactions on Cybernetics* **45** (4): 647–661.

123 Hu, Y., Gao, Y., and An, A. (2015). Accelerating multiagent reinforcement learning by equilibrium transfer. *IEEE Transactions on Cybernetics* **45** (7): 1289–1302.

124 Bowling, M. and Veloso, M. (2001). Rational and convergent learning in stochastic games. *International Joint Conference on Artificial Intelligence* **17** (1): 1021–1026, Lawrence Erlbaum Associates Ltd.

125 Weiß, G. (1995). *Adaptation and Learning in Multi-agent Systems, Some Remarks and a Bibliography,* 1–21. Berlin, Heidelberg: Springer.

126 Banerjee, B. and Peng, J. (2003). Adaptive policy gradient in multiagent learning. *Proceedings of the Second International Joint Conference on Autonomous Agents and Multiagent Systems,* Melbourne, Victoria (14–18 July 2003), pp. 686–692. ACM.

127 Banerjee, B. and Peng, J. (2002). Convergent gradient ascent in general-sum games. In: *Machine Learning: ECML* (eds. T. Elomaa, H. Mannila and H. Toivonen), 1–9. Berlin, Heidelberg: Springer.

128 Weinberg, M. and Rosenschein, J.S. (2004). Best-response multiagent learning in non-stationary environments. *Proceedings of the Third International Joint Conference on Autonomous Agents and Multiagent Systems* **2**: 506–513.

129 Shoham, Y., Powers, R., and Grenager, T. (2003). Multi-agent Reinforcement Learning: A Critical Survey. Technical Report, Computer Science Department, Stanford University, Stanford.

130 Hu, J. (2003). Best-response algorithm for multiagent reinforcement learning. *Proceedings of the International Conference on Machine Learning,* Washington, DC (21–24 August 2003).

131 Suematsu, N. and Hayashi, A. (2002). A multiagent reinforcement learning algorithm using extended optimal response. *Proceedings of the First International Joint Conference on Autonomous Agents and Multiagent Systems: Part 1,* Bologna Italy (July 2002), pp. 370–377. ACM.

132 Cortés-Antonio, P., Rangel-González, J., Villa-Vargas, L.A., et al. (2014). Design and implementation of differential evolution algorithm on FPGA for double-precision floating-point representation. *Acta Polytechnica Hungarica* **11** (4): 139–153.

133 Storn, R. and Price, K., et al. (1996). Minimizing the real functions of the ICEC'96 contest by differential evolution, In Proceedings of IEEE international conference on evolutionary computation. pp 842–844.

2

Improve Convergence Speed of Multi-Agent Q-Learning for Cooperative Task Planning

Learning-based planning algorithms are currently gaining popularity for their increasing applications in real-time planning and cooperation of robots. This chapter aims at extending traditional multi-agent Q-learning algorithms to improve their speed of convergence by incorporating two interesting properties, concerning (i) exploration of the team-goal and (ii) selection of joint action at a given joint state. The exploration of team-goal is realized by allowing the agents, capable of reaching their goals, to wait at their individual goal states, until remaining agents explore their individual goals synchronously or asynchronously. To avoid unwanted never-ending wait-loops, an upper bound to wait-interval, obtained empirically for the waiting team members, is introduced. Selection of joint action, which is a crucial problem in traditional multi-agent Q-learning, is performed here by taking the intersection of individual preferred joint actions of all the agents. In case the resulting intersection is a null set, the individual actions are selected randomly or otherwise following classical multi-agent Q-learning. It is shown both theoretically and experimentally that the extended algorithms outperform its traditional counterpart with respect to speed of convergence. To ensure selection of right joint action at each step of planning, we offer high rewards to exploration of the team-goal and zero rewards to exploration of individual goals during the learning phase. The introduction of the above strategy results in an enriched joint Q-table, the consultation of which during the multi-agent planning yields significant improvement in the performance of cooperative planning of robots. Hard-wired realization of the proposed learning-based planning algorithm, designed for object-transportation application, confirms the relative merits of the proposed technique over contestant algorithms.

Multi-agent Coordination: A Reinforcement Learning Approach, First Edition.
Arup Kumar Sadhu and Amit Konar.
© 2021 The Institute of Electrical and Electronics Engineers, Inc.
Published 2021 by John Wiley & Sons, Inc.

2.1 Introduction

Reinforcement learning (RL) [1–10] refers to a real-time learning paradigm, where an agent learns its environment with respect to a fixed goal by receiving reward/penalty [6] for its actions on the environment. The reward/penalty obtained by the agent for its sequence of actions is used to adapt its effective reward in a given state–action space [11–15]. The motivation of RL is to derive the optimal action at a given environmental state for which the agent would be able to derive the maximum reward. Such formulation of deriving optimal action at a given state based on the learned experience of interaction with the environment has plenty of interesting applications, including generating moves in a game [16, 17], and complex task-planning and motion-planning of a mobile robot in a constrained environment [18]. In RL, the environment is typically represented by a Markov Decision Process (MDP) with unknown state-transition probabilities and an unknown reward model [6]. The MDP provides the basic mathematical model of a discrete-event system [19].

Among the RL algorithms, Q-learning is most popular. Q-learning does not require any background knowledge of the agents' environment and thus is called model-free. This characteristic of Q-learning is advantageous [20] as learning can be performed without the knowledge of the environment. In Q-learning, optimal policy for each state–action pair is estimated through an iterative process using Dynamic Programming (DP) [21], realized with the well-known Bellman Equation (BE) [21]. In single agent Q-learning, the state-transitions are controlled by the agent itself. However, in a multi-agent environment, all the agents participate to select their individual actions and form a joint action in a joint state-space. Because of joint actions by the agents on the environment, the environment in multi-agent Q-learning (MAQL) [2, 12, 18, 22–51] appears as dynamic to an individual agent. Like single agent Q-learning, a MAQL too is described by a MDP, called Multi-agent MDP (MMDP) [23, 33].

Several extensions of the single agent Q-learning for multi-agent applications is available. The fundamental problems in MAQL, by which it significantly differs from its single-agent counterpart, include [2, 18, 22–51] (i) joint action selection, (ii) update policy selection for adaptation of the Q-table in joint state–action space, and (iii) exploration of the team-goal. Although the first two problems have been addressed in the literature, the last one remains unattended. In this paper, we provide a solution to MAQL with a motivation to deal with exploration of the team-goal and demonstrate its scope of applications in tight cooperative multi-agent planning.

Several approaches to action selection in a single agent are available. A few of these that deserve special mention includes ε-greedy exploration [6], Boltzmann strategy [15, 52] the extended Boltzmann strategy for Frequency Maximum Q-value (FMQ) heuristic [43], and also random selection. Selection of a joint action traditionally is done in two phases. First, individual actions are selected by any one of the above techniques. Next, the individual actions are combined to form a joint action. However, there are situations when the joint actions thus obtained are infeasible for a given environment. In Traditional MAQL (TMAQL), the researchers do not check the possibility of infeasible actions, as infeasible actions are penalized and thus automatically get forbidden in subsequent learning epochs.

Wang et al. introduced a novel technique for joint action selection in their proposed Sequential Q-Learning (SQL) using a two-step procedure [18]. In the first step, they employed the Boltzmann strategy for the individual action selection, and in the second step, they designed a specialized selection operation to avoid the same actions repeatedly. Besides joint action selection, there exists extensive literature on update policy in the Q-table. A few of these include Nash Q-learning (NQL) [27, 28], correlated Q-learning (CQL) [26], SQL [18], sparse Q-learning [48], heuristically accelerated MAQL [49], MAQL with equilibrium transfer (MAQLET) [46], and Frequency of the maximum reward Q-learning (FMRQ) [50]. These techniques have their individual merits depending on the nature of the problem selected.

Of the three problems in MAQL, we discussed above the major works on the first two. Unfortunately, there is hardly any work on the last problem on exploration of the team-goal. In many real-world problems, particularly where tight cooperation of the members is required, such as carrying a stick [53]/pushing a box [50] by two (or more) robots in an environment with plenty of obstacles. Here, the moves that ensure reaching of one or more (but not all) agents to their individual goals are no longer useful. Such moves, if executed during planning, may not allow the agents, who have reached their goals, to perform any further actions. Thus, there is an apparent deadlock as no team effort can keep the agents continue changing their states.

In this paper, we overcome the above problem by realization of the following strategy in the learning phase. The strategy includes allowing one or more agents, who could manage to reach their individual goals, to wait in their individual goal states for a significantly large time to give the remaining agents a chance to move to their respective (individual) goals synchronously or asynchronously. Such multiphase state-transition to the team-goal offers one way to overcome the limitation of single-phase goal transition. Here, the goal transition in the last phase only accumulates high (immediate) reward contributed by an agent for the team, thereby improving the entries in the Q-table for state-transitions for the team-goal. The Q-table thus obtained offers the team the additional benefit to identify the joint action leading to transition to the team-goal.

One question that may be raised is how long the agents, who could manage to reach their goals, wait for the other agents to reach their subsequent goals. A small waiting interval may not be enough to allow all agents to reach their goals. On the other hand, a large interval may keep the entire team waiting at their team-goal. Thus, selection of the right time-interval for the agents waiting at their individual goals is a crucial parameter, which in turn determines both the speed and planning performance of the agents.

The other important issue addressed in the chapter is the joint action selection. Here, the agents identify their preferred individual actions in combination with all possible actions by the other agents with an aim to determine the preferred joint action(s) of the team by taking the meet operation of such combinations. The joint action selection introduced above is useful for agents acting synchronously. As agents act synchronously, they do not require setting any priority to them like in [18]. In case no feasible joint action by the above method is available, the agents select individual actions randomly or by standard techniques (Boltzmann strategy and ε-greedy) used in traditional Q-learning [6, 15, 37, 43] to construct the joint action.

The incorporation of the above two strategies in the MAQL enhances the planning performance of multi-agent systems as the Q-tables, defined in joint state–action space, is enriched with high reward values for state-transitions concerning exploration of the team-goal in the next joint state. The reward values stored in the joint Q-table are also adapted with greater rewards for next joint states geographically closer to the team-goal. The resulting joint Q-table would offer the right selection of next joint state, helping the agents reach the team-goal by an optimal/near-optimal path for transition from the starting joint state to the goal state.

A fast cooperative multi-agent Q-learning (FCMQL) and its associated multi-agent planning algorithm have been developed using the above two strategies in both deterministic and stochastic environment. Experiments undertaken confirm that the proposed algorithms outperform their existing competitors with respect to convergence time in learning and successful team-task in planning. In addition, the joint action selection employing Imperialist Competitive Firefly Algorithm (ICFA) [53], modified noise-resistant Particle Swarm Optimization (MNPSO) [54, 55], Differential Evolution (DE) [56, 57], and multi-robot joint action learning by demonstration (MLbD) [58] algorithms are compared separately with the FCMQL-based multi-robot planning algorithms. The merits of the present work are now outlined below.

1) Two useful properties have been developed to speedup the convergence of MAQL algorithms. Property 2.1 establishes the principles used to overcome the exploration of the team-goal. Property 2.2 directs an alternative approach

to speedup the convergence of MAQL by identifying the preferred joint action for the team.

2) Incorporation of the above two properties in TMAQL (including NQL, variants of CQL, MAQLET, and FMRQ) results in significant improvement in speed of convergence.

3) In addition, because of an enriched Q-table to handle transitions to goal states, the proposed FCMQL-induced planning algorithm can successfully complete the plan to reach the team-goal, where TMAQL-based planning stops inadvertently.

4) Experiments have been developed to validate the performance of the proposed FCMQL with the contender algorithms in terms of the convergence speed and the run-time complexity as the performance metrics.

The rest of the chapter is structured as follows. Preliminaries of RL are reviewed in Section 2.3. Sections 2.4 and 2.5 introduce the proposed FCMQL algorithms and Section 2.6 deals with multi-agent cooperative planning algorithms. Section 2.7 includes experiments and results. The conclusions are listed in Section 2.8. The list of acronyms are listed in Table 2.1.

Table 2.1 List of acronyms.

Full form	Acronyms
Multi-agent Q-learning	MAQL
Traditional MAQL	TMAQL
Nash equilibrium	NE
Nash Q-learning	NQL
NQL with equilibrium transfer	NQLET
NQL with Property 2.1	NQLP1
NQL with Property 2.2	NQLP2
NQL with Properties 2.1 and 2.2	NQLP12
Correlated equilibrium	CE
Correlated Q-learning	CQL
Utilitarian Q-Learning	UQL
UQL with equilibrium transfer	UQLET
UQL with Property 2.1	UQLP1
UQL with Property 2.2	UQLP2
UQL with Properties 2.1 and 2.2	UQLP12
Egalitarian Q-learning	EQL

(Continued)

Table 2.1 (Continued)

Full form	Acronyms
EQL with equilibrium transfer	EQLET
EQL with Property 2.1	EQLP1
EQL with Property 2.2	EQLP2
EQL with Properties 2.1 and 2.2	EQLP12
Republican Q-learning	RQL
RQL with equilibrium transfer	RQLET
RQL with Property 2.1	RQLP1
RQL with Property 2.2	RQLP2
RQL with Properties 2.1 and 2.2	RQLP12
Libertarian Q-learning	LQL
LQL with equilibrium transfer	LQLET
LQL with Property 2.1	LQL1
LQL with Property 2.2	LQL2
LQL with Properties 2.1 and 2.2	LQLP12
Frequency of the maximum reward Q-learning	FMRQ
FMRQ with Property 2.1	FMRQP1
FMRQ with Property 2.2	FMRQP2
FMRQ with Properties 2.1 and 2.2	FMRQP12
Fast cooperative multi-agent Q-learning	FCMQL
Nash Q-induced multi-agent planning	NQIMP
Correlated Q-induced multi-agent planning	CQIMP
Contributed reward by agent i for the team	CR_i
Imperialist competitive firefly algorithm	ICFA
Modified noise-resistant particle swarm optimization	MNPSO
Differential Evolution	DE
Multi-robot joint action learning by demonstration	MLbD

2.2 Literature Review

Quite a few interesting works on the MAQL have been reported in the literature [18, 22–51]. Among the state-of-the-art MAQL algorithms, the following need special mention. In [24], Claus and Boutilier aimed at solving the coordination problem using two types of reinforcement learners. The first one, called independent learner (IL) [24], takes care of the learning behavior of individual agents by ignoring the presence of other agents. The second one, called joint action learner (JAL) [24], considers all agents including the self to learn at joint action-space. Unlike JAL, in Team Q-learning [51] proposed by Littman, an agent updates its Q-value at a joint state–action pair without utilizing associated agents' reward; rather the value function of the agent at the next joint state is evaluated by obtaining the maximum Q-value among the joint actions at the next joint state. In [37], Ville Könönen proposed Asymmetric-Q learning (AQL) algorithm, where the leader agents are capable of maintaining all the agents' Q-tables. However, the follower agents are not allowed to maintain all the agents' Q-tables and hence, they just maximize their own rewards. In AQL, agents always achieve the pure strategy Nash equilibrium (NE), although there does exist mixed strategy NE [27, 28]. In [27], Hu and Wellman extended the Littman's Minimax Q-learning [29] to general-sum-stochastic game (where summation of all agents' payoff is neither zero nor constant) [16, 59] by taking into account of other agents' dynamics using NE [27, 28, 60]. They also offered a proof of convergence of their algorithm [40]. In [41, 42], the authors selected one NE optimally in case of its multiple occurrences. In [30], Littman proposed Friend-or-Foe Q-learning algorithm for general-sum games. In this algorithm, the learner is instructed to treat each other agent either as a friend in Friend Q-learning (FQL), or as a foe in Foe Q-learning. Friend-or-Foe Q-learning provides a stronger convergence guarantee in comparison to that of the existing NE-based learning rule [27, 28]. In [26], Greenwald et al. proposed CQL employing correlated equilibrium (CE) [26] to generalize both NQL [27] and Friend-or-Foe Q-learning [30]. The bottlenecks of the above MAQL algorithms are update policy selection for adaptation of the Q-tables in joint state–action space and the curse of dimensionality with the increase in number of learning agents. Several attempts have been made to handle the curse of dimensionality in MAQL. Kok and Vlassis proposed Sparse Cooperative Q-learning in [48], where a sparse representation of the joint state–action space of the agents is done by identifying the need of coordination among the agents at a joint state. In [48], agents undertake coordination by their actions only in a few joint states. Hence, each agent maintains two Q-tables: one is the individual-action Q-table for uncoordinated joint states and other one is the joint action Q-table to represent the coordinated joint states. In case of uncoordinated states, a global Q-value is evaluated by adding the individual Q-values. In [47], authors offer a neural network-based approach for generalized representation of the state-space for multi-agent coordination. By such generalization, agents (here robots) can avoid collision with an obstacle or other robots by collecting minimum information from the sensors. In [49], Bianchi et al. proposed a novel algorithm to heuristically accelerate the TMAQL algorithms. In the literature of MAQL [18, 22–51] agents either converge to NE or CE.

The equilibrium-based MAQL algorithms [26, 27] are most popular for their inherent ability to determine optimal strategy (equilibrium) at a given joint state. In [46], Hu et al. identified the phenomenon of similar equilibria in different joint states and introduced the concept of equilibrium transfer to accelerate the state-of-the-art equilibrium-based MAQL (NQL and CQL). In equilibrium transfer, agents recycle the previously computed equilibria having very small transfer-loss. Recently in [50], Zhang et al. attempted to reduce the dimension of the Q-tables in NQL. The reduction is done by allowing the agents to store the Q-values in joint state–individual action space, instead of joint state–action space. However, with the best of our knowledge, there is no work in the literature, which considers simultaneous exploration of the individual goals (i.e. team-goal) of the agents.

In the state-of-the-art MAQL (NQL [27, 28] and CQL [26]), balancing exploration/exploitation during the learning phase is an important issue. Traditional approaches used to balance exploration/exploitation in MAQL are summarized here. The ε-greedy exploration [6], although has wide publicity, needs to tune the value of ε, which is time-costly. In the Boltzmann strategy [15], the action selection probability is controlled by tuning a control parameter (temperature) [15] and by utilizing the Q-values due to all actions at a given state. Here, the setting of temperature to infinity (zero) implies pure exploration (exploitation). Unfortunately, the Boltzmann strategy antagonistically affects the speed of learning [43]. Evolution of the Boltzmann strategy toward better performance is observed in Refs. [38, 43]. However, the above selection mechanisms are not suitable for selecting a joint action preferred for the team (all the agents) because of the dissimilar joint Q-values offered by the agents at a common joint state–action pair. There are traces of literature concerning joint action selection at a joint state during learning. In [54], Pugh and Martinoli employ a MNPSO, where each agent is considered as a swarm and they can communicate with each other. In [58], the joint action for multi-robot cooperation is selected by learning simultaneous demonstration [58].

2.3 Preliminaries

The section presents preliminaries of RL, single agent Q-learning, and MAQL concisely. In RL [6, 8], an agent interacts with the environment, by means of a 3-tuple <state (s), action (a), reward (r)>. A state refers to the current position of an agent (here robot) within an environment. By executing an action in the current state, the agent receives a scalar reward from the environment and moves to the next state. The scalar reward acts as a feedback for the agent on its immediate performance. Figure 2.1 provides a schematic overview of RL.

Figure 2.1 Block diagram of reinforcement leaning (RL).

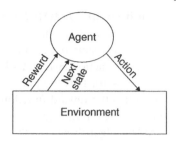

2.3.1 Single Agent Q-learning

Single agent Q-learning, proposed by Watkins and Dayan, is one of the most widely used RL techniques [20]. In single agent Q-learning, the environment is divided into a finite number of states. At any state, an agent has a finite set of actions, from which it can choose one according to a given policy. The agent learns optimal state–action value (Q-value) for each state–action pair using the principle of DP and BE [21]. In single agent Q-learning, the agent attempts to determine the optimal policy in order to maximize the sum of discounted expected rewards [11]. The single agent Q-learning update rule is given by (2.1) [20]:

$$Q(s,a) \leftarrow (1-\alpha)Q(s,a) + \alpha \left[r(s,a) + \gamma \sum_{s'} P\left[s' \mid (s,a)\right] \max_{a'} Q\left(s',a'\right) \right],$$

$$(2.1)$$

where $Q(s, a)$ and $r(s, a)$ are the Q-value and immediate reward, respectively, at state s due to action a, $a' \in \{a\}$ is the action in the next state $s' \in \{s\}$, $s' \leftarrow \delta(s, a)$ is the state-transition function, $\gamma \in [0, 1)$ denotes the discounting factor, and $\alpha \in [0, 1)$ refers to the learning rate. However, in the deterministic situation, the state-transition probability $P[s' \mid (s, a)]$ to reach the next state $s' \in \{s\}$ from the state s because of action a is unity. After infinite revisit of (s, a), Q-value $Q(s, a)$ turns to the optimal Q-value $Q^*(s, a)$.

2.3.2 Multi-agent Q-learning

Unlike single agent Q-learning presented above, in MAQL, the joint Q-value depends on the other agents' actions too. In MAQL, MDP is extended to MMDP [23, 32]. The definition of MMDP is given below.

Definition 2.1   A *MMDP* for m number of agents can be defined as a 5-tuple $\langle\{S\}, m, \{A\}, P_i, R_i\rangle$, where $\{S\} = \times_{i=1}^{m}\{s_i\}$ is the joint state space, $S \in \{S\}$ and $s_i \in \{s_i\}$ are the state of agent i, $\times$ denotes the Cartesian product, $\{A\} = \times_{i=1}^{m}\{a_i\}$ is the joint action space, $A \in \{A\}$ and $a_i \in \{a_i\}$ are the action of agent i, $P_i : \{S\} \times \{A\} \times \{S\} \to [0, 1]$ is the joint state-transition probability of agent i, and $R_i : \{S\} \times \{A\} \to R$ is the reward function at a joint state–action pair of agent i, where R is the set of real numbers.

MAQL algorithms [18, 22–51] usually are of three types: cooperative, competitive, and mixed [45]. In this paper, we deal with cooperative MAQL algorithms, where all the agents adapt Q-tables in a common environment. Because of the adaption in a common environment, the environment becomes dynamic, and an agreement is needed among the agents to attain optimal performance of the team. Such agreement is attained by adapting the joint Q-values in equilibrium, e.g. NE [60] and CE [26]. Both NE and CE employ (i) pure strategy and (ii) mixed strategy. The definitions of NE [60] and CE [26] are given below.

Definition 2.2   *NE* is a stable joint action (or strategy) at a given joint state (S) of a system that involves m interacting agents, such that no unilateral deviation (deviation of an agent independently) can occur as long as all the agents follow the same optimal joint action $A_N = \langle a_i^* \rangle_{i=1}^{m}$ at a joint state $S \in \{S\}$ for *pure strategy NE*. Further, for a *mixed strategy NE*, agents perform the joint action $A = \langle a_i \rangle_{i=1}^{m}$ with a probability $p^*(A) = \prod_{i=1}^{m} p_i^*(a_i)$, where $p_i^* : \{a_i\} \to [0, 1]$, $p^* : \{A\} \to [0, 1]$.

Let $a_i^* \in \{a_i\}$ be the optimal action of agent i at s_i and $A_{-i}^* \subseteq A$ be the optimal joint action profile of all agents except agent i at joint state $S = <s_j>_{j=1, j\neq i}^{m}$ and $Q_i(S, A)$ be the joint Q-value of agent i at S because of joint action $A \in \{A\}$. Then the condition of pure strategy NE at S is [60].

$$Q_i\left(S, a_i^*, A_{-i}^*\right) \geq Q_i\left(S, a_i, A_{-i}^*\right), \quad \forall i$$
$$\Rightarrow Q_i(S, A_N) \geq Q_i\left(S, A'\right), \quad \forall i \; \left[\text{where} \quad A_N = \langle a_i^*, A_{-i}^* \rangle \text{ and } A' = \langle a_i, A_{-i}^* \rangle\right]$$
$$(2.2)$$

and condition of mixed strategy NE at S is [60]

$$Q_i\left(S, p_i^*, p_{-i}^*\right) \geq Q_i\left(S, p_i, p_{-i}^*\right), \quad \forall i, \tag{2.3}$$

where $Q_i(S, p) = \sum_{\forall A} p(A) Q_i(S, A)$ and $p_{-i}^*(A_{-i}) = \prod_{j=1, j\neq i}^{m} p_j^*(a_j)$ be the joint probability of selecting joint action profile of all agents except agent i denoted by $A_{-i} \subseteq A$.

Agents follow (2.2) to evaluate pure strategy NE $A_N = \langle a_i^*, A_{-i}^* \rangle$ and (2.3) for mixed strategy NE $\langle p_i^*(a_i), p_{-i}^*(A_{-i}) \rangle$, respectively, at joint state S. Evaluation of NE employing Lemke–Howson method [61] is quiet efficient but limited to two agents problem only. In this chapter, to evaluate NE, a simple search method following [62] has been employed.

In NE, agents are allowed to maximize its own reward. However, in CE, the composite benefits of the agents are considered by selecting the individual actions jointly. In [26], authors outline four variants of CE: Utilitarian equilibrium (UE) (representing sum of all the agents' rewards), Egalitarian equilibrium (EE) (computed by taking minimum of all the agents' rewards), Republican equilibrium (RE) (obtained by taking maximum of all the agents' rewards), and Libertarian equilibrium (LE) (which multiplies all the agents' rewards) to evaluate a joint strategy (action).

Definition 2.3 *CE* at a joint state $S = \; <s_i>\;_{i=1}^{m}$ with m interacting agents is the pure strategy CE; A_C and mixed strategy CE, $p^*(A_C)$ if agents follow (2.4) and (2.5), respectively [26].

$$A_C = \underset{A}{\operatorname{argmax}}[\Phi(Q_i(S,A))], \tag{2.4}$$

$$p^*(A_C) = \underset{p(A)}{\operatorname{argmax}}\left[\Phi\left[\sum_{A} p(A)(Q_i(S,A))\right]\right], \tag{2.5}$$

where

$$\Phi \in \left\{\sum_{i=1}^{m}, \min_{i=1}^{m}, \max_{i=1}^{m}, \prod_{i=1}^{m}\right\}. \tag{2.6}$$

In [27], Hu and Wellman proposed NQL with the help of NE to update the reward of the agent at joint state–action space. Similarly, in [26], Greenwald et al. proposed CQL with the help of CE to update the reward of the agent at joint state–action space. Later in [46], Hu et al. attempted to accelerate the NQL and CQL by equilibrium transfer. Recently in [50], Zhang et al. attempted to reduce the dimension of the Q-tables in NQL. The reduction is done by allowing the agents to store the Q-values in joint state–individual action space, instead of storing them in joint state–action space. The above-mentioned NE/CE-based algorithms are summarized in Algorithm 2.1. In Algorithm 2.1, $r_i(S, A)$ refers to the immediate reward of agent i given by (2.7), where r_{max} and r_{min} are the maximum and minimum immediate rewards, respectively.

$$\begin{aligned}
r_i(S,A) &= r_{max}, &&\text{if agent } i \text{ reaches its individual goal,} \\
&= r_{min}, &&\text{if agent } i \text{ does not reach its individual goal,} \\
&= -r, &&\text{if agent } i \text{ violates constraint, } r \in R^+.
\end{aligned} \tag{2.7}$$

Algorithm 2.1   NE/CE-Based Multi-agent-Q Learning

Input: Current state s_i, $\forall i$, action set $\{a_i\}$, μ is a small positive threshold to stop the algorithm, $\gamma \in [0, 1)$ and $\alpha \in [0, 1)$;

Output: Joint Q-value of agent $iQ_i^*(S, A)$, $\forall S$, $\forall A$, $\forall i$;

Initialize: $Q_i(S, A) \leftarrow 0$, $\forall S$, $\forall A$, $\forall i$;

Repeat

  Observe the current state s_i, $\forall i$;

  Randomly select an action $a_i \in \{a_i\}$ at s_i and execute it $\forall i$;

  Receive $r_i(S, A)$, $\forall i$, evaluate next state $s_i' \leftarrow \delta_i(s_i, a_i)$, $\forall i$ to obtain next joint

  state $S' = <s_i'>_{i=1}^{m}$; $Q_i'(S, A) \leftarrow Q_i(S, A)$, $\forall i$;

Update:

$$Q_i(S,A) \leftarrow (1-\alpha)Q_i(S,A) + \alpha\left[r_i(S,A) + \gamma\sum_{S'}P_i[S'|(S,A)]\Psi Q_i(S')\right], \forall i \text{ // for stochastic}$$

$Q_i(S, A) \leftarrow (1-\alpha)Q_i(S, A) + \alpha[r_i(S, A) + \gamma \Psi Q_i(S')]$,

$\forall i$ //for deterministic, $\Psi \in \{NE, CE\}$ and $S \leftarrow S'$; //$\Psi Q_i(S')$ is the Q-value of agent i due to $\Psi \in \{NE, CE\}$ at joint state S'

Until $|Q_i'(S, A) - Q_i(S, A)| < \mu$, $\forall S$, $\forall A$, $\forall i$;

Obtain $Q_i^*(S, A) \leftarrow Q_i(S, A)$, $\forall S$, $\forall A$, $\forall i$.

Complexity analysis: To analyze complexities of Algorithm 2.1 [27, 50], let for *m* number of agents $\{S\}$ be the set of joint states and $\{A\}$ be the set of joint actions from each joint state $S \in \{S\}$. In NQL, CQL, and MAQLET, an agent maintains Q-table at joint state–action space. In the absence of communication [27], an agent has to maintain all the agents' Q-tables at joint state–action space. So, the *space complexity* of the NQL, CQL, and MAQLET algorithms is $m\,|\{S\}\|\{A\}|$. However, in FMRQ, an agent adapts Q-values at a joint state for each individual actions. Therefore, the *space complexity* of the FMRQ algorithms is $m\,|\{S\}\|\{a\}|$, where $\{a_1\} = \{a_2\} = \cdots = \{a_m\} = \{a\}$. Also in the TMAQL, an agent updates all the agents' Q-values at the current joint state–action pair by selecting the Q-values in the next joint state at NE/CE in each learning epoch. So, the *time complexity* to evaluate NE (considering pure strategy NE) is $(|\{A\}| - 1) \cdot |\{A\}|^{m-1} = O(|\{A\}|)^m$ and *time complexity* to evaluate the pure strategy CE is $(m-1)(|\{A\}| - 1) = O(m\,|\{A\}|)$.

2.4 Proposed MAQL

Algorithm 2.1 presented above suffers from two limitations: (i) exploration of the team-goal and (ii) joint action selection. In addition, overcoming these limitations derive additional benefit in subsequent planning stage to optimally select the team-goal. We here briefly outline the possible ways to overcome the limitations stated above.

In this section, we propose two important properties to overcome the above limitations and subsequently increase the speed of convergence of MAQL algorithms. In the first property, when one agent reaches its goal, it would remain idle, while its teammates continue exploration for their respective goals. The second property ascertains selection of a joint action at a joint state corresponding to the least reward of all the agents. It is shown that such selection accelerates the learning of the Q-table in MAQL algorithms. It is shown that the convergence speed of the proposed FCMQL algorithms is more than the same of the TMAQL (NQL, CQL, MAQLET, and FMRQ) algorithms. We now define a new term, called contributed reward by agent i, for the team denoted by CR_i.

Definition 2.4 The contributed reward by agent i to achieve the team-goal is a scalar quantity: $CR_i(S, A)$, defined at joint state S due to joint action A, is given by

$$\left. \begin{array}{rll} CR_i(S,A) &= r_{\max}, & \text{if all agents reach their goals simultaniously,} \\ &= r_{\min}, & \text{if atleast one agent is left to reach its goal,} \\ &= -r, & \text{if atleast one agent violates constraint, } r \in \mathrm{R}^+ \end{array} \right\},$$

$$(2.8)$$

where $r_{\max}$ and $r_{\min}$ are the maximum and minimum immediate rewards, respectively. Violation of constraints generally indicates collision among the teammates.

$$Q_i(S,A) \leftarrow (1-\alpha)Q_i(S,A) + \alpha \left[CR_i(S,A) + \gamma \sum_{S'} P_i \left[S' \mid (S,A) \right] \Psi Q_i \left(S' \right) \right],$$

$$(2.9)$$

where $\gamma \in [0, 1)$ and $\alpha \in [0, 1)$ refer to the discounting factor and learning rate, respectively. The joint state-transition function designed following TMAQL is given below:

$$\left.\begin{aligned}
\delta(S, A) &= \ <\delta_i(s_i, a_i) >_{i=1}^{m} \\
&= \left\langle s_i' \right\rangle_{i=1}^{m} \\
&= S' \\
&\in \{S\}
\end{aligned}\right\} \tag{2.10}$$

and $P_i[S' \mid (S, A)]$ denotes the joint state-transition probability of agent i to reach the next joint state $S' \in \{S\}$ from the joint state S because of joint action A. $\Psi \, Q_i(S')$ is the Q-value of agent i because of $\Psi \in \{NE, CE\}$ at next joint state S' and is evaluated by a simple search method [62].

2.4.1 Two Useful Properties

The properties based on which the FCMQL algorithms are being developed are discussed below. The properties are valid both in deterministic and stochastic situations. Property 2.1 is derived using Statute 2.1 given below.

Statute 2.1 *Unlike the TMAQL in the proposed FCMQL, when an agent moves to its goal state, it will not restart the learning process by randomly selecting a state (excluding its goal state); rather it waits in its goal state, and will restart learning along with all other agents, when the last agent moves to its individual goal state.*

Property 2.1 *In MAQL, if all the agents follow Statute 2.1, then the probability of exploring the team-goal monotonically increases with k in a learning episode, where k refers to the number of agents exploring their individual goals.*

Proof:
Let,
    l be the number of states in a given environment,
    m be the number of agents learning cooperatively in a given environment,
    j be the feasible actions for each agent.
    The proof is segregated into the following three components.

1) Here, agent 1 can occupy any one of l states in the next iteration. Consequently, agent 2 would occupy any one of $(l-1)$ possible next states. In the similar manner, it can be shown that agent m can occupy any one of $(l-m)$ possible next states. Thus, there would be as many as $l(l-1)\cdots(l-m+1) = {}^{l}P_m$ possible next joint states, where P denotes the permutation operator.
2) Thus, probability that the next joint state (S') is equal to the team-goal (G) due to a joint action (A) at joint state (S) is given by (2.11).

$$\Pr\Big(\big(S' = G\big) \mid (S, A)\Big) = \frac{1}{{}^{i}P_m}.$$

(2.11)

3) Now, each agent can have j feasible actions. So, two agents would have $j \times j = j^2$ joint actions. Proceeding similarly, m agents would have j^m possible joint actions. Thus, the probability of randomly selecting a joint action (A) at a joint state (S) from the joint action set ($\{A\}$) is given by (2.12).

$$\Pr(S, A) = \frac{1}{j^m}.$$

(2.12)

Now, probability that the next joint state (S') is the team-goal (G) after executing a joint action (A) randomly from the joint action set ($\{A\}$) at a joint state (S) given in (2.13) by conditional probability.

$$\Pr\Big((S, A) \cap \big(S' = G\big) : A \in \times_{i=1}^{m}\{a_i\}; S, S' \in \times_{i=1}^{m}\{s_i\}; G = {<}g_i{>}_{i=1}^{m}\Big) \quad \text{[g_i is the goal of agent i]}$$
$$= \Pr(S, A) \times \Pr\Big(\big(S' = G\big) \mid (S, A)\Big) \qquad\qquad\qquad \text{[since $\Pr(C \cap D) = \Pr(C)\cdot\Pr(D \mid C)$]}$$
$$= \frac{1}{j^m} \times \frac{1}{{}^{i}P_m}. \qquad\qquad\qquad\qquad\qquad\qquad\qquad\qquad \text{[by (2.11) and (2.12)]}$$

(2.13)

In general, suppose k agents have already reached their individual goals. Then by Statute 2.1, the number of active learning agents become $(m - k)$. So, one can rewrite (2.13) as in (2.14). In (2.14), $-k$ in suffix indicates that all except the k number of agents and $\{S\} = \{S_{-k}\} \cup \{S_{m-k}\}$, etc., where $(m - k)$ in the suffix indicates the joint state for $(m - k)$ agents.

$$\Pr\Big((S_{-k}, A_{-k}) \cap \big(S'_{-k} = G_{-k}\big) : A_{-k} \in \times_{n=1}^{m}\{a_n\}; S_{-k}, S'_{-k} \in \times_{n=1}^{m}\{s_n\}; G_{-k} = {<}g_n{>}_{n=1}^{m}; n \notin [1, k]\Big)$$
$$= \Pr(S_{-k}, A_{-k}) \times \Pr\Big(\big(S'_{-k} = G_{-k}\big) \mid (S_{-k}, A_{-k})\Big) \quad \text{[since $\Pr(C \cap D) = \Pr(C)\cdot P(D \mid C)$]}$$
$$= \frac{1}{j^{m-k}} \times \frac{1}{{}^{i}P_{m-k}}. \qquad\qquad\qquad\qquad\qquad \text{[since $m \leftarrow m - k$]}$$

(2.14)

Since the result obtained in (2.14) is a monotonically increasing function of k, with increase in k, the probability of exploring the team-goal monotonically increases. $\qquad\square$

Besides exploration of the team-goal, to speedup learning further, Property 2.2 is proposed. For the sake of convenience of the readers, the definition of preferred joint action is given below.

Definition 2.5 If $Q_i(S, A)$ refers to the Q-value of agent i at joint state S because of joint action A, then the set of *preferred joint actions* $\{A_i^p\}$ *of agent i*, is obtained by (2.15).

$$\{A_i^p\} = \arg\max_{A} [Q_i(S, A)]. \tag{2.15}$$

We also define the common preferred set of joint actions of m agents as

$$\{A^P\} = \bigcap_{i=1}^{m} \{A_i^P\}. \tag{2.16}$$

In case $\{A^P\} = \phi$, the agents would select their individual preferred actions randomly or by traditional selection techniques [6, 15, 43, 52].

In Property 2.2 introduced below, if at a joint state S only one joint action A remains non-utilized, then the probability to execute A at S becomes one, i.e. the joint action A is selected certainly for execution. This, in other words, indicates that the joint actions already taken in a joint state should not be repeated, until all the joint actions at that joint state have been explored.

Property 2.2 *In MAQL, if $\{A^P\}$ is the set of equally preferred joint action for the team at the joint state S where $\{A^P\} = \bigcap_{\forall i}\{A_i^P\} = \bigcap_{\forall i}\left\{ \arg\min_{A} [Q_i(S,A)] \right\} \neq \phi$ then $P(S, A^{P/}) > P(S, A^P)$, where $A^{P/}$ refers to the preferred joint action in the next iteration.*

Proof
Let at each state there exist j number of feasible actions for each of the m agents. Therefore, at a joint state (S) there are j^m number of feasible joint actions. Let joint action set for all the agents at joint state S are

$$\left. \begin{array}{l} \{A_i\} = \{A\}, \forall i \\ \text{and} \quad | \{A\} | = j^m, \forall i. \end{array} \right\} \tag{2.17}$$

In MAQL, the initial joint Q-values usually are assumed to be zero, i.e. $Q_i(S, A) = 0, \forall S, \forall A, \forall i$ at iteration $t = 0$. So, by Definition 2.5, preferred joint action set of agent $i = [1, m]$ at joint state S is

$$\{A_i^p\} = \underset{A}{\operatorname{argmin}}[Q_i(S,A)], \quad \forall i$$

$$= \{A_i\}, \quad \forall i.$$

$$\left[\text{since } Q_i(S,A) = 0, \; \forall S, \; \forall A, \; \forall i, \because \underset{A}{\operatorname{argmin}}[Q_i(S,A)] \text{ returns all } A \text{ for agent } i \text{ at } S \right]$$

$$= \{A\}, \quad \forall i. \quad [\text{by } (2.17)]$$

$$(2.18)$$

Now, by the given statement of Property 2.2, preferred joint action set of the team (m agents) at joint state S is

$$\{A^p\} = \overset{m}{\underset{i=1}{\cap}} \{A_i^p\}$$

$$= \overset{m}{\underset{i=1}{\cap}} \{A\} \quad [\text{by } (2.18)] \tag{2.19}$$

$$= \{A\}.$$

Therefore, probability to execute joint action A^p at the joint state S is

$$\Pr(S, A^p) = \frac{1}{|\{A^p\}|}$$

$$= \frac{1}{|\{A\}|}. \quad [\text{by } (2.19)] \tag{2.20}$$

Let after first iteration the joint Q-value of agent $x \in [1, m]$ has been improved because of preferred joint action $A_x^p \in \{A_x^p\} = \, < a_x, A_{-x} > $ at the joint state $S \in \{S\}$. So, joint Q-value of agent x at joint state S is

$$Q_x(S; a_x, A_{-x}) > Q_x(S; A), \forall A, A \neq \, < a_x, A_{-x} > , \tag{2.21}$$

where A_{-x} be the joint action except the action of agent x, $a_x \in \{a_x\}$. Therefore, updated preferred joint action set of agent $x \in [1, m]$ at joint state S by Definition 2.5 is

$$\left\{A_x^{p/}\right\} = \underset{A}{\operatorname{argmin}}[Q_x(S,A)]$$

$$= \{A_x^p\} - \{A_x^j\} \quad [\text{where, } \{A_x^j\} \text{ be the joint action set of agent } x$$

$$\text{containing action } a_x]$$

$$\subset \{A_x^p\}. \tag{2.22}$$

Therefore, by (2.17), (2.22), and the given statement of the Property 2.2, updated preferred joint action set $\{A^{p/}\}$ of the team (m agents) at joint state S is

$$\left\{A^{p\prime}\right\} = \bigcap_{\substack{i=1, \\ i \neq x}}^{m} \left\{A_i^p\right\} \cap \left\{A_x^{p\prime}\right\}$$

$$= \bigcap_{\substack{i=1, \\ i \neq x}}^{m} \left\{A\right\} \cap \left\{A_x^{p\prime}\right\} \quad [\text{by } (2.19)] \tag{2.23}$$

$$= \left\{A\right\} \cap \left\{A_x^{p\prime}\right\}$$

$$= \left\{A_x^{p\prime}\right\}. \quad \left[\text{since } \left\{A_x^{p\prime}\right\} \subset \left\{A\right\}, \quad x \in [1, m]\right]$$

Therefore, probability to execute joint action $A_x^{p\prime}$ at joint state S is

$$\Pr\left(S, A^{p\prime}\right) = \frac{1}{\left|\left\{A^{p\prime}\right\}\right|}$$

$$= \frac{1}{\left|\left\{A_x^{p\prime}\right\}\right|} \quad [\text{by } (2.23)]$$

$$> \frac{1}{\left|\left\{A_x^p\right\}\right|} \quad \left[\text{since } \left|\left\{A_x^{p\prime}\right\}\right| < \left|\left\{A_x^p\right\}\right| \text{ by } (2.22)\right] \tag{2.24}$$

$$= \frac{1}{\left|\left\{A\right\}\right|} \quad [\text{by } (2.17)]$$

$$= P(S, A^p). \quad [\text{by } (2.20)]$$

Hence, the Property is proved. $\qquad\qquad\qquad\qquad\qquad\qquad\qquad\square$

In Property 2.2, if an agent i receives a penalty (reward of $-r$ by (2.8)) at a joint state S because of a joint action A before improving its joint Q-value $Q_i(S, A)$ from the initialized value (generally zero), then the agent is trapped at the former joint state S. To overcome such problem, $Q_i(S, A)$ is re-initialized to zero. Such re-initialization improves the speed of convergence of the proposed FCMQL by avoiding the trapping at local minima.

2.5 Proposed FCMQL Algorithms and Their Convergence Analysis

In this section, we propose FCMQL algorithms with their convergence analysis, where FCMQL refers to a set of algorithms given by {NQLP12, EQLP12, UQLP12, RQLP12, LQLP12, FMRQP12}.

2.5.1 Proposed FCMQL Algorithms

In Algorithm 2.2, the proposed FCMQL algorithms enjoy the benefits of the proposed Properties 2.1 and 2.2, which are responsible for exploring the team-goal rapidly and speeding-up learning process, respectively. In Algorithm 2.2, we compute pure strategy NE, if it exists; otherwise, mixed strategy NE is evaluated. However, it may please be noted that in the proposed FMRQP12 and its associated variants, agents maintain Q-tables at joint state–individual action space denoted by $Q_i(S, a_i), \forall S, \forall a_i, \forall i$ [50].

Complexity analysis: To analyze the complexity of the proposed Algorithm 2.2, let there be m number of agents. Let $\{S\}$ and $\{A\}$ be the set of joint states and joint actions, respectively. The *space complexity* of the proposed FCMQL algorithms, except FMRQP12, is given by $m\,|\{S\}|\,\cdot\,|\{A\}|$, where for the latter the complexity is $m\,|\{S\}|\,\cdot\,|\{a\}|$, where $\{a_1\} = \{a_2\} = \cdots = \{a_m\} = \{a\}$. Now, referring to Property 2.1, the best- and worst-case time complexities in one learning epoch for an agent in the proposed FCMQL algorithms, in the absence of communication [28], are given by $(|\{a\}| - 1) = O(|\{a\}|)$ and $(|\{A\}| - 1)|\{A\}|^{m-1} = O(|\{A\}|^m)$, respectively.

Algorithm 2.2   Fast Cooperative Multi-agent Q-Learning (FCMQL)

> **A) Input:** Current state $s_i, \forall i$, joint action set $\{A\}$, μ is a small positive threshold to stop the algorithm, $\gamma \in [0, 1)$ and $\alpha \in [0, 1)$;
>
> **B) Output:** Joint Q-value of agent $iQ_i^*(S, A), \forall S, \forall A, \forall i$;
>
> **C) Initialize:** $Q_i(S, A) \leftarrow 0, \forall S, \forall A, \forall i$;
>
> **Repeat**
>   1) Observe the current state $s_i, \forall i$;
>   2) **If** $\underset{\forall i}{\cap}\{\underset{A}{arg\,min}[Q_i(S, A)]\} \neq \phi$
>   **Then** select a joint action $A \in \{A\}$ employing Property 2.2; // by Property 2.2
>   **Else** Randomly select an action $a_i \in \{a_i\}, \forall i$;
>   **End If;**
>   3) Receive immediate reward $r_i(s_i, a_i)$, $\forall i$ and evaluate CR_i by Definition 2.4;
>   4) Evaluate next state $s_i^/ \leftarrow \delta_i(s_i, a_i), \forall i$ and joint next state $S^/ = <s_i^/>_{i=1}^m$;

5) **If** $s_i = g_i$ holds for $i < m$ // g_i is the goal state of agent i
    Then the agent i waits at g_i, until $S_{-i} = G_{-i}$
      //where $-i$ indicates all except agent i
      or up to a finite time T_f obtained empirically;
    Else select a joint action $A \in \{A\}$ by step **2**;
End If;
6) **If** $s_i = g_i, \forall i$
    Then restart learning by randomly selecting a joint
    state (except team-goal state);
End If;
7) $Q_i'(S, A) \leftarrow Q_i(S, A), \forall i;$
8) **Update:** $Q_i(S, A) \leftarrow (1 - \alpha) Q_i(S, A) + \alpha [CR_i(S, A) +$
    $\gamma\ \Psi Q_i(S')]$;   //for deterministic

$$Q_i(S, A) \leftarrow (1 - \alpha)Q_i(S, A) + \alpha\left[CR_i(S, A) + \gamma \sum_{S'} P_i[S' \mid (S, A))]\Psi Q_i(S')\right];$$

    //for stochastic
  and $S \leftarrow S'$ //$\Psi\ Q_i(S')$ be the Q-value of agent i
      due to $\Psi \in \{NE,\ CE\}$ at joint state S'
Until $\mid Q_i'(S, A) - Q_i(S, A) \mid\ < \mu, \forall S, \forall A, \forall i;$
Obtain $Q_i^*(S, A) \leftarrow Q_i(S, A), \forall S, \forall A, \forall i.$

2.5.2 Convergence Analysis of the Proposed FCMQL Algorithms

The convergence of the proposed FCMQL is compared with the TMAQL in Theorem 2.1 and is given below.

Theorem 2.1 *The expected time of convergence of the proposed FCMQL is less than the same of the TMAQL.*

Proof
The expected time of convergence of FCMQL, T_e^F, decreases with an increase in the probability of exploring the team-goal, given by $\Pr(S, A) \times \Pr((S' = G) \mid (S, A))$ and also the joint action selection probability $\Pr(S, A)$. Thus, T_e^F can be modeled by an exponentially decreasing function of the joint probability of exploration of the team-goal and probability of joint action selection, i.e.

$$T_e^F = \exp\left\{-(\Pr(S, A))^2 \times \Pr\left(\left(S' = G\right) \mid (S, A)\right)\right\}. \tag{2.25}$$

It is important to note that the expression (2.25) is equally good for TMAQL. However, in TMAQL, the probabilities $\Pr(S, A)$ and $\Pr((S' = G) \mid (S, A))$ both remain constant over the learning epochs, whereas in FCMQL, the above two probabilities increase with increase in learning epochs. Thus, (2.25) transforms to (2.26) and (2.27) for TMAQL and FCMQL, respectively.

$$T_e^{TM} = \exp\left(-k\right), \tag{2.26}$$

for any positive real number k.

$$T_e^F = \exp\left(-k - \delta k\left(T_e^F\right)\right), \tag{2.27}$$

where $\delta k\left(T_e^F\right)$ is a linearly increasing function of T_e^F. A little algebra, given below, returns T_e^F as a nonlinear function of k:

$$
\begin{aligned}
&T_e^F \cdot \exp\left(\delta k\left(T_e^F\right)\right) = \exp\left(-k\right) \\
\Rightarrow\ &T_e^F \cdot \delta k\left(T_e^F\right) = \exp\left(-k\right) \quad \left[\text{as } \delta k\left(T_e^F\right) \to 0.\right] \\
\Rightarrow\ &T_e^F \cdot \left\{\beta \cdot T_e^F\right\} = \exp\left(-k\right) \quad \left[\text{by linear approximation of } \delta k\left(T_e^F\right)\right] \\
\Rightarrow\ &T_e^F = \sqrt{\frac{1}{\beta}} \exp\left(-k\right).
\end{aligned}
$$

$$\tag{2.28}$$

It is apparent from (2.26) and (2.28) that $T_e^F < T_e^{TM}$. Thus, the theorem follows. $\square$

2.6 FCMQL-Based Cooperative Multi-agent Planning

In this section, the proposed FCMQL-based cooperative multi-agent planning algorithms are discussed. In the proposed FCMQL-based multi-agent planning, agents move from the current joint state to the next joint state following the principle of pure strategy NE/CE, which is evaluated by utilizing the joint Q-tables adapted by the FCMQL and satisfying the task-constraint. Here, task-constraint refers to the constraint which agents have to satisfy during the planning phase in the deterministic and/or the stochastic environment. Consider the problem of object-carrying, where an object (stick, triangle, or square) needs to be transported to a desired location with the help of multiple robotic agents that hold the stick at its two extremities [53], triangle at its vertexes, and rectangle at its corners. Robots maintain a fixed distance between them to avoid falling off of the object carried by them. Holding the object without a fall is considered as a task-constraint. This is a problem, where cooperation of two (or more) robots is needed for the required transportation problem.

In TMAQL, the immediate reward is given in (2.7), and is designed to measure the individual agent's performance. However, in the proposed FCMQL, the immediate reward is given by (2.8) and is designed to measure the team performance. The benefit of such proposed reward function during the planning phase is realized and analyzed in the proposed FCMQL-based planning (Algorithm 2.3) and Theorem 2.2, respectively, in terms of optimal team performance, measured by the number of joint state-transitions required to reach the team-goal. The definition of the optimal team performance is given in Definition 2.6. The FCMQL-based cooperative multi-agent planning is given in Algorithm 2.3.

Definition 2.6 If the planning algorithm evaluates joint state-transitions following NE/CE, and the terminal state-transition ends at the team-goal, then the agents are called to have the *optimal team performance* considering the number of joint state-transitions required to reach the terminal (team-goal) joint state as the performance metric.

Theorem 2.2 shows that the non-team-goal state transitions cannot be a NE in the proposed NPQLP12-based multi-agent planning. However, it does a NE in the TMAQL-based multi-agent planning.

Theorem 2.2 *If all excluding at least one agent explores its individual goal state employing the proposed NPQLP12 or TMAQL due to joint action A_N at joint state S, then in the NQLP12-induced planning, A_N is not a NE, but in TMAQL-induced planning, A_N is a NE at S.*

Proof
Let the Q-values of agent $i \in [1, m]$ at joint state S due to all joint actions $A \in \{A\}$ is denoted by the set $\{Q_i(S, A) : A \in \{A\}\}$. Now, one can write

$$r_{\min} \leq Q_i(S, A) \leq r_{\max}, \quad \forall i, \tag{2.29}$$

where $r_{\min}$ and $r_{\max}$ are the minimum and maximum immediate rewards, respectively, of an agent. Let agent $x \in [1, m]$ explore its individual goal due to A_N at S and the subsequent joint Q-value of agent x adapted by the proposed NQLP12 is given by

$$Q_x(S, A_N) = r_{\min}. \quad [\text{by (2.8)}] \tag{2.30}$$

Again, by (2.29),

$$r_{\min} \le Q_x\left(S, A'\right). \quad \left[\text{where } x \in [1, m] \text{ and } A' \in \{A\}\right] \tag{2.31}$$

Combining (2.30) and (2.31), we obtain

$$Q_x(S, A_N) \le Q_x\left(S, A'\right), \quad A' \in \{A\}. \tag{2.32}$$

However, in the above situation, joint Q-value of agent x adapted by TMAQL is

$$Q_x(S, A_N) = r_{\max}. \quad [\text{by } (2.7)] \tag{2.33}$$

Again, by (2.29),

$$r_{\max} \ge Q_x\left(S, A'\right), \quad A' \in \{A\}. \quad \left[\text{where } x \in [1, m] \text{ and } A' \in \{A\}\right] \tag{2.34}$$

Combining (2.33) and (2.34), we obtain

$$Q_x(S, A_N) \ge Q_x\left(S, A'\right), \quad A' \in \{A\}. \tag{2.35}$$

Now, by the principle of multi-agent planning algorithm, let maximum joint Q-value of all except agent x at joint state S because of joint action A_N is $Q_{-x}(S, A_N)$ $\in \{Q_{-x}(S, A) : A \in \{A\}\}, \forall -x$. Therefore,

$$Q_{-x}(S, A_N) \ge Q_{-x}\left(S, A'\right), A' \in \{A\}, \forall -x. \tag{2.36}$$

By (2.32) and (2.36), we can conclude that $Q_i(S, A_N) \le Q_i(S, A')$ for $i = x$ and $Q_i(S, A_N) \ge Q_i(S, A'), \forall i, i \ne x$. Hence, by Definition 2.2, we say that in the proposed NQLP12-induced planning, the joint action A_N is not a NE at S. Again by (2.35) and (2.36), we conclude that $Q_i(S, A_N) \ge Q_i(S, A'), \forall i$. So, by Definition 2.2, we say that in TMAQL-induced planning, the joint action A_N is a NE at S. $\qquad \square$

By Theorem 2.2, one can confirm that in NQLP12-based cooperative multi-agent planning (Algorithm 2.3), an agent never executes a joint action, which results in a goal state-transition of at least one agent. However, in the TMAQL-induced planning, agents do prefer such joint actions. The agent which reaches its individual goal in the planning phase cannot move any more, resulting in low probability to reach the team-goal. Trivially, it can also be shown that in the other variants of the proposed FCMQL-induced multi-agent planning, agents do not prefer a joint action which leads to a non-team-goal state transition, except in the proposed RQLP12.

Algorithm 2.3   FCMQL-Based Cooperative Multi-agent Planning

Input: Q_i, ∀ i, feasible joint state S_F;

Output: NE (or CE) A_N (or A_C) at S_F;

Repeat

Observe current state s_i, ∀ i;

Evaluate NE (or CE), A_N (or A_C) following (2.2) (or (2.4)) and satisfying task constraint;

Execute A_N (or A_C) at S_F and go to next feasible joint state S_F' and $S_F \leftarrow S_F'$;

For multiple A_N (or A_C) solutions at S_F select the first one;

Until the task is complete.

2.7   Experiments and Results

This section includes four experiments. The first experiment is designed to examine the relative performance of the proposed FCMQL algorithms over the reference algorithms in view of the team-goal exploration, considering convergence speed as the performance metric. The second experiment is designed to compare the performance of the proposed Algorithm 2.3 over the reference algorithms. The third experiment examines the merits of the proposed Algorithm 2.3 over the existing ones, including joint action selection by MLbD [58], MNPSO [54, 55] DE [56, 57], and ICFA [53] algorithms, uses run-time complexity as the metric. The computer simulations undertaken for the experiments are coded and tested with an Intel(R) Core(TM) i7-3770 CPU with a clock speed of 3.40 GHz. Finally, in the last experiment, we examine the performance of the proposed Algorithm 2.3 in real environment with twin Khepera-II mobile robots (Appendix 2.A).

All the experiments are studied in 10 different 10 × 10 grid world maps given in Table 2.2. Figure 2.2 indicates map 1 (for deterministic) or 4 (for stochastic) in a two-agent system during the learning phase with 12 obstacles (marked as a black rectangle) and a team-goal <G1, G2>. Each agent can perform four actions: such as moving Left (L), Forward (F), Right (R), and Back (B). In case of stochastic environment, the state-transition probabilities are assigned as randomly generated constant values, satisfying the property of a Markovian matrix, where the sum of state-transition probabilities at each state is unity. Like the TMAQL algorithms, the starting positions can be selected randomly for a fixed team-goal state, which is predefined during the learning. To maintain uniformity, all the algorithms are initialized with identical joint starting states. Each grid in the multi-robots'

Table 2.2 Details of 10 × 10 grid maps.

Number of agents	Situation	Map	Team-goal	Joint starting state	Number of obstacles	Obstacle state number
2	Deterministic	1	81, 91	10, 20	12	9, 27, 40, 46, 52, 54, 58, 61, 63, 67, 82, 84
2		2	55, 65	45, 55	6	25, 48, 53, 57, 68, 75
2		3	55, 65	45, 55	8	25, 46, 48, 53, 57, 66, 68, 75
3		7	9, 20, 19	72, 81, 71	6	8, 28, 45, 49, 73, 86
4		8	81, 82, 92, 91	10, 20, 19, 9	7	16, 29, 33, 41, 47, 64, 83
2	Stochastic	4	81, 91	10, 20	12	9, 27, 40, 46, 52, 54, 58, 61, 63, 67, 82, 84
2		5	55, 65	45, 55	6	25, 48, 53, 57, 68, 75
2		6	55, 65	45, 55	8	25, 46, 48, 53, 57, 66, 68, 75
3		9	9, 20, 19	72, 81, 71	6	8, 28, 45, 49, 73, 86
4		10	81, 82, 92, 91	10, 20, 19, 9	7	16, 29, 33, 41, 47, 64, 83

workspace is assigned a positive integer to indicate its identity in the workspace with the help of mapping functions defined in Appendix 2.A.

The discounting factor γ is chosen as 0.9 and learning rate α is set to 0.1. On exploration of the team-goal, agents are awarded by (2.8), where maximum immediate reward $r_{max} = 100$, minimum immediate reward $r_{min} = 0$. In addition, the violation of constraint is penalized by a reward of $r = -1$.

Experiment 2.1 Study of Convergence Speed
This experiment aims at examining the relative superiority in convergence speed of the proposed FCMQL over the existing algorithms. The study includes: (i) convergence of state–action pairs with learning epochs, (ii) determining the number of times a given team-goal is explored within a fixed number of learning epochs, (iii) average reward of m agents, where the reward of an agent is the average of the entries in the Q-table, and (iv) convergence in state–action pairs with learning epochs, where joint action selection is done by Property 2.2.

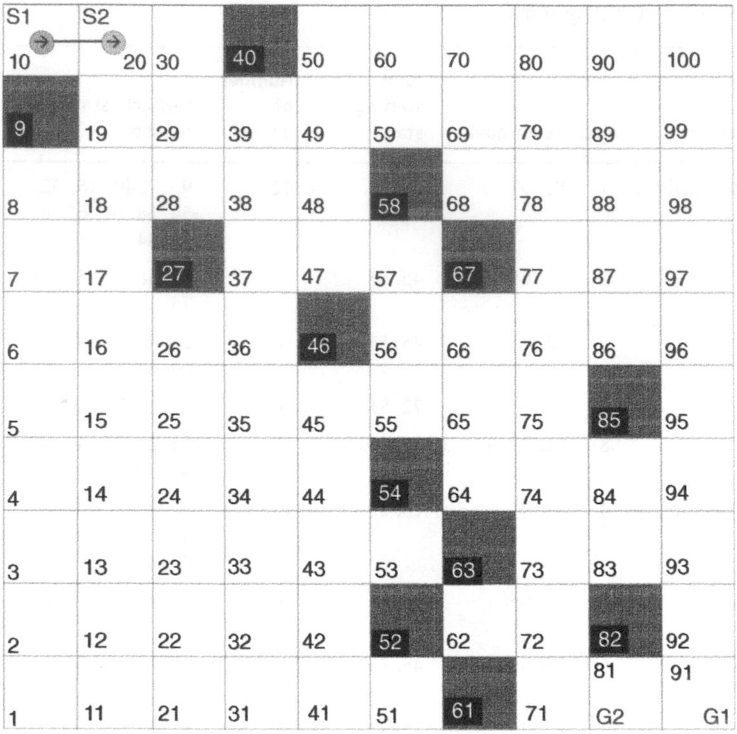

S1	S2								
10	20 30	40	50	60	70	80	90	100	
9	19	29	39	49	59	69	79	89	99
8	18	28	38	48	58	68	78	88	98
7	17	27	37	47	57	67	77	87	97
6	16	26	36	46	56	66	76	86	96
5	15	25	35	45	55	65	75	85	95
4	14	24	34	44	54	64	74	84	94
3	13	23	33	43	53	63	73	83	93
2	12	22	32	42	52	62	72	82	92
								81	91
1	11	21	31	41	51	61	71	G2	G1

Figure 2.2 Experimental workspace for two agents during the learning phase.

The results of the first study are given in Figure 2.3, developed for NQL and in Figures 2.A.1–2.A.3 (Appendix 2.A). It is apparent from Figures 2.3 and 2.A.1–2.A.3 that the FCMQL outperforms reference algorithms with respect to the number of joint state–action pairs converged (N_c). Here, the FMRQP12 is not compared with reference algorithms. As in FMRQ, an agent does not adapt its Q-value in joint state–action space; instead the Q-values are adapted in joint state–individual action space. However, FMRQP12 is compared in the later part of the same experiment.

It is interesting that in the second to seventh columns of Tables 2.A.1 and 2.A.2 (Appendix 2.A), the proposed FCMQL algorithms designed with Property 2.1 outperform the realization of FCMQL with Property 2.2 in the measure of N_c. But gradually at higher learning epochs (eighth, ninth, and 10th columns of Tables 2.A.1 and 2.A.2), the superiority of the proposed FCMQL algorithms realized with Property 2.2 is observed over the FCMQL designed with Property 2.1.

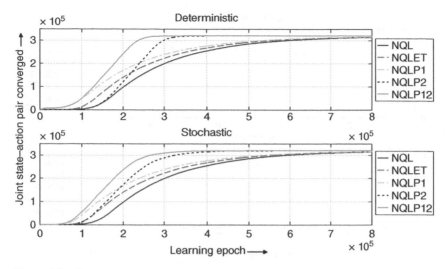

Figure 2.3 Convergence plot of NQLP12 and reference algorithms for two agents.

The result of the second study emphasizes that the proposed FCMQL, when developed with Property 2.1, yields a high count in the team-goal exploration in comparison to its traditional counterpart, including those developed with Property 2.2 (see Figure 2.A.4, Tables 2.A.3 and 2.A.4).

The third study reveals that the average reward of m agents, denoted by average of average reward (AAR) (where the reward of an agent being measured by its average Q-table value) evaluated for the proposed FCMQL exceeds that of the TMAQL. The high value in AAR of the agents indicates that early convergence in FCMQL in comparison to TMAQL (see Figures 2.4 and 2.A.5–2.A.7).

The last study dealing with convergence of joint state–action pairs with learning epochs, while embedding Property 2.2 in designing FCMQL, yields larger value in convergence of joint state–action pairs than the same obtained by the TMAQL (see Figures 2.5, 2.A.8, and 2.A.9).

Experiment 2.2 Planning Performance

The motivation of the present study is to examine the completion of a task in planning and is tested with the well-known object-carrying problem on a 10×10 grid-map by 2, 3, and 4 agents. Figures 2.6 and 2.A.10–2.A.14 offer the planed paths for robot team toward the predefined team-goal. It is worthwhile to note that the TMAQL-induced multi-agent planning fails to reach their team-goal, while the FCMQL-induced multi-agent planning is successful to complete the task.

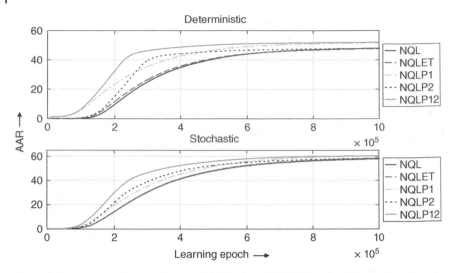

Figure 2.4 Average of average reward (AAR) plot of NQLP12 and reference algorithms for two agents.

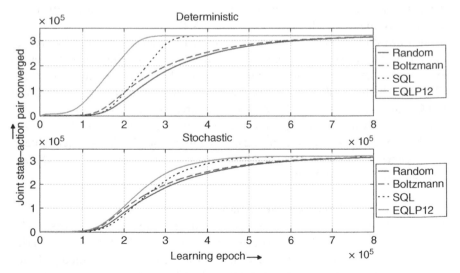

Figure 2.5 Joint action selection strategy in EQLP12 and reference algorithms for two agents.

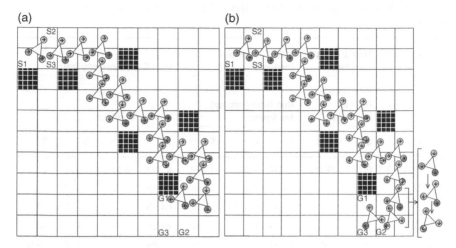

Figure 2.6 Cooperative path planning to carry a triangle by three robots in deterministic situation by: (a) NQIMP algorithm and (b) NQLP12-based cooperative multi-agent planning.

The reason behind the success of FCMQL lies in the enrichment of the Q-table because of incorporation of Property 2.1 in the learning phase. In Figure 2.6b, the arrows outside the environment indicate rotation of the triangle by robots for successful team-goal state-transition.

Experiment 2.3 Run-Time Complexity

This study includes run-time analysis of the proposed FCMQL-induced multi-agent planning along with a set of well-known algorithms from different domains. The algorithms used for comparison include: (i) ICFA [53], (ii) MNPSO [54, 55], (iii) DE [56, 57], and (iv) MLbD [58]. The run-time analysis reveals that the proposed FCMQL has the least run-time complexity in comparison to its contenders (see Tables 2.3 and 2.4).

For ICFA and DE, the objective functions used for the object-transportation task are as given in Refs. [53, 57], respectively. In MNPSO, population size is equal to the number of agents. Here, agents learn in a parallel and distributed fashion, so as to reduce the run-time requirement by the MNPSO with an increase in the number of agents. By varying the number of robots in MNPSO algorithm, different objects are transported. On the other hand, little progress is attained in the field of learning joint action by simultaneous demonstrations. MLbD is a novel technique to learn multi-robot joint action from simultaneous demonstrations as given in [58]. Here also agents learn sequence of individual actions obtained from

Table 2.3 Run-time complexity of Algorithm 2.3 over reference algorithms in deterministic situation.

| Algorithms | Map 1 (stick-carrying) | | Map 7 (triangle-carrying) | | | Map 8 (square-carrying) | | | |
| | Run-time (minute) for Agent | | Run-time (minute) for Agent | | | Run-time (minute) for Agent | | | |
	1	2	1	2	3	1	2	3	4
Algorithm 2.3	**0.195**	**0.191**	**0.244**	**0.246**	**0.242**	**0.309**	**0.313**	**0.310**	**0.304**
MLbD	14.24	14.54	20.57	21.05	20.56	27.56	28.06	27.39	28.10
ICFA	51.16	51.01	60.56	61.10	60.51	64.56	64.10	64.51	64.56
MNPSO	70.43	70.58	50.54	50.38	51.01	40.26	40.45	40.42	40.56
DE	90.45	90.56	86.54	86.34	86.38	79.45	79.34	79.34	79.04

The bold values' corresponding algorithm is outperforming the reference algorithms.

Table 2.4 Run-time complexity of Algorithm 2.3 over reference algorithms in stochastic situation.

| Algorithms | Map 4 (stick-carrying) | | Map 9 (triangle-carrying) | | | Map 10 (square-carrying) | | | |
| | Run-time (minute) for agent | | Run-time (minute) for agent | | | Run-time (minute) for agent | | | |
	1	2	1	2	3	1	2	3	4
Algorithm 2.3	**0.184**	**0.182**	**0.218**	**0.220**	**0.221**	**0.293**	**0.302**	**0.301**	**0.302**
MLbD	18.34	18.27	25.28	24.58	25.49	33.56	33.59	33.34	33.09
ICFA	52.27	53.10	60.76	60.25	60.17	63.59	63.55	63.45	63.57
MNPSO	71.54	71.52	51.34	51.65	52.04	39.45	39.34	39.32	39.12
DE	91.04	89.52	83.34	84.58	83.32	80.34	78.26	79.28	80.12

The bold values' corresponding algorithm is outperforming the reference algorithms.

demonstration with the help of HAMMER architecture [58]. The joint action plan is then identified by spatiotemporal clustering algorithm. Here, we compare the MLbD from [58] with the proposed Algorithm 2.3. In MLbD, agents need to communicate among themselves, which require an extra cost in terms of time and energy.

Table 2.5 Time taken by Khepera-II mobile robots to reach a team-goal with different speeds in Algorithm 2.3 [63].

Run-time obtained	Speed (unit)	Run-time (seconds)	
		Agent 1	Agent 2
Theoretically	2	8.75	9.14
	3	5.83	6.09
	5	3.50	3.66
Experimentally	2	11.71	12.43
	3	9.45	10.23
	5	8.28	9.36

Experiment 2.4 Real-Time Planning

This experiment is concerned with examining planning performance of the proposed FCMQL algorithms in the stick-carrying problem realized with twin Khepera-II robots (Appendix 2.A). The stick-carrying problem refers to determining the pathways to transfer stick from a given starting position to a fixed destination, where the robots hold the stick at its two ends. We consider a grid-world map for the robots with 6×6 square grids.

Figure 2.8 provides a snapshot of the experimental instance, when the robots reach the goal positions using the proposed FCMQL-induced planning. The path followed by the robots employing the reference algorithms also is shown in Figure 2.7. The experiments presented indicate that the simulated results presented earlier are realized in hardware.

2.8 Conclusions

The chapter aims at extending the TMAQL with two useful characteristic properties: exploration of the team-goal and the joint action selection. The incorporation of the first property ensures exploration of the team-goal by multiphased transitions of the agents asynchronously or synchronously to finally reach the team-goal, and thereby offer high reward values to such pre-goal state to the goal state transitions. The second property helps in identifying common preferred joint actions for the team, thus avoiding same joint actions at the same joint states and thereby enhancing the learning speed of the agents. The Q-table obtained in joint state–action space using the proposed FCMQL algorithms have been

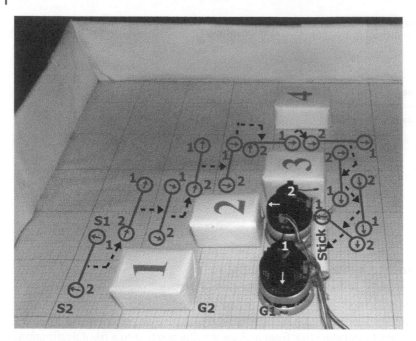

Figure 2.7 Cooperative path planning to carry a stick by two Khepera-II mobile robots using NQIMP algorithm.

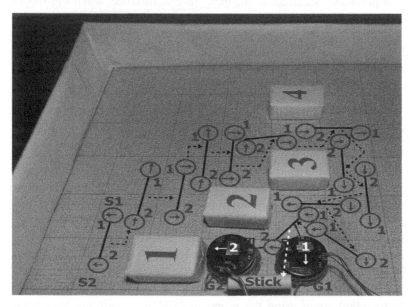

Figure 2.8 Cooperative path planning to carry a stick by two Khepera-II mobile robots using Algorithm 2.3.

employed in the multi-agent planning algorithm to autonomously select goal state-transitions from the pre-goal states based on their high reward values stored in the Q-table. TMAQL-induced planners occasionally fail to reach the team-goal as such state-transitions which might result in due to follow-up actions of Property 2.1 in FCMQL are missing from the Q-table obtained by TMAQL.

The convergence of the proposed FCMQL is shown in Theorem 2.1, that the expected convergence time of the proposed FCMQL algorithms is less than the same of TMAQL algorithms. The complexity analysis reveals the superiority of the proposed FCMQL algorithms over the TMAQL algorithms.

Four different experiments have been conducted to validate the performance of FCMQL and the FCMQL-based planning algorithms over the contender algorithms. In Experiment 2.1, the FCMQL algorithms outperform reference algorithms in terms of convergence rate, exploration of the team-goal, and the AAR parameter. In Experiment 2.2, Algorithm 2.3 outperforms reference algorithms considering successful completion of a task as the performance metric. In Experiment 2.3, the merit of Algorithm 2.3 is verified considering the run-time requirement as the performance metric over the reference algorithms: ICFA [53], MNPSO [51, 58], DE [56, 57], and MLbD [50] algorithms with respect to the well-known object-transportation problems. In Experiment 2.4, the superiority of Algorithm 2.3 is verified over contender algorithms utilizing in a real-time planning problem using twin Khepera-II mobile robots.

2.9 Summary

This chapter offers learning-based planning algorithms, by extending the traditional MAQL algorithms (NQL and CQL) for multi-robot coordination and planning. This extension is achieved by employing two interesting properties. The first property deals with the exploration of the team-goal (simultaneous success of all the robots) and the other property is related to the selection of joint action at a given joint state. The exploration of team-goal is realized by allowing the agents, capable of reaching their goals, to wait at their individual goal states, until remaining agents explore their individual goals synchronously or asynchronously. Selection of joint action, which is a crucial problem in traditional MAQL, is performed here by taking the intersection of individual preferred joint actions of all the agents. In case the resulting intersection is a null set, the individual actions are selected randomly or otherwise following classical techniques. The superiority of the proposed learning and learning-based planning algorithms are validated over contestant algorithms in terms of the speed of convergence and run-time complexity, respectively.

2.A   More Details on Experimental Results

2.A.1   Additional Details of Experiment 2.1

Two agents' individual state numbers s_1 and s_2 are mapped into a single integer S (joint state) by the mapping function:

$$S = (s_2 - 1) \times n + s_1 \tag{2.A.1}$$

for $n \times n$ grid map. For three and four agents, the mapping functions are given by (2.A.2) and (2.A.3), respectively, where s_3 and s_4 are the state of third and fourth agents, respectively.

$$S = (s_3 - 1) \times n^2 + (s_2 - 1) \times n + s_1, \tag{2.A.2}$$

$$S = (s_4 - 1) \times n^3 + (s_3 - 1) \times n^2 + (s_2 - 1) \times n + s_1. \tag{2.A.3}$$

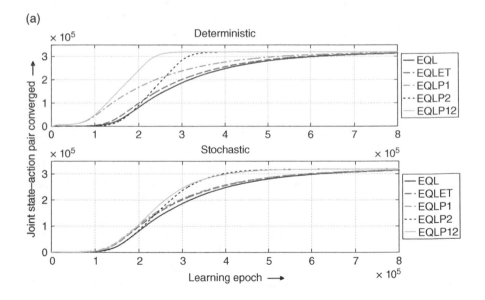

Figure 2.A.1   Convergence plot of FCMQL and reference algorithms for two agents. (a) EQLP12 and reference algorithms for two agents. (b) UQLP12 and reference algorithms for two agents. (c) RQLP12 and reference algorithms for two agents. (d) LQLP12 and reference algorithms for two agents.

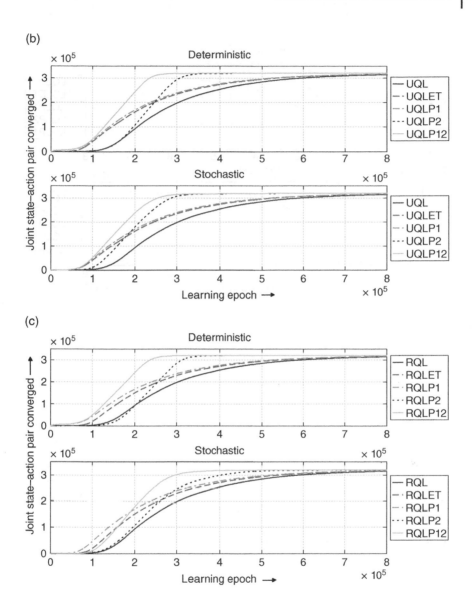

Figure 2.A.1 (Continued)

(d)

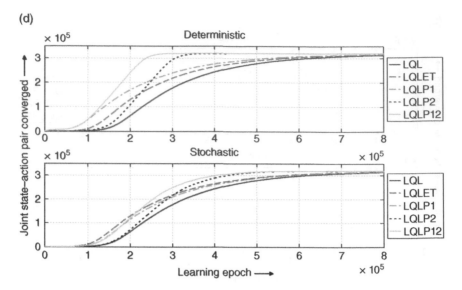

Figure 2.A.1 (Continued)

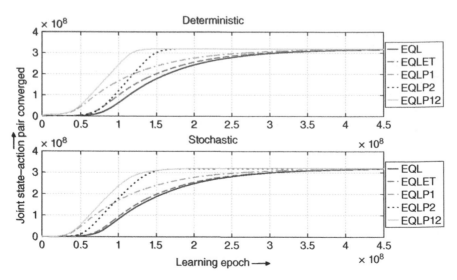

Figure 2.A.2 Convergence plot of EQLP12 and reference algorithms for three agents.

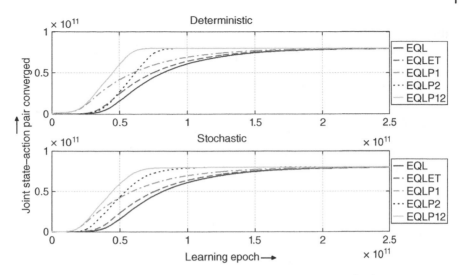

Figure 2.A.3 Convergence plot of EQLP12 and reference algorithms for four agents.

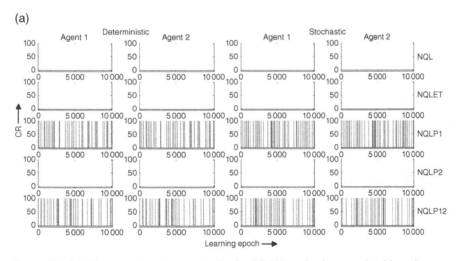

Figure 2.A.4 CR versus learning epoch plot for FCMQL and reference algorithms for two agents. (a) NQLP12 and reference algorithms for two agents. (b) EQLP12 and reference algorithms for two agents. (c) UQLP12 and reference algorithms for two agents. (d) RQLP12 and reference algorithms for two agents. (e) LQLP12 and reference algorithms for two agents. (f) FMRQP12 and reference algorithms for two agents.

(b)

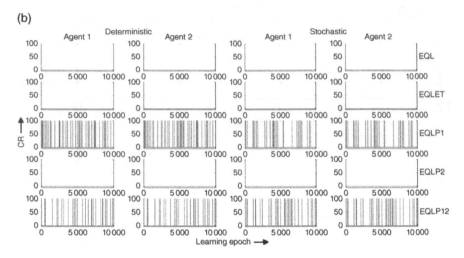

(c)

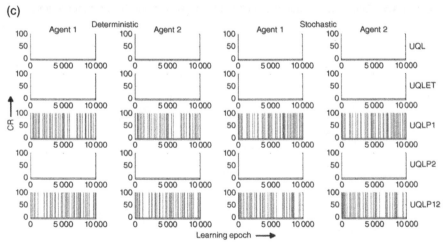

Figure 2.A.4 (Continued)

(d)

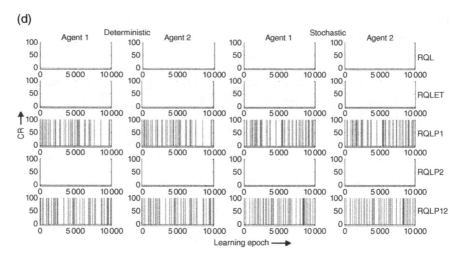

(e)

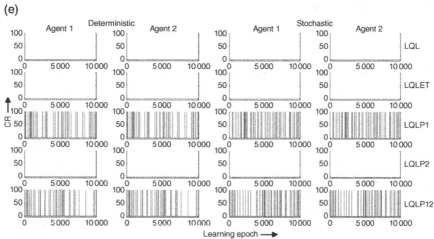

Figure 2.A.4 (Continued)

(f)

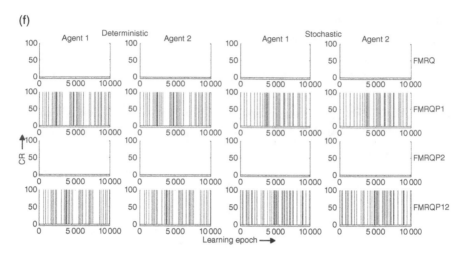

Figure 2.A.4 (Continued)

(a)

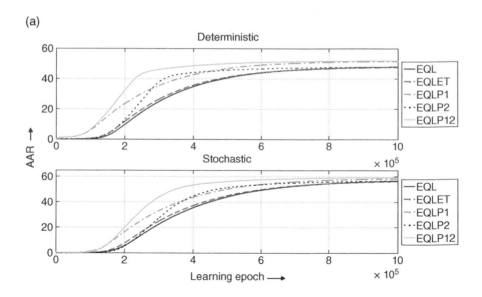

Figure 2.A.5 Average of average reward (AAR) plot of FCMQL and reference algorithms for two agents. (a) EQLP12 and reference algorithms for two agents. (b) UQLP12 and reference algorithms for two agents. (c) RQLP12 and reference algorithms for two agents. (d) LQLP12 and reference algorithms for two agents. (e) FMRQP12 and reference algorithms for two agents.

(b)

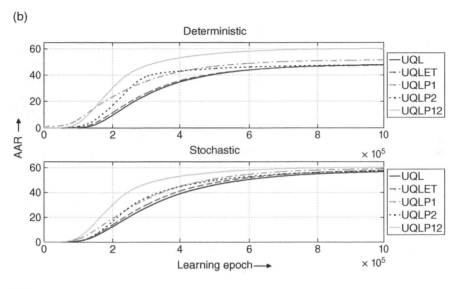

(c)

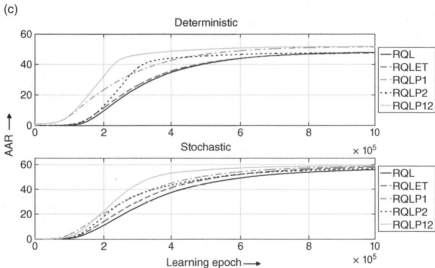

Figure 2.A.5 (Continued)

(d)

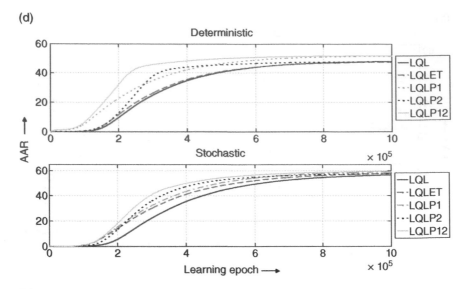

(e)

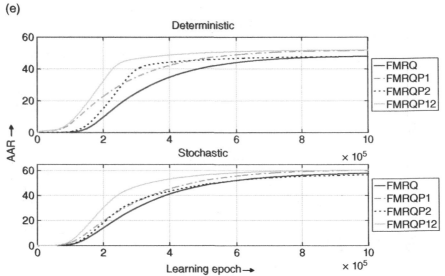

Figure 2.A.5 (Continued)

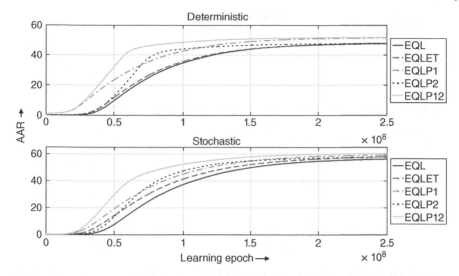

Figure 2.A.6 Average of average reward (AAR) plot of EQLP12 and reference algorithms for three agents.

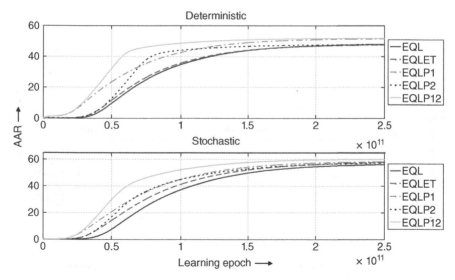

Figure 2.A.7 Average of average reward (AAR) plot of EQLP12 and reference algorithms for four agents.

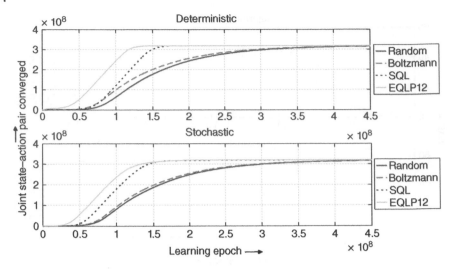

Figure 2.A.8 Joint action selection strategy in EQLP12 and reference algorithms for three agents.

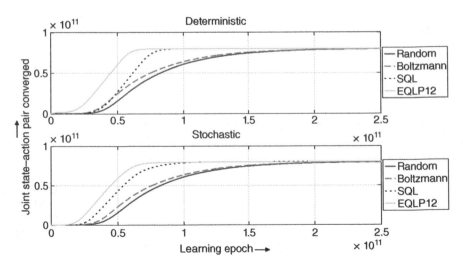

Figure 2.A.9 Joint action selection strategy in EQLP12 and reference algorithms for four agents.

Table 2.A.1 Number of joint state–action pair converged in deterministic situation for two agents.

	Number of joint state–action pair has been converged within								
	10^5 epochs in map			15×10^4 epochs in map			10^6 epochs in map		
Algorithms	**1**	**2**	**3**	**1**	**2**	**3**	**1**	**2**	**3**
NQL	2 976	2 965	2 979	30 060	30 057	30 061	318 314	318 312	318 317
NQLET	12 365	12 367	12 366	74 299	74 302	74 298	318 723	318 725	318 724
NQLP1	47 566	47 567	47 568	115 164	115 168	115 167	318 878	318 879	318 877
NQLP2	2 600	2 602	2 599	31 522	31 524	31 521	**319 968**	**319 968**	**319 968**
NQLP12	**48 846**	**48 847**	**48 844**	**142 010**	**142 011**	**142 014**	**319 968**	**319 968**	**319 968**
UQL	2 732	2 734	2 733	27 824	27 826	27 823	318 296	318 299	318 297
UQLET	40 726	40 727	40 729	105 388	105 387	105 390	318 795	318 798	318 799
UQLP1	45 834	45 833	45 836	113 614	113 615	113 618	318 858	318 861	318 860
UQLP2	2 910	2 909	2 912	27 140	27 141	27 143	**319 968**	**319 968**	**319 968**
UQLP12	**50 934**	**50 932**	**50 935**	**319 968**	**319 968**	**319 968**	**319 968**	**319 968**	**319 968**
EQL	2 388	2 390	2 389	20 834	20 835	20 834	318 230	318 229	318 228
EQLET	3 582	3 580	3 581	32 630	32 630	32 632	318 342	318 340	318 341
EQLP1	43 518	43 517	43 516	111 101	111 102	111 100	318 863	318 861	318 862
EQLP2	894	896	894	16 092	16 093	16 091	**319 968**	**319 968**	**319 968**
EQLP12	**48 524**	**48 526**	**48 525**	**141 596**	**141 597**	**141 599**	**319 968**	**319 968**	**319 968**
RQL	2 732	2 732	2 733	27 824	27 826	27 824	318 299	318 298	318 300
RQLET	19 648	19 649	19 648	88 577	88 575	88 576	318 667	318 668	318 666
RQLP1	43 256	43 254	43 255	110 322	110 321	110 323	318 954	318 955	318 953
RQLP2	1 096	1 097	1 098	16 820	16 821	16 822	**319 968**	**319 968**	**319 968**
RQLP12	**48 748**	**48 748**	**48 749**	**142 642**	**142 641**	**142 642**	**319 968**	**319 968**	**319 968**
LQL	1 377	1 379	1 378	14 067	14 067	14 068	317 953	317 954	317 955
LQLET	10 019	10 020	10 018	62 028	62 027	62 029	318 502	318 503	318 501
LQLP1	46 126	46 125	46 127	113 724	113 725	113 726	318 786	318 786	318 786
LQLP2	2 910	2 911	2 912	27 140	27 141	27 143	**319 968**	**319 968**	**319 968**
LQLP12	**47 954**	**47 955**	**47 954**	**140 408**	**140 408**	**140 410**	**319 968**	**319 968**	**319 968**

The bold values' corresponding algorithm is outperforming the reference algorithms.

Table 2.A.2 Number of joint state–action pair converged in stochastic situation for two agents.

	Number of joint state–action pair has been converged within								
	10^5 epochs in map			15×10^4 epochs in map			10^6 epochs in map		
Algorithms	4	5	6	4	5	6	4	5	6
NQL	12 365	12 366	12 363	74 299	74 302	74 301	318 723	318 724	318 723
NQLET	2 976	2 978	2 977	30 060	30 062	30 061	318 314	318 313	318 315
NQLP1	42 371	42 372	42 373	111 814	111 817	111 816	318 823	318 823	318 825
NQLP2	**11 472**	**11 471**	**11 475**	**82 937**	**82 939**	**82 938**	**319 937**	**319 938**	**319 939**
NQLP12	**54 705**	**54 708**	**54 706**	**147 816**	**147 815**	**147 818**	**319 948**	**319 951**	**319 950**
UQL	40 726	40 727	40 728	105 388	105 386	105 389	318 795	318 796	318 798
UQLET	2 732	2 733	2 735	27 824	27 827	27 826	318 296	318 295	318 299
UQLP1	45 768	45 765	45 769	113 985	113 986	113 987	318 822	318 824	318 821
UQLP2	**10 877**	**10 876**	**10 879**	**84 040**	**84 042**	**84 039**	**319 896**	**319 900**	**319 899**
UQLP12	**51 191**	**51 193**	**51 196**	**146 529**	**146 531**	**146 532**	**319 893**	**319 895**	**319 896**
EQL	2 388	2 390	2 387	20 834	20 833	20 836	318 228	318 230	318 231
EQLET	3 582	3 581	3 583	32 630	3 263	32 634	318 342	318 341	318 342
EQLP1	4 928	4 927	4 929	36 492	36 493	36 494	318 438	318 440	318 439
EQLP2	**1 738**	**1 740**	**1 739**	**20 824**	**20 823**	**20 825**	**319 810**	**319 812**	**319 811**
EQLP12	**3 759**	**3 761**	**3 760**	**34 658**	**34 660**	**34 661**	**319 803**	**319 806**	**319 804**
RQL	2 732	2 733	2 731	27 824	27 825	27 823	318 298	318 302	318 299
RQLET	19 648	19 647	19 649	88 575	88 577	88 576	318 667	318 669	318 668
RQLP1	45 653	45 654	45 655	113 840	113 839	113 842	318 820	318 819	318 822
RQLP2	**10 751**	**10 750**	**10 749**	**83 343**	**83 341**	**83 344**	**319 882**	**319 883**	**319 881**
RQLP12	**3 759**	**3 760**	**3 761**	**34 658**	**34 657**	**34 659**	**319 803**	**319 802**	**319 804**
LQL	1377	1379	1378	14 067	14 068	14 066	317 953	317 952	317 954
LQLET	10 018	10 020	10 019	62 028	62 027	62 029	318 502	318 501	318 504
LQLP1	6 362	6 364	6 363	46 961	46 960	46 963	318 486	318 485	318 487
LQLP2	**1 042**	**1 040**	**1 043**	**16 178**	**16 180**	**16 179**	**319 766**	**319 765**	**319 764**
LQLP12	**5 721**	**5 720**	**5 722**	**44 249**	**44 249**	**44 250**	**319 783**	**319 784**	**319 782**

The bold values' corresponding algorithm is outperforming the reference algorithms.

Table 2.A.3 Count of team-goal explored in the deterministic situation for two agents within.

Algorithms	15 000 epochs map			10 000 epochs map			5 000 epochs map		
	1	2	3	1	2	3	1	2	3
NQL	0	1	0	0	0	0	0	0	0
NQLET	1	0	0	0	0	0	0	0	0
NQLP1	55	65	70	37	38	41	16	20	27
NQLP2	0	1	1	0	0	0	0	0	0
NQLP12	57	66	68	38	39	40	18	22	26
UQL	1	1	0	0	0	0	0	0	0
UQLET	0	1	1	0	0	0	0	0	0
UQLP1	56	68	69	37	38	41	21	23	27
UQLP2	1	0	1	0	0	0	0	0	0
UQLP12	55	65	67	38	39	39	23	25	26
EQL	0	1	0	0	0	0	0	0	0
EQLET	1	0	2	0	0	0	0	0	0
EQLP1	57	69	70	38	39	41	18	23	25
EQLP2	1	2	0	0	0	0	0	0	0
EQLP12	56	62	68	38	39	40	20	22	26
RQL	1	0	1	0	0	0	0	0	0
RQLET	0	1	0	0	0	0	0	0	0
RQLP1	56	68	69	37	38	41	21	23	27
RQLP2	0	1	1	0	0	0	0	0	0
RQLP12	57	63	69	38	39	40	19	21	25
LQL	0	2	1	0	0	0	0	0	0
LQLET	1	0	1	0	0	0	0	0	0
LQLP1	55	62	68	37	38	40	20	24	27
LQLP2	1	0	1	0	0	0	0	0	0
LQLP12	56	61	68	38	39	41	22	23	26
FMRQ	0	1	0	0	0	0	0	0	0
FMRQP1	60	65	70	37	38	41	21	26	27
FMRQP2	2	1	0	0	0	0	0	0	0
FMQRP12	56	61	68	38	39	41	23	24	26

The bold values' corresponding algorithm is outperforming the reference algorithms.

Table 2.A.4 Count of team-goal explored in the stochastic situation for two agents within.

Algorithms	15 000 epochs map			10 000 epochs map			5 000 epochs map		
	4	5	6	4	5	6	4	5	6
NQL	1	0	0	0	0	0	0	0	0
NQLET	0	2	1	0	0	0	0	0	0
NQLP1	55	59	66	35	38	41	12	18	28
NQLP2	0	1	0	0	0	0	0	0	0
NQLP12	56	59	65	36	37	40	16	19	26
UQL	0	1	1	0	0	0	0	0	0
UQLET	1	0	0	0	0	0	0	0	0
UQLP1	57	58	63	37	38	41	18	22	25
UQLP2	0	1	1	0	0	0	0	0	0
UQLP12	55	57	65	36	39	40	15	21	27
EQL	0	2	1	0	0	0	0	0	0
EQLET	1	0	0	0	0	0	0	0	0
EQLP1	57	58	65	37	39	41	16	23	27
EQLP2	0	0	1	0	0	0	0	0	0
EQLP12	56	58	64	35	37	40	19	20	26
RQL	0	1	0	0	0	0	0	0	0
RQLET	1	0	2	0	0	0	0	0	0
RQLP1	55	59	65	34	37	39	21	22	25
RQLP2	0	2	1	0	0	0	0	0	0
RQLP12	56	58	65	35	39	41	17	21	26
LQL	0	2	1	0	0	0	0	0	0
LQLET	1	1	0	0	0	0	0	0	0
LQLP1	57	58	65	36	37	40	16	19	25
LQLP2	0	1	0	0	0	0	0	0	0
LQLP12	55	58	66	35	37	41	21	23	27
FMRQ	2	0	1	0	0	0	0	0	0
FMRQP1	56	58	64	37	38	40	18	22	26
FMRQP2	1	0	1	0	0	0	0	0	0
FMQRP12	56	57	65	35	38	41	21	24	26

The bold values' corresponding algorithm is outperforming the reference algorithms.

2.A.2 Additional Details of Experiment 2.2

(a) (b)

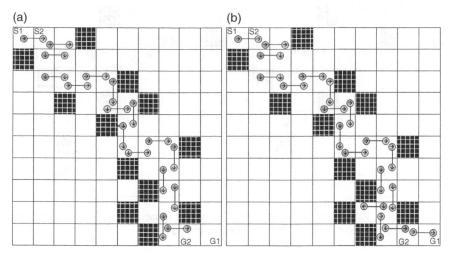

Figure 2.A.10 Path planning with stick in deterministic situation by: (a) NQIMP algorithm and (b) NQLP12-based cooperative multi-agent planning.

(a) (b)

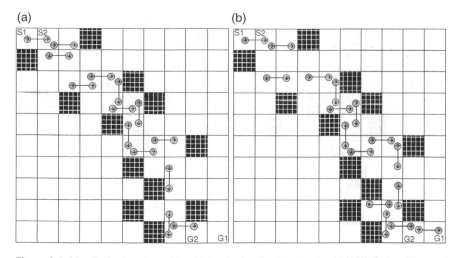

Figure 2.A.11 Path planning with stick in stochastic situation by: (a) NQIMP algorithm and (b) NQLP12-based cooperative multi-agent planning.

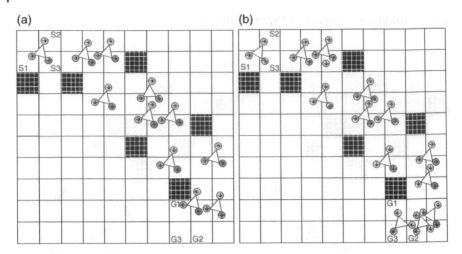

Figure 2.A.12 Path planning with triangle in stochastic situation by: (a) NQIMP algorithm and (b) NQLP12-based cooperative multi-agent planning.

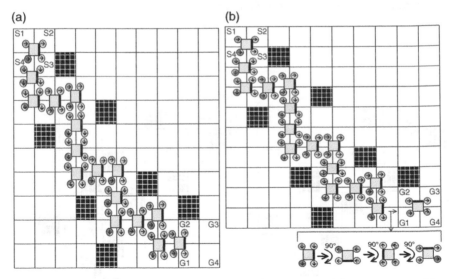

Figure 2.A.13 Path planning with square in stochastic situation by: (a) NQIMP algorithm and (b) NQLP12-based cooperative multi-agent planning.

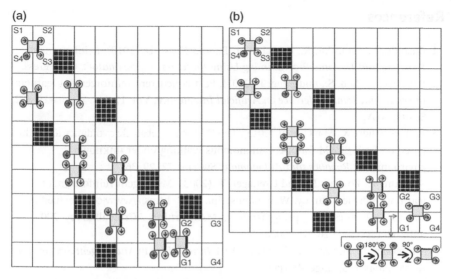

Figure 2.A.14 Path planning with square in deterministic situation by: (a) NQIMP algorithm and (b) NQLP12-based cooperative multi-agent planning.

2.A.3 Additional Details of Experiment 2.4

Details of Khepera-II mobile robot: Khepera-II is a miniature robot [64, 65], equipped with an onboard Microcontroller (Motorola 68331), and includes a flash memory of 512 KB and clock speed of 25 MHz, having 8 inbuilt infrared proximity sensors. 1 unit speed of Khepera II mobile robot is 0.08 mm/10 ms. Selected speeds in this experiment are 2 unit (0.16 mm/10 ms), 3 unit (0.24 mm/10 ms), and 5 unit (0.4 mm/10 ms). Considering one grid length of 80 mm (square grid), theoretically time taken by an agent to cover one grid length, with 2, 3, and 5 unit speed are 500, 333.33, and 200 ms, respectively [64, 65]. Assuming a circle of 40 mm radius inside each grid, Khepera-II has to cover 20π mm of the total circumference of the circle for 90° rotation. Therefore, theoretically time taken by an agent for one 90° rotation with 2, 3, and 5 unit speed are 392.7, 261.8, and 157 ms, respectively.

The stick-carrying problem has been realized in Figures 2.7 and 2.8 by controlling two Khepera-II mobile robots using pre-learned joint Q-tables. The stick length is one grid width and two robots can carry the stick if they occupy neighborhood cells. Each Khepera-II mobile robots (agents) are connected by wires to two different Pentium IV machines through serial port connections. Agents do not communicate between them while transporting the stick. The next joint states of the robots are determined by evaluating the NE employing the learned joint Q-tables, stored in the attached Pentium IV machine.

References

1 Busoniu, L., Babuska, R., De Schutter, B., and Ernst, D. (2010). *Reinforcement Learning and DynamicProgramming Using Function Approximators.* CRC Press.

2 Banerjee, B., Sen, S., and Peng, J. (2001). Fast concurrent reinforcement learners. *International Joint conference on Artificial Intelligence*, Vol. 17, No. 1, pp. 825–832, Seattle, WA.

3 Wen, S., Chen, X., Ma, C. et al. (2015). The Q-learning obstacle avoidance algorithm based on EKF-SLAM for NAO autonomous walking under unknown environments. *Robotics and Autonomous Systems* 72: 29–36.

4 Shoham, Y., Powers, R., and Grenager, T. (2003). Multiagent reinforcement learning: a critical survey, Web manuscript, 2003. https://www.cc.gatech.edu/classes/AY2009/cs7641_spring/handouts/MALearning_ACriticalSurvey_2003_0516.pdf (accessed 26 May 2020).

5 Srinivasan, D. and Jain, L.C. (eds.) (2010). *Innovations in Multi-agent Systems and Applications-1.* Springer-Verlag.

6 Sutton, R.S. and Barto, A.G. (1998). *Introduction to Reinforcement Learning.* MIT Press.

7 Buşoniu, L., Babuška, R., and De Schutter, B. (2010). Multi-agent reinforcement learning: an overview. In: *Innovations in Multi-Agent Systems and Applications-1* (ed. D. Srinivasan), 183–221. Springer.

8 Mitchell, T. (1997). *Machine Learning.* McGraw-Hill.

9 Sommer, N. and Ralescu, A. (2014). Developing a machine learning approach to controlling musical synthesizer parameters in real-time live performance. *Proceedings of the 25th Modern Artificial Intelligence and Cognitive Science Conference 2014, Spokane, Washington, USA, April 26, 2014* 1144: 61–67.

10 Dean, T., Allen, J., and Aloimonos, Y. (1995). *Artificial Intelligence: Theory and Practice.* Boston, MA: Addison-Wesley Publishing Company.

11 Pashenkova, E., Rish, I., and Dechter, R. (1996). Value iteration and policy iteration algorithms for Markov decision problem. *AAAI 96: Workshop on Structural Issues in Planning and Temporal Reasoning*, Portland, Oregon (5 August 1996).

12 Boutilier, C. (1999). Sequential optimality and coordination in multiagent systems. *Proceedings of the International Joint Conference on Artificial Intelligence*, Stockholm, Sweden (31 July to 6 August 1999), pp. 478–485. Vancouver, Canada: University of British Columbia.

13 Feinberg, E.A. (2010). Total expected discounted reward MDPS: existence of optimal policies. In: *Wiley Encyclopedia of Operations Research and Management Science* (eds. J.J. Cochran, L.A. Cox Jr., P. Keskinocak, et al.), 1–11. New York: State University of New York.

14 Kondo, T. and Ito, L. (2004). A reinforcement learning with evolutionary state recruitment strategy for autonomous mobile robots control. *Robotics and Autonomous Systems* 46 (2): 111–124.

15 Kaelbling, L.P., Littman, M.L., and Moore, A.W. (1996). Reinforcement learning: a survey. *Journal of Artificial Intelligence Research* 4: 237–285.

16 Von Neumann, J. and Morgenstern, O. (2007). *Theory of Games and Economic Behavior*, 60th Anniversary Commemorative Edition. Princeton University Press.

17 Sharma, R. and Gopal, M. (2010). Synergizing reinforcement learning and game theory-a new direction for control. *Applied Soft Computing* 10 (3): 675–688.

18 Wang, Y. and de Silva, C.W. (2008). A machine-learning approach to multi-robot coordination. *Engineering Applications of Artificial Intelligence* 21 (3): 470–484.

19 Cao, X.R. and Chen, H.-F. (1997). Perturbation realization, potentials, and sensitivity analysis of Markov processes. *IEEE Transactions on Automatic Control* 42 (10): 1382–1393.

20 Watkins, C.J. and Dayan, P. (1992). Q-learning. *Machine Learning* 8 (3–4): 279–292.

21 Bellman, R.E. (1957). Dynamic programming. *Proceedings of the National Academy of Science of the United States of America* 42 (10): 34–37.

22 Hu, Y., Gao, Y., and An, B. (2015). Multiagent reinforcement learning with unshared value functions. *IEEE Transactions on Cybernetics* 45 (4): 647–662.

23 Boutilier, C. (1996). Planning, learning and coordination in multiagent decision processes. *Proceedings of the 6th Conference on Theoretical Aspects of Rationality and Knowledge*, De Zeeuwse Stromen, The Netherlands (17–20 March 1996), pp. 195–210. Groningen, Netherlands: Morgan Kaufmann Publishers Inc.

24 Claus, C. and Boutilier, C. (1998). The dynamics of reinforcement learning in cooperative multiagent systems. *AAAI/IAAI*, Madison, WI (27–29 July 1998), pp. 746–752.

25 Georgios, C. and Boutilier, C. (2003). Coordination in multiagent reinforcement learning: a bayesian approach. *Proceedings of the Second International Joint Conference on Autonomous Agents and Multiagent Systems*, Melbourne, Australia (14–18 July 2003), pp. 709–716. ACM.

26 Greenwald, A., Hall, K., and Serrano, R. (2003). Correlated Q-learning. *International Conference on Machine Learning* 3: 242–249, Washington, DC.

27 Hu, J. and Wellman, M.P. (2003). Nash Q-learning for general-sum stochastic games. *The Journal of Machine Learning Research* 4: 1039–1069.

28 Hu, J. and Wellman, M.P. (1998). Multiagent reinforcement learning: theoretical framework and an algorithm. *International Conference on Machine Learning*, Madison, WI (24–27 July 1998), pp. 242–250.

29 Littman, M.L. (1994). Markov games as a framework for multiagent reinforcement learning. *Proceedings of the Eleventh International Conference on Machine Learning* 157: 157–163. Providence, RI: Brown University.

30 Littman, M.L. (2001). Friend-or-foe Q-learning in general-sum games. *International Conference on Machine Learning*, Williams College, Williamstown, MA (28 June to 1 July, 2001), pp. 322–328.

31 Littman, M.L. and Szepesvári, C. (1996). A generalized reinforcement learning model: convergence and applications. *International Conference on Machine Learning*, Bari, Italy (3–6 July 1996), pp. 310–318.

32 Mukhopadhyay, S. and Jain, B. (2001). Multi-agent Markov decision processes with limited agent communication. *Proceedings of the 2001 IEEE International Symposium on Intelligent Control, (ISIC'01)*, Mexico City, Mexico (5–7 September, 2001) pp. 7–12.

33 Sen, S., Mahendr, S. and Hale, J. (1994). Learning to coordinate without sharing information. *The Twelfth National Conference on Artificial Intelligence (AAAI-94)*, Seattle, WA (31 July to 4 August 1994), pp. 426–431.

34 Stone, P. and Sutton, R.S. (2001). Scaling reinforcement learning toward RoboCup soccer. *International Conference on Machine Learning*, Williams College, Williamstown, MA (28 June to 1 July 2001), pp. 537–544.

35 Wang, Y., Lang, H., and de Silva, C.W. (2008). Q-learning based multi-robot box-pushing with minimal switching of actions. *International Conference on Automation and Logistics, IEEE*, Qingdao, China (1–3 September 2008), pp. 640–643.

36 Tan, M. (1993). Multi-agent reinforcement learning: independent vs. cooperative agents. *Proceedings of the Tenth International Conference on Machine Learning*, University of Massachusetts, Amherst, MA (27–29 June 1993), Vol. 337.

37 Könönen, V. (2003). Asymmetric multiagent reinforcement learning. *International Conference on Intelligent Agent Technology*, Halifax, NS (13–17 October 2003), pp. 336–342.

38 Lauer, M. and Riedmiller, M. (2000). An algorithm for distributed reinforcement learning in cooperative multi-agent systems. *Proceedings of the Seventeenth International Conference on Machine Learning*, Stanford University, Stanford, CA (29 June to 2 July 2000).

39 Bowling, M. and Veloso, M. (2001). Rational and convergent learning in stochastic games. *International Joint Conference on Artificial Intelligence* 17 (1): 1021–1026. Lawrence Erlbaum Associates Ltd.

40 Bowling, M. (2000). Convergence problems of general-sum multiagent reinforcement learning. *International Conference on Machine Learning*, Stanford University, Stanford, CA (29 June to 2 July 2000), pp. 89–94.

41 Suematsu, N. and Hayashi, A. (2002). A multiagent reinforcement learning algorithm using extended optimal response. *Proceedings of the First International Joint Conference on Autonomous Agents and Multiagent Systems: Part 1*, Montreal, Quebec (13–17 May 2019), pp. 370–377. ACM.

42 Wang, X. and Sandholm, T. (2002). Reinforcement learning to play an optimal Nash equilibrium in team Markov games. *Advances in Neural Information Processing Systems* 15: 1571–1578.

43 Kapetanakis, S. and Kudenko, D. (2002). Reinforcement learning of coordination in cooperative multi-agent systems. *AAAI/IAAI*, Edmonton, Alberta (28 July to 1 August 2002), pp. 326–331.

44 Sadananada, R. (2006). Agent computing and multi-agent systems. *Proceedings of the 9th Pacific Rim International Workshop on Multi-Agents, (PRIMA)*, Guilin, China (7–8 August 2006), Vol. 4088.

45 Busoniu, L., Babuska, R., and De Schutter, B. (2008). A comprehensive survey of multiagent reinforcement learning. *IEEE Transactions on Systems, Man, and Cybernetics-Part C: Applications and Reviews* 38 (2): 156–172.

46 Hu, Y., Gao, Y., and An, B. (2015). Accelerating multiagent reinforcement learning by equilibrium transfer. *IEEE Transactions on Cybernetics* 45 (7): 1289–1302.

47 De Hauwere, Y.M., Vrancx, P., and Nowé, A. (2010). Learning multi-agent state space representations. *Proceedings of the 9th International Conference on Autonomous Agents and Multiagent Systems: Volume 1*, Downtown, Toronto (10–14 May 2010), pp. 715–722.

48 Kok, J.R. and Vlassis, N. (2004). Sparse cooperative Q-learning. *Proceedings of the Twenty-First International Conference on Machine Learning*, Louisville, KY (16–18 December 2004), p. 61. ACM.

49 Bianchi, R.A., Martins, M.F., Ribeiro, C.H., and Costa, A.H. (2014). Heuristically-accelerated multiagent reinforcement learning. *IEEE Transactions on Cybernetics* 44 (2): 252–265.

50 Zhang, Z., Zhao, D., Gao, J. et al. (2017). FMRQ-A multiagent reinforcement learning algorithm for fully cooperative tasks. *IEEE Transactions on Cybernetics* 47 (6): 1367–1379.

51 Littman, M.L. (2001). Value-function reinforcement learning in Markov games. *Cognitive Systems Research* 2 (1): 55–66.

52 Wang, Z., Shi, Z., Li, Y., and Tu, J. (2013). The optimization of path planning for multi-robot system using Boltzmann policy based Q-learning algorithm. *International Conference on Robotics and Biomimetics*, Shenzhen, China (12–14 December 2013), pp. 1199–1204.

53 Sadhu, A.K., Rakshit, P., and Konar, A. (2016). A modified imperialist competitive algorithm for multi-robot stick-carrying application. *Robotics and Autonomous Systems* 76: 15–35.

54 Pugh, J. and Martinoli, A. (2006). Multi-robot learning with particle swarm optimization. *Proceedings of the Fifth International Joint Conference on Autonomous Agents and Multiagent Systems*, Hakodate, Japan (8–12 May 2006), pp. 441–448.

55 Pugh, J., Zhang, Y., and Martinoli, A. (2005). Particle swarm optimization for unsupervised robotic learning. *Swarm Intelligence Symposium*, SWIS-CONF-2005-004, Pasadena, CA (8–10 June 2005), pp. 92–99.

56 Price, K.V. (1997). Differential evolution vs. the functions of the 2nd ICEO. *IEEE Proceedings of International Conference Evolutionary Computing*, Indianapolis (13–16 April 1997), pp. 153–157.

57 Rakshit, P., Konar, A., Bhowmik, P. et al. (2013). Realization of an adaptive memetic algorithm using differential evolution and Q-learning: a case study in multirobot path planning. *IEEE Transactions on Systems, Man, and Cybernetics: Systems* 3 (4): 814–831.

58 Martins, M.F. and Demiris, Y. (2010). Learning multirobot joint action plans from simultaneous task execution demonstrations. *Proceedings of the 9th International Conference on Autonomous Agents and Multiagent Systems: Volume 1*, Downtown, Toronto (10–14 May 2010), pp. 931–938.

59 Osborne, M.J. (2004). *An Introduction to Game Theory*, vol. 3(3). New York: Oxford University Press.

60 Nash, J. (1951). Non-cooperative games. *Annals of Mathematics* 54 (2): 286–295.

61 Cottle, R.W., Pang, J.S., and Stone, R.E. (1992). *The Linear Complementarity Problem*, vol. 60. Society for Industrial and Applied Mathematics.

62 Porter, R., Nudelman, E., and Shoham, Y.. (2008). Simple search methods for finding a Nash equilibrium. Games and Economic Behavior 63(2), pp. 642–662.

63 Sadhu, A.K., and Konar, A. (2017). Improving the speed of convergence of multi-agent Q-learning for cooperative task-planning by a robot-team. *Robotics and Autonomous Systems* 92, pp. 66–80.

64 Franzi, E. (1998). *Khepera BIOS 5.0 Reference Manual*. Lausanne: K-Team, SA.

65 K. U. M. Version (1999). *Khepera User Manual 5.02*. Lausanne: K-Team, SA.

3

Consensus Q-Learning for Multi-agent Cooperative Planning

Multi-robot cooperation entails planning by multiple robots for a common objective, where each robot/agent actuates upon the environment based on the sensory information received from the environment. Multi-robot cooperation employing equilibrium-based reinforcement learning is optimal in the sense of system resource (time and/or energy) utilization, because of the prior adaption of the environment by the robots. Unfortunately, robots cannot enjoy such benefit of reinforcement learning in the presence of multiple types of equilibria (here, Nash equilibrium or correlated equilibrium). In the above perspective, robots need to adapt with a strategy, so that robots can select the optimal equilibrium in each step of the learning. This chapter proposes consensus-based multi-agent Q-learning to address the bottleneck of the optimal equilibrium selection among multiple types. An analysis reveals that a consensus (joint action) is coordination-type pure strategy Nash equilibrium as well as pure strategy correlated equilibrium. The superiority of the proposed consensus-based multi-agent Q-learning algorithm over the traditional reference algorithms in terms of the average reward collection is shown in the experimental section. In addition, the proposed consensus-based planning algorithm is also verified considering multi-robot stick-carrying problem as a benchmark.

3.1 Introduction

Planning [1] refers to the execution of an action sequence, with an aim to achieve a predefined goal by optimally employing the system resource (time and/or energy). An agent (here, robot) can plan individually or in a group. While planning in a group, the agent may be cooperative or competitive toward the remaining group members. In this chapter, only the cooperative robots are considered and analyzed.

Multi-agent Coordination: A Reinforcement Learning Approach, First Edition.
Arup Kumar Sadhu and Amit Konar.
© 2021 The Institute of Electrical and Electronics Engineers, Inc.
Published 2021 by John Wiley & Sons, Inc.

Several techniques are available for planning in the literature, including Graphs [2], Voronoi diagrams [3], potential field [4], adaptive action selection [5], intention inference [6], cooperative conveyance [7], perceptual cues [8], and the like. All these require information about the environment, and thus are unable to function when the information about the environment is absent. Reinforcement Learning (RL) [9–18] fills this void.

RL is the model-free approach and hence it is preferred over other traditional planning approaches. There exist a number of RL algorithms [9–18]. Based on the number of agents involved, RL is of two types: single agent and multi-agent. Multi-Agent Reinforcement Learning (MARL) algorithms are of three types: cooperative, competitive, and mixed [19]. In this chapter, we focus only on cooperative MARL. Among the cooperative MARL algorithms, equilibrium-based MARL is one type [19], where each agent updates its joint Q-value at equilibrium. By equilibrium, an agent attains a balance condition among the agents. In the literature, there are two types of equilibria: Nash equilibrium (NE) [20] and correlated equilibrium (CE) [21]. In Nash Q-learning (NQL) [22, 23] and correlated Q-learning (CQL) [21], agents update Q-values at joint state–action space employing the NE and CE, respectively. As we are dealing only with the cooperative MAQL, so here only the coordination-type NE is considered. It is difficult to find out that which equilibrium (NE or CE) is optimal at a joint state. If agents are instructed to select any one type of equilibrium (either NE or CE) *a priori*, then there is a chance of missing the optimal solution.

To address the above problem, we introduce the concept of consensus [24, 25] in the domain of MARL, from the field of cooperative control [26] and potential games (PGs) [26]. A consensus is a coordination-type pure strategy NE [26]. In this paper, agents are instructed to update Q-values at consensus and proposed a novel consensus Q-learning (CoQL) algorithm. In addition, an analysis reveals that a consensus jointly satisfies the criterion of pure strategy NE as well as pure strategy CE. Experimental result demonstrates the superiority of the proposed CoQL algorithms over the reference algorithms in terms of the average of the average rewards (AAR) earned by the agents. The consensus-based multi-robot cooperative planning algorithm is also proposed and its superiority is shown over the reference algorithms considering path length and torque requirement by the robots as the performance metric. The merits of the chapter are:

1) The problem of selecting the equilibrium type in multi-agent system is addressed by proposing the CoQL algorithm.
2) Agents evaluate consensus (joint action) in each step of learning and planning phases.
3) It is shown by an analysis that a consensus at a joint state is a coordination-type pure strategy NE as well as pure strategy CE.

Table 3.1 List of acronyms.

Full form	Acronyms
Multi-agent Q-learning	MAQL
Nash equilibrium	NE
Nash Q-Learning	NQL
Correlated equilibrium	CE
Correlated Q-learning	CQL
Consensus Q-learning	CoQL
Utilitarian Q-learning	UQL
Egalitarian Q-learning	EQL
Republican Q-learning	RQL
Libertarian Q-learning	LQL

The rest of the chapter is structured as follows. Preliminaries of the Q-learning are given in Section 3.2. Section 3.3 introduces the concept of consensus. Section 3.4 proposes the consensus-based Q-learning and planning. Section 3.5 includes experiments and results. The conclusions are listed in Section 3.6. The list of acronyms are listed in Table 3.1.

3.2 Preliminaries

In RL, the learner works on the principle of reward/penalty received from the environment. Q-learning is an example of RL. This section briefly introduces the adaption mechanism of single agent Q-learning [27] and the state-of-the-art equilibrium-based multi-agent Q-learning (MAQL) algorithms. The state-of-the-art equilibrium-based MAQL includes NQL [22, 23] and the four variants of CQL [21].

3.2.1 Single Agent Q-Learning

The single agent Q-learning is proposed by Watkins and Dayan [27]. The recursive update rule of the single agent Q-learning for an agent, denoted by i, is given by (3.1) [27].

$$Q_i(s_i, a_i) \leftarrow (1 - \alpha)Q_i(s_i, a_i) + \alpha \left[r_i(s_i, a_i) + \gamma \sum_{\forall s_i'} P_i \left[s_i' \mid (s_i, a_i) \right] \max_{a_i'} Q_i \left(s_i', a_i' \right) \right],$$

$$(3.1)$$

where $\alpha \in (0, 1]$ refers to the learning rate, $\gamma \in (0, 1]$ denotes the discounting factor, $r_i(s_i, a_i)$ is the immediate reward received by the agent i because of action $a_i \in \{a_i\}$ at the current state $s_i \in \{s_i\} \cdot Q_i(s_i, a_i)$ refers to the sum of long-term discounted rewards or Q-value of agent i at state s_i because of action $a_i \cdot P_i\left[s_i' \mid (s_i, a_i)\right]$ is the probability of moving to the next state $s_i' \in \{s_i\}$ from current state s_i because of a_i. In the literature of Q-learning, $P_i\left[s_i' \mid (s_i, a_i)\right]$ is well known as the state-transition probability. On completion of the learning, an agent (here, robot) begins to plan. During the planning phase, it selects the action corresponding to the maximum Q-value in the current state, at each step of planning.

3.2.2 Equilibrium-Based Multi-agent Q-Learning

The Q-value adaption mechanism of single agent Q-learning is not applicable for MAQL. As in multi-agent system, each agent learns in a common environment, which results in a dynamic environment. Several attempts have been made to address such multi-agent dynamics [22, 23]. In cooperative MAQL, each agent attempts to maximize its own reward as well as the reward of the team. Such requirement can be attained by achieving a balanced condition among the agents, where no agent has any selfish intention to deviate from the balanced condition. In the literature of cooperative MAQL, the above-mentioned balanced condition is achieved following equilibrium, e.g. NE or CE, where each agent updates its optimal expected future reward at equilibrium. Equilibrium-based cooperative MAQL is one of the interesting learning-based multi-robot planning algorithms, where each robot has inherent capabilities to adapt equilibrium at the current joint state.

In this paper, we are interested only with the pure strategy NE/CE (or joint action). The definitions of pure strategy NE and pure strategy CE are, respectively, given in Definitions 3.1 and 3.2.

Definition 3.1 With m interacting agents' *pure strategy NE* at a joint state $S \in \{S\}$ is a joint action $A_N = \langle a_i^* \rangle_{i=1}^m$, such that no unilateral deviation (selfish deviation of an agent) can occur as long as all the agents follow the same optimal joint action $A_N = \langle a_i^* \rangle_{i=1}^m$ at S.

Assuming $a_i^* \in \{a_i\}$ be the optimal action of agent i at s_i and $A_{-i}^* \subseteq A$ be the optimal joint action profile of all agents except agent i at $S = <s_i>_{i=1}^m$ and $Q_i(S, A)$ be the joint Q-value of agent i at S because of joint action $A \in \{A\}$. Then the condition of pure strategy NE $A_N = \langle a_i^*, A_{-i}^* \rangle$ at S is

$$Q_i(S, A_N) \geq Q_i\left(S, a_i, A_{-i}^*\right), \quad \forall i. \tag{3.2}$$

Definition 3.2 With m interacting agents' *pure strategy CE* at a joint state (S) is the optimal pure strategy profile $A_{CE} = <a_1, a_2, ..., a_m>^*$, if and only if agents follow (3.3).

$$A_{CE} = \underset{A}{\text{argmax}}[\Psi(Q_i(S, A))], \tag{3.3}$$

where [21]

$$\Psi \in \left\{ \underset{\forall i}{\text{Min}}, \underset{\forall i}{\Sigma}, \underset{\forall i}{\text{Max}}, \underset{\forall i}{\Pi} \right\}. \tag{3.4}$$

Here, CE has four variants: Egalitarian equilibrium (EE), Utilitarian equilibrium (UE), Republican equilibrium (RE), and Libertarian equilibrium (LE). One problem of equilibrium-based MAQL is the selection of optimal equilibrium among the multiple types of equilibria. In addition, in the context of multi-robot cooperative planning problem, selection of optimal equilibrium refers to the selection of optimal joint action. In this context, the traditional equilibrium-based MAQL algorithm is given in Algorithm 3.1 [21–23].

Algorithm 3.1   Equilibrium-Based MAQL

Input: Current state s_i, $\forall i$, action set A_i at s_i, $\forall i$, $\alpha \in [0, 1)$ and $\gamma \in [0, 1)$;
Output: Optimal joint Q-value $Q_i^*(S, A)$, $\forall S, \forall A, \forall i$;
Begin
  Initialize: $Q_i(S, A) \leftarrow 0$, $\forall S, \forall A, \forall i$;
  Repeat
    Select an action $a_i \in A_i$, $\forall i$ randomly and execute it;
    Observe immediate rewards $r_i(S, A)$, $\forall i$;
    Evaluate $s_i' \leftarrow \delta_i(s_i, a_i)$, $\forall i$ to obtain $S' = <s_i'>_{i-1}^m$;
    $Q_i(S, A) \leftarrow (1 - \alpha)Q_i(S, A) + \alpha[r_i(S, A) + \gamma \cdot \Psi Q_i(S')]$, $\forall i$
                      and $S \leftarrow S'$; //$\Psi \in \{NE, CE\}$
  Until $Q_i(S, A)$, $\forall S, \forall A, \forall i$ converges;
  $Q_i^*(S, A) \leftarrow Q_i(S, A)$, $\forall S, \forall A, \forall i$;
End.

3.3 Consensus

In this section, the cooperative control problem employing PGs mainly focusing upon the consensus problem is briefly discussed. Here, cooperative control [24–26] refers to a planning problem (e.g. object-transportation) by autonomous agents, satisfying all the necessary constraints. One paradigm of cooperative control problem is the consensus problem with plenty of literature in computer science and in the field of distributed computing [28], where the challenge is to design the objective functions of the autonomous agents at a given joint state due to a joint action to realize the team objective amidst obstacles. Alternatively, the cooperative control problem (consensus problem) can also be deciphered by employing the concept of game-theory. In the context of cooperative control, PG has a big role to play [26]. In PG, agents require the perfect alignment between the team objective/potential function and the individual objective of the agent. A consensus in the PG is guaranteed to converge to a pure strategy NE with a potential function of increasing nature [26]. In Q-learning, individual objective is equivalent to the Q-value. The following definitions are required to understand the later sections of the paper. The definition of consensus is given by utilizing the concept that all the PGs are guaranteed to converge to a pure strategy NE as given in [26].

Definition 3.3 In a m player game, if $S \in \times_{i=1}^{m} S_i$ and $A \in \times_{i=1}^{m} A_i$ indicate the joint state and joint action, respectively, individual objective functions are $\{Q_i : S \times A \rightarrow \mathbb{R}\}_{i=1}^{m}$ and potential function denoted by $\Phi : S \times A \rightarrow \mathbb{R}$ satisfies

$$Q_i\left(S, a_i', A_{-i}\right) - Q_i\left(S, a_i'', A_{-i}\right) = \Phi\left(S, a_i', A_{-i}\right) - \Phi\left(S, a_i'', A_{-i}\right), \quad (3.5)$$

i.e. all players' objective functions are aligned with the potential function, then the game is an *Exact Potential game* (EPG), where $A_{-i} \in \times_{j=1, j \neq i}^{m} A_j$ and $a_i'', a_i' \in A_i$ [26].

Definition 3.4 In a m player game, if $S \in \times_{i=1}^{m} S_i$ and $A \in \times_{i=1}^{m} A_i$ indicate the joint state and joint action, respectively, individual objective functions $\{Q_i : S \times A \rightarrow \mathbb{R}\}_{i=1}^{m}$ and potential function denoted by $\Phi : S \times A \rightarrow \mathbb{R}$ satisfy

$$\left. \begin{array}{c} Q_i\left(S, a_i', A_{-i}\right) > Q_i\left(S, a_i'', A_{-i}\right) \\ \Phi\left(S, a_i', A_{-i}\right) > \Phi\left(S, a_i'', A_{-i}\right) \end{array} \right\}, \quad (3.6)$$

i.e. at least one player's objective function is aligned with the potential function, then the game is *weakly acyclic game* (WAG), where $A_{-i} \in \times_{j=1, j \neq i}^{m} A_j$ and $a_i'', a_i' \in A_i$ [26].

Definition 3.5 A *consensus* is a joint action $A^* = \langle a_i^*, A_{-i}^* \rangle \in \{A\}$ at a given joint state $S \in \{S\}$, which jointly maximizes the individual objective function $Q_i(S, a_i, A_{-i}), \forall A, \forall i$ or $Q_i\left(S, a_i^*, A_{-i}^*\right) \geq Q_i(S, a_i, A_{-i}), \forall A, \forall i$ and the potential function $\Phi(S, A)$ or $\Phi(S, A^*) \geq \Phi(S, A), \forall A$ [26].

3.4 Proposed CoQL and Planning

In the section, we proposed a novel CoQL. Subsequently, a consensus-based multi-robot cooperative planning algorithm is proposed.

3.4.1 Consensus Q-Learning

An example is given in Figure 3.1 to understand the importance of consensus in multi-robot cooperative planning. Let at a given joint state two robots 1 and 2 are synchronously cooperating with the action set, respectively, $A_1 = \{a, b\}$ and $A_2 = \{x, y\}$ having no communication among the robots. The reward matrices in two different joint states are given in Figure 3.1a and b. In Figure 3.1a, suppose, robots plan following the CE (UE) and then they have two solutions ax and by to cooperate by (3.3). In such situation, in the absence of communication among the robots, they cannot select one joint action to cooperate. But if they evaluate coordination-type NE (cooperative NE) by (3.2) and select the joint action ax, then the above problem can be addressed. However, Figure 3.1b contains two coordination-type NEs (ax and by) by (3.2) and again the same problem arises. Here, robots can go for evaluating the CE (UE or EE) by (3.3) and select joint action ax to cooperate.

It is interesting to note that both the robots receive maximum reward for the joint action, which satisfies the criterion of coordination-type NE (or pure strategy NE for brevity) and pure strategy CE jointly. Motivated by this observation, we are interested to find such an equilibrium, which is a pure strategy NE as well as pure strategy CE. To achieve this, we borrow the concept of consensus from PGs, which by definition is a pure strategy NE. In this paper, by a Theorem 3.1 we have shown that a consensus is also a pure strategy CE.

Theorem 3.1 In a PG, if $A^* = \langle a_i^*, A_{-i}^* \rangle \in \{A\}$ is a consensus point (joint action) at a given joint state $S \in \{S\}$, then at joint state S a consensus (A^*) is a pure strategy NE, A_N as well as a pure strategy CE, A_{CE}. Assuming there exist at least one coordination-type pure strategy NE.

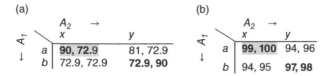

(a)

A_1 ↓ \ A_2 →	x	y
a	**90, 72.9**	81, 72.9
b	72.9, 72.9	**72.9, 90**

(b)

A_1 ↓ \ A_2 →	x	y
a	**99, 100**	94, 96
b	94, 95	**97, 98**

Figure 3.1 Equilibrium selection in multi-agent system. (a) Two UE (ax and by) and one NE (ax). (b) Two NE (ax and by) and one UE or EE (ax).

Proof

Since A^* is a consensus point, by Definition 3.5, we have:

$$Q_i\left(S, a_i^*, A_{-i}^*\right) \geq Q_i(S, a_i, A_{-i}), \quad \forall A, \quad \forall i$$

$$\Rightarrow Q_i\left(S, a_i^*, A_{-i}^*\right) \geq Q_i\left(S, a_i, A_{-i}^*\right), \quad \forall i. \quad (\because \langle a_i, A_{-i}^*\rangle \in \{A\}) \qquad (3.7)$$

$$\Rightarrow Q_i(S, A^*) \geq Q_i\left(S, a_i, A_{-i}^*\right), \quad \forall i. \qquad (\because \langle a_i^*, A_{-i}^*\rangle = A^*)$$

By (3.7) and Definition 3.1 we can say that

$$A^* = A_N \qquad (3.8)$$

at S. Again by Definition 3.5 at consensus, the inequality (3.9) holds.

$$\Phi(S, A^*) \geq \Phi(S, A), \quad \forall A. \qquad (3.9)$$

Now, by Definition 3.3 all players' objective functions are aligned with the potential function in an EPG and by Definition 3.4 in WAG, at least one agent's objective function is aligned with the potential function and hence $\Phi(S, A)$ is assumed as in (3.10).

$$\Phi(S, A) = \Omega[Q_i(S, A)], \qquad (3.10)$$

where

$$\Omega \in \left\{ \min_{\forall i}, \sum_{\forall i}, \max_{\forall i}, \prod_{\forall i} \right\}. \qquad (3.11)$$

Now, by (3.9),

$$\Phi(S, A^*) \geq \Phi(S, A), \quad \forall A$$

$$\Rightarrow \Omega[Q_i(S, A^*)] \geq \Omega[Q_i(S, A)], \quad \forall A \quad \left[\text{by (3.10) and } \Omega \in \left\{ \min_{\forall i}, \sum_{\forall i}, \max_{\forall i}, \prod_{\forall i} \right\}\right]$$

$$\Rightarrow \Omega[Q_i(S, A^*)] = \max_A [\Omega[Q_i(S, A)]]$$

$$\Rightarrow Q_j(S, A^*) = \max_A [\Omega[Q_i(S, A)]] \quad [\text{Let } \Omega[Q_i(S, A^*)] = Q_j(S, A^*), \quad j \in [1, m]]$$

$$\Rightarrow \arg_A[Q_j(S, A^*)] = \underset{A}{\mathrm{argmax}}[\Omega[Q_i(S, A)]]$$

$$\Rightarrow A^* = \underset{A}{\mathrm{argmax}}[\Omega[Q_i(S, A)]]$$

$$\Rightarrow A^* = A_{CE}. \quad [\text{by Definition 3.2}]$$

$$(3.12)$$

Algorithm 3.2   Consensus Q-Learning (CoQL)

Input: Current state s_i, $\forall i$, action set A_i at s_i, $\forall i$, $\alpha \in [0, 1)$ and $\gamma \in [0, 1)$;

Output: Optimal joint Q-value $Q_i^*(S, A)$, $\forall S$, $\forall A$, $\forall i$;

Begin

  Initialize: $Q_i(S, A) \leftarrow 0$, $\forall S$, $\forall A$, $\forall i$;

 Repeat

    Select an action $a_i \in A_i$, $\forall i$ randomly and execute it;

    Observe immediate rewards $r_i(S, A)$, $\forall i$;

    Evaluate $s_i' \leftarrow \delta_i(s_i, a_i)$, $\forall i$ to obtain $S' = <s_i'>_{i=1}^m$;

$$Q_i(S, A) \leftarrow (1-\alpha)\,Q_i(S, A) + \alpha\,[r_i(S, A) + \gamma \cdot \mathrm{Co}Q_i(S')], \forall i \left.\vphantom{\begin{matrix}a\\a\end{matrix}}\right\}$$

    and $S \leftarrow S'$; // Co = NE and CE   //Proposed

 Until $Q_i(S, A)$, $\forall S$, $\forall A$, $\forall i$ converges;

  $Q_i^*(S, A) \leftarrow Q_i(S, A)$, $\forall S$, $\forall A$, $\forall i$;

End.

So, to hold (3.9) in a PG, A^* should be a A_{CE}. Hence, by (3.8) and (3.12), we can say that a consensus A^* at a given joint state S is a A_N as well as A_{CE}.   ☐

So, in the CoQL and planning algorithms, instead of evaluating the pure strategy NE/CE at a joint state, a consensus is evaluated motivated by the cooperative control and PG, as a consensus is a pure strategy NE as well as a pure strategy CE as shown in the proposed Theorem. The proposed CoQL algorithm is given in Algorithm 3.2. The brace in Algorithm 3.2 indicates the difference between Algorithms 3.1 and 3.2.

3.4.2   Consensus-Based Multi-robot Planning

In multi-agent planning phase, each agent evaluates consensus by jointly satisfying (3.2) and (3.3) at a feasible joint state. It may be noted that for multiple consensuses at the given joint state, the consensus which appears first is selected. In this paper, we have considered the well-known stick-carrying problem, where each robot needs to reach its individual goal optimally without violating any constraint. Constraint violation refers to the collision with obstacle or the teammates and falling of stick following Algorithm 3.3. The brace in Algorithm 3.3 indicates the key contribution in the planning algorithm.

Algorithm 3.3   Consensus-Based Planning

Input: Feasible joint starting state S_F, joint goal state S_G and optimal joint Q-value $Q_i^*(S, A)$, $\forall i$;

Output: Consensus or joint action which is a NE as well as CE A_F^* at S_F;

Begin

  While $S_F \neq S_G$ **do Begin**

   For $A \in \{A\}$

   Evaluate consensus by jointly following (3.2) and (3.3) ; $\Big\}$ //Proposed

    If next feasible joint state S_F' satisfies all the constraints;

     Then $A_F^* \leftarrow A$ and $S_F \leftarrow S_F'$; $// S_F'$ is the next joint state

    End If;

   End for;

  End While;

End.

3.5   Experiments and Results

Two experiments are presented in this section. The first experiment is designed to study the relative performance of the CoQL over the reference algorithms, considering average reward collection by the agents as a performance metric. Another experiment is framed to study the relative performance of the consensus-based planning algorithm over the reference algorithms, considering multi-robot stick carrying problem as a benchmark in terms of state-transitions required to complete the task.

3.5.1   Experimental Setup

All the experiments related to learning are performed in ten different 10×10 grid world maps for two and three agents. However, for brevity, multi-robot planning is conducted for two agents only in 5×5 grid world maps. Each agent can execute one among the four possible actions (Left (L), Forward (F), Right (R), and Back (B)) at a state. As an agent reaches its goal state due to an action from a state, it receives maximum immediate reward of 100. Similarly, an agent receives zero (0) immediate reward for a non-goal state-transition. The constraint violation is penalized by a negated immediate reward (here, -1). In addition, to the above parameter setting the learning rate, α, and discounting factor, γ, are set to 0.1 and 0.9, respectively.

3.5.2 Experiments for CoQL

In this experiment, at each state an agent selects its action randomly from its individual action pool. In the next step, the agent updates its own as well as the remaining agents' Q-values at joint state–action space following Algorithm 3.2. AAR as given in (3.13) is considered as a performance metric of the learning algorithms for m number of learning agents.

$$AAR = \left(\sum_{i=1}^{m} \left(\sum_{\forall S} \left(\sum_{\forall A} (Q_i(S,A)) \right) \times \frac{1}{|\{A\}|} \right) \times \frac{1}{|\{S\}|} \right) \times \frac{1}{m}. \quad (3.13)$$

It is apparent from Figure 3.2 that the AAR collected by a team of two agents over the learning epoch (iteration) in CoQL is more than the same offered by the traditional NQL and different variants of CQL (EQL, UQL, RQL, and LQL). Similar experiment is conducted for three agents as shown in Figure 3.3.

3.5.3 Experiments for Consensus-Based Planning

In this experiment, performance of the consensus-based multi-robot cooperative planning algorithm has been tested considering the well-known stick-carrying problem as a benchmark. The stick-carrying problem refers to the transportation of a stick from starting position to the fixed destination optimally without violating any constraint. It is apparent from Figures 3.4 and 3.5 that the planning path offered by the consensus-based multi-agent cooperative planning algorithm is better than the same offered by the traditional learning-based planning path, in terms of the path length and the number of 90° turns. Minimization of the 90° turns

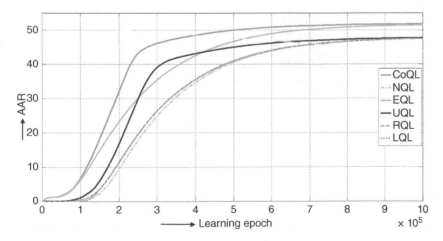

Figure 3.2 AAR versus learning epoch for two-agent system.

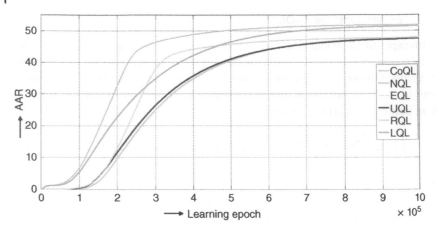

Figure 3.3 AAR versus learning epoch for three-agent system.

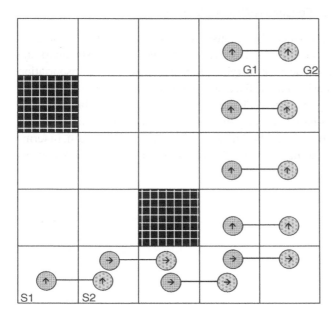

Figure 3.4 Planning path offered by the consensus-based multi-agent planning algorithm.

minimizes the torque requirement by the robots, and hence, saving in the energy consumption. Table 3.2 illustrates the planning performance of the proposed consensus-based planning algorithm over the NQL-based planning algorithm (here, NQL) in terms of the above explained metrics.

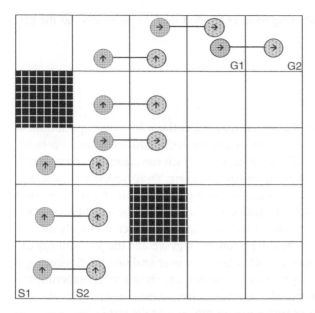

Figure 3.5 Planning path offered by the Nash Q-learning-based planning algorithm.

Table 3.2 Planning performance.

Planning algorithm	Number of state-transitions required		Number of 90° turns required	
	A_1	A_2	A_1	A_2
Consensus-based	7	7	2	2
NQL-based	7	7	3	3

3.6 Conclusions

The chapter proposes a novel CoQL algorithm for multi-robot cooperative planning. The proposed CoQL algorithm addresses the problem of equilibrium selection among different types of equilibria, by evaluating the consensus (joint action) at the current joint state. An analysis reveals that a consensus at a joint state is a pure strategy NE as well as pure strategy CE. The novelty of the CoQL lies in the adaption of the joint Q-values at consensus. The superiority of the proposed CoQL algorithm is verified over the reference algorithms in terms of the AAR earned by the agents against the learning epoch. In addition, consensus-based multi-robot cooperative planning algorithm is proposed and its superiority is verified over reference algorithms considering path length and torque requirement as the performance metrics.

3.7 Summary

In this chapter, it is shown that robots may select the suboptimal equilibrium in the presence of multiple types of equilibria (here, NE or CE). In the above perspective, robots need to adapt with such a strategy, which can select the optimal equilibrium in each step of the learning and the planning. To address the bottleneck of the optimal equilibrium selection among multiple types, this chapter presents a novel CoQL for multi-robot coordination, by extending the equilibrium-based MAQL algorithms. It is also shown that a consensus (joint action) jointly satisfies the conditions of the coordination-type pure strategy NE and the pure strategy CE. The superiority of the proposed CoQL algorithm over traditional reference algorithms in terms of the average reward collection are shown in the experimental section. In addition, the proposed consensus-based planning algorithm is also verified considering multi-robot stick-carrying problem as the test bed.

References

1 LaValle, S.M. (2006). *Planning Algorithms*. Cambridge University Press.
2 Luna, R. and Bekris, K.E. (2011). Efficient and complete centralized multi-robot path planning. *International Conference on Intelligent Robots and Systems (IROS)*, San Francisco, CA (2–30 September 2011), pp. 3268–3275. IEEE/RSJ.
3 Bhattacharya, P. and Gavrilova, M.L. (2008). Roadmap-based path planning: using the Voronoi diagram for a clearance-based shortest path. *IEEE Robotics and Automation Magazine* 15 (2): 58–66.
4 Gayle, R., Moss, W., Lin, M.C., and Manocha, D. (2009). Multi-robot coordination using generalized social potential fields. *IEEE International Conference on Robotics and Automation*, Kobe, Japan (12–17 May 2009), pp. 106–113.
5 Yamada, S. and Saito, J.Y. (2001). Adaptive action selection without explicit communication for multirobot box-pushing. *IEEE Transactions on Systems, Man, and Cybernetics, Part C: Applications and Reviews* 31 (3): 398–404.
6 Sugie, H., Inagaki, Y., Ono, S. et al. (1995). Placing objects with multiple mobile robots-mutual help using intention inference. *IEEE International Conference on Robotics and Automation, Proceedings* 2: 2181–2186.
7 Yamauchi, Y., Ishikawa, S., Uemura, N., and Kato, K. (1993). On cooperative conveyance by two mobile robots. *IEEE International Conference on Industrial*

Electronics, Control, and Instrumentation, Proceedings of the IECON'93, Lahaina, Hawaii (15–18 November 1993), pp. 1478–1481.

8 Kube, C.R. and Zhang, H. (1996). The use of perceptual cues in multi-robot box-pushing. *IEEE International Conference on Robotics and Automation, Proceedings* 3: 2085–2090.

9 Busoniu, L., Babuska, R., De Schutter, B., and Ernst, D. (2010). *Reinforcement Learning and Dynamic Programming Using Function Approximators*. CRC Press.

10 Banerjee, B., Sen, S., and Peng, J. (2001). Fast concurrent reinforcement learners. *International Joint Conference on Artificial Intelligence* 17 (1): 825–832. Seattle, WA.

11 Wen, S., Chen, X., Ma, C. et al. (2015). The Q-learning obstacle avoidance algorithm based on EKF-SLAM for NAO autonomous walking under unknown environments. *Robotics and Autonomous Systems* 72: 29–36.

12 Shoham, Y., Powers, R., and Grenager, T. (2003). Multiagent reinforcement learning: a critical survey, Web manuscript, 2003. https://www.cc.gatech.edu/classes/AY2009/cs7641_spring/handouts/MALearning_ACriticalSurvey_2003_0516.pdf (accessed 27 May 2020).

13 Srinivasan, D. and Jain, L.C. (eds.) (2010). *Innovations in Multi-agent Systems and Applications-1*. Springer-Verlag.

14 Sutton, R.S. and Barto, A.G. (1998). *Introduction to Reinforcement Learning*. MIT Press.

15 Buşoniu, L., Babuška, R., and De Schutter, B. (2010). Multi-agent reinforcement learning: an overview. In: *Innovations in Multi-Agent Systems and Applications-1* (ed. D. Srinivasan), 183–221. Springer.

16 Mitchell, T. (1997). *Machine Learning*. McGraw-Hill.

17 Sommer, N. and Ralescu, A. (2014). Developing a machine learning approach to controlling musical synthesizer parameters in real-time live performance. *Proceedings of the 25th Modern Artificial Intelligence and Cognitive Science Conference*, Spokane, Washington (26 April 2014), pp. 61–67.

18 Dean, T., Allen, J., and Aloimonos, Y. (1995). *Artificial Intelligence: Theory and Practice*. Boston, MA: Addison-Wesley Publishing Company.

19 Busoniu, L., Babuska, R., and De Schutter, B. (2008). A comprehensive survey of multiagent reinforcement learning. *IEEE Transactions on Systems, Man, and Cybernetics-Part C: Applications and Reviews* 38 (2): 156–172.

20 Nash, J. (1951). Non-cooperative games. *Annals of mathematics* 54 (2): 286–295.

21 Greenwald, A. and Hall, K. (2003). Correlated Q-learning. *International Conference on Machine Learning* 3: 242–249. Washington, DC.

22 Hu, J. and Wellman, M.P. (2003). Nash Q-learning for general-sum stochastic games. *The Journal of Machine Learning Research* 4: 1039–1069.

23 Hu, J. and Wellman, M.P. (1998). Multiagent reinforcement learning: theoretical framework and an algorithm. *International Conference on Machine Learning* 98: 242–250.

24 Kashyap, A., Başar, T., and Srikant, R. (2006). Consensus with quantized information updates. *Proceedings of the 45th IEEE Conference on Decision and Control*, San Diego, CA (13–15 December 2006).

25 Olfati-Saber, R., Fax, A., and Murray, R.M. (2007). Consensus and cooperation in networked multi-agent systems. *Proceedings of the IEEE* 95 (1): 215–233.

26 Marden, J.R., Arslan, G., and Shamma, J.S. (2009). Cooperative control and potential games. *IEEE Transactions on Systems, Man, and Cybernetics, Part B: Cybernetics* 39 (6): 1393–1407.

27 Watkins, C.J. and Dayan, P. (1992). Technical note Q-learning. *Machine Learning* 8 (3–4): 279–292.

28 Lynch, N.A. (1997). *Distributed Algorithms*. San Francisco, CA: Morgan Kaufmann.

4

An Efficient Computing of Correlated Equilibrium for Cooperative Q-Learning-Based Multi-Robot Planning

In traditional multi-agent Q-learning-induced planning, we need to evaluate Nash/correlated equilibrium at a given joint state during both learning and planning phases. Determination of such equilibrium being computationally expensive prohibits the planning in real time. This chapter introduces a novel approach to adapt composite rewards of all the agents in one Q-table in joint state–action space during learning, and uses these rewards to compute correlated equilibrium in the planning phase. Two schemes of multi-agent Q-learning have been proposed. If success of only one agent is enough to make the team successful, then Scheme-I is employed. However, if an agent's success is contingent upon other agents and simultaneous success of the agents is mandatory, then Scheme-II is employed. New algorithms for multi-agent learning/planning have been proposed, centering on the said schemes. It is shown that the correlated equilibrium obtained by the proposed algorithms and the traditional correlated Q-learning are identical. In order to restrict the exploration within the feasible joint states, constraint versions of the said algorithms are also proposed. An analysis is included to demonstrate the significant saving of computational time and space by the proposed algorithms. In addition, convergence analysis of the proposed algorithms is done. Experiments have been undertaken to validate the performance of the proposed algorithms in multi-robot planning on both simulated and real platforms.

4.1 Introduction

Reinforcement learning (RL) works on the principle of reward and penalty earned by an agent (robot) [1–8] from the environment. An agent is an autonomous body [9–12] capable of maintaining state-transitions [13, 14] freely in a given

Multi-agent Coordination: A Reinforcement Learning Approach, First Edition.
Arup Kumar Sadhu and Amit Konar.
© 2021 The Institute of Electrical and Electronics Engineers, Inc.
Published 2021 by John Wiley & Sons, Inc.

environment. In RL, an agent learns a policy π to maximize a *value function* $V^{\pi}(s)$ [15], at any environmental state s to achieve its (fixed) goal. Q-learning belongs to the family of RL algorithms. In Q-learning, the agent learns an optimal policy to select the best (optimal) action a at state s to maximize the sum of immediate reward and the value function of the next state s', discounted by a factor $0 \leq \gamma < 1$.

In single agent Q-learning [16, 17], the environment is stationary because the agent earns immediate reward due to its own action on the environment [18, 19]. However, in multi-agent scenario, the immediate reward obtained by an agent depends also on the other agents' actions on the environment, and thus the environment seems to be nonstationary [18–23]. Although the nonstationary behavior of the environment has not yet been modeled directly in multi-agent Q-learning (MAQL), its effect is considered by updating the joint state–action value function of the agents at equilibrium [24].

Several algorithms for MAQL have been proposed for both cooperative and competitive applications [18–34]. Among the equilibrium-based cooperative MAQL algorithms, Nash-Q learning (NQL) [21, 28] and Friend-Q learning (FQL) [23] algorithms need special mention. Both these algorithms allow each agent to optimize its reward (payoff) in joint state–action space, considering fixed strategies (pure or mixed) of all other agents among possible alternatives. Meanwhile, if an agent selects only one action with unity probability, then the agent is said to use a *pure strategy*. A *mixed strategy* is the assignment of a probability distribution over the available actions, indicating a possibility of being selected by an agent [35]. The strategy profile corresponding to Nash equilibrium (NE) [35–38] thus refers to the best joint strategy of all the agents that allow each agent to maximize its payoff, considering fixed strategies of all other agents. Such payoff updating policy offers maximum freedom to an agent to give its best choice. In [22], Greenwald et al. compared the relative performance of NQL and FQL algorithms with Correlated Q-learning (CQL), where the last one is used as the reference. Different variants of CQL exist in the literature based on the definition of Ω-equilibrium [22], where Ω usually takes any one of the four types: Utilitarian (U), Egalitarian (E), Republican (R), and Libertarian (L) by which an agent updates its future reward.

Curse of dimensionality is one of the prohibiting factors of the state-of-the-art equilibrium-based MAQL (NQL and CQL). Such bottleneck increases with the increase in number of learning agents while adapting Q-values in joint state–action space [39–41] by the state-of-the-art update policies. To address the curse of dimensionality in MAQL, Kok and Vlassis proposed the Sparse Cooperative Q-learning [40], where each agent maintains two Q-tables based on the requirement of coordination among the agents at a joint state. Zhang et al. successfully reduced the dimension of Q-tables in NQL, where unlike the traditional NQL, agents store Q-values in joint state–individual action space [41]. To accelerate the convergence of the state-of-the-art equilibrium-based MAQL (NQL and

CQL), Hu et al. introduced the concept of equilibrium transfer [39] by exploiting the previously computed equilibria in different joint states with negligible transfer-loss. However, with the best of our knowledge, there is no equilibrium-based MAQL in the literature, where agents adapt only one joint Q-table to accumulate the rewards of all agents.

The applicability of RL includes finance sector [42], gaming industry [31, 36], robotics [5, 10, 29, 33], and many more. In this chapter, proposed algorithms are tested in the test bed of multi-robot object-transportation problems [43, 44].

The ΩQ-learning (ΩQL) algorithms proposed in this chapter have two attractive features, which are not available in the traditional CQL. First, during the learning phase, an agent needs to adapt only one Q-table in joint state–action space unlike adapting m joint Q-tables for m agents in CQL. Second, the evaluation of the computationally expensive correlated equilibrium (CE) is avoided, following a tricky approach of computing it partially during the learning and the rest during the planning phases. This offers benefits in real-time planning as computation of a CE, which is time-costly, is avoided here by the proposed technique.

Two schemes of ΩQL have been proposed to serve two distinct types of MAQL-based planning applications. Scheme-I ensures the success of the team, if only one agent is successful to serve its goal. This is useful for weakly coupled multi-agent systems, where only one agent is active at a time to serve the fixed goal. For example, in a soccer game, only one person/agent at a time takes the ball ahead, serving its individual as well the team-goal. Scheme-II ensures simultaneous success of all the agents in a tightly coupled multi-agent system, such as long stick/big object carrying by multiple robots. Both the schemes adapt Q-tables in joint state–action space. However, there is a small difference in the adaptation mechanism of Q-values by the two schemes. Scheme-I is used to adapt a Q-table in joint state–action space based on the individual Q-values of the agents and the effect of coordination among the agents, received as feedback from the environment. Scheme-II adapts Q-table in joint state–action space by considering group (Ω) Immediate Reward (ΩIR) as a function of individual immediate rewards plus expected group (Ω) future reward as a function of individual expected future rewards discounted by a factor γ in [0, 1).

Scheme-I and -II have four variants depending on the functional form used to compute the Q-value in joint state–action space. We here use a general nomenclature $\Phi \in \left\{\Sigma_{i=1}^{m}, \mathrm{Min}_{i=1}^{m}, \mathrm{Max}_{i=1}^{m}, \Pi_{i=1}^{m}\right\}$ for a unified treatment of the four variants, for computing Q-values following U, E, R, and L equilibria, respectively.

During the planning phase [45], we obtain one of the four equilibria, depending on the choice of Φ in the preceding learning phases. The planned task is then executed following the obtained equilibrium. Sometimes to execute a plan, we need to satisfy certain constraints that appear naturally from the problem under consideration. For example, in a twin robot cooperation to carry a stick held by the robots at the two end-points of the stick [43], the stick-length is a constraint.

It acts as a constraint in planning as for all possible next positions of the robots, the separating distance should be equal to the stick length. The constraint can be handled at the planning phase but at the cost of extra time to identify feasible next states for the robots. Alternatively, the feasible joint state–actions can be learned during the learning phase, so that equilibrium obtained in the planning phase always falls in the feasible action-space. Here, we emphasized learning only at the feasible joint state–action space to speed up planning.

The main contributions of the chapter are briefly summarized below.

1) Unlike traditional CQL, where CE is evaluated both in learning and planning phases, here we need to compute CE partly in the learning and the rest in the planning phases, thereby requiring CE computation once only when learning-based planning is employed.
2) It has been proved that the CE obtained by the proposed schemes is the same as that obtained by the traditional CQL algorithms.
3) The computational cost to evaluate CE here is much smaller than that obtained by traditional CQL algorithms for the following reasons. Computation of CE in CQL requires consulting m Q-tables in joint state–action space for m agents, whereas in the present context, we use a single Q-table in the joint state–action space for evaluation of CE.
4) Complexity analysis undertaken here confirms the last point. Both time- and space-complexity-wise the proposed algorithms are less expensive than traditional CQL algorithms.
5) Problem-specific constraints are taken care of in the proposed ΩQL to avoid unwanted exploration of the infeasible state-space during the learning phase, thereby saving additional run-time complexity during the planning phase.
6) Experiments are undertaken to validate the proposed concepts in simulated and practical multi-agent robotic platform (here Khepera-environment).

The rest of the chapter is organized as follows. In Section 4.2, an overview of the single agent Q-learning and equilibrium-based MAQL algorithms are given. Proposed cooperative MAQL and corresponding planning algorithms are given in Section 4.3. Section 4.4 offers complexity analysis. Simulation and experimental results are presented in Section 4.5. Conclusions are given in Section 4.6.

4.2   Single-Agent Q-Learning and Equilibrium-Based MAQL

This section discusses the preliminary ideas concisely on single agent Q-learning and equilibrium-based MAQL algorithm for better understanding of the proposed methods.

4.2.1 Single Agent Q-Learning

In 1989, Watkins and Dayan [17] coined the single agent Q-learning, which is one of the most widely used RL techniques. It works by continuously updating an agent's state–action value (Q-value) by a fixed policy and earns a reward (or penalty) from the environment in each step of learning. The Q-learning update rule of an agent i is given in (4.1), assuming $\hat{Q}_i^*\left(s_i'\right)$ to be the expected (indicated by $\hat{}$) optimal (indicated by $*$) Q-value [3, 17] of agent i at next state $s_i' \in S_i$ and the expression of $\hat{Q}_i^*\left(s_i'\right)$ is given in the Appendix 4.A following the traditional representation [15, 21].

$$Q_i(s_i, a_i) \leftarrow (1-\alpha)Q_i(s_i, a_i) + \alpha\left[r_i(s_i, a_i) + \gamma \cdot \hat{Q}_i^*\left(s_i'\right)\right], \tag{4.1}$$

where $Q_i(s_i, a_i)$ and $r_i(s_i, a_i)$ are the Q-value and immediate reward, respectively, at a state $s_i \in S_i$ because of action $a_i \in A_i$ of agent i, $\alpha \in [0, 1)$ be the learning rate, $\gamma \in [0, 1)$ denotes the discounting factor, and $s_i' \leftarrow \delta_i(s_i, a_i)$ indicates the state-transition from state s_i to next state s_i' because of action a_i with state-transition probability $p_i\left(s_i' \mid (s_i, a_i)\right)$ of agent i.

4.2.2 Equilibrium-Based MAQL

Depending upon the type of tasks, MAQL can be classified into three categories: cooperative, competitive, and mixed [11]. Multi-agent cooperative scenario demands formulation of a joint policy, which benefits each agent individually and also the team. The analysis and further enhancement of the cooperative MAQL is carried out in this chapter.

In MAQL algorithm, more specifically in equilibrium-based MAQL, each agent updates Q-values individually in joint state–action space employing one of the following equilibria: NE [28] and CE [22] to update the expected joint Q-value at equilibrium of an agent at the joint next state. CE includes U-equilibrium (UE), E-equilibrium (EE), R-equilibrium (RE), and L-equilibrium (LE) [22].

Suppose in a m agent system, due to joint action $K \in \{K\} = A_1 \times A_2 \times \cdots \times A_m = \times_{i=1}^m A_i$ at joint state $G \in \{G\} = \times_{i=1}^m S_i$, the agent i earns an immediate reward $r_i(G, K)$ and $Q_i(G, K)$ be the Q-value of agent i because of joint action K at joint state G, where $\times$ denotes the Cartesian product. Now, following traditional representation [15, 21] of the expected joint Q-value at a given joint next state, $G' \in \{G\}$ because of mixed strategy Ω-equilibrium,

$$\Omega p^*\left(K' \mid G'\right) = \prod_{i=1}^m p_i^*\left(a_i' \mid s_i'\right), \tag{4.2}$$

for an agent i is given in (4.3),

$$\Omega \hat{Q}_i^* \left(G^{/} \right) = \sum_{\forall G^{/}} p \left(G^{/} \mid (G, K) \right) \sum_{\forall K^{/}} \Omega p^* \left(K^{/} \mid G^{/} \right) Q_i \left(G^{/}, K^{/} \right), \tag{4.3}$$

where

$$p \left(G^{/} \mid (G, K) \right) = \prod_{i=1}^{m} p_i \left(s_i^{/} \mid (s_i, a_i) \right) \tag{4.4}$$

be the joint state-transition probability and $K^{/} \in \{K\}$ be the joint action at joint next state $G^{/}$. The definition of CE is given below.

Definition 4.1 *CE* [22, 46] at a joint state $G = \ < s_i >_{i=1}^{m}$ with m interacting agents is the pure strategy CE, ΩK^* and mixed strategy CE, $\Omega p^*(K)$ if agents follow (4.5) and (4.6), respectively, for $\Omega \in \{U, E, R, L\}$.

$$\Omega K^* = \underset{K}{\mathrm{argmax}}[\Phi(Q_i(G, K))], \tag{4.5}$$

$$\Omega p^*(K) = \underset{\Omega p(K)}{\mathrm{argmax}} \left[\Phi \left[\sum_{K} \Omega p(K)(Q_i(G, K)) \right] \right], \tag{4.6}$$

where $\Phi \in \left\{ \sum_{i=1}^{m}, \underset{i=1}{\overset{m}{\mathrm{Min}}}, \underset{i=1}{\overset{m}{\mathrm{Max}}}, \prod_{i=1}^{m} \right\}$.

The CQL update rule is given in (4.7) [22] following the traditional representation [15, 21].

$$Q_i(G, K) \leftarrow (1 - \alpha)Q_i(G, K) + \alpha \left[r_i(G, K) + \gamma \cdot \Omega \hat{Q}_i^* \left(G^{/} \right) \right]. \tag{4.7}$$

CQL algorithm [22] is given in the supplemental file Appendix 4.A.

4.3 Proposed Cooperative MAQL and Planning

In CQL algorithm, the entries of the Q-tables of m-agents at a given joint state because of a joint action need not necessarily be the same. However, in the present formulation, an attempt is made to solve the CQL algorithm by efficiently employing the $\Omega \in \{U, E, R, L\}$ equilibrium, with the motivation to create single joint Q-table in joint state–action space by considering m Q-tables at individual state–action space and the environmental feedback about possible penalty due to multi-agent coordination at joint state–action space.

After each learning epoch, the results of adaptation of each agent's individual Q-tables are exploited to update the single Q-table in joint state–action space.

Two techniques are proposed, namely Scheme-I and -II, by efficiently employing the $\Omega \in \{U, E, R, L\}$-equilibrium to evaluate the single joint Q-table. To distinguish the nomenclatures of Scheme-I and –II, respectively, - and ~ are placed on the top of each symbol. The basis of proposed schemes with their applicability is provided below.

4.3.1 Proposed Schemes with Their Applicability

The chapter proposes two distinct schemes for addressing two types of situations that may arise during the MAQL-based multi-robot planning. In the first scheme, the success of the team is subject to the success of any one agent. Scheme-I is applicable for the weakly coupled multi-agent systems, where only one agent is enough at a time to serve the fixed team-goal. For example, suppose, m numbers of agents are assigned to transport a box from one location to another following Scheme-I, and let transportation of the box requires only one agent at a time. Once failure of an agent is detected, its nearest agent expresses cooperation toward the failed agent for successful transportation of the box. Here, the success of any one agent is enough to make the team successful. On the other hand, in the second scheme, the success of a team is contingent upon the simultaneous success of all the agents and it is applicable for the tightly coupled multi-agent system, such as long stick/ big object carrying by multiple robots [43, 44]. Therefore, in both schemes, agents adapt Q-tables depending upon the task requirement.

In the proposed Scheme-I-induced Q-learning (ΩQL-I), agents adapt the Q-table in joint state–action space exploiting the individual Q-values at individual state–action space and the effect of coordination among the agents, received as a feedback from the environment to be explained in the next section. However, in the proposed Scheme-II-induced Q-learning (ΩQL-II), agents adapt the Q-table in joint state–action space following the traditional MAQL rule by evaluating the ΩIR as a function of individual immediate rewards plus expected group (Ω) future reward as a function of individual expected future rewards discounted by a factor $0 \leq \gamma < 1$.

It may be notated that in the proposed ΩQL-II, at a joint state, G because of all the joint actions, $K \in \{K\}$, if an agent i receives less than or equal to ($\leq$) reward for EE (or LE) or greater than or equal to ($\geq$) reward for UE (or RE) than the same by the proposed ΩQL-I, then for EE (or LE), the joint action $K \in \{K\}$ corresponding to equal reward $\left(\Omega\overline{Q}(G,K) = \Omega\widetilde{Q}(G,K)\right)$ is preferred, as simultaneous success of all the agents is desired to make the team successful. On the other hand for UE (or RE), also the joint action, $K \in \{K\}$ corresponding to equal reward $\left(\Omega\overline{Q}(G,K) = \Omega\widetilde{Q}(G,K)\right)$ is preferred as success of any one agent is enough to make the team successful.

4.3.2 Immediate Rewards in Scheme-I and -II

In the literature of MAQL, agents receive only one type of immediate reward, i.e. immediate reward at joint state–action space. However, it is our observation that the immediate rewards at individual state–action space and immediate rewards at joint state–action space are often diverse. Hence, in this chapter, we have considered two types of immediate rewards for an agent i. First one is the immediate rewards at individual state–action space, $r_i(s_i, a_i)$, and the second one is the immediate rewards at joint state–action space during the multi-agent coordination, $d_i(G, K)$. The physical significance of such reward categorization is that an agent should not receive penalty or reward because of remaining agents' actions. For example, if each robot in a group individually receives immediate reward at joint state–action space and subsequently employs either Scheme-I or -II to obtain single Q-table at joint state–action space, then the penalty incurred by a robot due to possible collision with an obstacle might influence the identical Q-values offered by the Scheme-I or -II. The above phenomenon is not desired and hence such immediate reward categorization is done. The definition of the proposed immediate reward is given in Definition 4.2.

Definition 4.2 $\Omega \in \{U, E, R, L\}$ *immediate reward* (ΩIR), $R(G, K)$, is given by (4.8), where $\Phi \in \left\{ \Sigma_{i=1}^m, \text{Min}_{i=1}^m, \text{Max}_{i=1}^m, \Pi_{i=1}^m \right\}$.

$$R(G, K) = d_i(G, K), \qquad \text{if agent } i \text{ is penalized due to other agents}$$
$$= \Phi[r_i(s_i, a_i)], \qquad \text{otherwise.} \tag{4.8}$$

Trivially from (4.8), it can be inferred that

$$R(G, K) = \Phi[r_i(G, K)]. \tag{4.9}$$

4.3.3 Scheme-I-Induced MAQL

The Q-value offered by Scheme-I $\left(\Omega\overline{Q}(G, K) \right)$ is evaluated by obtaining the $\Phi \in \left\{ \Sigma_{i=1}^m, \text{Min}_{i=1}^m, \text{Max}_{i=1}^m, \Pi_{i=1}^m \right\}$ of the summation of individual Q-value $Q_i(s_i, a_i)$ and the immediate reward due to multi-agent coordination given by $d_i(G, K)$. For example, in multi-agent robotics, $d_i(G, K)$ is the penalty because of collision among the agents. The $\Omega\overline{Q}(G, K)$ is evaluated by the learning rule,

$$\Omega\overline{Q}(G, K) \leftarrow \Phi[Q_i(s_i, a_i) + d_i(G, K)] \tag{4.10}$$

at the joint state G because of joint action K. Assuming $K^* = \; <a_1, a_2, ..., a_m>^*$ be the jointly optimized individual actions (joint action) at joint state G, at the end of learning phase, agents evaluate the optimal pure strategy $\Omega \overline{K}^*$ corresponding to the maximum of $\Omega \overline{Q}(G, K)$, $\Omega \in \{U, E, R, L\}$ and is given by (4.11).

$$\Omega \overline{K}^* = \arg \max_{\overline{K}} \left[\Omega \overline{Q}(G, \overline{K}) \right]. \tag{4.11}$$

Note 4.1   As the CQL and the proposed Scheme-I-based learning algorithms share common environment and agents, both have same joint action set given by (4.12).

$$\{\overline{K}\} = \{K\}. \tag{4.12}$$

In ΩQL-I, the optimal mixed strategy $\Omega \overline{p}^*(K)$ is obtained by evaluating the maximum of the expected reward $\sum_{\forall K} \Omega \overline{p}(K) \Omega \overline{Q}(G, K)$, $\Omega \overline{p} : \{K\} \to [0, 1]$ and is given by (4.13).

$$\Omega \overline{p}^*(K) = \arg \max_{\Omega \overline{p}(K)} \left[\sum_{\forall K} \Omega \overline{p}(K) \left[\Omega \overline{Q}(G, K) \right] \right]. \tag{4.13}$$

On the other hand, Kok et al. observed that in most of the MAQL, agents required to coordinate their actions only in a few states, and in the remaining they act independently [40]. Motivated by their observations, Notes 4.2 and 4.3 are given below before proposing Theorems 4.1 and 4.2.

Note 4.2   Following the principle of [40], in CQL, Q-value of agent i at joint state G because of joint action K may be expressed by (4.14).

$$Q_i(G, K) = Q_i(s_i, a_i) + d_i(G, K), \tag{4.14}$$

where $d_i(G, K)$ is explained in Section 4.3.2, elements of G and K include s_i and a_i, respectively.

Note 4.3   Again, following the principle of [40], in CQL, the Q-value of agent i at joint state G because of joint action K setting $d_i(G, K) = 0$ may be expressed by (4.15).

$$Q_i'(G, K) = Q_i(s_i, a_i). \tag{4.15}$$

Theorem 4.1   *The optimal pure strategy, $\Omega \overline{K}^*$ induced by Scheme-I is an Ω-equilibrium, ΩK^* for $\Omega \in \{U, E, R, L\}$ attained in CQL.*

Proof

Here,

$$
\begin{aligned}
\Omega\overline{K}^* &= \arg\max_{\overline{K}} \left[\Omega\overline{Q}(G, \overline{K}) \right] && \text{[by (4.11)]} \\
&= \arg\max_{K} \left[\Omega\overline{Q}(G, K) \right] && \text{[by (4.12)]} \\
&= \arg\max_{K} \left[\Phi[Q_i(s_i, a_i) + d_i(G, K)] \right] && \left[\text{by (4.10) and } \Phi \in \left\{ \sum_{i=1}^{m}, \operatorname*{Min}_{i=1}^{m}, \operatorname*{Max}_{i=1}^{m}, \prod_{i=1}^{m} \right\} \right] \\
&= \arg\max_{K} \left[\Phi[Q_i(G, K)] \right] && \text{[by (4.14)]} \\
&= \Omega K^*. && \text{[by (4.5)]}
\end{aligned}
$$

$$(4.16)$$

Hence, the Theorem is proved. □

Theorem 4.2 *The optimal mixed strategy, $\Omega\overline{p}^*(K)$ induced by Scheme-I is an Ω-equilibrium, $\Omega p^*(K)$ for $\Omega \in \{U, E, R, L\}$ attained in CQL.*

Proof

Here,

$$
\begin{aligned}
\Omega\overline{p}^*(K) &= \arg\max_{\Omega\overline{p}(K)} \left[\sum_{\forall K} \Omega\overline{p}(K) \left[\Omega\overline{Q}(G, K) \right] \right] && \text{[by (4.13)]} \\
&= \arg\max_{\Omega\overline{p}(K)} \left[\sum_{\forall K} \Omega\overline{p}(K)\Phi[Q_i(s_i, a_i) + d_i(G, K)] \right] && \left[\text{by (4.10) and } \Phi \in \left\{ \sum_{i=1}^{m}, \operatorname*{Min}_{i=1}^{m}, \operatorname*{Max}_{i=1}^{m}, \prod_{i=1}^{m} \right\} \right] \\
&= \arg\max_{\Omega\overline{p}(K)} \left[\Phi\left(\sum_{\forall K} \Omega\overline{p}(K)[Q_i(s_i, a_i) + d_i(G, K)] \right) \right] && [\because \Phi \text{ is independent of K}] \\
&= \arg\max_{\Omega\overline{p}(K)} \left[\Phi\left(\sum_{\forall K} \Omega\overline{p}(K)[Q_i(G, K)] \right) \right] && \text{[by (4.14)]} \\
&= \arg\max_{\Omega p(K)} \left[\Phi\left(\sum_{\forall K} \Omega p(K)[Q_i(G, K)] \right) \right] && [\because \Omega\overline{p}: \{K\} \to [0,1], \quad \Omega p: \{K\} \to [0,1]] \\
&= \Omega p^*(K). && \text{[by (4.6)]}
\end{aligned}
$$

$$(4.17)$$

Hence, the Theorem is proved. □

It may be noted that, if among m agents at least one is required to successfully transport an object (e.g. small box-carrying) to a predefined goal state cooperatively for succeeding the team, then Scheme-I is useful. In Scheme-I, while an agent searches for its goal state, at the same time remaining agents keep on static (current state becomes the next state) by maintaining the equilibrium (cooperating) with the active one at that joint state. However, if in a task (e.g. long stick-carrying) all m agents need to reach their individual goal simultaneously to complete the assigned task, then Scheme-II is employed instead of Scheme-I. Details of Scheme-II are given below.

4.3.4 Scheme-II-Induced MAQL

In the traditional single agent Q-learning, two types of rewards are used: immediate reward and optimal future reward. The principle of ΩQL-II does not differ much from single agent Q-learning except the consideration of $R(G, K)$ at a given joint state G because of a joint action K and $\Omega\hat{Q}^*(G')$ at next joint state G'. Naturally, to optimize total reward, we need to optimize both $R(G, K)$ and $\Omega\hat{Q}^*(G')$. Definition of $R(G, K)$ is given in Definition 4.2 and $\Omega\hat{Q}^*(G')$ are formally defined in Definition 4.3 for convenience of the readers.

Definition 4.3 *Expected optimal* $\Omega \in \{U, E, R, L\}$ *Q-value at next joint state* G', $\Omega\hat{Q}^*(G')$ *is obtained by evaluating the* $\Phi \in \{\Sigma_{i=1}^m, \text{Min}_{i=1}^m, \text{Max}_{i=1}^m, \Pi_{i=1}^m\}$ *among the summation of expected optimal* Q-value of agent i at s_i', $\hat{Q}_i^*(s_i')$ *and the expected optimal change in immediate reward due to multi-agent coordination at joint next state* G', $\Delta\hat{Q}_i^*(G')$. $\Omega\hat{Q}^*(G')$ *is given by (4.18),*

$$\Omega\hat{Q}^*(G') = \Phi\left[\hat{Q}_i^*(s_i') + \Delta\hat{Q}_i^*(G')\right]. \tag{4.18}$$

where $\Omega\hat{Q}^*(G')$ and $\Delta\hat{Q}_i^*(G')$ are given by (4.19) and (4.20), respectively.

$$\Omega\hat{Q}^*(G') = \sum_{\forall G'} p\left(G' \mid (G, K)\right) \sum_{\forall K'} \Omega\widetilde{p}^*\left(K' \mid G'\right) \Omega\widetilde{Q}\left(G', K'\right), \tag{4.19}$$

$$\Delta\hat{Q}_i^*(G') = \sum_{\forall G'} p\left(G' \mid (G, K)\right) \sum_{\forall K'} \Omega p^*\left(K' \mid G'\right) d_i\left(G', K'\right), \tag{4.20}$$

where $\Omega\widetilde{p}^*(K' \mid G')$ be the probability of selecting joint action K' at joint next state G' in Scheme-II and the Ω Q-value by Scheme-II $\left(\Omega\widetilde{Q}(G, K)\right)$ following the principle of single agent Q-learning rule using Definitions 4.2 and 4.3 is given in (4.21).

$$\Omega\widetilde{Q}(G, K) \leftarrow (1 - \alpha)\Omega\widetilde{Q}(G, K) + \alpha\left[R(G, K) + \gamma.\Omega\hat{Q}^*(G')\right]. \tag{4.21}$$

At the end of learning phase, agents evaluate the optimal pure strategy $\Omega\widetilde{K}^*$ corresponding to the maximum of $\Omega\widetilde{Q}(G, K)$, $\Omega \in \{U, E, R, L\}$ and is given by (4.22).

$$\Omega \widetilde{K}^* = \arg\max_{\widetilde{K}} \left[\Omega \widetilde{Q}\left(G, \widetilde{K}\right) \right]. \tag{4.22}$$

Note 4.4 Similar to Note 4.1, the relation between joint action set in Scheme-II, $\left\{ \widetilde{K} \right\}$ and $\{K\}$ at a given joint state is given by (4.23).

$$\left\{ \widetilde{K} \right\} = \{K\}. \tag{4.23}$$

In ΩQL-II, the optimal mixed strategy $\Omega \widetilde{p}^*(K)$ is obtained by evaluating the maximum of the expected reward $\sum_{\forall K} \Omega \widetilde{p}(K) \Omega \widetilde{Q}(G, K)$, $\Omega \widetilde{p} : \{K\} \rightarrow [0, 1]$ and is given by (4.24).

$$\Omega \widetilde{p}^*(K) = \arg\max_{\Omega \widetilde{p}(K)} \left[\sum_{\forall K} \Omega \widetilde{p}(K) \left[\Omega \widetilde{Q}(G, K) \right] \right] \tag{4.24}$$

Lemmas 4.1 to 4.6 are required to prove Theorems 4.3 and 4.4.

Lemma 4.1 *The Inequality,* $\Psi(x_i) \pm \gamma \, \Psi(y_i) \leq \Psi(x_i \pm \gamma \, y_i)$, $\Psi \in \left\{ \text{Min}_{i=1}^m, \Pi_{i=1}^m \right\}$ *holds for any real values of* x_i, y_i, $\forall i$, $i \in [1, m]$ *and* $\gamma \in [0, 1)$, *where* $0 \in \{x_i\}$ *and* $0 \in \{y_i\}$.

Proof
Given x_i, y_i, $\forall i$, $i \in [1, m]$ as real values and $\gamma \in [0, 1)$,

For any $j \in [1, m]$ and $\Psi \in \underset{i=1}{\overset{m}{\text{Min}}}$,

$$x_j \geq \underset{i=1}{\overset{m}{\text{Min}}}(x_i) \text{ and } y_j \geq \underset{i=1}{\overset{m}{\text{Min}}}(y_i) \text{ always hold}$$

$$\therefore x_j \pm \gamma y_j \geq \underset{i=1}{\overset{m}{\text{Min}}}(x_i) \pm \gamma \underset{i=1}{\overset{m}{\text{Min}}}(y_i), \forall j, j \in [1, m]$$

$$\Rightarrow \underset{j=1}{\overset{m}{\text{Min}}}\left(x_j \pm \gamma y_j\right) \geq \underset{i=1}{\overset{m}{\text{Min}}}(x_i) \pm \gamma \underset{i=1}{\overset{m}{\text{Min}}}(y_i) \tag{4.25}$$

$$\Rightarrow \underset{i=1}{\overset{m}{\text{Min}}}(x_i \pm \gamma y_i) \geq \underset{i=1}{\overset{m}{\text{Min}}}(x_i) \pm \gamma \underset{i=1}{\overset{m}{\text{Min}}}(y_i) \quad [\because i, j \in [1, m]]$$

$$\therefore \underset{i=1}{\overset{m}{\text{Min}}}(x_i) \pm \gamma \underset{i=1}{\overset{m}{\text{Min}}}(y_i) \leq \underset{i=1}{\overset{m}{\text{Min}}}(x_i \pm \gamma y_i).$$

Similarly, if $\Psi \in \underset{i=1}{\overset{m}{\Pi}}$, $0 \in \{x_i\}$ and $0 \in \{y_i\}$, then

$$\prod_{i=1}^{m} (x_i) \pm \gamma \prod_{i=1}^{m} (y_i) \leq \prod_{i=1}^{m} (x_i \pm y_i). \tag{4.26}$$

Thus, the desired inequality holds. □

Lemma 4.2 *The Inequality,* $\Psi(x_i) \pm \gamma \, \Psi(y_i) \geq \Psi(x_i \pm \gamma \, y_i)$, $\Psi \in \left\{ \text{Max}_{i=1}^m, \Sigma_{i=1}^m \right\}$ *holds for any real values of* x_i, y_i, $\forall \, i$, $i \in [1, m]$ *and* $\gamma \in [0, 1)$.

Proof

Given x_i, y_i, $\forall \, i$, $i \in [1, m]$ as real values and $\gamma \in [0, 1)$,

For any $j \in [1, m]$ and $\Psi \in \underset{i=1}{\overset{m}{\text{Max}}}$,

$$x_j \geq \underset{i=1}{\overset{m}{\text{Max}}}(x_i) \text{ and } y_j \geq \underset{i=1}{\overset{m}{\text{Max}}}(y_i) \text{ always hold}$$

$$\therefore x_j \pm \gamma y_j \leq \underset{i=1}{\overset{m}{\text{Max}}}(x_i) \pm \gamma \underset{i=1}{\overset{m}{\text{Max}}}(y_i), \forall j, j \in [1, m]$$

$$\Rightarrow \underset{j=1}{\overset{m}{\text{Max}}}\left(x_j \pm \gamma y_j\right) \leq \underset{i=1}{\overset{m}{\text{Max}}}(x_i) \pm \gamma \underset{i=1}{\overset{m}{\text{Max}}}(y_i) \tag{4.27}$$

$$\Rightarrow \underset{i=1}{\overset{m}{\text{Max}}}(x_i \pm \gamma y_i) \leq \underset{i=1}{\overset{m}{\text{Max}}}(x_i) \pm \gamma \underset{i=1}{\overset{m}{\text{Max}}}(y_i) \quad [\because i, j \in [1, m]]$$

$$\therefore \underset{i=1}{\overset{m}{\text{Max}}}(x_i) \pm \gamma \underset{i=1}{\overset{m}{\text{Max}}}(y_i) \geq \underset{i=1}{\overset{m}{\text{Max}}}(x_i \pm \gamma y_i).$$

Similarly, if $\Psi \in \underset{i=1}{\overset{m}{\Sigma}}$, then

$$\therefore \sum_{i=1}^m (x_i) \pm \gamma \sum_{i=1}^m (y_i) \geq \sum_{i=1}^m (x_i \pm \gamma y_i). \tag{4.28}$$

Thus, the desired inequality holds. $\qquad\qquad\square$

Lemma 4.3 *The Inequality,* $(1 - \alpha)\Psi(x_i) \pm \alpha \, \Psi(y_i) \leq \Psi[(1 - \alpha)x_i \pm \alpha \, y_i]$, $\Psi \in \left\{ \text{Min}_{i=1}^m, \Pi_{i=1}^m \right\}$ *holds for any real values of* x_i, y_i, $\forall \, i$, $i \in [1, m]$ *and* $\alpha \in [0, 1)$, *where* $0 \in \{x_i\}$ *and* $0 \in \{y_i\}$.

Proof

Proof of Lemma 4.3 is similar to the proof of Lemma 4.1. $\qquad\qquad\square$

Lemma 4.4 *The Inequality,* $(1 - \alpha)\Psi(x_i) \pm \alpha \, \Psi(y_i) \geq \Psi[(1 - \alpha)x_i \pm \alpha y_i]$, $\Psi \in \left\{ \text{Max}_{i=1}^m, \Sigma_{i=1}^m \right\}$ *holds for any real values of* x_i, y_i, $\forall \, i$, $i \in [1, m]$ *and* $\alpha \in [0, 1)$.

Proof

Proof of Lemma 4.4 is similar to the proof of Lemma 4.2. $\qquad\qquad\square$

Now, if $\Delta\hat{Q}_i^*(G') = 0$, then let the expected Q-value at Ω-equilibrium of agent i at next joint state G', $\Omega\hat{Q}_i^*(G')$ is given in (4.29).

$$\Omega\hat{Q}_i^*(G') = \sum_{\forall G'} p\Big(G' \mid (G,K)\Big) \sum_{\forall K'} \Omega p^*\Big(K' \mid G'\Big) Q_i'\Big(G', K'\Big). \qquad (4.29)$$

Now, if $\Delta\hat{Q}_i^*(G') \neq 0$, (4.7) can be rewritten as in (4.30).

$$Q_i(G, K) \leftarrow (1 - \alpha)Q_i(G, K) + \alpha\Big[r_i(G, K) + \gamma \cdot \Big[\Omega\hat{Q}_i^*(G') + \Delta\hat{Q}_i^*(G')\Big]\Big]. \qquad (4.30)$$

Now, comparing (4.7) and (4.30), one can write

$$\Omega\hat{Q}_i^*(G') = \Omega\hat{Q}_i^*(G') + \Delta\hat{Q}_i^*(G'). \qquad (4.31)$$

Lemma 4.5 *If* $\Omega\hat{Q}_i^*(G') = \Omega\hat{Q}_i^*(G') + \Delta\hat{Q}_i^*(G')$, *then* $\Omega\hat{Q}_i^*(G') = \hat{Q}_i^*\big(s_i'\big) + \Delta\hat{Q}_i^*(G')$ *at the next joint state* $G' = \big\langle s_i'\big\rangle_{i=1}^m$.

Proof
By (4.30),

$$\Omega\hat{Q}_i^*(G') = \sum_{\forall G'} p\Big(G' \mid (G,K)\Big) \sum_{\forall K'} \Omega p^*\Big(K' \mid G'\Big) Q_i'\Big(G', K'\Big)$$

$$= \sum_{\forall G'} \prod_{j=1}^m p_j\Big(s_j' \mid (s_j, a_j)\Big) \sum_{\forall K'} \prod_{j=1}^m p_j^*\Big(a_j' \mid s_j'\Big) Q_i'\Big(G', K'\Big) \quad \text{[by (4.3) and (4.5)]}$$

$$= \prod_{j=1}^m \sum_{\forall s_j'} p_j\Big(s_j' \mid (s_j, a_j)\Big) \prod_{j=1}^m \sum_{\forall a_j'} p_j^*\Big(a_j' \mid s_j'\Big) Q_i\Big(s_i', a_i'\Big) \quad \text{[by (4.14), } Q_i'\Big(G', K'\Big) = Q_i\Big(s_i', a_i'\Big)$$

$$= \sum_{\forall s_i'} p_i\Big(s_i' \mid (s_i, a_i)\Big) \sum_{\forall a_i'} p_i^*\Big(a_i' \mid s_i'\Big) Q_i\Big(s_i', a_i'\Big)$$

$$\times \prod_{\substack{j=1, \\ j\neq i}}^m \sum_{\forall s_j'} p_j\Big(s_j' \mid (s_j, a_j)\Big) \prod_{\substack{j=1, \\ j\neq i}}^m \sum_{\forall a_j'} p_j^*\Big(a_j' \mid s_j'\Big), \quad [\because i,j \in [1,m]]$$

$$= \sum_{\forall s_i'} p_i\left(s_i' \mid (s_i, a_i)\right) \sum_{\forall a_i'} p_i^*\left(a_i' \mid s_i'\right) Q_i\left(s_i', a_i'\right)$$

$$\left[\because \sum_{\forall s_j'} p_j\left(s_j' \mid (s_j, a_j)\right) = 1 \text{ and } \sum_{\forall a_j'} p_j^*\left(a_j' \mid s_j'\right) = 1, \forall j \right] \tag{4.32}$$

$$= \hat{Q}_i^*\left(s_i'\right). \quad [\text{by (4.1)}]$$

Given, $\Omega \hat{Q}_i^*(G') = \Omega \hat{\mathbb{Q}}_i^*(G') + \Delta \hat{Q}_i^*(G')$,

$$\therefore \Omega \hat{Q}_i^*\left(G'\right) = \hat{Q}_i^*\left(s_i'\right) + \Delta \hat{Q}_i^*\left(G'\right). \quad [\text{by (4.32)}]$$

Hence, the Lemma is proved. $\qquad\square$

Lemma 4.6 $\Omega\widetilde{Q}(G,K) = \Phi[Q_i(G,K)]$ *for* $\Phi \in \left\{\Sigma_{i=1}^m, \text{Min}_{i=1}^m, \text{Max}_{i=1}^m, \Pi_{i=1}^m\right\}$ *holds for the equality cases of Lemmas 4.1–4.4.*

Proof
Here,

$$\Omega\widetilde{Q}(G,K) \leftarrow (1-\alpha)\Omega\widetilde{Q}(G,K) + \alpha\left[R(G,K) + \gamma.\Omega\hat{Q}^*\left(G'\right)\right] \quad [\text{by (4.21)}]$$

$$= (1-\alpha)^t \Omega\widetilde{Q}(G,K) + (1-\alpha)^{t-1}\alpha\left[R(G,K) + \gamma\Omega\hat{Q}^*\left(G'\right)\right]$$

$$+ (1-\alpha)^{t-2}\alpha\left[R(G,K) + \gamma\Omega\hat{Q}^*\left(G'\right)\right] + \cdots + (1-\alpha)\alpha\left[R(G,K) + \gamma\Omega\hat{Q}^*\left(G'\right)\right]$$

$$+ \alpha\left[R(G,K) + \gamma\Omega\hat{Q}^*\left(G'\right)\right]$$

[by recursively substituting (4.21), where, learning epoch $t \to \infty$]

$$= \Phi\left[(1-\alpha)^t Q_i(G,K)\right] + (1-\alpha)^{t-1}\alpha\left[R(G,K) + \gamma\Omega\hat{Q}^*\left(G'\right)\right]$$

$$+ (1-\alpha)^{t-2}\alpha\left[R(G,K) + \gamma\Omega\hat{Q}^*\left(G'\right)\right] + \cdots + (1-\alpha)\alpha\left[R(G,K) + \gamma\Omega\hat{Q}^*\left(G'\right)\right]$$

$$+ \alpha\left[R(G,K) + \gamma\Omega\hat{Q}^*\left(G'\right)\right]$$

$$\left[\because t \to \infty \text{ and } \alpha \in [0,1) \therefore (1-\alpha)^t \to 0, \text{ where } \Phi \in \left\{\sum_{i=1}^m, \text{Min}_{i=1}^m, \text{Max}_{i=1}^m, \prod_{i=1}^m\right\}\right]$$

$$= \Phi\left[(1-\alpha)^t Q_i(G,K)\right] + (1-\alpha)^{t-1}\alpha\left[\Phi[r_i(G,K)] + \gamma \cdot \Phi\left[\hat{Q}_i^*\left(s_i'\right) + \Delta\hat{Q}_i^*(G')\right]\right]$$

$$+ (1-\alpha)^{t-2}\alpha[\Phi[r_i(G,K)] + \gamma \cdot \Phi\left[\hat{Q}_i^*\left(s_i'\right) + \Delta\hat{Q}_i^*(G')\right]\right] + \cdots +$$

$$(1-\alpha)\alpha\left[\Phi[r_i(G,K)] + \gamma \cdot \Phi\left[\hat{Q}_i^*\left(s_i'\right) + \Delta\hat{Q}_i^*(G')\right]\right] + \alpha[\Phi[r_i(G,K)]$$

$$+ \gamma \cdot \Phi\left[\hat{Q}_i^*\left(s_i'\right) + \Delta\hat{Q}_i^*(G')\right]\right] \quad [\text{by } (4.9) \text{ and } (4.18)]$$

$$= \Phi\left[(1-\alpha)^t Q_i(G,K)\right] + (1-\alpha)^{t-1}\alpha\left[\Phi[r_i(G,K)] + \gamma \cdot \Phi\left[\Omega\hat{Q}_i^*(G')\right]\right]$$

$$+ (1-\alpha)^{t-2}\alpha[\Phi[r_i(G,K)] + \gamma \cdot \Phi\left[\Omega\hat{Q}_i^*(G')\right]\right] + \cdots + (1-\alpha)\alpha[\Phi[r_i(G,K)] + \gamma \cdot \Phi\left[\Omega\hat{Q}_i^*(G')\right]\right]$$

$$+ \alpha[\Phi[r_i(G,K)] + \gamma \cdot \Phi\left[\Omega\hat{Q}_i^*(G')\right]\right] \quad [\text{by Lemma } 4.5]$$

$$= \Phi\left[(1-\alpha)^t Q_i(G,K)\right] + (1-\alpha)^{t-1}\alpha\left[\Phi\left[r_i(G,K) + \gamma \cdot \Omega\hat{Q}_i^*(G')\right]\right]$$

$$+ (1-\alpha)^{t-2}\alpha\left[\Phi\left[r_i(G,K) + \gamma \cdot \Omega\hat{Q}_i^*(G')\right]\right] + \cdots + (1-\alpha)\alpha\left[\Phi\left[r_i(G,K) + \gamma \cdot \Omega\hat{Q}_i^*(G')\right]\right]$$

$$+ \alpha\left[\Phi\left[r_i(G,K) + \gamma \cdot \Omega\hat{Q}_i^*(G')\right]\right]$$

[by statement considering only the equalities in Lemmas 4.1 and 4.2]

$$= (1-\alpha)^{t-1}\Phi[(1-\alpha)Q_i(G,K)] + (1-\alpha)^{t-1}\Phi\left[\alpha\left[r_i(G,K) + \gamma.\Omega\hat{Q}_i^*(G')\right]\right]$$

$$+ (1-\alpha)^{t-2}\Phi[\alpha[r_i(G,K) + \gamma \cdot \Omega\hat{Q}_i^*(G')]\right] + \cdots + (1-\alpha)\Phi\left[\alpha\left[r_i(G,K) + \gamma \cdot \Omega\hat{Q}_i^*(G')\right]\right]$$

$$+ \Phi\left[\alpha\left[r_i(G,K) + \gamma \cdot \Omega\hat{Q}_i^*(G')\right]\right] [\because \Phi \text{ is independent of t and } \alpha]$$

$$= (1-\alpha)^{t-1}\Phi\left[(1-\alpha)Q_i(G,K) + \alpha\left[r_i(G,K) + \gamma \cdot \Omega\hat{Q}_i^*(G')\right]\right] + (1-\alpha)^{t-2}\Phi[\alpha[r_i(G,K)$$

$$+ \gamma \cdot \Omega\hat{Q}_i^*(G')]\right] + \ldots + (1-\alpha)\Phi\left[\alpha\left[r_i(G,K) + \gamma \cdot \Omega\hat{Q}_i^*(G')\right]\right] + \Phi\left[\alpha\left[r_i(G,K) + \gamma \cdot \Omega\hat{Q}_i^*(G')\right]\right],$$

[by statement considering only the equalities in Lemmas 4.3 and 4.4]

$$= (1-\alpha)^{t-1}\Phi[Q_i(G,K)] + (1-\alpha)^{t-2}\Phi\left[\alpha\left[r_i(G,K) + \gamma \cdot \Omega\hat{Q}_i^*(G')\right]\right] + \ldots$$

$$+ (1-\alpha)\Phi[\alpha[r_i(G,K) + \gamma \cdot \Omega\hat{Q}_i^*(G')]\right] + \Phi\left[\alpha\left[r_i(G,K) + \gamma \cdot \Omega\hat{Q}_i^*(G')\right]\right] \quad [\text{by } (4.7)]$$

$$= (1-\alpha)^{t-2}\Phi[(1-\alpha)Q_i(G,K)] + (1-\alpha)^{t-2}\Phi\left[\alpha\left[r_i(G,K) + \gamma \cdot \Omega\hat{Q}_i^*(G')\right]\right] + \cdots$$

$$+ (1-\alpha)\Phi\left[\alpha\left[r_i(G,K) + \gamma \cdot \Omega\hat{Q}_i^*(G')\right]\right] + \Phi\left[\alpha\left[r_i(G,K) + \gamma \cdot \Omega\hat{Q}_i^*(G')\right]\right]$$

which on further simplification returns

$$\Omega\tilde{Q}(G,K) = \Phi\left[(1-\alpha)Q_i(G,K) + \alpha\left[r_i(G,K) + \gamma \cdot \Omega\hat{Q}_i^*\left(G'\right)\right]\right]$$

$$= \Phi[Q_i(G,K)]. \quad [\text{by } (4.7)]$$

Hence, the Lemma is proved. $\qquad\square$

Theorem 4.3 *The optimal pure strategy, $\Omega\widetilde{K}^*$, induced by Scheme-II is an Ω-equilibrium, ΩK^* for $\Omega \in \{U, E, R, L\}$ attained in CQL, holds for the equality cases of Lemmas 4.1–4.4.*

Proof
Here,

$$
\begin{aligned}
\Omega\widetilde{K}^* &= \arg\max_{\widetilde{K}} \left[\Omega\widetilde{Q}\left(G, \widetilde{K}\right) \right] && \text{[by (4.22)]} \\
&= \arg\max_{K} \left[\Omega\widetilde{Q}(G, K) \right] && \text{[by (4.23)]} \\
&= \arg\max_{K} \left[\Phi[Q_i(G, K)] \right] && \text{[by Lemma 4.6]} \\
&= \Omega K^*. && \text{[by (4.5)]}
\end{aligned}
\tag{4.33}
$$

Hence, the Theorem is proved. $\qquad\square$

Theorem 4.4 *The optimal mixed strategy, $\Omega\widetilde{p}^*(K)$ induced by Scheme-II is an Ω-equilibrium, $\Omega p^*(K)$ for $\Omega \in \{U, E, R, L\}$ attained in CQL, holds for the equality cases of Lemmas 4.1–4.4.*

Proof
Here,

$$
\begin{aligned}
\Omega\widetilde{p}^*(K) &= \underset{\Omega\widetilde{p}(K)}{\arg\max} \left[\sum_{\forall K} \Omega\widetilde{p}(K) [\Omega\widetilde{Q}(G, K)] \right] && \text{[by (4.24)]} \\
&= \underset{\Omega\widetilde{p}(K)}{\arg\max} \left[\sum_{\forall K} \Omega\widetilde{p}(K) [\Phi[Q_i(G, K)]] \right] && \text{[by Lemma 4.6]} \\
&= \underset{\Omega\widetilde{p}(K)}{\arg\max} \left[\Phi \left[\sum_{\forall K} \Omega\widetilde{p}(K) [Q_i(G, K)] \right] \right] && [\because \Phi \text{ is independent of } K] \\
&= \underset{\Omega p(K)}{\arg\max} \left[\Phi \left[\sum_{\forall K} \Omega p(K) [Q_i(G, K)] \right] \right] && [\because \Omega\widetilde{p}: \{K\} \to [0,1], \Omega p: \{K\} \to [0,1]] \\
&= \Omega p^*(K). && \text{[by (4.6)]}
\end{aligned}
\tag{4.34}
$$

Hence, the Theorem is proved. $\qquad\square$

4.3.5 Algorithms for Scheme-I and II

Scheme-I and –II-induced ΩQL algorithms are proposed in Algorithm 4.1. Now, for further improvement, constraint version of ΩQL-I/ΩQL-II(CΩQL-I/ CΩQL-II) is given below.

Algorithm 4.1   Scheme-I and –II-Induced ΩQL (ΩQL-I and ΩQL-II)

Input: Learning rate $\alpha \in [0, 1)$ and discounting factor $\gamma \in [0, 1)$;
Output: Optimal joint Q-value $\Omega\overline{Q}^*(G, K)$, $\forall G$, $\forall K$; \\ for Scheme-I
     Optimal joint Q-value $\Omega\widetilde{Q}^*(G, K)$, $\forall G$, $\forall K$; \\ for Scheme-II
Begin
  Initialize: state s_i, $\forall i$, action set A_i at s_i, $\forall i$,
  $\Omega\overline{Q}(G, K) \leftarrow 0$, $\forall G$, $\forall K$ for Scheme-I and $\Omega\widetilde{Q}(G, K) \leftarrow 0$, $\forall G$, $\forall K$ for
  Scheme-II;
  Repeat
    1) Select an action $a_i \in A_i$, $\forall i$ by the Boltzmann strategy
       [47] and execute it for both the schemes;
    2) For both the schemes observe immediate rewards $r_i(s_i, a_i)$
       and $d_i(G, K)$, $\forall i$, evaluate next state $s'_i \leftarrow \delta_i(s_i, a_i)$, $\forall i$
       to obtain joint next state $G' = <s'_i>^m_{i=1}$ and individual
       Q-value
       $$Q_i(s_i, a_i) \leftarrow (1-\alpha)Q_i(s_i, a_i) + \alpha\left[r_i(s_i, a_i) + \gamma.\hat{Q}^*_i\left(s'_i\right)\right], \forall i;$$
    3) **Update:** Joint Q-value $\Omega\overline{Q}(G, K)$ by (4.10) for Scheme-I*
       and $\Omega\widetilde{Q}(G, K)$ by (4.21) for Scheme-II** and
       $$G \leftarrow G'; //\Omega \in \{U, E, R, L\}, \Phi \in \left\{\sum_{i=1}^m, Min^m_{i=1}, Max^m_{i=1}, \prod_{i=1}^m\right\}.$$
    Until $\Omega\overline{Q}(G, K)$, $\forall G$, $\forall K$ converges for Scheme-I and
    $\Omega\widetilde{Q}(G, K)$, $\forall G$, $\forall K$ converges for Scheme-II;
    $\Omega\overline{Q}^*(G, K) \leftarrow \Omega\overline{Q}(G, K)$, $\forall G$, $\forall K$ for Scheme-I and $\Omega\widetilde{Q}^*(G, K) \leftarrow$
    $\Omega\widetilde{Q}(G, K)$, $\forall G$, $\forall K$ for Scheme-II;
  End.
  * In Scheme-I, suppose, there is a group of two robots, R1 and
    R2. R1 attempts to transport a box from one location to a
    fixed goal G. Once R1 fails, R2 takes in charge and
    continues the box transportation. If R2 reaches the goal
    state G, then it receives the maximum individual
    immediate reward, 100 (say). At the same time, R1

```
    receives the minimum individual immediate reward, i.e. 0.
    In the above circumstance, we choose RE for group
    immediate reward evaluation, because the success of one
    agent is enough to make the successful. Group immediate
    reward = max(100, 0) = 100.
 ** In Scheme-II, for the stick-carrying problem [44], both R1
    and R2 should receive 100 rewards to make the team
    successful. Here, EE is employed to evaluate the group
    immediate reward = min(100, 100) = 100.
```

4.3.6 Constraint ΩQL-I/ΩQL-II(CΩQL-I/CΩQL-II)

In constraint ΩQL (CΩQL) algorithms, agents have to satisfy one or more task constraints to determine next feasible joint state from a set of next joint states. For example, in the stick-carrying problem, two robots (agents) transport a stick from a given location to the other in their environment by holding it at two ends of the stick. During transportation, the stick should not collide with any obstacle. The transportation of a fixed-length stick without having encountered an obstacle by the stick acts as a task constraint that the agents have to maintain throughout their journey. Similarly, in triangle-carrying problem, three robots carry a triangle satisfying the above-mentioned constraint.

If joint next state (G') does not satisfy task constraint(s) after selecting a joint action (K) from a feasible joint state (G_F), then the next joint state (G') is removed from the feasible joint Q-table and also the joint action (K) is dropped from the feasible joint state (G_F), otherwise the joint action is executed for learning. It is apparent that $G_F \subseteq G$ and $K_F \subseteq K$, where G and K are joint state and joint action of the agents, respectively. The constraint ΩQL-I/ΩQL-II(CΩQL-I/CΩQL-II) algorithm mentioning the changes as compared with ΩQL (Algorithm 4.1) is given in Algorithm 4.2.

4.3.7 Convergence

In [40], Kok et al. mentioned that in most of the MAQL, agents require coordinating their actions only in a few states, while acting independently in the remaining states. Based on their observations, we jointly optimize a combination of

---

Algorithm 4.2   Constraint ΩQL-I/ΩQL-II (CΩQL-I/CΩQL-II)

Input: As in Algorithm 4.1 plus task constraints;
Output: Optimal Q-values for feasible joint state-action space;
Begin
  Initialize: Same as Algorithm 4.1;
Repeat
  1) Select action as in Algorithm 4.1;
  2) Receive immediate rewards $r_i(s_i, a_i)$, $\forall i$ and $d_i(G, K)$, $\forall i$
     as in Algorithm 4.1 and evaluate joint next state
     $G^/ = \langle s_i^/ \rangle_{i=1}^m$ and individual Q-value $Q_i(s_i, a_i)$, $\forall i$ as
     in Algorithm 4.1;
  3) **Update:** $\Omega\overline{Q}(G_F, K_F)$ for Scheme-I and $\Omega\widetilde{Q}(G_F, K_F)$ for Scheme-
     II; //F in the suffix indicates the feasible
  4) If the feasibility checking fails, then delete the G_F
     from the joint Q-table and drop the K_F taken at the
     current joint state;
Until $\Omega\overline{Q}(G_F, K_F)$, $\forall G_F$, $\forall K_F$ converges for Scheme-I and
$\Omega\widetilde{Q}(G_F, K_F)$, $\forall G_F$, $\forall K_F$ converges for Scheme-II;
$\Omega\overline{Q}^*(G_F, K_F) \leftarrow \Omega\overline{Q}(G_F, K_F)$, $\forall G_F$, $\forall K_F$ for   Scheme-I   and
$\Omega\widetilde{Q}^*(G_F, K_F) \leftarrow \Omega\widetilde{Q}(G_F, K_F)$, $\forall G_F$, $\forall K_F$
for Scheme-II;
End.

(i) individual Q-function and (ii) the change in the individual Q-functions because of the multi-agent coordination. The function used to combine the above two is determined based on the choice of type of equilibrium. In the present chapter, to consider the change in Q-values due to multi-agent coordination, we classify the immediate reward (Section 4.3.2) into two types, one defined in individual state–action space, and the other in the joint state–action space. Theorems (4.1, 4.2) and (4.3, 4.4), respectively, lead to the optimal global policy for deterministic and stochastic cases for both Scheme-I and -II. Convergence proofs of the proposed algorithms are offered by Theorem 4.5 and 4.6, respectively, for Scheme-I and-II. To propose Theorems 4.5 and 4.6 Lemmas 4.7–4.9 are the prerequisites.

Lemma 4.7 $\alpha \,|\, [R_t(G, K) - R^*(G, K)]\,| \,= 0, \forall\, t$ *holds for* $\alpha \in [0, 1)$, *where t is the learning epoch.*

Proof
By (4.9),

$$\alpha \,|\, [R_t(G,K) - R^*(G,K)]\,| \,= \alpha \big|\Phi\big[r_i^t(G,K)\big] - \Phi\big[r_i^*(G,K)\big]\big|. \tag{4.35}$$

For $\Phi \in \left\{ \underset{i=1}{\overset{m}{\text{Min}}}, \underset{i=1}{\overset{m}{\Pi}} \right\}$, (4.35) becomes

$$\alpha \,|\, [R_t(G,K) - R^*(G,K)]\,| \,\leq \alpha \big|\Phi\big[r_i^t(G,K) - r_i^*(G,K)\big]\big|, \quad \text{[by Lemma 4.1 with } \gamma = 1]$$
$$\alpha \,|\, [R_t(G,K) - R^*(G,K)]\,| \,= 0. \qquad\qquad [\because r_i^t(G,K) = r_i^*(G,K), \forall t, \forall i]$$
$$\tag{4.36}$$

For $\Phi \in \left\{ \underset{i=1}{\overset{m}{\text{Max}}}, \underset{i=1}{\overset{m}{\Sigma}} \right\}$, (4.35) becomes

$$\alpha \,|\, [R_t(G,K) - R^*(G,K)]\,| \,\leq \alpha\,\Phi\big|\big[r_i^t(G,K) - r_i^*(G,K)\big]\big|,$$
$$[\because |\,\Phi(a_i) - \Phi(b_i)\,| \,\leq \Phi\,|\,a_i - b_i\,|]$$
$$\alpha \,|\, [R_t(G,K) - R^*(G,K)]\,| \,= 0. \qquad\qquad [\because r_i^t(G,K) = r_i^*(G,K), \forall t, \forall i]$$
$$\tag{4.37}$$

Hence, by (4.36) and (4.37), the Lemma holds. $\qquad\qquad\qquad\qquad\square$

Lemma 4.8 $\gamma \big|\big[\Omega \hat{Q}_t^*(G') - \Omega \hat{Q}^*(G')\big]\big| = 0$, *holds for* $\gamma \in [0, 1)$ *as learning epoch* $t \rightarrow \infty$.

Proof
By (4.18),

$$\gamma \big|\big[\Omega \hat{Q}_t^*\big(G'\big) - \Omega \hat{Q}^*\big(G'\big)\big]\big|$$
$$= \gamma \big|\Phi\big[\hat{Q}_i^{t*}\big(s_i'\big) + \Delta\hat{Q}_i^{t*}\big(G'\big)\big] - \Phi\big[\hat{Q}_i^*\big(s_i'\big) + \Delta\hat{Q}_i^*\big(G'\big)\big]\big|. \tag{4.38}$$

Now, we have two cases:
Case I: For, $\Phi \in \left\{ \underset{i=1}{\overset{m}{\text{Min}}}, \underset{i=1}{\overset{m}{\Pi}} \right\}$ (4.38) becomes

$$\gamma \left\| \left[\Omega \hat{Q}_t^* \left(G' \right) - \Omega \hat{Q}^* \left(G' \right) \right] \right\|$$

$$\leq \gamma \left| \Phi \left[\hat{Q}_i^{t*} \left(s_i' \right) + \Delta \hat{Q}_i^{t*} \left(G' \right) - \hat{Q}_i^* \left(s_i' \right) - \Delta \hat{Q}_i^* \left(G' \right) \right] \right| \quad \text{[by Lemma 4.1 with } \gamma = 1]$$

$$= \gamma \left| \Phi \left[\left[\hat{Q}_i^{t*} \left(s_i' \right) - \hat{Q}_i^* \left(s_i' \right) \right] + \left[\Delta \hat{Q}_i^{t*} \left(G' \right) - \Delta \hat{Q}_i^* \left(G' \right) \right] \right] \right|$$

$$= \gamma \left| \Phi \left[\sum_{\forall s_i'} p_i \left(s_i' \mid (s_i, a_i) \right) \sum_{\forall a_i'} p_i^* \left(a_i' \mid s_i' \right) \left[Q_i^t \left(s_i', a_i' \right) - Q_i^* \left(s_i', a_i' \right) \right] \right. \right.$$

$$\left. \left. + \sum_{\forall G'} p \left(G' \mid (G, K) \right) \sum_{\forall K'} p^* \left(K' \mid G' \right) \left[d_i^t \left(G', K' \right) - d_i^* \left(G', K' \right) \right] \right] \right|$$

[by (4.A.1) and (4.20)]

$$\left[Q_i^* \left(s_i', a_i' \right) \text{ is the maximum individual Q-value of agent } i \text{ at } \left(s_i', a_i' \right) \right.$$

$$\left. \text{and } d_i^t \left(G', K' \right) = d_i^* \left(G', K' \right), \forall t, \forall i \right]$$

$$= \gamma \left| \Phi \left[\sum_{\forall s_i'} p_i \left(s_i' \mid (s_i, a_i) \right) \sum_{\forall a_i'} p_i^* \left(a_i' \mid s_i' \right) \left[Q_i^t \left(s_i', a_i' \right) - Q_i^* \left(s_i', a_i' \right) \right] \right] \right|.$$

$$(4.39)$$

Case II: For $\Phi \in \left\{ \underset{i=1}{\overset{m}{\text{Max}}}, \underset{i=1}{\overset{m}{\Sigma}} \right\}$, (4.38) becomes

$$\gamma \left\| \left[\Omega \hat{Q}_t^* \left(G' \right) - \Omega \hat{Q}^* \left(G' \right) \right] \right\|$$

$$\leq \gamma \Phi \left| \left[\hat{Q}_i^{t*} \left(s_i' \right) + \Delta \hat{Q}_i^{t*} \left(G' \right) - \hat{Q}_i^* \left(s_i' \right) - \Delta \hat{Q}_i^* \left(G' \right) \right] \right| \left[\because \mid \Phi(a_i) - \Phi(b_i) \mid \ \leq \Phi \mid a_i - b_i \mid \right]$$

$$= \gamma \Phi \left| \left[\hat{Q}_i^{t*} \left(s_i' \right) - \hat{Q}_i^* \left(s_i' \right) \right] + \left[\Delta \hat{Q}_i^{t*} \left(G' \right) - \Delta \hat{Q}_i^* \left(G' \right) \right] \right|$$

$$= \gamma \Phi \left| \sum_{\forall s_i'} p_i \left(s_i' \mid (s_i, a_i) \right) \sum_{\forall a_i'} p_i^* \left(a_i' \mid s_i' \right) \left[Q_i^t \left(s_i', a_i' \right) - Q_i^* \left(s_i', a_i' \right) \right] + \right.$$

$$\left. \sum_{\forall G'} p \left(G' \mid (G, K) \right) \sum_{\forall K'} p^* \left(K' \mid G' \right) \left[d_i^t \left(G', K' \right) - d_i^* \left(G', K' \right) \right] \right|$$

[by (4.A.1) and (4.20)]

$$\left[Q_i^* \left(s_i', a_i' \right) \text{ is the maximum individual Q-value of agent } i \text{ at } \left(s_i', a_i' \right) \right.$$

$$\left. \text{and } d_i^t \left(G', K' \right) = d_i^* \left(G', K' \right), \forall t, \forall i \right]$$

$$= \gamma \Phi \left| \sum_{\forall s_i'} p_i \left(s_i' \mid (s_i, a_i) \right) \sum_{\forall a_i'} p_i^* \left(a_i' \mid s_i' \right) \left[Q_i^t \left(s_i', a_i' \right) - Q_i^* \left(s_i', a_i' \right) \right] \right|.$$

$$(4.40)$$

Now as $t \to \infty$ by [17] $Q_i^t\left(s_i^{\prime}, a_i^{\prime}\right) \to Q_i^*\left(s_i^{\prime}, a_i^{\prime}\right)$. So, from (4.39) and (4.40) $\gamma\left|\left[\Omega\hat{Q}_t^*(G^{\prime}) - \Omega\hat{Q}^*(G^{\prime})\right]\right| = 0$, as $t \to \infty$.

Hence, the Lemma holds. $\qquad\square$

Lemma 4.9 *If* $|\Omega\widetilde{Q}_{t-k}(G,K) - \Omega\widetilde{Q}^*(G,K)| = \Delta\widetilde{Q}_{t-k}(G,K)$, *then* $(1-\alpha)|\left[\Omega\widetilde{Q}_{t-1}\right.$ $(G,K) - \Omega\widetilde{Q}^*(G,K)]\left.\right| = (1-\alpha)^k\Delta\widetilde{Q}_{t-k}(G,K)$, *where,* $\alpha \in [0, 1)$, $k \in \mathrm{R}^+$ *and* t *is the learning epoch.*

Proof
By (4.21),

$$(1-\alpha)\left|\left[\Omega\widetilde{Q}_{t-1}(G,K) - \Omega\widetilde{Q}^*(G,K)\right]\right|$$

$$= (1-\alpha)\left|\left[(1-\alpha)\Omega\widetilde{Q}_{t-2}(G,K) + \alpha\left[R_{t-2}(G,K) + \gamma \cdot \Omega\hat{Q}_{t-2}^*\left(G^{\prime}\right)\right]\right] - \left[(1-\alpha)\Omega\widetilde{Q}^*(G,K) + \alpha\left[R^*(G,K) + \gamma \cdot \Omega\hat{Q}^*\left(G^{\prime}\right)\right]\right]\right|$$

$$= (1-\alpha)\left|(1-\alpha)\left[\Omega\widetilde{Q}_{t-2}(G,K) - \Omega\widetilde{Q}^*(G,K)\right] + \alpha[R_{t-2}(G,K) - R^*(G,K)] + \gamma\left[\Omega\hat{Q}_{t-2}^*\left(G^{\prime}\right) - \gamma \cdot \Omega\hat{Q}^*\left(G^{\prime}\right)\right]\right|$$

$$\leq (1-\alpha)\left|(1-\alpha)\left[\Omega\widetilde{Q}_{t-2}(G,K) - \Omega\widetilde{Q}^*(G,K)\right] + \alpha[R_{t-2}(G,K) - R^*(G,K)]\right| + (1-\alpha)\left|\gamma\left[\Omega\hat{Q}_{t-2}^*\left(G^{\prime}\right) - \gamma \cdot \Omega\hat{Q}^*\left(G^{\prime}\right)\right]\right| \quad (\because |a+b| \leq |a| + |b|)$$

$$\leq (1-\alpha) \mid (1-\alpha)\left[\Omega\widetilde{Q}_{t-2}(G,K) - \Omega\widetilde{Q}^*(G,K)\right] \mid + (1-\alpha) \mid \alpha[R_{t-2}(G,K) - R^*(G,K)] \mid + (1-\alpha)\left|\gamma\left[\Omega\hat{Q}_{t-2}^*\left(G^{\prime}\right) - \gamma \cdot \Omega\hat{Q}^*\left(G^{\prime}\right)\right]\right| \quad (\because |a+b| \leq |a| + |b|)$$

$$= (1-\alpha)^2\left|\left[\Omega\widetilde{Q}_{t-2}(G,K) - \Omega\widetilde{Q}^*(G,K)\right]\right| + (1-\alpha)\alpha|[R_{t-2}(G,K) - R^*(G,K)]| + (1-\alpha)\gamma\left|\left[\Omega\hat{Q}_{t-2}^*\left(G^{\prime}\right) - \gamma \cdot \Omega\hat{Q}^*\left(G^{\prime}\right)\right]\right|$$

$$= (1-\alpha)^2\left|\left[\Omega\widetilde{Q}_{t-2}(G,K) - \Omega\widetilde{Q}^*(G,K)\right]\right| + (1-\alpha)\gamma\left|\left[\Omega\hat{Q}_{t-2}^*\left(G^{\prime}\right) - \gamma \cdot \Omega\hat{Q}^*\left(G^{\prime}\right)\right]\right|$$

[by Lemma 4.7]

$$= (1-\alpha)^2\left|\Omega\widetilde{Q}_{t-2}(G,K) - \Omega\widetilde{Q}^*(G,K)\right| \quad \text{[by Lemma 4.8 with } t \to \infty.]$$

$$= (1-\alpha)^k\left|\Omega\widetilde{Q}_{t-k}(G,K) - \Omega\widetilde{Q}^*(G,K)\right|$$

[For $k \in \mathrm{R}^+$ and continuing recursively employing (4.21)]

$$= (1-\alpha)^k\Delta\widetilde{Q}_{t-k}(G,K). \quad \text{[by statement]}$$

$$(4.41)$$

Hence, the Lemma holds. $\qquad\square$

Theorem 4.5 *The proposed Scheme-I-induced Ω Q-learning converges* $\left[\Omega\bar{Q}_t(G,K) \to \Omega\bar{Q}^*(G,K)\right]$ *as learning epoch* $t \to \infty$.

Proof
By (4.10),

$$\left| \Omega\bar{Q}_t(G,K) - \Omega\bar{Q}^*(G,K) \right| = \left| \Phi\left[Q_i^t(s_i,a_i) + d_i^t(G,K)\right] - \Phi\left[Q_i^*(s_i,a_i) + d_i^*(G,K)\right]\right|.$$
(4.41)

Now, we have two cases:

Case I: For $\Phi \in \left\{ \underset{i=1}{\overset{m}{\text{Min}}}, \underset{i=1}{\overset{m}{\Pi}} \right\}$, (4.41) becomes

$$\left| \Omega\bar{Q}_t(G,K) - \Omega\bar{Q}^*(G,K) \right| \quad \text{[by Lemma 4.1 with } \gamma = 1\text{]}$$
$$\leq \left| \Phi\left[Q_i^t(s_i,a_i) + d_i^t(G,K) - Q_i^*(s_i,a_i) - d_i^*(G,K)\right]\right|$$
$$= \left| \Phi\left[Q_i^t(s_i,a_i) - Q_i^*(s_i,a_i)\right] + \left[d_i^t(G,K) - d_i^*(G,K)\right]\right| = \left| \Phi\left[Q_i^t(s_i,a_i) - Q_i^*(s_i,a_i)\right]\right|$$

[for any agent i at a fixed (G,K) $d_i(G,K)$ is constant]

$$= \left| \Phi\left[\Delta Q_i^t(s_i,a_i)\right]\right|.$$
(4.42)

Here, $\Delta Q_i^t(s_i,a_i)$ refers to the error in Q-value of agent i at tth iteration.

Case II: For $\Phi \in \left\{ \underset{i=1}{\overset{m}{\text{Max}}}, \underset{i=1}{\overset{m}{\Sigma}} \right\}$, (4.41) becomes

$$\left| \Omega\bar{Q}_t(G,K) - \Omega\bar{Q}^*(G,K) \right|$$
$$\leq \left| \Phi\left[Q_i^t(s_i,a_i)\right] + \Phi\left[d_i^t(G,K)\right] - \Phi\left[Q_i^*(s_i,a_i)\right] - \Phi\left[d_i^*(G,K)\right]\right| \quad \text{[by Lemma 4.2 with } \gamma = 1\text{]}$$
$$= \left| \Phi\left[Q_i^t(s_i,a_i)\right] - \Phi\left[Q_i^*(s_i,a_i)\right] + \Phi\left[d_i^t(G,K)\right] - \Phi\left[d_i^*(G,K)\right]\right|$$
$$\leq \left| \Phi\left[Q_i^t(s_i,a_i)\right] - \Phi\left[Q_i^*(s_i,a_i)\right]\right| + \left| \Phi\left[d_i^t(G,K)\right] - \Phi\left[d_i^*(G,K)\right]\right| \quad [\because |a+b| \leq |a| + |b|]$$
$$\leq \Phi\left|\left[Q_i^t(s_i,a_i) - Q_i^*(s_i,a_i)\right]\right| + \Phi\left|\left[d_i^t(G,K) - d_i^*(G,K)\right]\right|$$

$[\because |\Phi[a_i] - \Phi[b_i]| \leq \Phi|[a_i + b_i]| = \Phi|[Q_i^t(s_i,a_i) - Q_i^*(s_i,a_i)]|$
[for any agent i at a fixed (G,K) $d_i(G,K)$ is constant]

$$= \left| \Phi\left[\Delta Q_i^t(s_i,a_i)\right]\right|.$$
(4.43)

Now, by [17] as learning epoch $t \to \infty$, $\Delta Q_i^t(s_i,a_i) \to 0$. Hence, the Scheme-I-induced Ω Q-learning converges $\left[\Omega\bar{Q}_t(G,K) \to \Omega\bar{Q}^*(G,K)\right]$ as $t \to \infty$. $\qquad\square$

Theorem 4.6 *The proposed Scheme-II-induced Ω Q-learning converges* $\left[\Omega\tilde{Q}_t(G,K) \to \Omega\tilde{Q}^*(G,K)\right]$ *as learning epoch* $t \to \infty$.

Proof
By (4.21),

$$\mid \left[\Omega \tilde{Q}_t(G,K) \right] - \left[\Omega \tilde{Q}^*(G,K) \right] \mid$$

$$= \left| \left[(1-\alpha)\Omega \tilde{Q}_{t-1}(G,K) + \alpha \left[R_t(G,K) + \gamma \cdot \Omega \hat{Q}_t^* \left(G' \right) \right] \right.\right.$$
$$\left.\left. - \left[(1-\alpha)\Omega \tilde{Q}^*(G,K) + \alpha \left[R^*(G,K) + \gamma \cdot \Omega \hat{Q}^* \left(G' \right) \right] \right] \right| \right.$$

$$= \left| (1-\alpha) \left[\Omega \tilde{Q}_{t-1}(G,K) - \Omega \tilde{Q}^*(G,K) \right] \right.$$
$$\left. + \alpha [R_t(G,K) - R^*(G,K)] + \gamma \left[\Omega \hat{Q}_t^* \left(G' \right) - \Omega \hat{Q}^* \left(G' \right) \right] \right|$$

$$\leq \mid (1-\alpha) \left[\Omega \tilde{Q}_{t-1}(G,K) - \Omega \tilde{Q}^*(G,K) \right] +$$
$$\alpha [R_t(G,K) - R^*(G,K)] \mid \left| \gamma \left[\Omega \hat{Q}_t^* \left(G' \right) - \Omega \hat{Q}^* \left(G' \right) \right] \right| \quad [\because \mid a+b \mid \leq \mid a \mid + \mid b \mid]$$

$$\leq \mid (1-\alpha) \left[\Omega \tilde{Q}_{t-1}(G,K) - \Omega \tilde{Q}^*(G,K) \right] \mid +$$
$$\mid \alpha [R_t(G,K) - R^*(G,K)] \mid + \left| \gamma \left[\Omega \hat{Q}_t^* \left(G' \right) - \Omega \hat{Q}^* \left(G' \right) \right] \right| \quad [\because \mid a+b \mid \leq \mid a \mid + \mid b \mid]$$

$$= (1-\alpha) \mid \left[\Omega \tilde{Q}_{t-1}(G,K) - \Omega \tilde{Q}^*(G,K) \right] \mid + \alpha \mid [R_t(G,K) - R^*(G,K)]$$
$$\mid + \gamma \left| \left[\Omega \hat{Q}_t^* \left(G' \right) - \Omega \hat{Q}^* \left(G' \right) \right] \right|$$

$$= (1-\alpha)^k \Delta \tilde{Q}_{t-k}(G,K). \quad [\text{by Lemma } 4.7 - 4.9]$$

$$(4.44)$$

Now, $\because \alpha \in [0, 1)$, with $k \to \infty$, $(1-\alpha)^k \Delta \tilde{Q}_{t-k}(G,K) \to 0$, where k is the dummy variable indicating the learning epoch. Hence, the Scheme-II-induced Ω Q-learning converges $\left[\Omega \tilde{Q}_t(G,K) \to \Omega \tilde{Q}^*(G,K) \right]$ as learning epoch $t \to \infty$. $\square$

4.3.8 Multi-agent Planning

Multi-agent planning is followed by multi-agent learning. In Correlated-Q-induced Planning (CQIP) algorithm [22, 46], m number of agents plan to reach a predefined joint goal state by determining CE using m joint Q-tables. In the proposed multi-agent planning algorithms, the (strategy or CE) joint action corresponding to the (maximum expected) maximum joint Q-value offered by the proposed multi-agent planning algorithms is selected. Two alternatives of multi-agent planning algorithms are proposed. The first one, called Ω Multi-agent Planning (ΩMP), does not require to satisfy task constraints as it has already been undertaken during the learning phase (by CΩQL-I and CΩQL-II algorithms). The ΩMP algorithm is given in Algorithm 4.3. However, in case the task constraint (e.g. fixed stick length or triangle structure) is not undertaken during the learning

---

Algorithm 4.3 Ω Multi-agent Planning (ΩMP)

Input: Feasible joint state G_F, Goal state G_L, $\Omega \overline{Q}^*(G_F, K_F)$ for Scheme-I and $\Omega \widetilde{Q}^*(G_F, K_F)$ for Scheme-II;
Output: Optimal feasible joint action (or CE) K_F^* at G_F;
Begin
　While $G_F \neq G_L$ **do Begin**
　　For $K_F \in \{K_F\}$
　　　If $\Omega \overline{Q}^*(G_F, K_F^*) \geq \Omega \overline{Q}^*(G_F, K_F)$ // for Scheme-I
　　　　$\Omega \widetilde{Q}^*(G_F, K_F^*) \geq \Omega \widetilde{Q}^*(G_F, K_F)$ // for Scheme-II
　　　　　Then $K_F^* \leftarrow K_F$ and $G_F \leftarrow G_F'$; // G_F' is the joint next state

　　　End If;
　　End for;
　End While;
End.

---

phase (as happens to be in ΩQL-I and ΩQL-II), task constraint(s) are to be satisfied during the planning phase. Constraint ΩMP(CΩMP) algorithm takes into account the task constraint during the planning phase. To handle the task constraint (stick-length) in CΩMP algorithm, the policy given in Algorithm 4.4 is adapted.

Algorithm 4.4 Constraint Ω Multi-agent Planning (CΩMP)

Input: Feasible joint state G_F, Goal state G_L, $\Omega \overline{Q}^*(G, K)$ for Scheme-I and $\Omega \widetilde{Q}^*(G, K)$ for Scheme-II;
Output: Optimal feasible joint action (or CE) K_F^* at G_F;
Begin
　While $G_F \neq G_L$ **do Begin**
　　For $K \in \{K\}$
　　　　If $\Omega \overline{Q}^*(G_F, K^*) \geq \Omega \overline{Q}^*(G_F, K)$ // for Scheme-I
　　　　　$\Omega \widetilde{Q}^*(G_F, K^*) \geq \Omega \widetilde{Q}^*(G_F, K)$ // for Scheme-II
　　　　　and feasible joint next state G_F' satisfies task constraints;
　　　　Then $K_F^* \leftarrow K$ and $G_F \leftarrow G_F'$; // G_F' is the joint next state

　　　End If;
　　End for;
　End While;
End.

Let the space (grids) between the agents (robots) holding a stick called intermediate state. Since the stick lies over the intermediate space, it is difficult to ascertain whether the region containing the next (front/back) intermediate state is occupied by an obstacle or not. To handle this problem, an agent has to check whether joint Q-value of the next intermediate space is nonzero (as Q-values are initialized as zero). A nonzero Q-value indicates that the next joint state is free from obstacles.

4.4 Complexity Analysis

In this section, evaluation of the space- and time-complexities of the proposed learning and planning algorithms in deterministic settings and comparing them, respectively, with the CQL and CQIP algorithms are done for $\Omega \in \{E, R\}$. The time-complexity for $\Omega \in \{U, L\}$ is shown in the Appendix 4.A and the space-complexity is not shown as it does not vary with the variation of Ω. However, the run-time complexities of the proposed and existing algorithms for $\Omega \in \{U, E, R, L\}$ are given in Section 4.5. For simplicities, let us assume that

$$|S_1| = |S_2| = \cdots = |S_m| = |S| \tag{4.45}$$

$$\text{and} \quad |A_1| = |A_2| = \cdots = |A_m| = |A| \tag{4.46}$$

Now, the cardinality of joint state set

$$
\begin{aligned}
|\{G\}| &= |S_1 \times S_2 \times \cdots \times S_m| \\
&= |S_1| \cdot |S_2| \cdots \cdots |S_m| \\
&= |S|^m. \quad \text{[by (4.45)]}
\end{aligned}
$$

Further, the cardinality of joint action set

$$
\begin{aligned}
|\{K\}| &= |A_1 \times A_2 \times \cdots \times A_m| \\
&= |A_1| \cdot |A_2| \cdots \cdots |A_m| \\
&= |A|^m. \quad \text{[by (4.46)]}
\end{aligned}
$$

Let t_{CQIP} and $t_{C\Omega MP}$ be the number of steps required to satisfy task constraint in one epoch during the planning phase by CQIP and CΩMP algorithms, respectively. In CQIP algorithm, task constraint is satisfied for m joint Q-tables and in CΩMP algorithm, task constraint is satisfied for one joint Q-table, so $t_{CQIP} > t_{C\Omega MP}$. Also, let $t_{C\Omega QL\text{-}I}$ and $t_{C\Omega QL\text{-}II}$ are the number of steps required to satisfy task constraint in one learning epoch by CΩQL-I and CΩQL-II algorithms, respectively. Comparison of the CQL and CQIP algorithms with the proposed ΩQL, CΩQL, and Ω-induced planning algorithms (ΩMP and CΩMP) are given below.

4.4.1 Complexity of CQL

Complexities of Correlated-Q-induced learning and planning algorithms are given below.

4.4.1.1 Space Complexity
Learning
In CQL algorithm, agents maintain their own Q-tables in joint state–action space. Hence, the space requirement for a joint Q-table is $|S|^m \cdot |A|^m$. Assuming there is no communication among the agents, during the learning phase, each agent has to maintain all agent's joint Q-tables individually by observing other agents state, action, and rewards. So, in CQL algorithm, space complexity (SC) of one agent is

$$SC_{CQL} = m \cdot |S|^m \cdot |A|^m = O(m \cdot |S|^m \cdot |A|^m). \tag{4.47}$$

Planning
In the CQIP phase, agents need the same number of joint Q-tables as required during the learning phase. Hence, SC of CQIP algorithm is given by

$$SC_{CQIP} = m \cdot |S|^m \cdot |A|^m = O(m \cdot |S|^m \cdot |A|^m). \tag{4.48}$$

4.4.1.2 Time Complexity
Learning
In CQL, during the learning phase for $\Omega \in \{E, R\}$, an agent has to find out CE among all the joint actions. Therefore, in CQL algorithm, time complexity (TC) in a single learning epoch is

$$TC_{CQL} = (m-1)|A|^m + (|A|^m - 1) = O(m|A|^m). \tag{4.49}$$

Planning
For $\Omega \in \{E, R\}$ during the CQIP phase, except finding CE agents have to satisfy task constraint. Therefore, in CQIP algorithm, TC is

$$TC_{CQIP} = (m-1)|A|^m + (|A|^m - 1) + t_{CQIP} > O(m|A|^m). \tag{4.50}$$

4.4.2 Complexity of the Proposed Algorithms

Complexities of the proposed learning and planning algorithms are given below.

4.4.2.1 Space Complexity

Learning

In ΩQL algorithms, an agent maintains m agents' Q-tables at individual state–action space and one joint Q-table. Hence, during the learning phase, SC in ΩQL algorithms is

$$SC_{\Omega QL} = m \cdot |S| \cdot |A| + |S|^m \cdot |A|^m > O(|S|^m \cdot |A|^m). \tag{4.51}$$

Planning

During the planning phase, in CΩMP, agents need only one joint Q-table to plan. Hence, SC in CΩMP algorithm is

$$SC_{C\Omega MP} = |S|^m \cdot |A|^m = O(|S|^m \cdot |A|^m). \tag{4.52}$$

4.4.2.2 Time Complexity

Learning

For $\Omega \in \{E, R\}$ in ΩQL algorithms, TC in a single learning epoch is the number of comparisons required to update joint Q-value for a joint state–action pair. In ΩQL-I and CΩQL-I, during the learning phase, an agent has to evaluate m individual Q-values by $m(|A| - 1)$ comparisons and evaluate the $\Phi \in \left\{\text{Min}_{i=1}^m, \text{Max}_{i=1}^m\right\}$ among the summation of m individual Q-values and $d_i(G, K)$ by $(m - 1)$ comparisons. Hence, TC during the learning phase in ΩQL-I and CΩQL-I (satisfying task constraint) algorithms are, respectively,

$$TC_{\Omega QL-I} = m \cdot (|A| - 1) + (m - 1) \approx O(m \cdot |A|) \tag{4.53}$$

and

$$TC_{C\Omega QL\ I} = m \cdot (|A| - 1) + (m - 1) + t_{C\Omega QL-I} > O(m \cdot |A|). \tag{4.54}$$

In ΩQL-II and CΩQL-II, during the learning phase, each agent has to find out the ΩIR and $\Omega\hat{Q}^*$. For that, an agent requires $2(m - 1)$ number of comparisons. Also agents update m individual Q-values by $m \cdot (|A| - 1)$ comparisons. Hence, TC during the learning phases in ΩQL-II and CΩQL-II (satisfying task constraint) algorithms are given, respectively, in (4.55) and (4.56).

$$TC_{\Omega QL-II} = m \cdot (|A| - 1) + 2(m - 1) \approx O(m \cdot |A|), \tag{4.55}$$

$$TC_{C\Omega QL-II} = m \cdot (|A| - 1) + 2(m - 1) + t_{C\Omega QL-II} > O(m \cdot |A|). \tag{4.56}$$

Planning

During the planning phase, agents evaluate optimal joint action (CE) corresponding to the maximum joint Q-value at a given joint state. Hence, TC in ΩMP and CΩMP (satisfying task constraint) algorithms are

$$TC_{\Omega MP} = (|A|^m - 1) = O(|A|^m)$$ (4.57)

and

$$TC_{C\Omega MP} = (|A|^m - 1) + t_{C\Omega MP} > O(|A|^m).$$ (4.58)

Space-complexity Analysis of Stick-Carrying and Triangle-Carrying Problem

SC of CΩQL algorithms ($SC_{C\Omega QL}$) and ΩMP algorithm ($SC_{\Omega MP}$) depend on the task to be solved. In the context of stick-carrying and triangle-carrying problems, a description is given below. In a grid map, usually there exist three types of cells, called Corner cell (c), Wall cell (w), and Other Cell (oc). From Figure 4.1 it is observed that in an $n \times n$ grid map, the number of Corner cells (C_c), Wall cells (C_w), and Other cells (C_{oc}) are 4, $4(n-2)$, and $(n-2)^2$, respectively. An analysis of Figure 4.2 indicates that in a two-agent system ($m = 2$), from a c, w, and oc there exist 3, 5, and 8 feasible joint states, respectively, for an agent. Therefore, assuming F_k be the number of feasible joint states from state k in an $n \times n$ grid map, the total number of feasible joint states by CΩQL algorithm is

$$m \times \sum_{k \in \{c, w, oc\}} C_k \times F_k = 2[4 \times 3 + 4(n-2) \times 5 + (n-2)^2 \times 8],$$ (4.59)

which on simplification returns

$$m \times \sum_{k \in \{c, w, oc\}} C_k \times F_k = 16n^2 - 24n + 8, \text{ i.e., } O(n^2),$$ (4.60)

Corner cell	Wall cell	Corner cell
Wall cell	Other cell	Wall cell
Corner cell	Wall cell	Corner cell

Figure 4.1 Corner cell, boundary cell, and other cell.

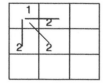 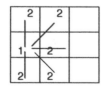 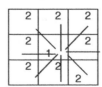

Figure 4.2 Feasible joint states for two-agent systems in stick-carrying problem.

while that in ΩQL algorithm, for $m = 2$ is

$$(n \times n)^m = (n \times n)^2 = (n)^4, \text{i.e., } O(n^4). \tag{4.61}$$

Similarly, for triangle-carrying problem $m = 3$ and total space complexity in CΩQL algorithm is

$$m \times \sum_{k \in \{c, w, oc\}} C_k \times F_k = 24n^2 - 48n + 24, \text{ i.e., } O(n^2) \tag{4.62}$$

and space complexity in ΩQL algorithm for $m = 3$ is

$$(n \times n)^m = (n \times n)^3 = (n)^6, \text{i.e., } O(n^6). \tag{4.63}$$

From (4.60)–(4.63) we conclude

$$SC_{\Omega QL} > SC_{C\Omega QL}. \tag{4.64}$$

As only learned joint state–action pairs are utilized to plan,

$$\therefore SC_{C\Omega MP} > SC_{\Omega MP}. \tag{4.65}$$

4.4.3 Complexity Comparison

Comparisons of complexities between CQL and proposed algorithms are given below.

4.4.3.1 Space Complexity
From (4.47) and (4.51),

$$
\begin{aligned}
\frac{SC_{\Omega QL}}{SC_{CQL}} &= \frac{m \cdot |S| \cdot |A| + |S|^m \cdot |A|^m}{m \cdot |S|^m \cdot |A|^m} \\
&= \frac{|S| \cdot |A|}{|S|^m \cdot |A|^m} + \frac{1}{m} \\
&\approx \frac{1}{|S|^{m-1} \cdot |A|^{m-1}} \quad \text{[after approximation]} \\
&< 1.
\end{aligned}
\tag{4.66}
$$

From (4.48) and (4.52),

$$
\begin{aligned}
\frac{SC_{C\Omega MP}}{SC_{CQIP}} &= \frac{|S|^m \cdot |A|^m}{m \cdot |S|^m \cdot |A|^m} \\
&= \frac{1}{m}.
\end{aligned}
\tag{4.67}
$$

$\therefore$SC of CΩMP is $\frac{1}{m}$ of the SC in CQIP.

We by (4.64) and (4.66) obtain,

$$SC_{CQL} > SC_{\Omega QL} > SC_{C\Omega QL}. \tag{4.68}$$

We by (4.65) and (4.67) obtain,

$$SC_{CQIP} > SC_{C\Omega MP} > SC_{\Omega MP}. \tag{4.69}$$

4.4.3.2 Time Complexity
From (4.49) and (4.54),

$$\frac{TC_{C\Omega QL\text{-}I}}{TC_{CQL}} = \frac{m \cdot (|A| - 1) + (m - 1) + t_{C\Omega QL\text{-}I}}{(m - 1)|A|^m + (|A|^m - 1)}$$

$$\approx \frac{1}{|A|^{m-1}} \quad \text{[after approximation]} \tag{4.70}$$

$$< 1.$$

From (4.53), (4.54), and (4.70),

$$TC_{CQL} > TC_{C\Omega QL\text{-}I} > TC_{\Omega QL\text{-}I}. \tag{4.71}$$

From (4.49) and (4.56),

$$\frac{TC_{C\Omega QL\text{-}II}}{TC_{CQL}} = \frac{m \cdot (|A| - 1) + 2(m - 1) + t_{C\Omega QL\text{-}II}}{(m - 1)|A|^m + (|A|^m - 1)}$$

$$\approx \frac{1}{|A|^{m-1}} \quad \text{[after approximation]} \tag{4.72}$$

$$< 1.$$

From (4.55), (4.56), and (4.72),

$$TC_{CQL} > TC_{C\Omega QL\text{-}II} > TC_{\Omega QL\text{-}II}. \tag{4.73}$$

Again from (4.50) and (4.58),

$$\frac{TC_{C\Omega MP}}{TC_{CQIP}} = \frac{(|A|^m - 1) + t_{C\Omega MP}}{(m - 1)|A|^m + (|A|^m - 1) + t_{CQIP}} \quad (t_{C\Omega MP} < t_{CQIP})$$

$$\approx \frac{1}{m}. \quad \text{[after approximation]} \tag{4.74}$$

From (4.57), (4.58), and (4.74), we obtain,

$$TC_{CQIP} > TC_{C\Omega MP} > TC_{\Omega MP}. \tag{4.75}$$

4.5   Simulation and Experimental Results

This section provides three experiments on multi-agent cooperation: one is Experiment 4.1 where complexity analysis of the proposed and the existing algorithms are shown. Second one is Experiment 4.2 (for $\Omega = R$) in which success of any one agent is enough to make the team successful. The last one is Experiment 4.3 (for $\Omega = E$) where simultaneous success of all the agents is needed to make the team successful. Experiment 4.1 provides experiments on cooperation of multiple mobile robots (agents) during the learning phase in the framework of object-transportation (stick-carrying and triangle-carrying) problem. The stick-carrying (triangle-carrying) problem [43] refers to transposition of the stick (triangle) from a given location to a desired destination in the given workspace by two (three) robots, where the stick (triangle) is held at its end-points (vertices). In Experiment 4.2, two agents cooperatively transport an object (box) from a given location to a predefined destination. Agents cooperate among themselves by moving (passing) the box to another agent with an aim to achieve success. In Experiment 4.3, two/three agents transport a stick/triangle from a given location to a predefined destination. Obstacles are added to the workspace to add complexity for all the mentioned Experiments. These Experiments are undertaken to study the performance of the proposed learning and planning algorithms to compare their performance with equilibrium-based MAQL (NQL, FQL, and CQL) algorithms. The performance metric used during the learning phase is the number (or percentage) of converged Q-values in joint state–action pair required with learning epochs and run-time complexity per learning epoch, while that during the planning phase includes only the run-time required to completely execute the plan.

4.5.1   Experimental Platform

Both computer simulations (for stick-carrying, triangle-carrying problem, and box-carrying) and hardware testing (for stick-carrying and box-carrying problem) are performed to compare the relative performance of the proposed and existing algorithms.

4.5.1.1   Simulation

The simulation is done employing MATLAB GUI (graphical user interface) R2015a version on an i7-3370 processor desktop computer with clock speed of 3.40 GHz. The individual grid size in computer simulation is fixed at 20×20 pixels. The total arenas in computer simulation are considered as of 5×5 unit grids size and 9×9 unit grids size.

In the present chapter, learning is conducted only in simulation, either by mimicking a real-world environment or by generating an arbitrary environment to avoid any damage of the real-robot. On the other hand, in simulation, planning is straightforward, where at the current joint state each agent evaluates the CE employing the identical Q-table maintained by each agent in joint state–action space, and moves to the next state by adding a fixed length in the direction of the action executed. In case of multiple equilibria, agents select the CE, which appears first.

4.5.1.2 Hardware

The hardware testing is done with two Khepera-II mobile robots [48, 49], equipped with an onboard Microcontroller (Motorola 68331) having a flash memory of 512 kB and a clock speed of 25 MHz. It has eight inbuilt active infrared proximity sensors and they are the well-known semiconductor (GaAs)-type proximity sensors [50]. In addition, both motor axes consist of an incremental encoder for position and speed measurement of the robot [48, 49]. Considering 2 unit and 5 unit speed (1 unit $= 0.08$ mm/10 ms), the stick-carrying problem is realized by connecting two robots through serial ports to two different Pentium IV desktop computers with clock speed of 2 GHz.

As already discussed, to avoid damage of the real-robot, learning is conducted in simulation only and subsequently the planning is done in real time. During the planning phase, the next positions of the robots are determined employing the proposed Ω-induced joint Q-table for CΩMP, ΩMP algorithms and the Correlated-Q-induced joint Q-tables for CQIP algorithm stored in both the Pentium IV machines. As the joint Q-table maintained by each Pentium IV machine (or robot) is identical, hence, robots do not require communicating with fellow robots as well as with fellow robots' computers during coordination (i.e. evaluation of CE). In the perspective of implementation, robots identify the change in states (next state) by measuring the distance traversed, in the direction of the action executed using incremental encoders. The individual grid size in hardware testing is fixed at 80 mm $\times$ 80 mm. Total arena for hardware testing is 9×9 unit grids (720 mm $\times$ 720 mm).

Both in computer simulation and hardware testing, each agent cooperates by selecting one set of actions among two sets. The first one consists of five actions: Left (L), Forward (F), Right (R), Back (B), and Pause (P) from a state. The second one includes nine actions, which are Left (L), Left-Forward (LF), Forward (F), Forward-Back (FB), Right (R), Right-Back (RB), Back (B), and Pause (P) from a state.

4.5.2 Experimental Approach

Experimental approaches for both learning and planning phases are given below.

4.5.2.1 Learning Phase

In the present chapter, it is assumed that agents can observe other agents' state, action, and reward, i.e. the environment can be represented as a Multi-agent Markov Decision Process (MMDP) [3]. Hence, in the above perspective, interagent communication is not required. The parameters required during the learning phase of the ΩQL-I, CΩQL-I, ΩQL-II, CΩQL-II, NQL, FQL, and CQL algorithms are set as follows: discounting factor $\gamma = 0.90$, learning rate $\alpha = 0.2$ and maximum immediate reward $= 100$. In NQL, FQL, and CQL algorithms, a reward of -1 (penalty) is given to an agent, when it hits other agents besides when hitting an obstacle or boundary wall in the proposed Experiments 4.1, 4.2, and 4.3. However, in ΩQL-I, CΩQL-I, ΩQL-II. and CΩQL-II algorithms, an agent receives the same reward (-1) due to penalty (hitting an obstacle or the boundary wall). In ΩQL-I and ΩQL-II, because of the collision among the agents and in CΩQL-I and CΩQL-II, because of collision among the agents as well as collision between the stick (or triangle) with an obstacle results in a reward of -1, however, individually agents are not penalized for the former cause. In simulation, the system joint state-transition probabilities are assigned as randomly generated constant values assuming the workspace to be slippery, satisfying the property of a Markovian matrix, subject to the sum of state-transition probabilities at each state is unity, and slippery workspace is the cause of uncertainty. In hardware, experiments are conducted only in the deterministic environment. To determine convergence performance of NQL, FQL, CQL, ΩQL-I, CΩQL-I, ΩQL-II, and CΩQL-II algorithms, the number (or percentage) of joint state–action pairs having converged Q-values after each learning epoch (N_{algo}) is accumulated in an array to plot with respect to the learning epoch, where $algo \in \{$NQL, FQL, CQL, ΩQL-I, CΩQL-I, ΩQL-II, CΩQL-II$\}$. The plots are shown under Experiment 4.1. In case of CQL, the average of N_{algo} among the four variants of CQL is done before comparison.

4.5.2.2 Planning Phase

To study the total execution time in the planning phase (Experiments 4.2 and 4.3), the run-time complexity of ΩMP, CΩMP, and CQIP algorithms are evaluated utilizing the 'run & time' button in MATLAB GUI. To study the run-time complexity during hardware test by Khepera-II mobile robot, a stop watch is used. Let T_{algo} be the run-time complexity of the $algo \in \{$CQIP, CΩMP, ΩMP$\}$. For multiple solutions (joint action or equilibrium), the solution which appears first is selected by all the agents. Let Si be the starting position of robot Ri and Gi is the goal position of the robot, $i \in \{1, 2, 3\}$. Real-time planning with Khepera-II mobile robots is followed after learning by computer simulation. Results for Experiments 4.1, 4.2, and 4.3 are given below.

4.5.3 Experimental Results

Experiments 4.1, 4.2, and 4.3 are given below in detail.

Experiment 4.1 Performance Test of the Proposed Learning Algorithms

The motivation of this experiment is to examine the convergence of the ΩQL-I, CΩQL-I (Figures 4.3a, 4.4a, and 4.5a), and ΩQL-II, CΩQL-II (Figures 4.3b, 4.4b, and 4.5b) algorithms with learning epoch for a two/three agent system. In Figures 4.3–4.5, all the algorithms are run for 20 times separately in an obstacle-free 5×5 grid map and the mean from the above 20 runs is evaluated. It is apparent from Figure 4.3 that for both the schemes $N_{CQL} > N_{\Omega QL} > N_{C\Omega QL}$, $\Omega \in \{E, U, R, L\}$. This is supported by (4.68) and (4.69). It is also observed from Figure 4.3 that $N_{\Omega QL-I} \approx N_{\Omega QL-II}$, $N_{C\Omega QL-I} \approx N_{C\Omega QL-II}$, and $N_{NQL} \approx N_{FQL} \approx N_{CQL}$. Further, the learning epochs required for convergence of NQL exceeds the same for ΩQL algorithms, which in turn exceeds the same for CΩQL algorithms. This is supported by (4.73) and (4.75). Hence, it is apparent from Figure 4.3 that CΩQL algorithms outperform NQL, FQL, CQL, and ΩQL algorithms in terms of speed of convergence. In Figure 4.3, a fluctuation is observed in the curves of CΩQL because of task-constraint checking (here, maintaining stick length in stick-carrying problem). Table 4.1 offers the average of the percentage of joint state–action pair converged. It is apparent that Table 4.1 supports (4.68), (4.69), (4.73), and (4.75). Similar inferences can be drawn from Figures 4.4 and 4.5.

Table 4.2 shows the superiority of the proposed schemes in terms of the run-time complexity of single learning epoch over the equilibrium-based MAQL including CQL for two agents.

Experiment 4.2 Object (Box)-Carrying By Scheme-I-Based Proposed Planning Algorithms

The motivation of this experiment is to transport a box by two agents from a given starting position to the desired destination utilizing the earlier experimental

(a)

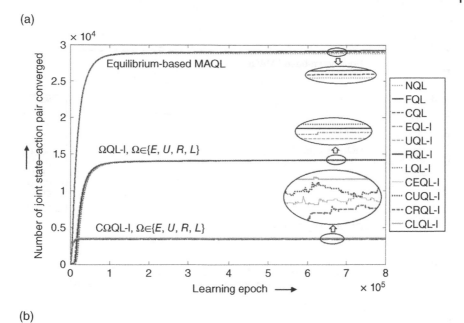

(b)

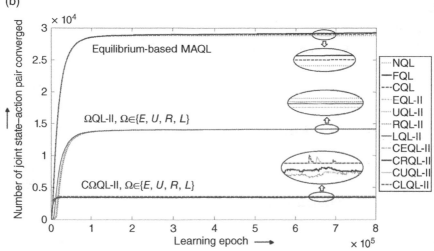

Figure 4.3 Convergence comparison of ΩQL, CΩQL, NQL, FQL, and CQL algorithms for two agents five actions, where $\Omega \in \{U, E, R, L\}$. (a) Scheme-I and (b) Scheme-II.

(a)

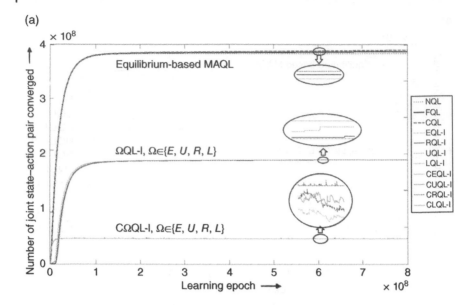

(b)

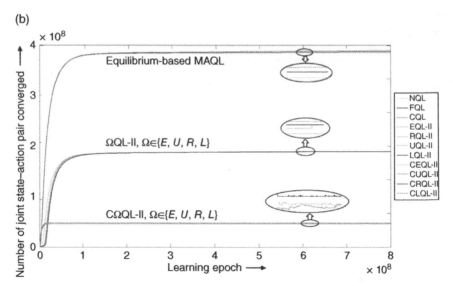

Figure 4.4 Convergence comparison of ΩQL, CΩQL, NQL, FQL, and CQL algorithms for three agents five actions, where $\Omega \in \{U, E, R, L\}$. (a) Scheme-I and (b) Scheme-II.

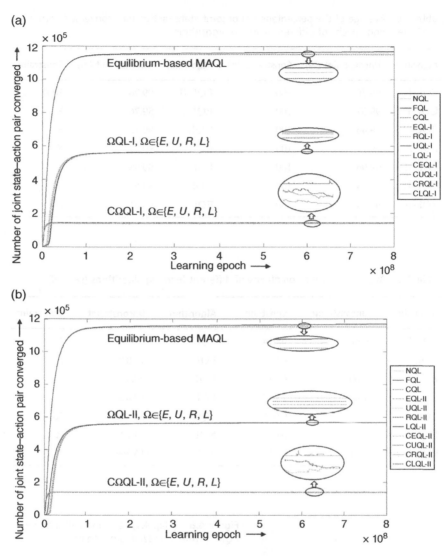

Figure 4.5 Convergence comparison of ΩQL, CΩQL, NQL, FQL, and CQL algorithms for two agents nine actions, where Ω ∈ {U, E, R, L}. (a) Scheme-I and (b) Scheme-II.

platform and approach for $\Omega = R$. Corresponding simulation and experimental results for the planning paths are shown in Figures 4.6 and 4.7. In Map 4.1 (Figures 4.6 and 4.7), there are seven obstacles and two agents (robots). Each agent has a gripper to grip the box with an aim to transport it from one position to

Table 4.1 Average of the percentage (%) of joint state–action pair converged within 1×10^5 learning epochs of different learning algorithms.

Algorithm	Unconstraint (%)	Constraint (%)	Algorithm	Unconstraint (%)	Constraint
EQL-I	99.76	100	LQL-II	99.96	100%
UQL-I	99.57	100	EQL	89.76	X
RQL-I	99.46	100	UQL	90.75	X
LQL-I	99.78	100	RQL	90.17	X
EQL-II	99.96	100	LQL	89.98	X
UQL-II	99.84	100	NQL	89.67	X
RQL-II	99.84	100	FQL	90.61	X

Table 4.2 Average run-time complexity of different learning algorithms (second).

Algorithm	Unconstraint	Constraint	Algorithm	Unconstraint	Constraint
EQL-I	0.008	0.014	LQL-II	1.011	1.017
UQL-I	0.019	0.023	EQL	12.019	X
RQL-I	0.008	0.015	UQL	22.018	X
LQL-I	1.008	1.015	RQL	12.020	X
EQL-II	0.010	0.016	LQL	32.801	X
UQL-II	0.021	0.025	NQL	14.201	X
RQL-II	0.012	0.016	FQL	16.206	X

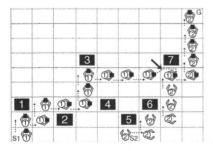

Figure 4.6 (Map 4.1) Planning with box by CQIP, CΩMP, and ΩMP algorithms.

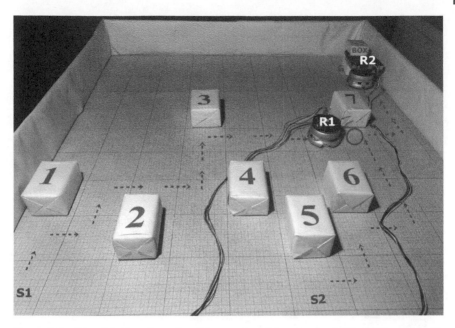

Figure 4.7 (Map 4.1) Planning using Khepera-II mobile robot by CQIP, CΩMP, and ΩMP algorithms, the planned path of which is given in Figure 4.6 also.

another. If two or more than two robots gather, then they exchange the box (indicated by thick arrow in Figure 4.6 and by a circle in Figure 4.7), motivated by the principle of market-based multi-robot coordination [51]. In Figure 4.7, two Khepera-II mobile robots are employed in real time, for box transportation task. In real time, only robot 2 (R2) has a gripper to grip the box (Figure 4.7) and robot 1 (R1) transports the same by carrying it on its top.

Table 4.3 provides the mean of the run-time complexity of the 20 runs of the CQIP, CΩMP, and ΩMP algorithms. It is apparent from Table 4.3 that $T_{CQIP} > T_{CΩMP} > T_{ΩMP}$, which is supported by (4.75). Hence, it is apparent from Table 4.3 that ΩMP algorithm outperforms the existing algorithms in terms of run-time complexity.

Experiment 4.3 Stick- or Triangle-Carrying By Model-II-Based Proposed Planning Algorithms

The motivation of this experiment is to transport a stick (by twin agents) or a triangle (by three agents) from a given starting position to the desired destination

Table 4.3 Average run-time complexity of different planning algorithms (second).

		Proposed planning algorithms	
Map	CQIP algorithm	CΩMP	ΩMP
4.1 (Figure 4.4)	15.93	10.92	8.90
4.1 (Figure 4.5) with 2 unit speed	28.84	23.75	21.92
4.1 (Figure 4.5) with 5 unit speed	18.65	13.65	11.97

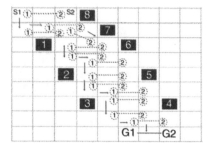

Figure 4.8 (Map 4.2) Planning with stick by CQIP, CΩMP, and ΩMP algorithms.

utilizing the above explained experimental platform and approach for $\Omega = E$. To transport a stick, an agent is contingent upon other agents, where all the agents have to reach their individual goal simultaneously to successfully complete the task. In Map 4.2 (Figures 4.8 and 4.9), two robots transport a fixed length stick from a given joint state to the joint next state, indicated by arrows avoiding eight obstacles. In Figures 4.8 and 4.9, robots follow optimal strategy (CE) using ΩMP or CΩMP algorithm. On the other hand, in CQIP, robots evaluate the same CE using m joint Q-tables obtained after CQL. Similarly, in Map 4.3 (Figure 4.10), three robots transport a triangle from a given joint state to the joint next state, indicated by arrows avoiding seven obstacles.

Table 4.4 provides the mean of the run-time complexity of the 20 runs of the CQIP, CΩMP, and ΩMP algorithms. By Table 4.4, one can conclude that $T_{CQIP} > T_{C\Omega MP} > T_{\Omega MP}$, which supports (4.75). Hence, it is apparent from Table 4.4 that ΩMP algorithm outperforms the existing algorithms in terms of run-time complexity.

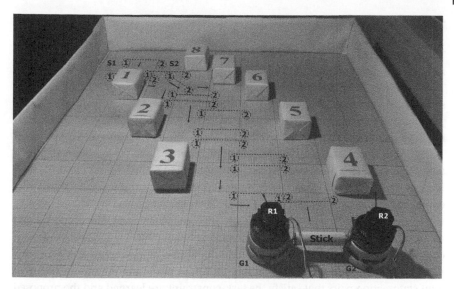

Figure 4.9 (Map 4.2) Path planning using Khepera-II mobile robot by CQIP, CΩMP, and ΩMP algorithms, the planned path of which is given in Figure 4.6 also.

Figure 4.10 (Map 4.3) Path planning with triangle employing CQIP, CΩMP, and ΩMP algorithms.

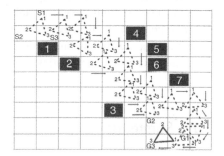

Table 4.4 Average run-time complexity of different planning algorithms (second).

Map	CQIP algorithm	Proposed planning algorithms	
		CΩMP	ΩMP
4.2 (Figure 4.8)	29.31	15.91	10.31
4.3 (Figure 4.10)	37.92	20.13	16.11
4.2 (Figure 4.9) with 2 unit speed	39.72	20.31	15.31
4.2 (Figure 4.9) with 5 unit speed	34.55	17.63	13.46

4.6 Conclusion

The chapter introduces a new approach to MAQL and learning-based multi-agent planning by efficiently fusing the CE and the proposed principles of Scheme-I and -II. The principles adapted in the proposed schemes yield a single Q-table in joint state–action space, which contains sufficient information to plan by employing the proposed multi-agent planning algorithms. Also the task-constraint is considered during the learning phase to further reduce the space-, time-, and run-time complexities.

CE is efficiently employed in the proposed Scheme-I and -II to obtain single Q-table in joint state–action space. The Q-table obtained from Scheme-I and -II, with less computational cost than the CQL, contains sufficient information to plan by employing the proposed ΩMP and CΩMP. This is also proved by Theorems 4.1–4.4. Convergence analyses of both the schemes are provided in Theorems 4.5 and 4.6, respectively. Although CΩMP plans well, it needs to satisfy the task-constraint (e.g. stick length in stick-carrying problem) during the planning phase. To save the run-time for task-constraint satisfaction, CΩQL is proposed, where only feasible joint state–action pairs that satisfy the task-constraint are learned and the proposed ΩMP follows the CΩQL. An analysis reveals that both time- and space-complexities of proposed learning and planning algorithms are significantly less than those of the CQL. A further reduction in complexity is obtained by dropping the infeasible joint state–action pairs from the joint Q-table.

Simulation and practical experimental results are given to validate the superiority of the proposed algorithms over the reference algorithms considering space-, time-, and run-time complexities as the performance metrics.

4.7 Summary

Unlike CQL, this chapter proposes an attractive approach to adapt composite rewards of all the agents in one Q-table in joint state–action space during learning, and subsequently these rewards are employed to compute correlated equilibrium in the planning phase. Two separate schemes of MAQL have been proposed. If success of only one agent is enough to make the team successful, then Scheme-I is employed. However, if an agent's success is contingent upon other agents and simultaneous success of the agents is required, then Scheme-II is employed. It is also shown that the CE obtained by the proposed algorithms and by the traditional CQL is identical. In order to restrict the exploration within the feasible joint states, constraint versions of the said algorithms are also proposed. Complexity analysis and experiments have been undertaken to validate the performance of the proposed algorithms in multi-robot planning on both simulated and real platforms.

Appendix 4.A Supporting Algorithm and Mathematical Analysis

The expected optimal Q-value of an agent i at next state $s_i^/ \in S_i$ is denoted by $\hat{Q}_i^*\left(s_i^/\right)$ and is expressed in (4.A.1).

$$\hat{Q}_i^*\left(s_i^/\right) = \sum_{\forall s_i^/} p_i\left(s_i^/ \mid (s_i, a_i)\right) \sum_{\forall a_i^/} p_i^*\left(a_i^/ \mid s_i^/\right) Q_i\left(s_i^/, a_i^/\right) \qquad (4.A.1)$$

Here, $a_i^/ \in A_i$ is the action at $s_i^/$. $Q_i\left(s_i^/, a_i^/\right)$ be the Q-value of agent i at next state $s_i^/ \in S_i$ because of action $a_i^/ \in A_i$. $p_i^* : A_i \rightarrow [0,1]$ is the optimal probability distribution over A_i.

Algorithm 4.A.1 Correlated Q-Learning (CQL)

Input: Learning rate $a \in [0, 1)$ and discounting factor $\gamma \in [0, 1)$;
Output: Optimal joint Q-value $Q_i^*(G, K)$, $\forall G, \forall K, \forall i$;
Begin
  Initialize: Current state s_i, action set A_i at s_i, joint Q-value $Q_i(G, K) \leftarrow 0$, $\forall G, \forall K, \forall i$;
  Repeat
  Randomly select an action $a_i \in A_i$, $\forall i$ and execute it;
  Observe joint immediate reward $r_i(G, K)$, $\forall i$;
  Evaluate next state $s_i^/ \leftarrow \delta_i(s_i, a_i)$, $\forall i$ to obtain joint next state $G^/ = < s_i^/ >_{i=1}^m$ for m agents;
  $Q_i(G, K) \leftarrow (1 - a)Q_i(G, K) + a\big[r_i(G, K) + \gamma.\Omega\hat{Q}_i^*(G^/)\big]$, $\forall i$ and $G \leftarrow G^/$; $//\Omega \in \{U, E, R, L\}$
  Until $Q_i(G, K)$, $\forall G, \forall K, \forall i$ converges;
  $Q_i^*(G, K) \leftarrow Q_i(G, K)$, $\forall G, \forall K, \forall i$;
End.

Table 4.A.1 Time-complexity analysis.

	Algorithm	$\Omega = U$	$\Omega = L$
Learning	CQL	$m\|A\|^m + (\|A\|^m - 1)$	$N^m\|A\|^m + (\|A\|^m - 1)$
	ΩQL-I	$m(\|A\| - 1) + m$	$m(\|A\| - 1) + N^m$
	CΩQL-I	$m(\|A\| - 1) + m + t_{C\Omega QL\text{-}I}$	$m(\|A\| - 1) + N^m + t_{C\Omega QL\text{-}I}$
	ΩQL-II	$m(\|A\| - 1) + 2m$	$m(\|A\| - 1) + 2N^m$
	CΩQL-II	$m(\|A\| - 1) + 2m + t_{C\Omega QL\text{-}I}$	$m(\|A\| - 1) + 2N^m + t_{C\Omega QL\text{-}I}$
Planning	CQIP	$m\|A\|^m + (\|A\|^m - 1) + t_{CQIP}$	$N^m\|A\|^m + (\|A\|^m - 1) + t_{CQIP}$
	ΩMP	$(\|A\|^m - 1)$	$(\|A\|^m - 1)$
	CΩMP	$(\|A\|^m - 1) + t_{C\Omega MP}$	$(\|A\|^m - 1) + t_{C\Omega MP}$

The time-complexity for $\Omega \in \{U, L\}$ are given in Table 4.A.1 for the traditional as well as for the proposed algorithms. Let N be the maximum number of digits required to represent one Q-value all agents' Q-values.

It is apparent from Table 4.A.1 and earlier complexity analysis in Section 4.4 that the time-complexity of the proposed planning algorithms does not vary with the variation of Ω.

References

1 Busoniu, L., Babuska, R., De Schutter, B., and Ernst, D. (2010). *Reinforcement Learning and Dynamic Programming Using Function Approximators*. New York: CRC Press.

2 Poole, D.L. and Mackworth, A.K. (2010). *Artificial Intelligence: Foundations of Computational Agents*. Cambridge University Press.

3 Sutton, R.S. and Barto, A.G. (1998). *Introduction to Reinforcement Learning*. Cambridge, MA: MIT Press.

4 Mitchell, T.M. (1997). *Machine Learning*. McGraw-Hill.

5 Pradhan, S.K. and Subudhi, B. (2012). Real-time adaptive control of a flexible manipulator using reinforcement learning. *IEEE Transactions on Automation Science and Engineering* 9 (2): 237–249.

6 Vrancx, P., Verbeeck, K., and Nowe, A. (2008). Decentralized learning in markov games. *IEEE Transactions on Systems, Man and Cybernetics (Part B: Cybernetics)* 38 (4): 976–981.

7 Leng, J., Jain, L., and Fyfe, C. (2007). Convergence analysis on approximate reinforcement learning. In: *Knowledge Science, Engineering and Management* (eds. Z. Zhang and J. Siekmann), 85–91. Berlin, Heidelberg: Springer.

8 Park, S. and Roh, K.S. (2016). Coarse-to-fine localization for a mobile robot based on place learning with a 2-D range scan. *IEEE Transactions on Robotics* https://doi.org/10.1109/TRO.2016.2544301.

9 Kamkarian, P. and Hexmoor, H. (2013). A human inspired collision avoidance strategy for moving agents. *Proceedings of IEEE Federated Conference on Computer Science and Information System,* Kraków, Poland (8–11 September 2013), pp. 63–67.

10 Ng, A.Y., Coates, A., Diel, M. et al. (2006). Autonomous inverted helicopter flight via reinforcement learning. In: *Experimental Robotics IX* (eds. O. Khatib, V. Kumar and G. Pappas), 363–372. Berlin, Heidelberg: Springer.

11 Busoniu, L., Babuska, R., and De Schutter, B. (2008). A comprehensive survey of multiagent reinforcement learning. *IEEE Transactions on Systems, Man, and Cybernetics, Part C: Applications and Reviews* 38 (2): 156–172.

12 Hu, Y., Gao, Y., and An, B. (2014). Accelerating multiagent reinforcement learning by equilibrium transfer. *IEEE Transactions on Cybernetics* 45 (7): 1289–1302.

13 Samejima, K. and Omori, T. (1999). Adaptive internal state space construction method for reinforcement learning of a real-world agent. *Neural Networks* 12 (7): 1143–1155.

14 Mahadevan, S. (1994). To discount or not to discount in reinforcement learning: a case study comparing R learning and Q learning. *International Conference on Machine Learning* New Brunswick, NJ (10–13 July 1994), pp. 164–172.

15 Littman, M.L. (2001). Value-function reinforcement learning in Markov games. *Cognitive Systems Research* 2 (1): 55–66.

16 Konar, A., Chakraborty, I.G., Singh, S.J. et al. (2013). A deterministic improved Q-learning for path planning of a mobile robot. *IEEE Transactions on Systems, Man, And Cybernetics: Systems* 43 (5): 1–13.

17 Watkins, C.J. and Dayan, P. (1992). Q-learning. *Machine Learning* 8 (3–4): 279–292.

18 Bin, Z. and Lin, Z. (2014). Consensus of high-order multi-agent systems with large input and communication delays. *Automatica* 50 (2): 452–464.

19 D. Chakraborty and P. Stone, "Multiagent learning in the presence of memory-bounded agents," *Autonomous Agents and Multi-agent Systems,* Elsevier, vol. 28 no. 2, pp. 182-213, 2014.

20 Shoham, Y., Powers, R., and Grenager, T. (2003). Multi-agent reinforcement learning: a critical survey, Web manuscript, 2003. https://www.cc.gatech.edu/classes/AY2009/cs7641_spring/handouts/MALearning_ACriticalSurvey_2003_0516.pdf (accessed 27 May 2020).

21 Hu, J. and Wellman, M.P. (2003). Nash Q-learning for general-sum stochastic games. *The Journal of Machine Learning Research* 4: 1039–1069.

22 Greenwald, A., Hall, K., and Serrano, R. (2003). Correlated Q-learning. *International Conference on Machine Learning* 3: 242–249, Washington, DC.

23 Littman, M.L. (2001). Friend-or-foe Q-learning in general-sum games. *International Conference on Machine Learning* 1: 322–328, MA, USA.

24 Bowling, M. (2000). Convergence problems of general-sum multiagent reinforcement learning. *International Conference on Machine Learning*: 89–94.

25 Sen, S., Mahendr, S., and Hale, J. (1994). Learning to coordinate without sharing information. *Association for the Advancement of Artificial Intelligence*, Washington (31 July to 4 August 1994), pp. 426–431.

26 Tan, M. (1993). Multi-agent reinforcement learning: independent vs. cooperative agents. *Proceedings of the Tenth International Conference on Machine Learning*, Amherst, MA (27–29 June 1993). Vol. 337.

27 Yanco, H. and Stein, L. (1993). An adaptive communication protocol for cooperating mobile robots. *Proceedings of the 2nd International Conference on Simulation of Adaptive Behavior*, Chicago (August 1993), pp. 478–485. Cambridge MA: The MIT Press.

28 Hu, J. and Wellman, M.P. (1998). Multiagent reinforcement learning: theoretical framework and an algorithm. *International Conference on Machine Learning* 98: 242–250.

29 Muelling, K., Boularias, A., Mohler, B. et al. (2014). Learning strategies in table tennis using inverse reinforcement learning. *Biological Cybernetics* 108 (5): 603–619.

30 Claus, C. and Boutilier, C. (1998). The dynamics of reinforcement learning in cooperative multiagent systems. *Association for the Advancement of Artificial Intelligence/American Association for Artificial Intelligence*, Madison, WI (26–30 July 1998), pp. 746–752.

31 Leng, J., Fyfe, C., and Jain, L. (2008). Simulation and reinforcement learning with soccer agents. *Multiagent and Grid Systems* 4 (4): 415–436.

32 Littman, M.L. and Stone, P. (2005). A polynomial-time Nash equilibrium algorithm for repeated games. *Decision Support Systems* 39 (1): 55–66.

33 Peters, J., Vijayakumar, S., and Schaal, S. (2003). Reinforcement learning for humanoid robotics. *Proceedings of the International Conference on Humanoid Robots*, Las Vegas (27–31 October 2003), pp. 1–20.

34 Boutilier, C. (1996). Planning, learning and coordination in multiagent decision processes. *Proceedings of the 6th Conference on Theoretical Aspects of Rationality and Knowledge*, De Zeeuwse Stromen, Netherlands (17–20 March 1996), pp. 195–210. Morgan Kaufmann Publishers Inc.

35 Polak, B. (2007). Game Theory. Yale University. http://oyc.yale.edu/economics/econ-159 (accessed 27 May 2020).

36 Nash, J. (1951). Non-cooperative games. *Annals of Mathematics* 54 (2): 286–295.

37 Fan, Q., Zeitouni, K., Xiong, N. et al. (2017). Nash equilibrium-based semantic cache in mobile sensor grid database systems. *IEEE Transactions on Systems, Man, and Cybernetics: Systems* 47 (9): 2550–2561.

38 Barreiro-Gomez, J., Obando, G., and Quijano, N. (2017). Distributed population dynamics: optimization and control applications. *IEEE Transactions on Systems, Man, and Cybernetics: Systems* 47 (2): 304–314.

39 Hu, Y., Gao, Y., and An, B. (2015). Accelerating multiagent reinforcement learning by equilibrium transfer. *IEEE Transactions on Cybernetics* 45 (7): 1289–1302.

40 Kok, J.R. and Vlassis, N. (2004). Sparse cooperative Q-learning. *Proceedings of the Twenty-First International Conference on Machine Learning*, Banff, Alberta (4–8 July 2004), p. 61. ACM.

41 Zhang, Z., Zhao, D., Gao, J. et al. (2017). FMRQ-a multiagent reinforcement learning algorithm for fully cooperative tasks. *IEEE Transactions on Cybernetics* 47 (6): 1367–1379.

42 Eilers, D., Dunis, C.L., von Mettenheim, H.J., and Breitner, M.H. (2014). Intelligent trading of seasonal effects: a decision support algorithm based on reinforcement learning. *Decision Support Systems* 64: 100–108.

43 Sadhu, A.K., Rakshit, P., and Konar, A. (2016). A modified imperialist competitive algorithm for multi-robot stick-carrying application. *Robotics and Autonomous Systems* 76: 15–35.

44 Sadhu, A.K. and Konar, A. (2017). Improving the speed of convergence of multi-agent Q-learning for cooperative task-planning by a robot-team. *Robotics and Autonomous Systems* 92: 66–80.

45 de Weerdt, M. and Clement, B. (2009). Introduction to planning in multiagent systems. *Multiagent and Grid Systems* 5 (4): 345–355.

46 Greenwald, A., Hall, K., and Zinkevich, M. (2007). Correlated Q-learning. *Journal of Machine Learning Research* 1 (1): 1–30.

47 Kaelbling, L.P., Littman, M.L., and Moore, A.W. (1996). Reinforcement learning: a survey. *Journal of Artificial Intelligence Research*: 237–285.

48 Franzi, E. (1998). *Khepera BIOS 5.0 Reference Manual*. K-Team, SA.

49 K. U. M. Version (1999). *Khepera User Manual 5.02*. K-Team, SA.

50 Siemens Semiconductor Group. SFH 900-a low cost miniature reflex optical sensor app note 26. SFH900 Datasheet.

51 Dias, M.B. (2004). Traderbots: a new paradigm for robust and efficient multi-robot coordination in dynamic environments. Doctoral dissertation. Carnegie Mellon University Pittsburgh.

5

A Modified Imperialist Competitive Algorithm for Multi-Robot Stick-Carrying Application

This chapter proposes a novel evolutionary optimization approach of solving a multi-robot stick-carrying problem. The problem refers to determine the time-optimal trajectory of a stick, being carried by two robots, from a given starting position to a predefined goal position amidst static obstacles in a robot world map. The problem has been solved using a new hybrid evolutionary algorithm (EA). Hybridization, in the context of evolutionary optimization framework, refers to developing new algorithms by synergistically combining the composite benefits of global exploration and local exploitation capabilities of different ancestor algorithms. The chapter proposes a novel approach to embed the motion dynamics of fireflies of the Firefly Algorithm (FA) into a sociopolitical evolution-based meta-heuristic search algorithm, known as the Imperialist Competitive Algorithm (ICA). The proposed algorithm also uses a modified random walk strategy based on the position of the candidate solutions in the search space to effectually balance the trade-off between exploration and exploitation. Thirteen other state-of-the-art techniques have been used here to study the relative performance of the proposed Imperialist Competitive Firefly Algorithm (ICFA) with respect to run-time and accuracy (offset in objective function from the theoretical optimum after termination of the algorithm). Computer simulations undertaken on a well-known set of 25 benchmark functions reveal that the incorporation of the proposed strategies into the traditional ICA makes it more efficient in both run-time and accuracy. The performance of the proposed algorithm has then finally been studied on the real-time multi-robot stick-carrying problem. Experimental results obtained for both simulation and real frameworks indicate that the proposed algorithm-based stick-carrying scheme outperforms other state-of-the-art techniques with respect to two standard metrics defined in the literature. The application justifies the importance of the proposed hybridization and parameter adaptation strategies in practical systems.

Multi-agent Coordination: A Reinforcement Learning Approach, First Edition.
Arup Kumar Sadhu and Amit Konar.
© 2021 The Institute of Electrical and Electronics Engineers, Inc.
Published 2021 by John Wiley & Sons, Inc.

5.1 Introduction

Multi-robot coordination has emerged as an important part of robotics research since late 1980s [1]. The problem of coordination of multiple robots arises in numerous applications, for example, in factory environment (to transfer materials and products between workstations), in patient-carrying systems in hospitals/airports, and in defense and security systems. Coordination in multi-agent robotics aims at synchronizing and harmonizing the simultaneous actions of multiple robotic agents in pursuit of a specific goal. One of the crucial challenges for multi-agent coordination systems is to design appropriate coordination strategies between the robotic agents that enable them to perform effectively and time optimally in complex workspace. There exists extensive literature on multi-robot coordination employing different approaches including graphs [2], Voronoi diagrams [3], potential field [4], adaptive action selection [5], intention inference [6], cooperative conveyance [7], and perceptual cues [8]. The traditional mathematical model of a multi-robot coordination system can be recast in the settings of an optimization problem [9] with an aim to efficiently utilize the system resources. The objective of optimization here is to determine optimal robotic actions based on the sensory readings collected from the environment by the robots to meet one or more desired objectives of the problem. Thus, optimization of the objective functions, characterizing the functionality of a multi-robot coordination system, provides the feasible solutions for the qualitative system performance. The chapter proposes a novel formulation of a multi-robot stick-carrying system as an optimization problem. The stick-carrying problem [10] includes two robots to jointly carry a stick from an assigned initial position to a specified final position in a given environment, without collision with the given obstacles near the robots and the stick, constrained by the constant distance (equal to the stick length) between the robots. The sensory data of the robots, offering the range measurements of the stick from the nearby obstacles and the workspace boundary, are the input variables of the optimization problem while the output variables being the necessary amount of rotation and translation of the stick (by the robots) to transfer it in small steps toward the goal. The primary objective function of the stick-carrying optimization problem in this context is concerned with the minimization of the time consumed by the robots (i.e. the length of the path to be traversed by the robots) for complete traversal of the planned trajectory. In other words, we expect the robots to plan the local trajectory, so that the stick is shifted from a given position to the next position (subgoal) in a time-optimal sense avoiding collision with the obstacles or the boundary of the world map in the robots' workspace. The optimization algorithm is executed for each local planning step to carry the stick by a small distance. A sequence of local planning ultimately transports the stick to the desired goal position.

In the past decades, a plethora of computing algorithms has been proposed in the domain of numerical function optimization. Traditional derivative-based optimization techniques, such as Newton–Raphson method, quasi-Newton strategy, and steepest descent learning algorithm, and the like, completely rely on the derivative information of the objective function guiding the direction of search in the fitness landscape. These methods perform satisfactorily when the objective function to be optimized is globally concave over the search space. However, in real-world scenario, the objective functions are sometimes found to be irregular and multimodal comprising multiple local optima, saddle points, and discontinuities. Traditional gradient-based optimization algorithms are, therefore, ineffective to capture the global optima of these non-differentiable functions.

Since early 1990s, EAs have emerged as a derivative-free stochastic global optimizer with capability of providing promising results to optimize the non-differentiable functions of the real-world problems. EAs with the real-valued vector representation of the potential solutions of a complex physical system have earned wide popularity due to their flexibility and simple search strategy in the high-dimensional hyperspace and robust performance in the dynamic environment. They commence with a population of trial solutions, symbolizing the potential solutions of the problem. The relative integrity of a solution can be assessed by evaluating its associated objective function value (often called fitness). New solutions are then generated by population-based evolutionary procedure. Finally, a greedy selection step is employed being inspired by Darwinian principle of the survival of the fittest. The selection step is responsible for filtering and promoting better candidate solutions from the candidate pool to the next evolutionary generation.

The radical reduction in the computational time in the recent past coupled with the increasing demand to solve complex real-world problems has enhanced the quest for more proficient nature-inspired meta-heuristics. It is to be noted that two fundamental processes drive the evolution of an EA population – the diversification process, which enables exploring different regions of the search space and the intensification process, which ensures the exploitation of previous knowledge about the fitness landscape. The effects of such exploration and exploitation processes need to be competently balanced by an EA for its qualitative performance both w.r.t computational accuracy and run-time complexity over different fitness landscapes.

However, the superiority of an EA in optimizing different objective functions is subjected to the No Free Lunch Theorem (NFLT) [11]. According to NFLT, the expected effectiveness of any two traditional EAs across all possible optimization problems is identical. A self-evident implication of NFLT is that the elevated performance of one EA, say A, over other EA, say B, for one class of optimization problems is counterbalanced by their respective performances over another class. It is therefore practically difficult to devise a universal EA that would solve all the problems. This apparently paves the way for hybridization of EAs with other optimization strategies, machine learning techniques, and heuristics. In evolutionary computation paradigm, hybridization [12] refers to the process of integrating the attractive features of two or more EAs synergistically to develop a new hybrid EA. The hybrid EA is expected to outperform its ancestors w.r.t both accuracy and complexity over application-specific or general benchmark problems. The fusion of EAs through hybridization hence can be regarded as the key to overcome their individual limitations.

In this chapter, we propose a simple yet very powerful hybrid EA by collegially coalescing the attributes of two global optimizers – the traditional ICA [13, 14] and the traditional FA [15]. ICA is a novel sociopolitically motivated population-based meta-heuristic, which has revealed remarkable performance in variant fields of optimization problems. The population individuals of ICA, resembling the countries in the world, are categorized as imperialist (best countries) and colonies (rest of the population) based on their associated objective function values. The entire population is subsequently divided into a number of subpopulations, known as empires, each consisting of an imperialist and a number of colonies (randomly selected based on the ruling power of the respective imperialist). The foundation of ICA is rooted in three elementary operations: (i) assimilation, which allows the possible movement of the colonies to their respective imperialist (strengthening exploitation), (ii) revolution, which brings out sudden change in the countries' sociopolitical views (preventing premature convergence of ICA), and (iii) the imperialistic competition, which reinforces the powerful empires with an attempt to collapse the weakest one. There exists a vast literature on the modification and application of ICA. Among these the following contributions need special mentioning.

A new EA has been proposed in [16] by combining ICA, Differential Evolution (DE) [17], and K-means clustering algorithm. ICA is also successfully hybridized with EA [18] and Genetic Algorithm (GA) [19]. ICA is treated as a local search strategy to develop a new memetic algorithm in [20]. A new variant of ICA has been introduced in [21] by strengthening the interaction among the imperialists of all the empires. A modified version of ICA is proposed in [22] based on the attraction and repulsion profiles between countries in an empire and is applied to solve a brushless direct current wheel motor design problem. A hybrid ICA, along with an artificial neural network, is implemented in [23] for oil flow rate prediction combining the local search facility of back-propagation and the global search ability of ICA. Seven different chaotic maps are utilized in [24] to improve the convergence characteristics of traditional ICA. Chaos has also been employed in [25] to adapt the angle of movement of colonies in ICA. In [26], an adaptive colony-radius selection strategy is proposed for improvement in the assimilation policy of ICA. ICA has also been extended to solve constrained optimization policy in [27] equipped with a classical penalty technique.

In [28], ICA is used to solve the dynamic economic dispatch problem while ICA is utilized for parameter identification of a reduced detailed R-C-L-M model of transformer in [29]. The capability of ICA to efficiently control the traffic of a metropolis is studied in [30]. ICA has also shown its potential to design a novel rotor configuration [31]. In [32], promising results are obtained for optimal design of a brushless doubly fed induction generator using ICA. ICA has also been successfully applied for clustering [33] and optimizing epoxy adhesive layer in fiberglass [34]. ICA has also been utilized to optimize the skeletal structures [35] and for solving the integrated product mix-outsourcing optimization problem [36]. The efficiency of ICA has also been validated in the field of template matching [37], IIR filter design [38], nonlinear multiple response [39], graph coloring problem [40], PID controller tuning [41], and scheduling in a hybrid flexible flow-shop [42]. A comparative study carried out in [43] exposes superiority of ICA over Particle Swarm Optimization (PSO) in solving the inverse problem in eddy current nondestructive evaluation.

On the other hand, FA is a population-based meta-heuristic search algorithm for numerical function optimization that draws inspiration from the collective behavior and biochemical properties of fireflies. The motion dynamic of fireflies is derived from four properties of the social interaction between a group of mobile agents – following, dispersion, aggregation, and homing. In [44], a fuzzy controller is employed to adaptively tune FA parameters for its better performance. In contrast, a novel strategy employing optimal deviation-based FA-tuned fuzzy membership function is introduced in [45] for multi-objective unit commitment problem. Another multi-objective variant of FA, adaptively tuning its control parameters using beta distribution, is proposed in [46]. A high convergence speed is obtained in [47] by using a Gaussian probability distribution-based position renewal of fireflies. FA has been extensively applied to many optimization fields, including annual crop planning problem [48], complex and nonlinear problem [49], data mining [50], digital image processing [51], structural size and shape optimization [52], hybrid flow-shop scheduling problems [53], QAP problem [54], queuing system optimization [55], economic emissions load dispatch problem [56], object tracking [57], traveling salesman problem [58], and so on. According to [59] FA outperforms PSO in finding optimal solutions of noisy nonlinear continuous mathematical models in the presence of higher levels of noise. A hybridized version of FA is found in [60] for forecasting day-ahead electricity price. FA has also been successfully hybridized with cellular learning automata in [61]. A speciation-based FA has been implemented in [62] to solve dynamic optimization problem. A detailed description of hybridization aspects of FA with learning automata, GA, and directed direction-based search is provided in [63].

In our proposed hybrid stratagem, the foraging behavioral dynamic of fireflies in FA is used to assimilate the colonies of ICA. The proposed assimilation dynamic enforces the colonies within an empire to follow the sociopolitical aspects of all relatively better countries, even including the imperialist, of the same dominion empire. It, in turn, increases the explorative revelation of the colonies in the empire. For improving the performance of the hybrid algorithm further, we modulate the step-size for random movement of each firefly according to its relative position in the search space, such that an inferior solution is driven by the explorative force while a qualitative solution should be confined in its local neighborhood in the search space. This chapter also recommends a novel approach of evaluating the threshold value for uniting empires, accelerating the convergence speed. Combinations of the FA-type motion dynamic along with the adaptive step-size and search range-based threshold computation do not impose any serious computational overhead on the traditional ICA as evident from the simulation results.

The complicated real-world fitness landscape, induced by uncertain and imprecise environment, encompasses multimodality, deception, and isolation. Explorative and exploitative capabilities are two cornerstones of EA that determine its efficacy in tracking the global optimum in such ill-conditioned/diverse fitness landscape. Hence the performance of EA is constrained by a trade-off between two antagonist processes: exploration and exploitation. Exploitation favors good convergence speed by orienting the search toward the desired global optimum through local refinement, whereas exploration aids in searching new promising regions in a large search space without getting stuck at the local basins of attraction. In population-based EAs, the explorative power is manipulated by the population diversity. A population consisting of almost identical candidates has a low exploration power. Generally, the search space is vigorously explored by the trial solutions (using the search operators) in the earlier generations of EAs with a high population variance. The population gradually loses its diversity during the convergence toward the global optimum (via greedy selection) through evolutionary generations. In the earlier explorative phases of optimization problems, low population diversity could induce premature convergence toward a suboptimal solution. In this article, we analyze the evolution of the population variance of ICFA and its two parent algorithms including the traditional ICA and FA over generations delineating its impact on their explorative power. The simulation results reveal that the proposed hybrid algorithm realized with the traditional ICA and the traditional FA (hereafter referred to as ICFA) enjoys a greater potential of balancing the explorative and exploitative powers as compared to individual balancing propensity of the original ICA and FA.

Experiments have been undertaken to test the expertise of the proposed hybrid algorithm on a test-suite of 25 benchmark functions [64]. The performance of the proposed ICFA is compared with ICA with DE (ICA-DE) [16], Interaction

Enhanced ICA using Artificial Imperialists (ICAAI) [21], Memetic ICA (Memetic-ICA) [20], ICA with Adaptive Radius of Colonies Movement (ICAR) [26], Social-Based Algorithm (SBA) [65], Hybrid Evolutionary ICA (HEICA) [18], Chaotic ICA (CICA) [24], Modify ICA with K-means (K-MICA) [33], Recursive ICA with GA (R-ICA-GA) [19], the traditional Artificial Bee Colony (ABC) [66], traditional FA [15], the traditional ICA [13], and the traditional global best PSO [67]. Experiments reveal that the proposed realization outperforms other competitor algorithms both by computational accuracy and run-time complexity.

Lastly, the efficacy of the proposed hybrid EA is validated in the present context of the proposed multi-robot stick-carrying problem. Here too, the performance of the proposed algorithm is compared with the state-of-the-art techniques for the same application and the results are in favor of the proposed algorithm. Experiments undertaken further to compare the relative performance of the ICFA-based path-planner with other swarm/EA-based design reveal that the proposed ICFA-based planner outperforms other realizations. We have arrived at this conclusion by performing comparative analysis of the contender algorithms, used to plan the time-optimal trajectory of the stick, by using two performance metrics, which have been previously used in the existing literature [37].

The chapter is divided into five sections. Section 5.2 provides the formulation of the multi-robot stick-carrying problem. Section 5.3 overviews the traditional ICA and FA. The section then explores the proposed hybridization mechanism along with the experimental settings for the benchmarks and simulation strategies. Computer simulation of multi-robot stick-carrying problem in conjunction with the experiments with Khepera-II mobile robots is given in Section 5.4. Section 5.5 concludes the chapter with future research direction.

5.2 Problem Formulation for Multi-Robot Stick-Carrying

The problem is demonstrated by considering two homogeneous robots, capable of jointly carrying a stick (by transporting it through a desired angle and distance) from a given starting position to a given goal position avoiding collision with static obstacles in the workspace. There exist two different planning approaches to address the stick-carrying problem: (i) local planning and (ii) global planning. The global planning is concerned with the planning of the entire trajectory of the robots with the stick from the given initial position to the final position. Contrarily, in the local planning, the local movement of the system (the robots with the stick) is executed optimally in small steps toward the goal. The local planning has more flexibility than the global counterpart for the following reasons. First, it can take care of dynamic obstacles. Second, local planning requires small time to determine the next position of the stick only, rather than deriving the entire trajectory of motion for the robots carrying the stick. Here, the local planning is used for its time-efficiency.

The stick-carrying problem undertaken here is aimed at minimizing the time required by the robots for the execution of each local plan of transportation of the stick. In the present context, this is realized by minimizing the distance between the next positions of the robots with respect to their goal position. It ensures that the robots will follow the shortest path, in turn reducing time required to execute the plan. In order to take care that the next position of the stick is not in the close vicinity of obstacles, a penalty is introduced. It offers a large (or a small) penalty when the next position is close enough to (or far away from) any obstacle.

The mathematical model of the stick-carrying problem is configured with the distances of the stick as well as the robots, R1 and R2, from the sidewall of the workspace as input variables (Figure 5.1) and the next position of the robots (carrying the stick) as output (estimator) variables. The mathematical model is recast as minimizing an objective function, concerned with the optimal selection of the next position of the system (i.e. the robots with the stick) avoiding collision with obstacles for execution of each local plan. The hybrid evolutionary/swarm algorithm to be proposed is used to determine the next local position of the stick to satisfy the objective. Figure 5.1 provides the distance measures and (5.1) combines these distances into a single entity [68]. Here,

$$d = \min(d_{w1}, d_{w2}) + \min(d_{l1}, d_{l2}) + \min(d_{w3}, d_{w4}), \tag{5.1}$$

where the parameters used on the right side of (5.1) represent range-measures (indicated in Figure 5.1) and R1 and R2 represent the centers of gravity of two robots carrying the stick.

The following principles are used for formulating the problem:

1) The robots first determine their next positions in order to align themselves with the goal and thus plan for a local motion at that current position.

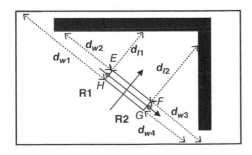

Figure 5.1 Diagram illustrating the calculation of *d*.

2) This alignment may result in a possible collision with static obstacles, if the determined next position of either of the robots or the stick has already been occupied by a static obstacle. Under this circumstance, the robots should turn left or right by certain angle and hence new next positions are to be determined.

3) While planning locally, the most important issue to be taken care of is the distance between two robots. If the distance becomes greater than the stick length, the stick will fall.

4) If the robots can align themselves toward the goal position of the stick without any collision satisfying the distance constraint between them, the local motion will be executed.

Let (x_i, y_i) and (x_i', y_i') be the current and the next positions of the robot R_i with θ_i representing its angle of rotation for $i = [1, 2]$. Furthermore, $(x_{i\text{-}goal}, y_{i\text{-}goal})$ is regarded as the goal position of R_i for $i = [1, 2]$. So, for unit time interval, we have

$$
\begin{aligned}
x_i' &= x_i + v_i \times \cos \theta_i, \\
y_i' &= y_i + v_i \times \sin \theta_i.
\end{aligned}
\tag{5.2}
$$

To ensure that the robots should follow the shortest path, we need to minimize (i) the total Euclidean distance traversed by robots from current position (x_i, y_i) to the next position (x_i', y_i') and (ii) the expected Euclidian distance to be covered from the next position (x_i', y_i') to the goal position $(x_{i\text{-}goal}, y_{i\text{-}goal})$, which is given by (5.3).

$$
f = \sum_{i=1}^{2} \sqrt{(x_i - x_i')^2 + (y_i - y_i')^2} + \sqrt{\left(x_i' - x_{i\text{-}goal}\right)^2 + \left(y_i' - y_{i\text{-}goal}\right)^2}.
\tag{5.3}
$$

Combining (5.2) and (5.3), we have the primary objective function to be minimized as given in (5.4).

$$
f = \sum_{i=1}^{2} v_i + \sqrt{\left(x_i + v_i \cos \theta_i - x_{i\text{-}goal}\right)^2 + \left(y_i + v_i \sin \theta_i - y_{i\text{-}goal}\right)^2}.
\tag{5.4}
$$

Simultaneously, the robots need to satisfy the equality constraint of (5.5) for successfully carrying the stick to execute each local step of the entire task.

$$
d_{1,2} = l.
\tag{5.5}
$$

Here, $d_{1,2}$ is the distance between the robots and l represents the length of the stick.

In a nutshell, the optimization problem here includes an objective function f, concerning minimization of the Euclidean distance between the current positions of the robots with their respective goal positions, avoiding collision with obstacles and subjected to the equality constraint as in (5.5). Hence, the objective function for the proposed optimization problem is given by

$$f = \sum_{i=1}^{2} v_i + \sqrt{\left(x_i + v_i \cos\theta_i - x_{i\text{-}goal}\right)^2 + \left(y_i + v_i \sin\theta_i - y_{i\text{-}goal}\right)^2}$$
$$- \lambda(d_{1,2} - l) + 2^{-d} \times K.$$
(5.6)

Here, λ is the Lagrangian multiplier, which needs to be evaluated to satisfy (5.5). The last term in (5.6) is the penalty where K is a constant. The last term offers a large (or a small) value when the next position is close enough to (or far away from) any obstacle in the workspace.

5.3 Proposed Hybrid Algorithm

In this section, first the traditional ICA and then the FA are overviewed. It then proposes their hybridization methodology following the simulation strategies to substantiate the merit of the proposed algorithm over their traditional counterparts.

5.3.1 An Overview of ICA

ICA is a population-based stochastic algorithm, which is inspired by the sociopolitical evolution and the imperialistic competitive policy of a government to extend its power beyond its boundaries. It has earned wide popularity because of its noticeable performance in computational optimization with respect to the quality of solutions [13]. Like any other EAs, ICA starts with an initial population of solutions, called countries. The countries are classified into two groups – imperialists and colonies, based on their power (which is inversely proportional to their objective function values). The colonies (weaker countries) with their relevant imperialist (stronger country) form some empires. In each empire, the imperialist pursues an assimilation policy to improve the economy, culture, and political situation of its colonies, thus winning their loyalty. Moreover, the empires take part in the imperialistic competition in an attempt to gain more colonies. In ICA, the assimilation of colonies toward their respective imperialists along with the competition among empires eventually results in just one empire in the world with all the other countries as colonies of that unique empire. An overview of the main steps of the ICA is presented next.

5.3.1.1 Initialization

ICA starts with a population P_t of NP, D-dimensional countries, $\vec{X}_i(t) = \{x_{i,1}(t), x_{i,2}(t), x_{i,3}(t), ..., x_{i,D}(t)\}$ for $i = [1, NP]$ representing the candidate solutions, at the current generation $t = 0$ by randomly initializing in the range $\left[\vec{X}^{\min}, \vec{X}^{\max}\right]$, where $\vec{X}^{min} = \{x_1^{min}, x_2^{min}, ..., x_D^{min}\}$ and $\vec{X}^{max} = \{x_1^{max}, x_2^{max}, ..., x_D^{max}\}$. Thus, the d-th component (sociopolitical feature) of the i-th country at $t = 0$ is given by

$$x_{i,d}(0) = x_d^{min} + rand(0,1) \times (x_d^{max} - x_d^{min}), \tag{5.7}$$

where $rand(0,1)$ is a uniformly distributed random number lying between 0 and 1 and $d = [1, D]$. The objective function value $f\left(\vec{X}_i(0)\right)$ of the country $\vec{X}_i(0)$ is evaluated for $i = [1, NP]$.

5.3.1.2 Selection of Imperialists and Colonies

The population P_0 is sorted in ascending order of $f\left(\vec{X}_i(0)\right)$ for minimization problem with $i = [1, NP]$. The first N countries with less cost function values are selected as imperialists while the remaining $M = NP - N$ countries are declared as colonies. Hence, the population individuals are categorized into two groups of countries – imperialists and colonies.

5.3.1.3 Formation of Empires

The empire under the j-th imperialist is constructed based on its ruling power. To accomplish this, first the normalized power of the j-th imperialist country, p_j, is evaluated by (5.8) with $f\left(\vec{X}_{NP}(0)\right)$ representing the objective function value of the weakest country in the current sorted population P_0.

$$p_j = \frac{f\left(\vec{X}_{NP}(0)\right) - f\left(\vec{X}_j(0)\right)}{\sum\limits_{l=1}^{N} f\left(\vec{X}_{NP}(0)\right) - f\left(\vec{X}_l(0)\right)}. \tag{5.8}$$

It is evident from (5.8) that better the j-th imperialist (i.e. less objective function value $f\left(\vec{X}_j(0)\right)$ for minimization problem), higher is the difference $f\left(\vec{X}_{NP}(0)\right) - f\left(\vec{X}_j(0)\right)$ leading to the enhancement of its corresponding ruling power, p_j. Now the initial number of colonies under in the j-th empire, denoted by n_j is computed by (5.9):

$$n_j = \left\lfloor M \times p_j \right\rfloor, \tag{5.9}$$

such that $\sum\limits_{j=1}^{N} n_j = M. \tag{5.10}$

Here, $\lfloor\ \rfloor$ represents the floor function. According to (5.9), the stronger imperialists with higher ruling power now possess larger empires. Hence p_j symbolizes the fraction of the colonies occupied by the j-th imperialist. Subsequently, the j-th empire is formed by randomly selecting n_j countries from M colonies provided that there will be no common colony between two different empires. Hence, the number of countries within the j-th empire including its imperialist is $n_j + 1$. Let the k-th country belonging to the j-th empire is denoted by $\vec{X}_k^j(t)$ (at generation $t = 0$) for $k = [1, n_j + 1]$. The countries within the j-th empire are now sorted in ascending order of their objective function values such that the imperialist $\vec{X}_1^j(t)$ in the j-th empire attains the first rank. This step is repeated for $j = [1, N]$.

5.3.1.4 Assimilation of Colonies

Each imperialist country now attempts to improve its empire by enhancing the sociopolitical influences of its colonies. To accomplish this, each country $\vec{X}_k^j(t)$ in the j-th empire now moves toward its corresponding imperialist $\vec{X}_1^j(t)$ by changing its characteristic features following (5.11) for $k = [2, n_j + 1]$.

$$\vec{X}_k^j(t + 1) = \vec{X}_k^j(t) + \beta \times rand(0, 1) \times \left(\vec{X}_1^j(t) - \vec{X}_k^j(t) \right). \tag{5.11}$$

Here, $rand(0, 1)$ is a uniformly distributed random number lying between 0 and 1 and β is the assimilation coefficient. The objective function value of the modified colony $f\left(\vec{X}_k^j(t + 1) \right)$ is evaluated for $k = [2, n_j + 1]$. After assimilation, all the countries in the j-th empire are sorted in ascending order of the objective function values and the first ranked country is declared as the imperialist $\vec{X}_1^j(t + 1)$ of the same empire for the next generation (i.e. $t = t + 1$). The step is repeated for $j = [1, N]$.

5.3.1.5 Revolution

Revolution creates sudden fluctuation in the economic, cultural, and political aspects of countries in an empire. The colonies in an empire are now equipped with the power of randomly changing their sociopolitical attributes instead of being assimilated by their corresponding imperialist. It resembles the mutation of trial solutions in the traditional EA. The revolution rate η in the algorithm indicates the percentage of colonies in each empire, which will undergo the revolution process. A high value of revolution rate therefore fortifies the explorative power at a cost of poor exploitation capability. Hence, a moderate value of revolution rate is favored. Revolution is implemented by randomly selecting $\eta \times n_j$ countries (including the imperialist) in the j-th empire (for $j = [1, N]$) and then they are replaced by randomly initialized countries characterized by new sociopolitical nature. After revolution, as in case of assimilation, all the countries in each empire are sorted in ascending order of the objective function values so that its imperialist is at the first position. The step is repeated for all empires.

5.3.1.6 Imperialistic Competition

All the N empires now participate in an imperialistic competition to take possession of colonies of other weaker empires based on their ruling power. The colonies of the weaker empires will be gradually eluded from the ruling power of their corresponding imperialists and will be thereafter controlled by some other stronger empires. Consequently, the weaker empires will be losing their power and ultimately may be eradicated from the competition. The imperialistic competition along with the collapse mechanism will progressively result in an increment in the power of more dominant empires and diminish the power of weaker ones. The imperialistic competition encompasses the following steps.

5.3.1.6.1 Total Empire Power Evaluation

Once an empire is constructed under the dominance of the j-th imperialist $\vec{X}_1^j(t + 1)$, the power of the respective empire is compositely influenced by the objective function value of $\vec{X}_1^j(t + 1)$ as well as the constituent colonies $\vec{X}_k^j(t + 1)$ (after assimilation) under the respective j-th empire for $k = [2, n_j + 1]$. The total objective function value of the j-th empire is evaluated as follows:

$$tc_j = f\left(\vec{X}_1^j(t + 1)\right) + \xi \cdot \frac{1}{n_j} \sum_{k=2}^{n_j+1} \vec{X}_k^j(t + 1). \tag{5.12}$$

Here, $\xi < 1$ is a positive number that regulates the influence of the constituent colonies to control the ruling power of the empire. A minuscule value of ξ causes the total power of the j-th empire to be determined by its imperialist $\vec{X}_1^j(t + 1)$ only, while increasing the value of ξ accentuates the importance of the colonies in deciding the total power of the respective empire. The N empires now are sorted in ascending order of tc_j for $j = [1, N]$. Then the normalized possession power of the j-th empire, pp_j, is evaluated by (5.13) with tc_N representing the total objective function value of the weakest empire in the current population P_t.

$$pp_j = \frac{tc_N - tc_j}{\sum_{l=1}^{N} tc_N - tc_l}. \tag{5.13}$$

It is evident from (5.13) that stronger the j-th empire (i.e. less the total objective function value tc_j for minimization problem), higher is the possession power, pp_j, which consecutively increases its probability of seizing colonies from weaker empires. This step is repeated for $j = [1, N]$.

5.3.1.6.2 Reassignment of Colonies and Removal of Empire

The empire with least possession power is interpreted as being defeated in the competition. Let the weakest colony of this weakest empire be denoted as $\vec{X}_{worst}$, which is now removed from the dominance of its currently ruling imperialist and reassigned as a new colony to one of the stronger empires based on their possession probabilities. It is noteworthy that $\vec{X}_{worst}$ will not be possessed by the most powerful empires, but stronger the empire, more likely to possess $\vec{X}_{worst}$. To accomplish this, the possession probability of the j-th empire is computed as follows for $j = [1, N]$:

$$prob_j = pp_j - rand(0, 1). \tag{5.14}$$

Now $\vec{X}_{worst}$ is assigned as a new colony to the j-th empire for which the possession probability $prob_j$ is maximum. However, if the worst colony consists of only its imperial before exclusion operation (i.e. $\vec{X}_{worst}$ is the imperialist of the weakest empire), the removal of $\vec{X}_{worst}$ will result in the collapse of the weakest empire.

5.3.1.6.3 Union of Empires

The disagreement between two empires may be assessed by the difference in their respective sociopolitical features. This dissimilarity between any two empires, j and l, is evaluated by taking the Euclidean distance between the respective imperialists $\vec{X}_1^{j}(t + 1)$ and $\vec{X}_1^{l}(t + 1)$ as in (5.15) for $j, l = [1, N]$.

$$Dist_{j,l} = \left\| \vec{X}_1^{j}(t + 1) - \vec{X}_1^{l}(t + 1) \right\|. \tag{5.15}$$

If $Dist_{j,l}$ is less than a predefined threshold, Th, the two empires are merged into one empire. The stronger country among $\vec{X}_1^{j}(t + 1)$ and $\vec{X}_1^{l}(t + 1)$ is declared as the imperialist of the newly formed empire.

After each evolution, we repeat from Section 5.3.1.4 until one of the following conditions for convergence is satisfied. Stop criteria include a bound by the number of iterations, achieving a sufficiently low error or aggregations thereof.

5.4   An Overview of FA

In FA [15], a potential solution to an optimization problem is encoded by the position of a firefly in the search space and the light intensity at the position of the firefly corresponds to the fitness of the associated solution. Each firefly changes its position iteratively by flying toward brighter fireflies at more attractive location in the fitness landscape to obtain optimal solutions.

5.4.1   Initialization

FA commences with a population P_t of NP, D-dimensional firefly positions, $\vec{X}_i(t) = \{x_{i,1}(t), x_{i,2}(t), x_{i,3}(t), ..., x_{i,D}(t)\}$ for $i = [1, NP]$ by randomly initializing in the search range $\left[\vec{X}^{\min}, \vec{X}^{\max}\right]$, where $\vec{X}^{\min} = \{x_1^{\min}, x_2^{\min}, ..., x_D^{\min}\}$ and $\vec{X}^{\max} = \{x_1^{\max}, x_2^{\max}, ..., x_D^{\max}\}$ at the current generation $t = 0$. Thus, the d-th component (sociopolitical feature) of the i-th firefly at $t = 0$ is given by

$$x_{i,d}(0) = x_d^{\min} + rand(0, 1) \times \left(x_d^{\max} - x_d^{\min}\right), \tag{5.16}$$

where $rand(0, 1)$ is a uniformly distributed random number lying between 0 and 1 and $d = [1, D]$. The objective function value $f\left(\vec{X}_i(0)\right)$ (which is inversely proportional to the light intensity for minimization problem) of the i-th firefly is evaluated for $i = [1, NP]$.

5.4.2   Attraction to Brighter Fireflies

Now the firefly $\vec{X}_i(t)$ is attracted toward the positions of the brighter fireflies $\vec{X}_j(t)$ for $i, j = [1, NP]$ but $i \neq j$ such that $f\left(\vec{X}_j(t)\right) < f\left(\vec{X}_i(t)\right)$ for minimization problem. Now the attractiveness $\beta_{i,j}$ of $\vec{X}_i(t)$ toward $\vec{X}_j(t)$ is proportional to the light intensity seen by adjacent fireflies. However, attractiveness $\beta_{i,j}$ decreases exponentially with the distance between them, denoted by $r_{i,j}$ as given in (5.17).

$$\beta_{i,j} = \beta_0 \exp\left(-\gamma \times r_{i,j}^m\right), \qquad m \geq 1, \tag{5.17}$$

where β_0 denotes the maximum attractiveness experienced by the i-th firefly at its own position (i.e. at $r_{i,j} = r_{i,i} = 0$) and γ is the light absorption coefficient, which controls the variation of $\beta_{i,j}$ with $r_{i,j}$. This parameter is responsible for the convergence speed of FA. A setting of $\gamma = 0$ leads to constant attractiveness while γ approaching infinity is equivalent to the complete random search [15]. In (5.17), m is a positive constant representing a nonlinear modulation index. The distance between $\vec{X}_i(t)$ and $\vec{X}_j(t)$ is computed using the Euclidean norm as follows:

$$r_{i,j} = \left\| \vec{X}_i(t) - \vec{X}_j(t) \right\|. \tag{5.18}$$

This step is repeated for $i, j = [1, N]$.

5.4.3 Movement of Fireflies

The firefly at position $\vec{X}_i(t)$ moves toward a more attractive position $\vec{X}_j(t)$ occupied by a brighter firefly (i.e. $f\left(\vec{X}_j(t)\right) < f\left(\vec{X}_i(t)\right)$) for $j = [1, N]$ but $i \neq j$ following the dynamic given in (5.19).

$$\vec{X}_i(t) = \vec{X}_i(t) + \beta_{i,j} \times \left(\vec{X}_j(t) - \vec{X}_i(t)\right) + \alpha \times (rand(0,1) - 0.5). \tag{5.19}$$

The first term in the position updating formula (5.19) represents the i-th firefly's current position. The second term in (5.19) denotes the change in the position of the firefly at $\vec{X}_i(t)$ due to the attraction toward the brighter firefly at $\vec{X}_j(t)$. Hence, it is apparent that the brightest firefly with no more attractive firefly in the current sorted population P_t will have no motion due to the second term and may get stuck at the local optima. To circumvent the problem, the last term is introduced in (5.19) for the random movement of the fireflies with a step-size of $\alpha \in (0, 1)$. Here, $rand(0, 1)$ is a random number generator uniformly distributed in the range $(0, 1)$. This step is repeated for $i = [1, NP]$. After completion of its journey mediated by the brighter ones, the updated position of the i-th firefly is represented by $\vec{X}_i(t + 1)$ for $i = [1, NP]$.

After each evolution, the Sections 5.4.2 and 5.4.3 are repeated until one of the following conditions for convergence is satisfied. The conditions include restraining the number of iterations, maintaining error limits, or the both, whichever occurs earlier.

5.5 Proposed ICFA

In our proposed hybridization stratagem, the light-intensity-based attraction-driven movement of fireflies is embedded into the modified version of ICA to utilize the composite benefits of the explorative and exploitative capabilities of both the ancestor algorithms. The fitness profile-based colonizing behavior of the countries in ICA provides them the local exploitation capability surrounding the local optima (as discovered by their imperialists). In addition, the imperialistic competition eventually helps the algorithm to converge toward the desired global optimum. On the other hand, FA draws inspiration from the self-organizing behavior of fireflies, which offers it potential for global exploration. The information of a better position in the search space, as acquired by a brighter firefly, is distributed among others through the motion dynamic as evident from (5.19). These facts have motivated us to propose a new hybrid algorithm, named ICFA. In ICFA, the intensification process is controlled by the formation and revolution of empires (clusters) in the search space by ICA, while the diversification is influenced by the foraging behavior of fireflies.

In the modified ICA, each colony tries to contribute to the improvement of its governing empire by improving its sociopolitical attributes following a new assimilation policy. This is different from the traditional ICA where the revolution of a colony is instigated by the features of its respective imperialist only. Hence, the evolving colony is not guided by the experience of more powerful colonies within the same empire. This issue is resolved here being inspired by the self-organizing dynamics (5.19) of the fireflies in the traditional FA. In the present context, the sociopolitical features of the assimilating colony are stimulated by that of all other powerful colonies within the same empire including its imperialist. This is implemented here by the assimilation dynamic in (5.20) employed by the k-th colony $\vec{X}_k^j(t)$ within the j-th empire for $k = [2, n_j + 1]$. Here, it is presumed that the countries in the j-th empire are sorted in ascending order of their respective objective function values such that the imperialist $\vec{X}_1^j(t)$ occupies the first position.

$$\vec{X}_k^j(t) = \vec{X}_k^j(t) + \beta_{k,l}^j \times \left(\vec{X}_l^j(t) - \vec{X}_k^j(t) \right) + \alpha \times (rand(0,1) - 0.5)$$
$$\text{if } f\left(\vec{X}_l^j(t) \right) < f\left(\vec{X}_k^j(t) \right). \tag{5.20}$$

Expression (5.20) indicates that the colony $\vec{X}_k^j(t)$ follows the nature of a stronger colony $\vec{X}_l^j(t)$ (including the imperialist $\vec{X}_1^j(t)$) with $f\left(\vec{X}_l^j(t) \right) < f\left(\vec{X}_k^j(t) \right)$ in the j-th empire. The k-th modernized country is now represented by $\vec{X}_k^j(t+1)$.

Again, it is noteworthy that the random movement of a firefly (or a colony) with step-size α in (5.19) (or in (5.20)) in traditional FA helps the population individuals to avoid local optima by their expedition proficiency. Particularly, the convergence of fireflies toward the global optimum greatly relies on the step-size (α) profile. However, in the traditional FA, α is taken to be constant for all fireflies in the current population. It indicates that α assists in the exploration of the fireflies in the fitness landscape irrespective of their fitness. Consequently, fireflies in vicinity of the global optimum may be deviated away (with α value greater than the requirement) and may get trapped at local optima. Contrarily, fireflies far away from the global optimum in the fitness landscape (with α smaller than necessity) may not be given any opportunity to be attracted toward the global optimum. To overcome this problem, α, used for the random movement of a firefly, needs to be modulated with its relative position with respect to the current best firefly position.

It in turn ensures that the best candidate solution should search in the local neighborhood with a small step-size to prevent the omission of the global optimum whereas a poor performing member should participate in the global search to explore promising regions in the search space. Under this proposed scheme, the step-size value $\alpha_{i,d}$ assigned to the d-th positional component of the i-th firefly at location $\vec{X}_i(t)$ is varied based on its spatial distance from the best firefly rather than being constant as outlined in (5.21) for $d = [1, D]$. It is apparent that in the sorted population $\vec{X}_1(t)$ corresponds to the position of the brightest firefly.

$$\alpha_{i,d} = \alpha_{\min} + (1 - \alpha_{\min}) \times rand(0,1) \times \frac{|X_{1,d}(t) - X_{i,d}(t)|}{X_d^{\max} - X_d^{\min}}. \qquad (5.21)$$

Here, |.| represents the absolute value and $rand(0, 1)$ is a uniformly distributed random number lying in $(0, 1)$. It is apparent from (5.21) that if $X_{i,d}(t)$ is close to $X_{1,d}(t)$, $\alpha_{i,d}$ reduces to its small minimum value $\alpha_{\min}$ confining $X_{i,d}(t)$ in its small neighborhood. Again, if the difference $|X_{i,d}(t) - X_{1,d}(t)|$ increases and approaches to $X_d^{\max}(t) - X_d^{\min}(t)$, $\alpha_{i,d}$ also approaches to unity offering $X_{i,d}(t)$ a large magnitude of perturbation. Apparently, the step-size is now treated as a D-dimensional vector as symbolized by $\vec{\alpha}_i = \{\alpha_{i,1}, \alpha_{i,2}, ..., \alpha_{i,D}\}$ with its d-th component $\alpha_{i,d} \in (\alpha_{\min}, 1)$.

Moreover, in the traditional ICA, the dissimilarity threshold, Th, used for uniting two empires is kept as a predefined constant disregarding the search space dimension. It is obvious that the selection of threshold, being responsible for the union of empires, determines the performance of ICA. In the proposed work, a new empirical formula is recommended to calculate the threshold as in (5.22) with the search range $\left[\vec{X}^{\min}, \vec{X}^{\max}\right]$ and D and N as the search space dimension and number of empires, respectively.

$$Th = \frac{\|\vec{X}^{\max} - \vec{X}^{\min}\|}{N \times D}. \qquad (5.22)$$

Motivated by these observations, we extend the traditional ICA with the proposed strategies of hybridization with α modulated FA and uniting threshold Th selection. The extended ICA, called ICFA, is similar to the traditional ICA except for the assimilation of the colonies and the union of the empires that are given below.

5.5.1 Assimilation of Colonies

The assimilation of the k-th country $\vec{X}_k^j(t)$ under the sorted j-th empire (led by the imperialist $\vec{X}_1^j(t)$) is performed by the following two steps for $k = [1, n_j + 1]$ and $j = [1, N]$.

5.5.1.1 Attraction to Powerful Colonies

The distance between the k-th and l-th countries, $\vec{X}_k^j(t)$ and $\vec{X}_l^j(t)$, under the j-th empire is computed using the Euclidean norm as follows:

$$r_{k,l}^j = \left\| \vec{X}_k^j(t) - \vec{X}_l^j(t) \right\|. \tag{5.23}$$

Now, as in case of FA, the country $\vec{X}_k^j(t)$ is attracted toward a more powerful one $\vec{X}_l^j(t)$ (including the respective imperialist) with an attractiveness $\beta_{k,l}^j$ for $k, l = [1, n_j + 1]$ but $k \neq l$ such that $f\left(\vec{X}_l^j(t) \right) < f\left(\vec{X}_k^j(t) \right)$. The associated attractiveness $\beta_{k,l}^j$ is evaluated by (5.24).

$$\beta_{k,l}^j = \beta_0 \exp\left(-\gamma \times \left(r_{k,l}^j \right)^m \right) \quad m \geq 1, \tag{5.24}$$

where β_0 and γ are same as defined in (5.17).

5.5.1.2 Modification of Empire Behavior

The country $\vec{X}_k^j(t)$ updates its sociopolitical features inspired by the stronger one $\vec{X}_l^j(t)$ in the same empire following the dynamic given in (5.25) for $k, l = [1, n_j + 1]$ but $k \neq l$ provided $f\left(\vec{X}_l^j(t) \right) < f\left(\vec{X}_k^j(t) \right)$.

$$\vec{X}_k^j(t+1) = \vec{X}_k^j(t) + \beta_{k,l}^j \times \left(\vec{X}_l^j(t) - \vec{X}_k^j(t) \right) + \vec{\alpha}_k^j \times (rand(0,1) - 0.5). \tag{5.25}$$

The D-dimensional step-size vector $\vec{\alpha}_k^j$ for random movement in (5.25) is now modulated based on the relative sociopolitical aspects of the country $\vec{X}_k^j(t)$ with respect to that of its respective imperialist $\vec{X}_1^j(t)$ (with least objective function value in the j-th empire) as given in (5.26) for $d = [1, D]$.

$$\alpha_{k,d}^j = \alpha_{\min} + (1 - \alpha_{\min}) \times rand(0,1) \times \frac{|X_{1,d}^j(t) - X_{k,d}^j(t)|}{X_d^{\max} - X_d^{\min}}. \tag{5.26}$$

Here, $rand(0, 1)$ is a uniformly distributed random number lying in $(0, 1)$. It is apparent from (5.26) that the imperialist $\vec{X}_1^j(t)$ is assigned with a step-size $\alpha_{\min}$ for all its components. After each movement of a country, the j-th empire is sorted in ascending order of the objective function values of its constituent countries so that the first rank is always occupied by the imperialist $\vec{X}_1^j(t)$. The step is repeated for $k = [1, n_j + 1]$. At the end of this step, the modified country is demoted by $\vec{X}_k^j(t + 1)$ for $k = [1, n_j + 1]$.

5.5.1.3 Union of Empires

The dissimilarity $Dist_{j,l}$ between any two empires, j and l, is evaluated by taking the Euclidean distance between the respective imperialists $\vec{X}_1^j(t + 1)$ and $\vec{X}_1^l(t + 1)$ as in (5.15) for $j, l = [1, N]$. The two empires are merged into one empire if $Dist_{j,l}$ is less than the threshold, Th, as computed using (5.22). The stronger country among $\vec{X}_1^j(t + 1)$ and $\vec{X}_1^l(t + 1)$ is declared as the imperialist of the newly formed empire and the rest is treated as a colony under the former one. The algorithm for ICFA is as follows.

Algorithm 5.1 Imperialist Competitive Firefly Algorithm (ICFA)

```
Begin

1) Initialize a population of NP, D-dimensional countries X⃗ᵢ(t) at
   generation t = 0 using (5.7) and evaluate f(X⃗ᵢ(t)) for i = [1, NP];
2) Sort Pₜ in ascending order of cost function values and select the
   top N countries as the imperialists with the remaining M = NP − N
   countries as colonies;
3) Assign randomly selected nⱼ colonies under the j-th imperialist,
   based on its power pⱼ as computed using (5.9) and (5.8), respec-
   tively, for j = [1, N];
4) While termination condition is not reached do

   Begin

4.1) For each empire j = 1 to N do begin

   Sort the countries in the j-th empire in ascending order of their
   respective cost function values with the imperialist X⃗₁ʲ(t) at
   the first position;
```

For each country under the j-th empire $k = 1$ to $n_j + 1$ **do begin**
For each country under the j-th empire $k = 1$ to $n_j + 1$ **do begin**

    If $f\left(\vec{X}_1^{\,j}(t)\right) < f\left(\vec{X}_k^{\,j}(t)\right)$ **then do**

      a) Evaluate the distance $r_{k,1}^{\,j}$ and hence the attraction $\beta_{k,1}^{\,j}$ between $\vec{X}_k^{\,j}(t)$ and $\vec{X}_1^{\,j}(t)$ using (5.23) and (5.24), respectively;

      b) Compute the step-size of random movement of $\vec{X}_k^{\,j}(t)$ using (5.26);

      c) Update the sociopolitical nature of $\vec{X}_k^{\,j}(t)$ using (5.25);

      d) Sort the countries in the j-th empire in ascending order of their respective cost function values with the imperialist $\vec{X}_1^{\,j}(t)$ at the first position;

    End If.
    End For.

    Denote the updated country with $\vec{X}_k^{\,j}(t+1)$;
  End For.
End For.

4.2) **For** each empire $j = 1$ to N **do begin**

    i) Randomly select $\eta \times n_j$ countries from the j-th empire and perform revolution by re-initialization;

    ii) Sort the countries in the j-th empire in ascending order of their respective cost function values with its imperialist at the first position;

  End For.

4.3) Evaluate the possession power pp_j and the possession probability $prob_j$ of the j-th empire using (5.13) and (5.14), respectively, for $j = [1, N]$;

4.4) Sort the empires in descending order of the possession power pp_j for $j = [1, N]$. Identify the worst colony $\vec{X}_{worst}$ of the weakest empire $\vec{X}_N(t+1)$ and reassign $\vec{X}_{worst}$ as a colony of new empire, j, with the largest possession probability $prob_j$ for $j \in [1, N]$;

4.5) **If** $\vec{X}_{worst}$ was the only country in the N-th empire **then** the N-th empire collapses with $N \leftarrow N - 1$;

  End If.

4.6) Evaluate the disagreement threshold Th and the dissimilarity $Dist_{j,1}$ between any two imperialists $\vec{X}_j(t+1)$ and $\vec{X}_1(t+1)$ using (5.22) and (5.15), respectively. Combine the j-th and 1-th empires if $D_{j,1} < Th$. The stronger among $\vec{X}_j(t+1)$ and $\vec{X}_1(t+1)$ will be considered as the imperialist of the combined empire while the remaining will be treated as its colony. Decrement the number of colonies by setting $N \leftarrow N - 1$. This is done for $j, 1 = [1, N]$;

4.7) Set $t \leftarrow t + 1$;

  End While.
End.

5.6 Simulation Results

The performance of the proposed ICFA algorithm is examined here with respect to the minimization of 25 benchmark functions recommended in [64].

5.6.1 Comparative Framework

The comparative framework includes ICA with DE (ICA-DE) [16], Interaction Enhanced ICA using Artificial Imperialists (ICAAI) [21], Memetic ICA (Memetic-ICA) [20], ICA with Adaptive Radius of Colonies Movement (ICAR) [26], Social-Based Algorithm (SBA) [65], Hybrid Evolutionary ICA (HEICA) [18], Chaotic ICA (CICA) [24], Modify ICA with K-means (K-MICA) [33], Recursive ICA with GA (R-ICA-GA) [19], the traditional Artificial Bee Colony (ABC) [66], the traditional FA [15], the traditional ICA [67], and the traditional PSO [54]. The above traditional evolutionary/swarm optimization algorithms are chosen because of their wide popularity in solving numerical single objective optimization problems.

5.6.2 Parameter Settings

To make the comparison fair, the populations for all the algorithms (over all problems tested) are initialized using the same random seeds and the population size is kept at 50. We employ the best parametric setup for all these algorithms as prescribed in their respective sources. In our proposed ICFA, the initial number of empires N is taken to be $\sqrt{NP}$, which is equal to 7 for a population size NP of 50 and α_{min} is taken to be 0.3 so that maximum permissible value of step-size is 1. The maximum attractiveness β_0 and the light absorption coefficient γ both are taken to be 1 with the nonlinear modulation index m determined by $\sqrt{D \times \max\limits_{j=1}^{D}\left(\left|X_j^{max} - X_j^{min}\right|\right)}$ as described in [69].

5.6.3 Analysis on Explorative Power of ICFA

The explorative and exploitative capabilities of an algorithm can be assessed by the population variance. Let $\overrightarrow{X}_i(t)$ be the D-dimensional i-th solution of the population P_t at generation t. The variance of the population P_t considering all its NP solutions is given by (5.27).

$$V(P_t) = \frac{1}{D}\sum_{j=1}^{D}\left(\frac{1}{NP}\sum_{i=1}^{NP}x_{i,j}^2 - \left(\frac{1}{NP}\sum_{i=1}^{NP}x_{i,j}\right)^2\right). \tag{5.27}$$

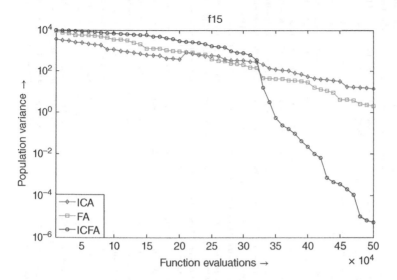

Figure 5.2 Evolution of the expected population variance.

Figure 5.2 shows the evolution of the population variance over FEs for f15 in case of 50-*D* problem. The plots of other functions are omitted for the sake of space economy. The plot indicates that ICA offers a good level of exploitation capability from the initiation of the algorithm, whereas FA performs better in balancing the diversification at the earlier exploration stage and gradually converges to the optimal point with a relatively smaller population variance. However, it is evident that ICFA outperforms the rest two ancestors in providing a well trade-off between high explorative and exploitative powers, which prevail during the earlier and later phases of the search, respectively. Hence, it can be concluded that the hybridization of ICA and FA has empowered ICFA with better exploration and exploitation capabilities.

5.6.4 Comparison of Quality of the Final Solution

Here, we test the relative performance of our algorithm with other competitor algorithms using 25 benchmark functions [64] of 10, 30, and 50 dimensions. The experiments are conducted for 50 independent runs. For lack of space, the mean and standard deviation (within parenthesis) of the benchmarks function values of 25 independent runs for each of the 14 algorithms are presented in Table 5.1 for 30-*D* problems only. Please note that the results excluded follow a similar trend like those reported in Table 5.1. Maximum number of function evaluations (Max_FEs) is set at 300 000 for 30-*D*.

Table 5.1 Comparative analysis of performance of the proposed ICFA with other algorithms based on solution quality for f01 to f25.

Functions	ICFA	ICA-DE	ICAAI	Memetic ICA	ICAR	SBA	HEICA	CICA	K-MICA	R-ICA-GA	ABC	FA	ICA	PSO	Stat. sig.
f01	0.00e+00 (0.00e+00)	2.88e−29 (1.99e-27)	1.10e−26 (2.74e-26)	1.94e−23 (2.95e-25)	3.39e−22 (4.59e-24)	3.82e−21 (4.75e-23)	4.42e−21 (5.20e-20)	5.70e−20 (5.30e-18)	6.34e−17 (5.54e-17)	6.39e−16 (5.60e-17)	6.70e−14 (5.94e-16)	6.70e−14 (6.41e-15)	7.75e−10 (6.53e-11)	7.79e−10 (6.71e-10)	+
f02	1.22e−04 (8.31e−04)	3.24e−04 (1.13e-03)	2.32e−03 (1.30e-03)	2.67e−03 (1.93e-02)	1.19e−01 (3.11e-01)	1.93e−01 (3.42e-01)	2.21e−01 (3.48e+00)	2.67e−01 (4.52e+02)	3.07e−01 (4.58e+02)	4.58e−01 (4.75e+02)	4.86e−01 (4.96e+02)	4.94e−01 (5.28e+02)	5.76e−01 (5.35e+03)	7.65e−01 (5.56e+03)	+
f03	1.97e−01 (1.37e+00)	1.04e+00 (1.50e+00)	1.56e+00 (1.75e+00)	1.78e+00 (1.77e+00)	1.80e+01 (2.44e+01)	2.38e+01 (2.46e+01)	3.54e+01 (3.31e+01)	3.83e+02 (3.84e+01)	4.09e+03 (4.09e+01)	4.89e+03 (4.31e+02)	5.25e+03 (5.69e+02)	6.23e+03 (5.81e+02)	6.71e+04 (5.50e+02)	6.71e+04 (5.88e+02)	+
f04	1.37e−05 (0.00e+00)	1.53e−04 (4.58e-26)	1.90e−04 (1.13e-25)	2.00e−04 (1.15e-23)	2.66e−04 (1.84e-22)	3.28e−03 (2.17e-20)	3.71e−03 (2.35e-20)	3.97e−02 (3.15e-16)	3.98e−02 (3.69e-16)	5.27e−02 (4.21e-14)	5.30e−02 (4.57e-10)	5.45e−01 (4.82e-03)	6.53e+01 (5.55e-01)	6.42e−01 (5.23e-02)	+
f05	1.03e−11 (4.59e−09)	2.54e−10 (6.95e-08)	3.74e−10 (1.01e-08)	1.06e−09 (1.01e-08)	1.60e−09 (1.27e-07)	3.09e−08 (1.81e-07)	3.76e−08 (1.84e-06)	5.42e−07 (2.79e-05)	5.72e−07 (3.01e-04)	5.78e−04 (3.84e-04)	6.08e−03 (4.05e-04)	6.39e−03 (5.60e-03)	6.97e−03 (7.37e-03)	6.73e−03 (6.08e-02)	+
f06	7.34e−01 (3.67e−05)	9.53e−01 (5.77e-05)	1.06e+00 (1.69e-04)	1.28e+00 (1.92e-04)	1.67e+00 (2.36e-03)	1.67e+00 (2.58e-03)	2.45e+00 (2.72e-02)	2.81e+00 (2.82e-01)	2.92e+00 (3.42e-01)	3.59e+00 (3.43e+00)	4.35e+00 (5.46e+00)	5.97e+00 (6.30e+00)	6.61e+00 (6.69e+01)	6.31e+00 (6.59e+01)	+
f07	1.10e−05 (8.56e−01)	1.30e−05 (1.28e+00)	1.41e−05 (1.32e+00)	1.18e−05 (2.14e+00)	1.64e−04 (2.57e+00)	2.07e−04 (3.05e+00)	2.47e−04 (3.12e+00)	3.15e−03 (3.40e+00)	3.82e−03 (4.37e+00)	4.02e−03 (4.80e+00)	4.53e−02 (5.21e+00)	4.54e−02 (5.42e+00)	5.74e−01 (6.50e+00)	5.12e−01 (5.46e+00)	+
f08	2.45e+01 (1.19e−02)	2.65e+01 (1.29e-02)	3.55e+01 (1.36e-02)	3.57e+01 (1.45e-02)	3.72e+01 (1.58e-01)	3.85e+01 (1.59e-01)	4.10e+01 (1.61e-01)	4.35e+01 (2.10e-01)	4.51e+01 (2.17e-01)	5.56e+01 (3.01e+00)	5.68e+01 (3.04e+00)	5.72e+01 (3.29e+01)	7.57e+01 (5.96e+01)	6.13e+01 (5.91e+01)	+
f09	0.00e+00 (2.20e−28)	4.82e−24 (3.59e-26)	1.55e−23 (1.66e-25)	1.80e−23 (1.83e-22)	1.83e−22 (2.96e-22)	2.07e−22 (3.21e-18)	2.23e−21 (3.42e-18)	2.86e−19 (3.55e-17)	3.07e−19 (3.82e-16)	4.16e−19 (4.04e-13)	4.21e−10 (5.11e-12)	4.97e−10 (5.60e-10)	8.85e−09 (7.74e-09)	6.33e−09 (6.50e-09)	+
f10	1.59e+01 (5.95e−06)	1.26e+01 (2.74e-06)	1.62e+01 (1.38e-05)	1.83e+01 (3.33e-04)	2.57e+01 (4.34e-04)	2.76e+01 (4.45e-03)	3.42e+01 (5.57e-03)	3.64e+01 (5.75e-02)	4.36e+01 (5.89e-02)	4.75e+01 (6.00e-01)	5.57e+01 (6.04e+00)	6.19e+01 (6.45e+00)	6.39e+01 (7.23e+00)	7.91e+01 (8.32e+00)	−
f11	2.07e−03 (1.29e−13)	1.21e−02 (3.41e-12)	1.28e−02 (4.50e-12)	1.67e−02 (2.67e-11)	3.35e−02 (1.17e-10)	3.50e−01 (3.29e-10)	4.03e−01 (3.42e-10)	4.26e−01 (3.50e-09)	4.32e+00 (3.65e-09)	5.20e+00 (4.77e-09)	5.63e+00 (4.98e-08)	6.01e+00 (5.72e-08)	6.20e+00 (5.72e-08)	6.33e+00 (5.85e-08)	+
f12	2.58e−04 (6.10e−05)	7.93e−04 (1.42e-04)	1.04e−03 (1.74e-04)	1.21e−03 (1.87e-04)	2.73e−03 (2.04e-04)	3.02e−03 (2.79e-04)	3.17e−03 (2.91e-03)	3.63e−02 (3.02e-03)	4.54e−02 (3.68e-03)	4.61e−02 (4.39e-02)	5.05e−02 (4.59e-02)	5.60e−02 (5.62e-02)	5.77e−02 (5.81e-02)	6.81e−02 (5.88e-02)	+
f13	1.26e−01 (0.00e+00)	1.58e−01 (1.89e-19)	1.88e−01 (1.19e-19)	2.37e−01 (1.24e-18)	2.60e−01 (2.11e-15)	2.92e−01 (3.77e-14)	2.95e−01 (3.92e-14)	3.42e−01 (4.66e-13)	3.83e−01 (4.66e-11)	5.16e−01 (4.68e-10)	6.44e−01 (4.88e-09)	6.51e−01 (4.90e-09)	6.66e−01 (6.17e-08)	6.88e−01 (7.99e-07)	+
f14	1.09e+00 (1.76e−01)	1.09e+00 (1.76e-01)	1.33e+00 (1.85e-01)	1.33e+00 (2.03e-01)	1.58e+00 (2.40e-01)	2.58e+00 (2.69e-01)	2.63e+00 (4.08e-01)	2.99e+00 (4.08e-01)	3.22e+00 (4.31e-01)	3.37e+00 (5.11e-01)	4.12e+00 (5.77e-01)	4.51e+00 (6.15e-01)	5.98e+00 (6.34e-01)	7.87e+00 (8.87e-01)	NA
f15	9.15e−02 (1.23e−03)	1.11e−01 (3.48e-03)	1.13e−01 (6.73e-03)	1.25e−01 (2.23e-02)	1.82e−01 (2.27e-02)	2.18e−01 (2.85e-02)	2.96e+00 (3.71e-02)	2.97e+00 (3.71e-02)	3.29e+00 (4.27e-01)	4.16e+00 (4.46e-01)	4.18e+00 (4.58e-01)	4.87e+00 (5.02e-01)	4.89e+00 (5.73e-01)	5.72e+00 (5.78e-01)	+

f16	**4.63e+01** (1.04e−04)	1.07e+02 (1.47e−04)	1.86e+02 (1.56e−04)	1.96e+02 (1.68e−04)	2.96e+02 (1.78e−03)	3.08e+02 (2.02e−03)	3.20e+02 (2.41e−02)	3.62e+02 (4.67e−02)	3.68e+02 (4.70e−02)	4.46e+02 (4.72e−01)	5.45e+02 (4.73e−01)	6.12e+02 (4.86e−01)	6.60e+02 (5.46e+00)	6.70e+02 (5.91e+00)	+
f17	**0.00e+00** (7.63e−08)	0.25e+02 (1.06e−07)	1.23e+02 (1.32e−07)	2.25e+02 (1.34e−07)	2.70e+02 (1.69e−06)	2.97e+02 (1.88e−04)	3.22e+02 (2.01e−04)	3.23e+02 (2.38e−04)	3.29e+02 (3.31e−04)	4.21e+02 (4.03e−03)	5.05e+02 (4.25e−02)	5.39e+02 (5.16e−02)	5.49e+02 (5.35e−01)	6.41e+02 (6.42e+01)	+
f18	**1.27e+02** (1.79e−05)	1.46e+02 (1.85e−05)	1.65e+02 (2.45e−05)	2.98e+02 (2.91e−05)	3.15e+02 (3.21e−05)	3.82e+02 (3.78e−04)	4.25e+02 (4.07e−04)	4.45e+02 (4.29e−04)	4.51e+02 (4.63e−04)	4.53e+02 (4.63e−04)	4.75e+02 (5.39e−03)	4.78e+02 (5.83e−03)	4.96e+02 (5.89e−03)	5.61e+02 (6.08e−03)	+
f19	1.33e+02 (1.08e−06)	**1.04e+02** (4.44e−07)	1.53e+02 (1.15e−06)	2.22e+02 (1.27e−060)	3.35e+02 (1.34e−06)	3.65e+02 (2.56e−05)	3.80e+03 (2.83e−05)	3.81e+03 (3.13e−05)	4.47e+03 (4.39e−05)	4.51e+03 (4.87e−04)	4.53e+03 (5.34e−04)	5.04e+03 (5.40e−04)	6.57e+03 (6.52e−04)	6.95e+03 (7.08e−04)	−
f20	**3.31e−03** (1.13e−01)	1.04e−02 (1.37e−01)	1.83e−02 (1.69e−01)	2.43e−01 (1.89e−01)	2.75e+00 (2.31e−01)	3.39e+00 (2.51e−01)	3.64e+00 (2.76e−01)	3.67e+01 (2.97e−01)	3.71e+01 (3.09e+00)	4.10e+02 (3.09e+00)	4.70e+03 (4.78e+00)	5.18e+03 (4.81e+00)	5.28e+03 (4.92e+01)	5.82e+03 (5.15e+01)	+
f21	**2.51e+02** (1.08e+00)	3.29e+02 (1.17e+00)	3.64e+02 (1.39e+00)	4.73e+02 (2.84e+00)	4.77e+02 (3.07e+00)	4.00e+02 (3.60e+00)	5.69e+02 (4.11e+00)	5.28e+03 (5.24e+00)	6.38e+03 (5.38e+01)	7.53e+03 (5.77e+01)	7.65e+03 (5.83e+01)	7.75e+03 (5.97e+01)	8.21e+03 (6.18e+01)	8.64e+03 (6.92e+01)	+
f22	**1.08e+02** (0.00e+00)	1.52e+02 (1.59e+00)	1.78e+02 (3.35e+00)	1.95e+02 (3.69e+00)	2.03e+02 (4.07e+00)	2.32e+02 (4.28e+00)	3.22e+02 (4.87e+00)	3.46e+02 (5.60e+00)	3.46e+02 (5.70e+00)	3.73e+02 (6.05e+00)	3.92e+02 (6.15e+00)	4.75e+02 (6.50e+00)	5.52e+02 (6.92e+00)	5.95e+02 (6.92e+00)	+
f23	**3.38e+02** (0.00e+00)	4.72e+02 (5.22e−18)	4.48e+02 (1.84e−17)	5.02e+02 (1.46e−14)	5.10e+02 (3.39e−13)	5.38e+02 (3.86e−09)	5.62e+03 (4.06e−08)	5.66e+03 (4.07e−06)	6.10e+03 (4.30e−05)	6.17e+03 (4.40e−04)	6.91e+03 (5.38e−04)	7.23 e+03 (5.91e−03)	7.30 e+03 (6.03e−02)	7.87e+03 (6.49e−02)	+
f24	**1.29e+02** (3.57e−17)	**1.29e+02** (3.57e−17)	1.46e+02 (1.44e−16)	1.62e+02 (1.45e−15)	1.78e+02 (1.89e−14)	1.84e+03 (2.91e−12)	1.93e+03 (3.11e−10)	1.97e+03 (3.43e−09)	2.53e+03 (3.75e−07)	3.42e+03 (3.95e−07)	3.49e+03 (4.48e−06)	3.77e+03 (5.97e−05)	4.44e+03 (6.11e−05)	4.86e+03 (6.63e+01)	NA
f25	**1.36e+02** (1.17e+00)	2.44e+02 (1.21e+00)	2.73e+02 (1.93e+00)	2.99e+02 (1.94e+00)	3.16e+02 (2.06e+00)	4.01e+02 (2.10e+00)	4.34e+02 (2.33e+00)	5.10e+02 (2.79e+00)	5.16e+02 (3.26e+00)	6.01e+02 (3.59e+01)	6.02e+02 (4.53e+01)	6.51e+02 (5.49e+01)	6.54e+02 (5.89e+01)	6.89e+02 (6.57e+01)	+

Comparative analysis is tabulated in Table 5.1. To identify the best algorithm (in this case ICFA) at a glance its corresponding values are bolded.

In the last column of Table 5.1, the statistical significance level of the difference of the means (of the final accuracies) of the best two algorithms, obtained using t-test with 25 samples, is reported. Here, "+" indicates that the t value of 49 degrees of freedom is significant at a 0.05 level of significance by two-tailed test, while "−" means the difference of the means is not statistically significant and "NA" stands for Not Applicable, referring to the cases for which two or more algorithms achieve the same best accuracy results.

5.6.5 Performance Analysis

A close scrutiny of Table 5.1 indicates that the performance of the proposed ICFA has remained effectually and consistently superior to that of the other algorithms. It is noteworthy that out of 25 benchmark instances, in 21 cases ICFA outperforms its nearest neighbor competitor in a statistically significant fashion. In three cases, (f10 and f19) ICA-DE, which remains the second best algorithm, has achieved the best average accuracy surpassing ICFA. It is evident from Table 5.1 that ICFA performs consistently better than all algorithms over most of the 25 benchmark instances, and the advantage of ICFA is very prominent as well.

In order to compare the speeds of different algorithms, we present the time taken by each algorithm to converge to the prescribed threshold value of the objective function for the minimization problem of 100-D search space in Table 5.2. The simulation results in Table 5.2 apparently substantiate the highest convergence speed of the proposed ICFA as compared to its other 13 contestants.

To compare the relative speed of convergence and quality of solution (accuracy) of ICFA with its 13 competitors, we plot the mean objective function values taken over 25 runs versus FEs over four representative benchmark instances (f05, f07, f17, and f20) for different settings of problem dimensions in Figures 5.3–5.6. The plots for all the functions are omitted for space economy. In Figures 5.3–5.6, the Max_FEs is set to be 100 000, 300 000, and 500 000 for 10-D, 30-D, and 50-D problems, respectively. It is observed from Figures 5.3–5.6 that ICFA outperforms all other algorithms in terms of convergence speed and solution quality.

In Figure 5.4, plot of accuracy versus run-time complexity for all 14 algorithms over the benchmark function f25 is presented with Max_FEs of 500 000 for 50-D problem. It is to be noted that the accuracy corresponds to absolute difference between the best-of-the-run value $f\left(\vec{X}_{best}\right)$ (obtained after the termination of the algorithm) and the theoretical optimum $f*$ of a particular objective function, i.e. $\left| f\left(\vec{X}_{best}\right) - f* \right|$. This provides a visual means of illustrating the performance of the algorithms with respect to both accuracy and FEs/run-time. In order to have uniformity in order of magnitude, the x- and the y-coordinates are scaled appropriately and then we refer to the distance of a point from the origin as a measure

Table 5.2 Comparative analysis of performance of the proposed ICFA with other algorithms based on convergence time in seconds for f01 to f25.

Functions	Tolerance	ICFA	ICA-DE	ICAAI	Memetic ICA	ICAR	SBA	HEICA	CICA	K-MICA	R-ICA-GA	ABC	FA	ICA	PSO
f01	1.00e−18	24.742	27.809	108.375	137.003	213.684	278.096	412.032	468.265	524.497	565.394	566.416	577.663	627.761	645.142
f02	2.00e−14	31.957	42.212	190.793	204.307	228.951	256.775	276.649	298.114	330.707	356.942	377.611	437.234	441.208	454.723
f03	4.00e−02	35.716	54.877	85.719	86.560	86.560	151.270	223.543	232.788	241.192	289.094	414.312	426.918	1 554.722	489.107
f04	2.00e−04	44.991	46.230	222.895	280.683	359.109	404.514	584.069	693.453	864.752	899.838	1 190.840	1 197.032	1 203.223	1 271.330
f05	1.00e−10	56.435	66.432	354.738	570.807	738.502	964.245	980.369	1 206.112	1 241.586	1 354.457	1 699.522	1 886.566	2 438.024	2 028.461
f06	4.00e−02	65.785	74.136	368.645	509.179	606.941	729.145	800.430	975.587	1 120.194	1 242.397	1 317.756	1 323.866	1 751.577	1 344.233
f07	3.00e−05	71.749	72.299	224.046	259.784	384.8657	412.356	426.101	501.700	531.939	607.538	716.125	801.345	874.195	1 213.701
f08	2.00e−01	80.550	85.743	195.016	225.752	289.344	393.212	463.163	474.822	518.277	519.337	526.756	549.013	594.587	552.193
f09	2.00e−02	82.757	108.455	452.986	879.839	1 520.119	1 568.031	2 060.219	2 068.930	2 121.198	2 386.892	2 700.498	2 748.410	2 883.435	2 974.904
f10	3.00e−03	83.044	87.470	299.377	416.525	609.168	632.598	991.851	1 239.163	1 473.458	1 496.888	3 358.236	5 987.554	12 183.370	6 430.112
f11	1.00e−10	87.984	136.390	335.992	410.024	586.563	879.845	936.792	1 059.230	1 104.789	1 261.396	1 312.649	1 383.833	1 765.384	2 007.413
f12	8.00e−02	103.247	116.073	1 154.319	1 346.705	1 513.440	2 103.425	2 218.857	2 622.869	3 078.184	3 283.396	3 341.112	3 347.525	3 629.692	3 719.472
f13	9.00e−02	103.916	104.565	184.451	223.420	326.037	357.212	462.427	467.623	474.118	494.901	567.643	618.302	758.589	775.475
f14	7.00e−04	113.784	146.048	431.003	679.753	684.679	756.102	758.565	770.880	844.766	898.949	943.281	1 098.442	1 155.088	1 293.009
f15	7.00e−01	117.032	144.925	312.086	374.504	2 145.597	2 360.156	3 881.580	6 807.394	8 406.839	8 874.969	9 577.165	11 157.105	11 332.653	12 795.561
f16	9.00e−03	120.138	177.510	81.890	87.284	622.757	2 049.704	2 093.837	2 407.667	2 505.739	2 540.064	2 785.244	2 795.051	2 834.280	3 442.327
f17	1.00e−01	120.310	131.810	293.698	302.544	337.929	360.930	375.084	461.778	470.624	485.663	5 051.256	5 316.646	6 015.507	6 227.819
f18	2.00e−01	123.131	123.131	574.288	622.956	958.769	1 065.840	1 241.046	1 620.661	1 990.541	2 710.835	3 022.314	3 178.053	3 650.137	4 263.361
f19	3.00e−02	128.413	168.148	327.428	185.883	325.722	3 871.156	4 280.442	5 184.280	5 798.208	6 633.832	8 339.188	8 782.580	9 925.168	11 801.059
f20	2.00e+00	152.039	164.528	323.989	360.189	427.159	428.969	477.839	765.629	948.439	1 035.319	1 076.949	1 136.679	1 174.689	1 230.799
f21	4.00e+01	152.635	201.814	250.264	324.213	743.142	863.356	1 366.070	1 653.855	1 690.283	1 850.569	2 032.712	2 112.854	2 549.997	3 398.782
f22	2.00e+00	156.405	184.566	1 869.495	2 129.448	2 166.275	2 751.169	4 180.911	7 603.627	9 639.926	9 661.589	10 983.017	25 995.306	34 443.781	60 439.088
f23	7.00e+01	165.270	207.414	224.767	243.773	269.390	329.714	428.049	437.966	444.576	454.493	472.672	545.391	2 247.674	4 016.065
f24	2.00e+02	180.090	266.919	543.129	571.715	618.167	1 032.661	1 386.410	1 486.460	1 650.828	1 915.2471	19 581.26	6 860.587	7 432.303	8 254.144
f25	2.00e+02	182.976	365.211	1 437.141	1 659.379	2 266.331	2 718.715	3 296.535	4 178.080	4 259.568	11 852.711	120 00.870	12 371.267	20 445.927	28 965.063

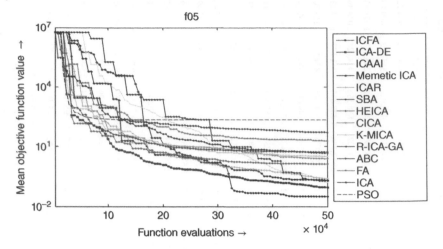

Figure 5.3 Relative performance in mean best objective function versus function evaluation for f05 with Max_FEs = 500 000.

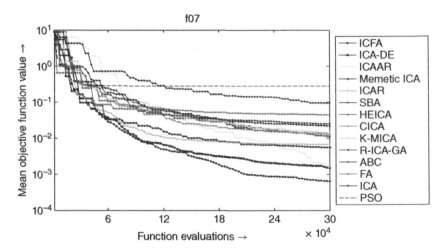

Figure 5.4 Relative performance in mean best objective function versus function evaluation for f07 with Max_FEs = 300 000.

of its performance. The smaller the measure, the better is the performance of the algorithm. The relative performance of two algorithms is symbolized by "$\geq$." Using this convention, Figure 5.4 reveals that the performance of the 14 algorithms, respectively, is ICFA $\geq$ ICA-DE $\geq$ ICAAI $\geq$ Memetic ICA $\geq$ ICAR $\geq$ SBA $\geq$ HEICA $\geq$ CICA $\geq$ K-MICA $\geq$ R-ICA-GA $\geq$ ABC $\geq$ FA $\geq$ ICA $\geq$ PSO.

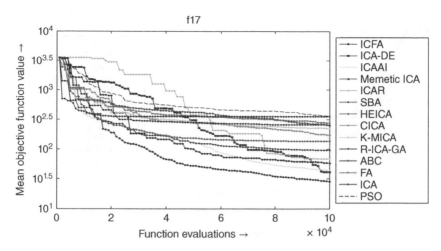

Figure 5.5 Relative performance in mean best objective function versus function evaluation for f17 with Max_FEs = 100 000.

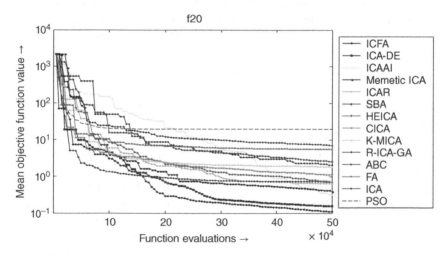

Figure 5.6 Relative performance in mean best objective function versus function evaluation for f20 with Max_FEs = 500 000.

The scalability of an algorithm signifies the consistency in its qualitative performance with the growth of dimensionality of the search space. Increase of dimensions indicates a rapid growth of the hyper-volume of the search space and this, in turn, decelerates the convergence speed of most of the global

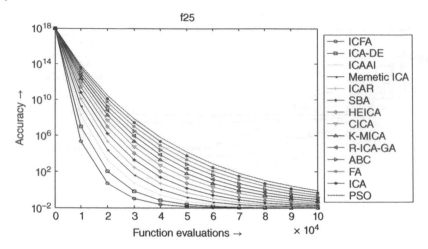

Figure 5.7 Relative performance in accuracy versus function evaluation for ICFA over other competitive algorithms for f25 with Max_FEs = 5×10^6.

optimizers. Figure 5.7 illustrates the scalability of the 14 algorithms over two benchmark functions delineating the variation of the average computational cost (measured in number of FEs required to yield a predefined accuracy threshold) to capture the global optimum with the enhancement in the dimensionality of the search space. It can be observed that ICFA requires smaller number of FEs to achieve the threshold value irrespective of the problem dimensions. Hence, the superiority of the proposed ICFA over other algorithms is prominent as well (Figure 5.8).

A non-parametrical statistical test, known as Friedman two-way analysis of variances by ranks [51], is also performed on the mean of the objective function values for 50 independent runs of each of the 14 algorithms, for 50-*D* problems. Additionally, we use Iman-Davenport test as a variant of Friedman test that provides better statistics [52]. Table 5.3 summarizes the rankings obtained by the Friedman procedure. The results emphasize ICFA as the best algorithm, so the post-hoc analysis [40] is applied with ICFA as the control method. With the level of significance $\alpha = 0.05$, both the Friedman and the Iman-Davenport statistics explain significant differences in operators with test values of 275.7054 and 20 591.88, respectively, and $p < 0.001$ (the estimated probability of rejecting the null hypothesis (H_0) of a study question when that hypothesis is true).

In the post-hoc analysis, the Bonferroni–Dunn test [53] is employed over the results of the Friedman procedure. The outcome of the analysis provides a measure of the level of significance of the superiority of the control algorithm over each of the remaining algorithms (i.e. when the null hypothesis is rejected). For the

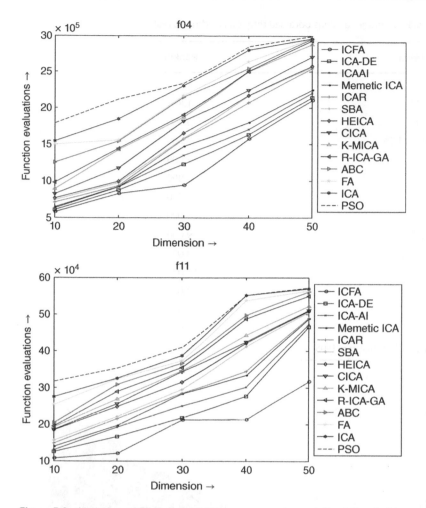

Figure 5.8 Variation of FEs required for convergence to predefined threshold accuracy (1.00e – 08) with increase in search space dimensionality for f04 and f11.

Bonferroni–Dunn test, a critical difference (CD) [53] is calculated which for these data appears as 2.639. It elucidates that the performance of two algorithms is significantly different, only if their corresponding average Friedman ranks differ by at least a CD. It is pictorially depicted in Figure 5.9. It can be perceived that only ICA-DE and ICAAI, the null hypothesis cannot be rejected with any of the tests for $\alpha = 0.05$. The performance of other 11 algorithms, however, may be regarded as significantly poor than the ICFA in the present context.

Table 5.3 Average rankings obtained through Friedman's test

Algorithm	Ranking
ICFA	1.117
ICA-DE	1.883
ICAAI	3.000
Memetic ICA	4.000
ICAR	5.000
SBA	6.000
HEICA	7.000
CICA	8.000
K-MICA	9.000
R-ICA-GA	10.00
ABC	11.00
FA	12.00
ICA	13.00
PSO	14.00
Critical difference $\alpha = 0.05$	2.639

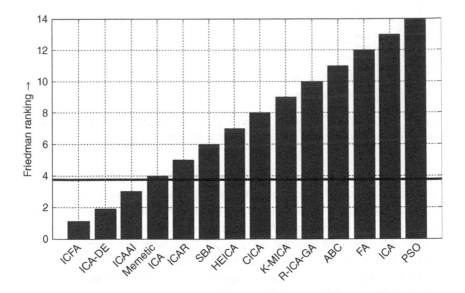

Figure 5.9 Graphical representation of Bonferroni–Dunn's procedure considering ICFA as a control method.

5.7 Computer Simulation and Experiment

Here, the proposed algorithm is employed to carry a fixed length stick from a starting position to a fixed destination by twin robots (multi-robot stick-carrying problem) both in computer simulation and real-time environment. To analyze the performance of the proposed multi-robot stick-carrying problem, the following performance metrics [68] are used.

5.7.1 Average Total Path Deviation (ATPD)

Let P_{ik} be a path from the starting point S_i to the goal point G_i generated by the i-th robot in the k-th run of the algorithm. If $P_{i,1}, P_{i,2}, ..., P_{ik}$ are the paths generated over k runs, then the average total path traversed ($ATPT$) by the i-th robot is given by $\sum_{j=1}^{k} P_{i,j}/k$ and the average path deviation (APD) is evaluated by measuring the difference between $ATPT$ and the ideal shortest path between S_i to G_i. If the geometrically ideal path in a particular workspace is $P_{i\text{-}ideal}$, then the APD is given by $P_{i\text{-}ideal} - \sum_{j=1}^{k} P_{i,j}/k$. Therefore, for two robots in the workspace, the average total path deviation ($ATPD$) is $\sum_{i=1}^{2} P_{i=ideal} - \sum_{j=1}^{k} P_{i,j}/k$.

5.7.2 Average Uncovered Target Distance (AUTD)

Given a goal position G_i and the current position C_i of a robot on a 2-dimensional workspace, where G_i and C_i are 2-dimensional vectors, the uncovered distance of robot i is $\|G_i - C_i\|$, where $\|.\|$ denotes the Euclidean norm. For two robots, uncovered target distance $UTD = \sum_{i=1}^{2} \|G_i - C_i\|$. Now, for k runs of the program, we evaluate the average of $UTDs$ and call it the average uncovered target distance ($AUTD$). For all experiments conducted in this study, we have considered $k = 10$.

5.7.3 Experimental Setup in Simulation Environment

The multi-robot stick-carrying problem is implemented in C on a Pentium processor. The experiment is performed with two similar soft-bots of circular cross-sections of radius 6 pixels and 10 differently shaped obstacles. While performing the experiments, old obstacles are retained and new obstacles are added in the workspace. The experiments are accomplished with equal velocities for two robots in a given run of the program; however, the velocities are regulated over different runs of the same program. Some instances of the workspace of the robots, employing different evolutionary optimization algorithms, are given in Figure 5.10. It reveals that the robots successfully follow the shortest path with minimum path deviation in case of ICFA-based realization of the multi-robot stick-carrying problem.

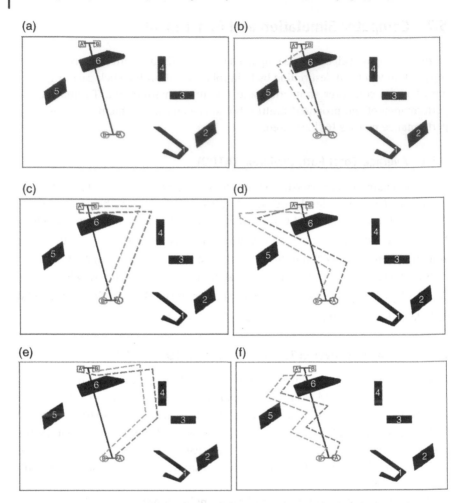

Figure 5.10 Initial (a) and final configuration of the world map after execution of the
(b) ICFA-, (c) ICA-DE-, (d) ICAAI-, (e) FA-, and (f) ICA-based simulations with
5 obstacles requiring 23, 29, 32, and 34 steps, respectively.

5.7.4 Experimental Results in Simulation Environment

First, we plot *ATPT* by varying the number of obstacles from 2 to 10 by generating
paths using five different algorithms, including ICFA, ICA-DE, ICAAI, FA, and
ICA. It is worth mentioning from Figure 5.11 that ICFA has the least *ATPT* in comparison to other algorithms irrespective to the number of obstacles.

The second study on performance analysis is undertaken by plotting *ATPD* by
generating paths by five different evolutionary/swarm algorithms (as used in

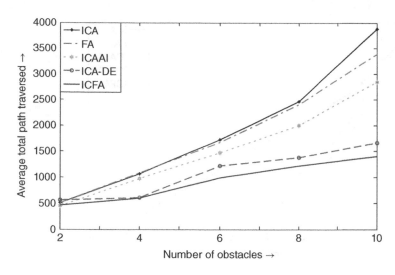

Figure 5.11 Average total path traversed versus number of obstacles.

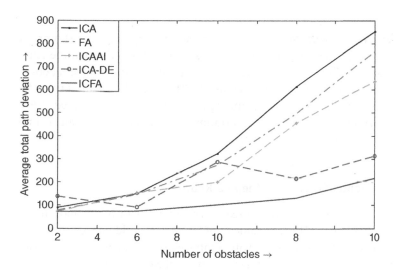

Figure 5.12 Average total path deviation versus number of obstacles.

ATPT). Figure 5.11 provides the results of *ATPD* computation when the number of obstacles varies from 2 to 10. Here too, we observe that ICFA outperforms the remaining four algorithms as *ATPD* remains the smallest for ICFA-based simulation irrespective to the number of obstacles (Figure 5.12).

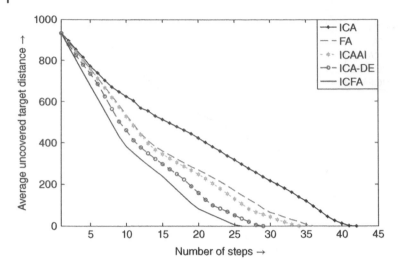

Figure 5.13 Average uncovered target distance versus number of steps with number of obstacles = 5 (constant).

The last analysis on performance is undertaken by comparing *AUTD* over the number of planning steps. Figure 5.13 provides a plot of *AUTD* when the paths are planned using the five algorithms referred to above with the number of obstacles = 5. It is apparent from Figure 5.13 that *AUTD* returns the smallest value for ICFA irrespective of the number of planning steps. In brief, the proposed ICFA-based stick-carrying methodology outperforms the remaining four algorithms with respect to all three popular metrics.

5.7.5 Experimental Setup with Khepera Robots

The experiment is also undertaken in real environment with two homogeneous Khepera-II mobile robots [70, 71] (diameter of 7 cm) in a world map of 8 × 6 grids of equal size. Each robot is equipped with 8 infrared sensors, 2 motor-driven side wheels, and one caster wheel with a flash memory of 512 KB, and a Motorola 68 331, 25 MHz processor. The range sensors placed at fixed angles have limited range-detection capabilities. The robot represents measured range data in the scale: [0, 1023]. When the distance of the obstacle from the sensor exceeds 5 cm, it is represented by zero. When an obstacle is approximately 2 cm away from the sensor, it corresponds to 1023.

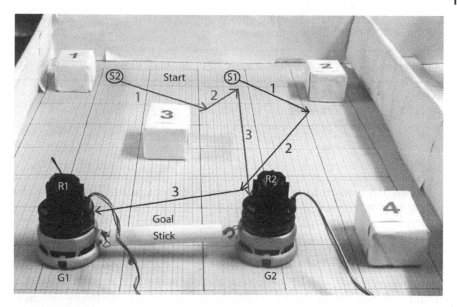

Figure 5.14 Final configuration of the world map after experiment using Khepera-II mobile robots.

The robots are controlled by two Pentium-IV personal computers (PCs) through wired connections. An optimization algorithm-based control program determining the next position of each robot from its current position is run on the attached Pentium machine with the range data obtained from sensory measurements of the robots. The necessary commands for controlling motor movements are transferred to the robots from their connected computers. One sample run of the stick-carrying problem on the Khepera environment is given in Figure 5.14. The experiment is performed on 20 different world maps of different grid counts, each with five different obstacle maps, and in all the 100 environments, the robots could successfully follow the shortest paths avoiding collision with the obstacles.

5.7.6 Experimental Results with Khepera Robots

Results of the experiments performed are summarized in Table 5.4. Three performance metrics, namely (i) total number of steps taken to reach the goal, (ii) *ATPT*, and (iii) *ATPD* have been used here too to determine the relative merits of ICFA over other algorithms. Table 5.4 substantiates that ICFA outperforms the remaining four algorithms with respect to all the three metrics.

Table 5.4 Comparison of number of steps, average path traversed, and average total path deviation (ATPD) by the Khepera robots.

Algorithms	Total number of steps	ATPT (in.)	ATPD (in.)
ICFA	**10**	**41.2**	7.5
ICA-DE	13	44.2	9.5
ICAAI	16	45.7	12.1
FA	18	48.3	13.7
ICA	22	52.0	16.4

Comparative analysis is tabulated in Table 5.4. To identify the best algorithm (in this case ICFA) at a glance its corresponding values are bolded. 7.5 is the ATPD corresponding to the ICFA.

5.8 Conclusion

The most intriguing issue of the present chapter is the unique formulation of a multi-robot stick-carrying problem in the framework of an evolutionary optimization problem. The integrity of the work lies in online optimization of the trajectory of the stick (carried by the robots) in a sequence of local steps from the predefined starting position to a given goal position without collision with obstacles in the workspace. The stick-carrying optimization problem is then solved using the proposed hybrid evolutionary optimization algorithm.

The chapter also introduced a novel approach for efficiently employing both ICA and FA to develop a hybrid algorithm with an aim to utilize the composite benefits of the explorative and exploitative capabilities of both ancestor algorithms. The potential of local exploitation is captured by the colonizing behavior of countries (representing candidate solutions) surrounding the respective imperialist (representing the local optima in the search space) of the traditional ICA. Alternatively, the global explorative proficiency of FA is signified by the self-organizing behavior of fireflies (representing candidate solutions) based on their light intensity (symbolizing the fitness) profile. The merit of the proposed hybridization policy lies in devising two interesting stratagems to realize the communal benefits of the two ancestor algorithms: (i) integration of the light intensity (fitness)-induced motion dynamics of fireflies in the traditional ICA and (ii) modulation of step-size for random motion of fireflies based on the best position in the search space (discovered so far). The chapter also recommends a new policy of evaluating the threshold value for union of colonies (set of candidate solutions) based on search space dimensions.

The incorporation of firefly motion dynamics of the traditional FA in the traditional ICA is significant due to its efficacy of distributing the information of the promising regions in the search space among the fireflies (candidate solutions) through the brighter ones (quality solutions with better fitness). The strategy thus allows each country (candidate solution) of ICA to improve its sociopolitical characteristics by following the more powerful countries (quality solutions with better fitness) in the colony, not only being guided by the respective imperialist country (local optima). Hence, it evades the possibility of the search strategy to get stuck at local optima.

The second strategy provides a unique estimate of step-size for random movement of fireflies based on their position in the search space relative to the so far best position. It differs from the conventional approach, which considers equal step-size for random movement of all fireflies irrespective of their fitness, thereby offering a poor convergence rate in most of the real-world applications. In the proposed alternative approach, the step-size for random motion is decreased for a brighter firefly (quality solution with better fitness) to confine its search process in close proximity of the best position discovered so far. It thus assists in the local exploitation of quality solutions. Contrarily, the fireflies far away from the best location in the search space are assigned with a large value of step-size to inspire them in global exploration.

The experimental study undertaken reveals the effectiveness of the proposed hybrid algorithm in counterbalancing the trade-off between the global exploration and the local exploitation. It is capable of maintaining large population variance to ensure population diversity at earlier explorative phase of ICFA, while confining the search process in the local neighborhoods at later exploitative phase by preserving low population diversity. We have then undertaken a comparative study of the proposed ICFA algorithm with 13 state-of-the-art hybrid/traditional evolutionary/swarm algorithms. The efficacy of all the 14 contender algorithms is scrutinized with respect to the test suit of 25 CEC 2005 benchmark functions. The relative performance of all the algorithms has been compared based on the solution quality and the convergence time. The quality performance of ICFA is substantiated by the reported simulation results. The experimental study clearly reveals that ICFA outperforms its competitor algorithms with respect to the computational accuracy and the run-time complexity required for convergence, irrespective of settings of problem dimension.

Three nonparametric tests including the Friedman test, the Iman-Davenport statistic, and the Bonferroni–Dunn post-hoc analysis are used to validate the statistical significance of the results. The results of both the Friedman and the Iman–Davenport tests affirm the rejection of the null hypothesis, concerned with the equivalent performance of all the contender algorithms. Moreover, ICFA emerges as the winner achieving the highest average Friedman rank. The outcome of the Bonferroni–Dunn test further reveals that apart from ICA-DE and ICAAI, the remaining 11 algorithms are outperformed by ICFA in a statistically significant manner.

Finally, the proposed ICFA is employed to handle the multi-robot stick-carrying problem. The experiments undertaken reveal that the ICFA-based program here too outperforms all its competitors with respect to two parameters AUTD and ATPD. The experiments performed with Khepera-II mobile robots also indicate that ICFA outperforms other realizations in real environment, thereby justifying the merit of the proposed algorithm.

A potential extension of the proposed multi-robot stick-carrying problem is to consider noise contaminating the sensory measurements of the robots. In real-world problems, the sensory data of the robots are often found to be contaminated with noise due to sensor aging or noisy ambience or faulty measurement procedure. The application of traditional/hybrid evolutionary/swarm optimization algorithms may fail to solve such practical multi-robot coordination problems. The existing algorithms are biased toward the selection of candidate solutions with better fitness measures over evolutionary generations. However, this conventional fitness-based selection of candidate solutions may lead the search process toward suboptimal or deceptive regions in the search space in the presence of noise. Hence, new robust selection strategy needs to be incorporated in the traditional/hybrid evolutionary/swarm algorithms to cope with the uncertainty involved in the noisy sensory data of the robots. Although the quality performance of ICFA is evident on different complicated fitness landscapes, there is still scope to further amend its effectiveness to capture the global optima in the real-world multimodal objective surface. It can be accomplished by the online tuning of the algorithm control parameters to learn the objective space characteristics using, for instance, machine-learning methods.

5.9 Summary

This chapter hybridizes the FA and the ICA. The above explained hybridization results in the ICFA, which is employed to determine the time-optimal trajectory of a stick, being carried by two robots, from a given starting position to a predefined goal position amidst static obstacles in a robot world map. The motion dynamics of fireflies of the FA is embedded into the sociopolitical evolution-based metaheuristic ICA. Also the trade-off between the exploration and exploitation is balanced by modifying the random walk strategy based on the position of the candidate solutions in the search space. The superiority of the proposed ICFA is studied considering run-time and accuracy as the performance metrics. Finally, the proposed algorithm has been verified in real-time multi-robot stick-carrying problem.

Appendix 5.A   Additional Comparison of ICFA

In order to compare the speeds of different competitive algorithms listed under Section 5.6.1, we record the number of FEs the algorithm takes to reach below a predefined cutoff value of the objective function for the minimization problem. A lower number of FEs corresponds to a faster algorithm. Table 5.A.1 details the

Table 5.A.1 No of successful runs out of 25 runs and success performance in parenthesis (success performance = mean (fes for successful runs) × (# of total runs)/(# of successful runs)) for f01 to f25.

Functions	Tolerance	ICFA	ICA-DE	ICAAI	Memetic ICA	ICAR	SBA	HEICA	CICA	K-MICA	R-ICA-GA	ABC	FA	ICA	PSO
f01	1.00e−18	**25** **(2.42e+03)**	25 (2.72e+03)	25 (1.06e+04)	24 (1.34e+04)	24 (2.09e+04)	24 (2.72e+04)	23 (4.03e+04)	23 (4.58e+04)	22 (5.13e+04)	21 (5.53e+04)	21 (5.54e+04)	21 (5.65e+04)	21 (6.14e+04)	20 (6.31e+04)
f02	2.00e−14	**24** **(4.02e+03)**	24 (5.31e+03)	23 (2.40e+04)	23 (2.57e+04)	22 (2.88e+04)	22 (3.23e+04)	22 (3.48e+04)	21 (3.75e+04)	21 (4.16e+04)	21 (4.49e+04)	21 (4.75e+04)	20 (5.50e+04)	19 (5.55e+04)	18 (5.72e+04)
f03	4.00e−02	**25** **(4.25e+03)**	24 (6.53e+03)	24 (1.02e+04)	24 (1.33e+04)	24 (1.03e+04)	24 (1.80e+04)	23 (2.66e+04)	23 (2.77e+04)	22 (2.87e+04)	21 (3.44e+04)	21 (4.93e+04)	21 (5.08e+04)	21 (1.85e+05)	21 (5.82e+04)
f04	2.00e−04	**25** **(2.18e+03)**	24 (2.24e+03)	24 (1.08e+04)	24 (1.36e+04)	24 (1.74e+04)	23 (1.96e+04)	23 (2.83e+04)	23 (3.36e+04)	21 (4.19e+04)	21 (4.36e+04)	21 (5.77e+04)	19 (5.80e+04)	19 (5.83e+04)	18 (6.16e+04)
f05	1.00e−10	**25** **(1.75e+02)**	25 (2.06e+02)	24 (1.10e+03)	2~ (1.77e+03)	23 (2.29e+03)	23 (2.99e+03)	23 (3.04e+03)	23 (3.74e+03)	22 (3.85e+03)	22 (4.20e+03)	21 (5.27e+03)	21 (5.85e+03)	21 (7.56e+03)	21 (6.29e+03)
f06	4.00e−02	**25** **(3.23e+03)**	24 (3.64e+03)	23 (1.81e+04)	23 (2.50e+04)	22 (2.98e+04)	22 (3.58 e+04)	22 (3.93e+04)	21 (4.79e+04)	21 (5.50e+04)	21 (6.10e+04)	20 (6.47e+04)	20 (6.50e+04)	19 (8.60e+04)	19 (6.60e+04)
f07	3.00e−05	**25** **(5.22e+02)**	24 (5.26e+02)	24 (1.63e+03)	24 (1.89e+03)	23 (2.80e+03)	23 (3.00e+03)	23 (3.10e+03)	22 (3.65e+03)	22 (3.87e+03)	21 (4.42e+03)	21 (5.21e+03)	20 (5.83e+03)	19 (6.36e+03)	18 (8.83e+03)
f08	2.00e−01	**25** **(7.60e+03)**	25 (8.09e+03)	25 (1.84e+04)	25 (2.13e+04)	25 (2.73e+04)	23 (3.71e+04)	23 (4.37e+04)	22 (4.48e+04)	22 (4.89e+04)	21 (4.90e+04)	20 (4.97e+04)	20 (5.18e+04)	19 (5.61e+04)	19 (5.21e+04)
f09	2.00e−02	**24** **(1.90e+02)**	24 (2.49e+02)	23 (1.04e+03)	23 (2.02e+03)	22 (3.49e+03)	23 (3.60e+03)	21 (4.73e+03)	21 (4.75e+03)	20 (4.87e+03)	20 (5.48e+03)	20 (6.20e+03)	19 (6.31e+03)	19 (6.62e+03)	19 (6.83e+03)
f10	3.00e−03	**24** **(3.19e+02)**	24 (3.36e+02)	24 (1.15e+03)	24 (1.60e+03)	23 (2.34e+03)	23 (2.43e+03)	22 (3.81e+03)	21 (4.76e+03)	21 (5.66e+03)	20 (5.75e+03)	19 (1.29e+04)	19 (2.30e+04)	18 (4.68e+04)	19 (2.47e+04)
f11	1.00e−10	**25** **(3.09e+03)**	25 (4.79e+03)	25 (1.18e+04)	25 (1.44e+04)	24 (2.06e+04)	23 (3.09e+04)	23 (3.29e+04)	23 (3.72e+04)	23 (3.88e+04)	21 (4.43e+04)	20 (4.61e+04)	19 (4.86e+04)	19 (6.20e+04)	20 (7.05e+04)
f12	8.00e−02	**25** **(1.61e+03)**	25 (1.81e+03)	25 (1.80e+04)	24 (2.10e+04)	24 (2.36e+04)	23 (3.28e+04)	22 (3.46e+04)	22 (4.09e+04)	22 (4.80e+04)	21 (5.12e+04)	21 (5.21e+04)	21 (5.22e+04)	20 (5.66e+04)	20 (5.80e+04)
f13	9.00e−02	**25** **(8.00e+03)**	25 (8.05e+03)	23 (1.42e+04)	22 1.72e+04)	21 (2.51e+04)	21 (2.75e+04)	20 (3.56e+04)	20 (3.60e+04)	20 (3.65e+04)	19 (3.81e+04)	19 (4.37e+04)	19 (4.76e+04)	19 (5.84e+04)	19 (5.97e+04)
f14	7.00e−04	**25** **(4.62e+02)**	25 (5.93e+02)	24 (1.75e+03)	24 (2.76e+03)	24 (2.78e+03)	24 (3.07e+03)	23 (3.08e − +03)	23 (3.13e+03)	22 (3.43e+03)	22 (3.65e+03)	21 (3.83e+03)	20 (4.46e+03)	20 (4.69e+03)	18 (5.25e+03)
f15	7.00e−01	**25** **(6.00e+02)**	25 (7.43e+02)	25 (1.60e+03)	25 (1.92e+03)	24 (1.10e+04)	24 (1.21e+04)	24 (1.99e+04)	23 (3.49e+04)	22 (4.31e+04)	22 (4.55e+04)	22 (4.91e+04)	21 (5.72e+04)	21 (5.81e+04)	21 (6.56e+04)

(Continued)

Table 5.A.1 (Continued)

Functions	Tolerance	ICFA	ICA-DE	ICAAI	Memetic ICA	ICAR	SBA	HEICA	CICA	K-MICA	R-ICA-GA	ABC	FA	ICA	PSO
f16	9.00e−03	**24** **(2.45e+03)**	24 (3.62e+03)	23 (1.67e+03)	23 (1.78e+03)	22 (1.27e+04)	22 (4.18e+04)	21 (4.27e+04)	21 (4.91e+04)	21 (5.11e+04)	20 (5.18e+04)	20 (5.68e+04)	20 (5.70e+04)	19 (5.78e+04)	19 (7.02e+04)
f17	1.00e−01	**25** **(1.36e+03)**	25 (1.49e+03)	23 (3.32e+03)	23 (3.42e+03)	22 (3.82e+03)	21 (4.08e+03)	21 (4.24e+03)	21 (5.22e+03)	21 (5.32e+03)	20 (5.49e+03)	20 (5.71e+04)	19 (6.01e+04)	19 (6.80e+04)	19 (7.04e+04)
f18	2.00e−01	**25** **(2.53e+03)**	25 (2.53e+03)	24 (1.18e+04)	24 (1.28e+04)	24 (1.97e+04)	23 (2.19e+04)	21 (2.55e+04)	20 (3.33e+04)	20 (4.09e+04)	19 (5.57e+04)	18 (6.21e+04)	18 (6.53e+04)	18 (7.50e+04)	17 (8.76e+04)
f19	3.00e−02	**24** **(7.53e+03)**	24 (9.86e+03)	24 (1.92e+04)	23 (1.09e+04)	23 (1.91e+04)	23 (2.27e+05)	22 (2.51e+05)	21 (3.04e+05)	20 (3.40e+05)	20 (3.89e+05)	20 (4.89e+05)	19 (5.15e+05)	19 (5.82e+05)	18 (6.92e+05)
f20	2.00e+00	**25** **(8.40e+03)**	24 (9.09e+03)	23 (1.79e+04)	22 (1.99e+04)	22 (2.36e+04)	22 (2.37e+04)	21 (2.64e+04)	21 (4.23e+04)	20 (5.24e+04)	19 (5.72e+04)	19 (5.95e+04)	19 (6.28e+04)	19 (6.49e+04)	18 (6.80e+04)
f21	4.00e+01	**25** **(4.19e+03)**	25 (5.54e+03)	24 (6.87e+03)	24 (8.90e+03)	23 (2.04e+04)	23 (2.37e+04)	22 (3.75e+04)	22 (4.54e+04)	21 (4.64e+04)	21 (5.08e+04)	21 (5.58e+04)	21 (5.80e+04)	21 (7.00e+04)	20 (9.33e+04)
f22	2.00e+00	**24** **(7.22e+02)**	24 (8.52e+02)	24 (8.63e+03)	23 (9.83e+03)	23 (1.00e+04)	22 (1.27e+04)	22 (1.93e+04)	21 (3.51e+04)	21 (4.45e+04)	19 (4.46e+04)	19 (5.07e+04)	19 (1.20e+05)	18 (1.59e+05)	18 (2.79e+05)
f23	7.00e+01	**25** **(2.00e+02)**	24 (2.51e+02)	24 (2.72e+02)	24 (2.95e+02)	23 (3.26e+02)	22 (3.99e+02)	22 (5.18e+02)	21 (5.30e+02)	20 (5.38e+02)	20 (5.50e+02)	20 (5.72e+02)	19 (6.60e+02)	19 (2.72e+03)	18 (4.86e+03)
f24	2.00e+02	**24** **(5.04e+02)**	24 (7.47e+02)	24 (1.52e+03)	23 (1.60e+03)	23 (1.73e+03)	22 (2.89e+03)	22 (3.88e+03)	20 (4.16e+03)	20 (4.62e+03)	20 (5.36e+03)	20 (5.48e+03)	20 (1.92e+04)	20 (2.08e+04)	19 (2.31e+04)
f25	2.00e+02	**24** **(2.47e+02)**	23 (4.93e+02)	23 (1.94e+03)	23 (2.24e+03)	22 (3.06e+03)	22 (3.67e+03)	22 (4.45e+03)	22 (5.64e+03)	21 (5.75e+03)	20 (1.60e+04)	19 (1.62e+04)	17 (1.67e+04)	17 (2.76e+04)	17 (3.91e+04)

Comparative analysis is tabulated in Table 5.A.1. To identify the best algorithm (in this case ICFA) at a glance its corresponding values are bolded.

number of runs (out of 25) that successfully locate the optimum solution (within the given tolerance) as well as the success performance attained by the algorithms to converge within the prescribed threshold value. Table 5.A.1 designates that the number of runs that converge below a prespecified threshold value is also greater for ICFA over most of the benchmark problems considered here. This indicates the higher robustness of the algorithm as compared to its other 13 contestants.

References

1 Fong, T., Nourbakhsh, I., and Dautenhahn, K. (2003). A survey of socially interactive robots. *Robotics and Autonomous Systems* 42 (3): 143–166.
2 Luna, R. and Bekris, K.E. (2011). Efficient and complete centralized multi-robot path planning. *International Conference on Intelligent Robots and Systems (IROS), IEEE/RSJ*, San Francisco, CA (25–30 September 2011), pp. 3268–3275.
3 Bhattacharya, P. and Gavrilova, M.L. (2008). Roadmap-based path planning-using the Voronoi diagram for a clearance-based shortest path. *IEEE Robotics and Automation Magazine* 15 (2): 58–66.
4 Gayle, R., Moss, W., Lin, M.C., and Manocha, D. (2009). Multi-robot coordination using generalized social potential fields. *IEEE International Conference on Robotics and Automation*, Kobe, Japan (12–17 May 2009), pp. 106–113.
5 Yamada, S. and Saito, J.Y. (2001). Adaptive action selection without explicit communication for multirobot box-pushing. *IEEE Transactions on Systems, Man, and Cybernetics, Part C: Applications and Reviews* 31 (3): 398–404.
6 Sugie, H., Inagaki, Y., Ono, S. et al. (1995). Placing objects with multiple mobile robots-mutual help using intention inference. *IEEE International Conference on Robotics and Automation, Proceedings* 2: 2181–2186.
7 Yamauchi, Y., Ishikawa, S., Uemura, N., and Kato, K. (1993). On cooperative conveyance by two mobile robots. *IEEE International Conference on Industrial Electronics, Control, and Instrumentation, Proceedings of the IECON'93*, Piscataway, NJ (15–18 November 1993), pp. 1478–1481.
8 Kube, C.R. and Zhang, H. (1996). The use of perceptual cues in multi-robot box-pushing. *IEEE International Conference on Robotics and Automation, Proceedings* 3: 2085–2090.
9 Rakshit, P., Konar, A., Das, S. et al. (2014). Uncertainty management in differential evolution induced multi-objective optimization in presence of measurement noise. *IEEE Transactions on Systems, Man, and Cybernetics: Systems* 44 (7): 922–937.
10 Das, P., Sadhu, A.K., Vyas, R.R. et al. (2015). Arduino based multi-robot stick-carrying by artificial bee colony optimization algorithm. *Third International Conference on Computer, Communication, Control and Information Technology (C3IT), IEEE*, Adisaptagram, Hoogly, West Bengal (7–8 February 2015), pp. 1–6.

11 Wolpert, D.H. and Macready, W.G. (1997). No free lunch theorems for optimization. *IEEE Transactions on Evolutionary Computation* 1 (1): 67–82.

12 Pugalendhi, G.K., Chellasamy, R., Durairaj, D., and Aruldoss Albert Victoire, T. (2014). Hybrid ant bee algorithm for fuzzy expert system based sample classification. *IEEE/ACM Transactions on Computational Biology and Bioinformatics* 11 (2): 347–360.

13 Gargari, E.A. and Lucas, C. (2007). Imperialist competitive algorithm: an algorithm for optimization inspired by imperialistic competition. *IEEE Congress in Evolutionary Computation, CEC*, Singapore (25–28 September 2007), pp. 4661–4667.

14 Kamkarian, P. and Hexmoor, H. (2013). Exploiting the imperialist competition algorithm to determine exit door efficacy for public buildings. *Simulation: Transactions of The Society for Modeling and Simulation International* 89 (12): 24–51, Sage Pub.

15 Yang, X.S. (2009). Firefly algorithms for multimodal optimization, Stochastic Algorithms: foundations and Applications. *SAGA, Lecture Notes in Computer Sciences* 5792: 169–178.

16 Narimani, R. and Narimani, A. (2013). A new hybrid optimization model based on imperialistic competition and differential evolution meta-heuristic and clustering algorithms. *Applied Mathematics in Engineering, Management and Technology* 1 (2): 1–9.

17 Subudhi, B. and Jena, D. (2011). A differential evolution based neural network approach to nonlinear system identification. *Applied Soft Computing* 11 (1): 861–871.

18 Ramezani, F., Lotfi, S., and Soltani-Sarvestani, M.A. (2012). A hybrid evolutionary imperialist competitive algorithm (HEICA). In: *Intelligent Information and Database Systems*, Part I, LNAI, vol. 7196 (eds. N.T. Nguyen, K. Jearanaitanakij, A. Semalat, et al.), 359–368. Berlin, Heidelberg: Springer.

19 Khorani, V., Razavi, F., and Ghoncheh, A. (2010). A new hybrid evolutionary algorithm based on ICA and GA: recursive-ICA-GA. *Proceedings of the International Conference on Artificial Intelligence*, Las Vegas, NV (12–15 July, 2010), pp. 131–140.

20 Nozarian, S. and Jahan, M.V. (2012). A novel memetic algorithm with imperialist competition as local search. *International Proceedings of Computer Science & Information Technology*, Hong Kong, China (April 2012). Vol. 30.

21 Lin, J.L., Tsai, Y.H., Yu, C.Y., and Li, M.S. (2012). Interaction enhanced imperialist competitive algorithms. *Algorithms* 5 (4): 433–448.

22 Coelho, L.D.S., Afonso, L.D., and Alotto, P. (2012). A modified imperialist competitive algorithm for optimization in electromagnetic. *IEEE Transactions on Magnetics* 48 (2): 579–582.

23 Ahmadi, M.A., Ebadi, M., Shokrollahi, A., and Majidi, S.M.J. (2013). Evolving artificial neural network and imperialist competitive algorithm for prediction oil flow rate of the reservoir. *Applied Soft Computing* 13 (2): 1085–1098, Elsevier.

24 Talatahari, S., Farahmand Azar, B., Sheikholeslami, R., and Gandomi, A.H. (2012). Imperialist competitive algorithm combined with chaos for global optimization. *Communications in Nonlinear Science and Numerical Simulation* 17 (3): 1312–1319, Elsevier.

25 Bahrami, H., Faez, K., and Abdechiri, M. (2010). Imperialist competitive algorithm using chaos theory for optimization (CICA). *Proceedings of the 12th International Conference on Computer Modelling and Simulation (UKSim), IEEE*, Cambridge, UK (24–26 March 2010), pp. 98–103.

26 Bahrami, H., Abdechiri, M., and Meybodi, M.R. (2012). Imperialist competitive algorithm with adaptive colonies movement. *International Journal of Intelligent Systems and Applications (IJISA)* 4 (2): 49–57.

27 Zhang, Y., Wang, Y., and Peng, C. (2009). Improved imperialist competitive algorithm for constrained optimization. *International Forum on Computer Science-Technology and Applications, IFCSTA, IEEE* 1: 204–207.

28 Mohammadi-ivatloo, B., Rabiee, A., Soroudi, A., and Ehsan, M. (2012). Imperialist competitive algorithm for solving non-convex dynamic economic power dispatch. *Energy* 44 (1): 228–240, Elsevier.

29 Rashtchi, V., Rahimpour, E., and Shahrouzi, H. (2012). Model reduction of transformer detailed RCLM model using the imperialist competitive algorithm. *IET Electric Power Applications* 6 (4): 233–242.

30 Khorani, V., Razavi, F., and Disfani, V.R. (2011). A mathematical model for urban traffic and traffic optimization using a developed ICA technique. *IEEE Transactions on Intelligent Transportation Systems* 12 (4): 1024–1036.

31 Gorginpour, H., Jandaghi, B., and Oraee, H. (2013). A novel rotor configuration for brushless doubly-fed induction generators. *IET Electric Power Applications* 7 (2): 106–115.

32 Gorginpour, H., Oraee Mirzamani, H., and McMaho, R. (2014). Electromagnetic-thermal design optimization of the brushless doubly-fed induction generator. *IEEE Transactions on Industrial Electronics* 61 (4): 1710–1721.

33 Niknam, T., Taherian, E.F., Pourjafarian, N., and Rousta, A. (2011). An efficient hybrid algorithm based on modified imperialist competitive algorithm and K-means for data clustering. *Engineering Applications of Artificial Intelligence* 24 (2): 306–317.

34 Mozafari, H., Abdi, B., and Ayob, A. (2012). Optimization of adhesive-bonded fiber glass strip using imperialist competitive algorithm. *Procedia Technology* 1: 194–198, Elsevier.

35 Kaveh, A. and Talatahari, S. (2010). Optimum design of skeletal structures using imperialist competitive algorithm. *Computers and Structures* 88 (21): 1220–1229, Elsevier.

36 Nazari-Shirkouhi, S., Eivazy, H., Ghodsi, R. et al. (2010). Solving the integrated product mix-outsourcing problem using the imperialist competitive algorithm. *Expert Systems with Applications* 37 (12): 7615–7626, Elsevier.

37 Duan, H., Xu, C., Liu, S., and Shao, S. (2010). Template matching using chaotic imperialist competitive algorithm. *Pattern Recognition Letters* 31 (13): 1868–1875, Elsevier.

38 Sharifi, M. and Mojallali, H. (2013). Design of IIR digital filter using modified chaotic orthogonal imperialist competitive algorithm. *Proceedings of the 13th Iranian Conference on Fuzzy Systems (IFSC), IEEE,* Qazvin, Iran (27–29 August 2013), pp. 1–6.

39 Bashiri, M. and Bagheri, M. (2013). Using imperialist competitive algorithm in optimization of nonlinear multiple responses. *International Journal of Industrial Engineering* 24 (3): 229–235.

40 Emami, H. and Lotfi, S. (2013). Graph colouring problem based on discrete imperialist competitive algorithm. *International Journal of Foundations of Compututer Science and Technology* 3 (4): 1–12.

41 Lin, J.L., Cho, C.W., and Chuan, H.C. (2013). Imperialist competitive algorithms with perturbed moves for global optimization. *Applied Mechanics and Materials* 284–287: 3135–3139.

42 Karimi, N., Zandieh, M., and Najafi, A.A. (2011). Group scheduling in flexible flow shops: a hybridized approach of imperialist competitive algorithm and electromagnetic-like mechanism. *International Journal of Production Research* 49 (16): 4965–4977.

43 Hamel, A., Mohellebi, H., and Feliachi, M. (2012). Imperialist competitive algorithm and particle swarm optimization comparison for eddy current non-destructive evaluation. *Przeglad Elektrotechniczny* 88 (9A): 285–289.

44 Bidar, M. and Rashidy, H.K. (2013). Modified firefly algorithm using fuzzy tuned parameters. *Proceedings of the 13th Iranian Conference on Fuzzy Systems (IFSC), IEEE,* Qazvin, Iran (27–29 August 2013), pp. 1–4.

45 Chandrasekaran, K. and Simon, S.P. (2013). Optimal deviation based firefly algorithm tuned fuzzy design for multi-objective UCP. *IEEE Transactions on Power Systems* 28 (1): 460–471.

46 Coelho, L.D.S., Bora, T.C., Schauenburg, F., and Alotto, P. (2013). A multiobjective firefly approach using beta probability distribution for electromagnetic optimization problems. *IEEE Transactions on Magnetics* 49 (5): 2085–2088.

47 Farahani, S.M., Abshouri, A.A., Nasiri, B., and Meybodi, M.R. (2011). A Gaussian firefly algorithm. *International Journal of Machine Learning and Computing* 1 (5): 448–453.

48 Chetty, S. and Adewumi, A.O. (2014). Comparison study of swarm intelligence techniques for the annual crop planning problem. *IEEE Transactions on Evolutionary Computation* 18 (2): 258–268.

49 Abdullah, A., Deris, S., Mohamad, M.S., and Hashim, S.Z.M. (2012). A new hybrid firefly algorithm for complex and nonlinear problem. *Distributed Computing and*

Artificial Intelligence, Springer, AISC 151, Salamanca, Spain (22–24 May 2013), pp. 673–680.

50 Banati, H. and Bajaj, M. (2011). Fire fly based feature selection approach. *International Journal of Computer Science Issues* 8, issue 4, no. 2: 473–480.

51 Horng, M.H. and Jiang, T.W. (2010). The codebook design of image vector quantization based on the firefly algorithm. *International Conference on Computer Communication and the Internet,* Kaohsiung, Taiwan (10–12 November 2010), pp. 438–447.

52 Abidin, Z.Z., Arshad, M.R., and Ngah, U.K. (2011). A simulation based fly optimization algorithm for swarms of mini-autonomous surface vehicles application. *Indian Journal of Geo-Marine Sciences* 40 (2): 250–266.

53 Huang, S.J., Liu, X.Z., Su, W.F., and Yang, S.H. (2013). Application of hybrid firefly algorithm for sheath loss reduction of underground transmission systems. *IEEE Transactions on Power Delivery* 28 (4): 2085–2092.

54 Durkota, K. (2011). Implementation of a discrete firefly algorithm for the QAP problem within the sage framework. Bachelor Thesis. Czech Technical University.

55 Kwiecień, J. and Filipowicz, B. (2012). Firefly algorithm in optimization of queueing systems. *Bulletin of the Polish Academy of Sciences Technical Sciences* 60 (2): 363–368.

56 Apostolopoulos, T. and Vlachos, A. (2011). Application of the firefly algorithm for solving the economic emissions load dispatch problem. *International Journal of Combinatorics* 2011: 523806, 23 pages.

57 Gao, M.L., He, X.H., Luo, D.S. et al. (2013). Object tracking using firefly algorithm. *IET Computer Vision* 7 (4): 227–237.

58 Jati, G.K. (2011). Evolutionary discrete firefly algorithm for travelling salesman problem. *International conference on adaptive and intelligent systems,* Klagenfurt, Austria (6–8 September 2011), pp. 393–403. Springer, Berlin, Heidelberg.

59 Pal, S.K., Rai, C.S., and Singh, A.P. (2012). Comparative study of firefly algorithm and particle swarm optimization for noisy non-linear optimization problems. *International Journal of Intelligent Systems and Applications* 4 (10): 50–57.

60 Mandal, P., Haque, A.U., Meng, J. et al. (2013). A novel hybrid approach using wavelet, firefly algorithm, and fuzzy ARTMAP for day-ahead electricity price forecasting. *IEEE Transactions on Power Systems* 28 (2): 1041–1051.

61 Hassanzadeh, T. and Meybodi, M.R. (2012). A new hybrid algorithm based on firefly algorithm and cellular learning automata. *Proceedings of the 20th Iranian Conference on Electrical Engineering (ICEE), IEEE,* Tehran, Iran (15–17 May 2012), pp. 628–633.

62 Nasiri, B. and Meybodi, M.R. (2012). Speciation based firefly algorithm for optimization in dynamic environments. *International Journal Artificial Intelligence* 8 (12): 118–132.

63 Farahani, S.M., Abshouri, A.A., Nasiri, B., and Meybodi, M.R. (2012). Some hybrid models to improve firefly algorithm performance. *International Journal Artificial Intelligence* 8 (S12): 97–117.

64 Suganthan, P.N., Hansen, N., Liang, J.J. et al. (2005). Problem Definitions and Evaluation Criteria for the CEC 2005 Special Session on Real-Parameter Optimization. *KanGAL Report 2005005*.

65 Ramezani, F. and Lotfi, S. (2013). Social-based algorithm (SBA). *Applied Soft Computing* 13 (5): 2837–2856, Elsevier.

66 Karaboga, D. (2005). An Idea Based on Honey Bee Swarm for Numerical Optimization. *Technical Report-TR06*. Erciyes University.

67 Chakraborty, J. and Konar, A. (2008). A distributed multi-robot path planning using particle swarm optimization. *Proceedings of the 2nd National Conference on Recent Trends in Information Systems*, Kolkata, India (7–9 February 2008), pp. 216–221.

68 Rakshit, P., Konar, A., Bhowmik, P. et al. (2013). Realization of an adaptive memetic algorithm using differential evolution and Q-learning: a case study in multirobot path planning. *IEEE Transactions on Systems, Man, and Cybernetics: Systems* 43 (4): 814–831.

69 Yan, X., Zhu, Y., Wu, J., and Chen, H. (2012). An improved firefly algorithm with adaptive strategies. *Advanced Science Letters* 16 (1): 249–254.

70 Franzi, E. (1998). *Khepera BIOS 5.0 Reference Manual*. K-Team, SA.

71 K. U. M. Version (1999). *Khepera User Manual 5.02*. Lausanne: K-Team, SA.

6

Conclusions and Future Directions

This chapter concludes the book. Here novelties, originality of book are reclaimed and the future research directions are indicated.

6.1 Conclusions

The book identifies a few fundamental problems in multi-robot coordination and proposes solutions to handle these problems by extending the traditional evolutionary algorithm (EA) and multi-agent Q-learning (MAQL). Chapter 1 provides the preliminaries of Reinforcement Learning (RL) and EA in view of the multi-robot coordination. Chapter 2 proposes two useful characteristic properties for exploration of the team-goal and joint action selection in multi-agent system. The incorporation of the first property with traditional MAQL (TMAQL) ensures exploration of the team-goal by multi-phased transitions of the agents asynchronously or synchronously to finally reach the team-goal, and thereby offer high reward values to such pre-goal state to the goal state-transitions. The second property helps in identifying common preferred joint actions for the entire team, thus avoiding same joint actions at the same states and thereby enhancing the learning speed of the agents. The Q-table obtained in joint state–action space using the proposed fast cooperative multi-agent Q-learning (FCMQL) algorithms have been employed in the multi-agent planning algorithm to autonomously select goal state-transitions (team-goal) from the pre-goal states based on their high reward values stored in the Q-table. TMAQL-induced planners occasionally fail to reach the team-goal as such state-transitions that might result in due to follow-up actions of Property 2.1 in FCMQL are missing from the Q-table obtained by TMAQL. It is shown in a Theorem 2.1 that the expected convergence time of the proposed FCMQL algorithms is less than the same of TMAQL algorithms. The complexity

Multi-agent Coordination: A Reinforcement Learning Approach, First Edition.
Arup Kumar Sadhu and Amit Konar.
© 2021 The Institute of Electrical and Electronics Engineers, Inc.
Published 2021 by John Wiley & Sons, Inc.

analysis reveals the superiority of the proposed FCMQL algorithms over the TMAQL algorithms.

Chapter 3 proposes a novel Consensus Q-learning (CoQL) algorithm for multi-robot cooperative planning. The proposed CoQL algorithm addresses the problem of equilibrium selection among multiple equilibria, by evaluating the consensus (joint action) at the current joint state. An analysis reveals that a consensus at a joint state is a pure strategy Nash equilibrium (NE) as well as pure strategy correlated equilibrium (CE). The novelty of the CoQL lies in the adaption of the joint Q-values at consensus. The superiority of the proposed CoQL algorithm is verified over the reference algorithms in terms of the average of the average rewards (AAR) earned by the agents against the learning epoch. In addition, consensus-based multi-robot cooperative planning algorithm is proposed and its superiority is verified over reference algorithms, considering path length and torque requirement as the performance metrics.

Chapter 4 introduces a novel approach to correlated Q-learning (CQL) and subsequent multi-robot planning. Two models are proposed in this chapter. The principles adapted in the proposed models yield a single Q-table in joint state–action space, which contains sufficient information to plan by employing the proposed multi-agent planning algorithms. The Q-table obtained from model-I and -II have less computational cost than the traditional CQL. An analysis reveals that both time- and space-complexities of proposed learning and planning algorithms are significantly less to those of the CQL. A further reduction in complexity is obtained by dropping the infeasible joint state–action pairs from the joint Q-table. Unlike traditional CQL, in the proposed models, computation of the CE is done partly in the learning and partly in the planning phases, thereby requiring CE computation once. It has been proved in a Theorem that the CE obtained by the proposed models is same as that obtained by the traditional CQL algorithms.

Chapter 5 introduces a novel approach for efficiently employing both Imperialist Competitive Algorithm (ICA) and Firefly Algorithm (FA) to develop a hybrid algorithm with an aim to utilize the composite benefits of the explorative and exploitative capabilities of both ancestor algorithms. The potential of local exploitation is captured by the colonizing behavior of countries (representing candidate solutions) surrounding the respective imperialist (representing the local optima in the search space) of the traditional ICA. Alternatively, the global explorative proficiency of FA is signified by the self-organizing behavior of fireflies (representing candidate solutions) based on their light intensity (symbolizing the fitness) profile. The merit of the proposed hybridization policy lies in devising two interesting stratagems to realize the communal benefits of the two ancestor algorithms: (i) integration of the light intensity (fitness)-induced motion dynamics of fireflies in the traditional ICA and (ii) modulation of step-size for random motion of fireflies based on the best position in the search space (discovered so far). The chapter also recommends a new policy of evaluating the threshold value for union of colonies (set of candidate solutions) based on search space dimensions.

Finally, all the proposed learning and planning algorithms are verified first in simulation and then are implemented for real-time planning using Khepera mobile robots. The proposed learning-based planning and ICFA are employed to handle the multi-robot object-transportation tasks. The experiments performed with Khepera mobile robots also indicate that the proposed algorithms outperform other realizations in real environment, thereby justifying the merit of the proposed algorithms.

6.2 Future Directions

Cooperative robots have wide applications in flexible manufacturing systems (FMS) and factory automation, where the servicing robots picks up items from the conveyer and places the items again once the operation on the item by the servicing robot is over. In the defense sector, cooperative robots would find applications in landmine/water mine clearing. In building construction/repair, robot team is a good choice as the skyscrapers invite high risks for the masons or their assistants. We hope for the best, when a pair of robots might serve as a surgeon and nurse, where the latter may assist the former in surgery.

The above dreams will be realized in near future by extending the book in the following dimension: (i) multi-agent Fuzzy-Q learning, (ii) multi-agent reinforcement learning employing function approximation techniques, (iii) multi-agent reinforcement learning for distributed Q-learning with the flavor of partially observable Markov decision process, (iv) optimal trajectory generation in the presence of dynamic obstacles employing PrEference Appraisal Reinforcement Learning, (v) efficient strategies for mixed coordination, and (vi) deep reinforcement learning.

Index

Multi-agent Coordination: A Reinforcement Learning Approach, First Edition.
Arup Kumar Sadhu and Amit Konar.
© 2021 The Institute of Electrical and Electronics Engineers, Inc.
Published 2021 by John Wiley & Sons, Inc.

Printed and bound by CPI Group (UK) Ltd, Croydon, CR0 4YY

27/10/2024

14580471-0002